WORKING PEOPLE IN ALBERTA

WORKING CANADIANS: *Books from the* CCLH

Series editors: Alvin Finkel and Greg Kealey

The Canadian Committee on Labour History is Canada's organization of historians and other scholars interested in the study of the lives and struggles of working people throughout Canada's past. Since 1976, the CCLH has published *Labour/Le Travail*, Canada's pre-eminent scholarly journal of labour studies. It also publishes books, now in conjunction with AU Press, that focus on the history of Canada's working people and their organizations. The emphasis in this series is on materials that are accessible to labour audiences as well as university audiences rather than simply on scholarly studies in the labour area. This includes documentary collections, oral histories, autobiographies, biographies, and provincial and local labour movement histories with a popular bent.

A History

WORKING PEOPLE
IN ALBERTA

ALVIN FINKEL

with contributions by JASON FOSTER,
WINSTON GERELUK, JENNIFER KELLY AND
DAN CUI, JAMES MUIR, JOAN SCHIEBELBEIN,
JIM SELBY, *and* ERIC STRIKWERDA

AU PRESS

Published by AU Press, Athabasca University
1200, 10011 – 109 Street, Edmonton, AB, T5J 3S6

ISBN 978-1-926836-58-4 (print)
ISBN 978-1-926836-59-1 (PDF)
ISBN 978-1-926836-60-7 (epub)

A volume in Working Canadians: Books from the CCLH
ISSN 1925-1831 (print)   1925-184X (digital)

Library and Archives Canada Cataloguing in Publication

Working people in Alberta : a history / edited by Alvin Finkel.

(Working Canadians, books from the CCLH, ISSN 1925-1831)
Issued also in electronic formats.
ISBN 978-1-926836-58-4

1. Labor—Alberta—History.
2. Working class—Alberta—History.
3. Alberta—Economic conditions.
4. Alberta—Economic policy.
I. Finkel, Alvin, 1949–
II. Series: Working Canadians (Edmonton, Alta.)

HD8109.A42W67 2011   331.097123   C2011-905733-6

Cover and interior design by Natalie Olsen, Kisscut Design.
Printed and bound in Canada by Marquis Book Printers.

We acknowledge the financial support of the Government of
Canada through the Canada Book Fund (CBF) for our publishing
activities.

Assistance provided by the Government of Alberta, Alberta Multi-
media Development Fund.

 Canadian Committee on Labour History

 Government of Alberta

 Canada Council for the Arts   Conseil des Arts du Canada

For Neil Reimer, 1921–2011
in recognition of his unparalleled contribution to the
betterment of the lives of working people in Alberta

CONTENTS

ACKNOWLEDGEMENTS

Our greatest debt in the production of this book is to the Alberta Labour History Institute (ALHI) for its over two hundred interviews with Alberta trade union leaders and rank-and-file workers, covering events from the 1930s to the present. The ALHI, working with the Alberta Federation of Labour (AFL) on Project 2012 — an organizational effort to commemorate the founding of the AFL in 1912 — suggested that a book of this kind would be a fitting way to celebrate the occasion and asked Alvin Finkel to undertake its research and writing. We thank both the ALHI and the AFL, as well as everyone involved with Project 2012, for their inspiration and ongoing encouragement.

We are also grateful to the anonymous reviewers for AU Press who provided incisive suggestions that we attempted to incorporate in our revisions. Editors Joyce Hildebrand and Pamela MacFarland Holway have raised important questions and improved the organization of our materials as well as our prose. Ron Patterson took charge of the collection of images, while Natalie Olsen is responsible for the book's elegant design.

We thank the Alberta Federation of Labour and the Alberta Union of Provincial Employees for their financial support for the research and production of this book. They donated to the project with no strings attached. No official of either union body asked for or received an opportunity to read any of the chapters as they were written or before they were finalized. In short, the book is not an official history of any union organization, though it was timed to appear for the centennial celebration of the AFL so as to contribute to reflections on labour's past in Alberta and on lessons for its future. While three of the authors — Jim Selby, Winston Gereluk, and Jason Foster — are past employees of the federation, none had any relationship with it at the time they wrote their chapters. This book is solely the product of its authors, and no one exercised any censorship or any attempt to impose particular points of views on any of the authors. The authors are all activists and/or sympathizers with the labour movement and work in labour-related fields. But this is an effort to tell the history of working people to the best of our abilities, not to whitewash anything within Alberta labour history or to give only one side of the story in internecine union battles.

As we were preparing this book, we were saddened by the death of Neil Reimer, one of the great heroes of the Alberta labour movement. Neil's lifelong efforts as a trade union organizer, trade union official, politician, and social activist have resulted in better representation and better working conditions for Alberta workers, and have improved social policies for Alberta workers and seniors. Always committed to education for and about working people in Alberta, Neil became an early member of ALHI; he conducted many interviews and agreed to be interviewed at length himself on several occasions. His efforts to create more autonomy for Canadian workers led to the creation of an independent Canadian union, the Energy and Chemical Workers Union (ECWU), in an area where American-led unions once prevailed in Canada. The ECWU was one of the three Canadian unions that merged in 1992 to form the Communications, Energy, and Paperworkers Union of Canada.

Neil's successful efforts to organize refinery workers in Alberta in the 1950s defied the common wisdom that the entire oil industry was beyond the reach of unionism. The Oil Workers International Union rewarded his efforts by making him its Canadian director. Under his leadership, the union fought not only for better wages but also for improved safety standards and greater union involvement in enforcing safety. An officer of the Canadian Labour Congress as well as his own union, Neil played a big role in the creation of the national New Democratic Party and became the party's first Alberta leader. To the end of his days, he remained active in both union and political work, serving during his retirement in many capacities, including president of the Alberta Council on Aging. A towering figure in the trade union and social justice communities in Alberta, Neil will be remembered for his storytelling, humour, and abundant humanity, which inspired all of the authors of this book.

WORKING PEOPLE IN ALBERTA

INTRODUCTION
THOSE WHO BUILT ALBERTA

ALVIN FINKEL

Most Canadians — and even many Albertans — view Alberta as a rich, placid province where the streets are paved with gold, thanks to the province's fossil fuel riches. In this view, Alberta is a one-class, one-party province where meaningful political debates about social values are absent. Certainly, one book, published in 2009, portrays recent immigrants to Alberta from other provinces as viewing their new home as the "second promised land," a place with low taxes and little government interference in people's daily lives.[1] An earlier study, however, demonstrates that this perspective on the province is too simplistic and ignores evidence that many, perhaps even most Albertans embrace communitarian values rather than the conservative values that are often attributed to them.[2]

Often lost in such discussions is the fact that Alberta has a capitalist economy in which some owners of capital have become very rich and some who must work for a living have done rather less well. The working people who built and continue to build the province of Alberta often vanish from the story when the focus is on constitutional battles between Edmonton and Ottawa, and on the mythological, individualist "mavericks" whom some wish to portray as embodying the true Alberta spirit.[3] While entrepreneurial individuals have certainly played a role in the history of the Prairies, their contribution has been modest relative to that of the workers, farmers, and small-business operators who have always formed the overwhelming majority of the population. It is a history of this majority, and especially its working-class component, that this book tells. It is a history in which entrepreneurs give way to trade union organizers and groups like the Industrial Workers of the World, the CCF, and the Communist Party; the Hunger Marchers of 1932; the Gainers' strikers and the "Dandelions" of the 1980s; the mostly female Calgary laundry workers who put the brakes on Ralph Klein's efforts to destroy the public sector in the 1990s; and the Lakeside Packers workers, most of whom belonged to a visible minority, who organized against all the odds within a classically reactionary community in the early twenty-first century.

In an earlier effort to portray the history of Alberta workers, Warren Caragata produced *Alberta Labour: A Heritage Untold* in 1979, a lively history of working people in Alberta that focused on union struggles.[4] Caragata was a staffer at the Alberta Federation of Labour (AFL), and writing the book was one of his assigned duties. Caragata evidently enjoyed a fair degree of independence in writing the book — although, according to AFL staff members at the time, AFL president Harry Kostiuk, reflecting Cold War sentiments that were still strong in the labour movement, made him abbreviate or remove certain passages that emphasized the major role played by Communists within certain labour struggles. Nonetheless, Caragata produced an excellent history of working-class struggles, incorporating material from interviews with some participants in those struggles. I strongly recommend that those interested in Alberta labour history make use of Caragata's study, in addition to the present work, to explore developments between 1883 and 1956, the period on which *Alberta Labour* concentrates.

Alberta Labour reflects the time and circumstances in which it was written. Historians were only beginning to shift from histories of "great men" and institutions toward social history, so the book contains little about workers who tried but failed to organize trade unions or about women, Aboriginals, and people of colour.

This book attempts to build on Caragata's achievement while also discussing the history of workers in the province in the thirty-five years since Caragata did most of his research. But it is more than simply an update, since a key focus of *Working People in Alberta: A History* is the incorporation of social history approaches to the history of working people. In this respect, our work is greatly aided by the over two hundred interviews that have been videographed and transcribed by the Alberta Labour History Institute (ALHI). ALHI was formed in 1999 by trade unionists and academics who felt that too much of the history of Alberta had been told from the point of view of the elites and too little from the perspective of its working people. Many labour pioneers and union activists were aging, and if they were not interviewed soon, their stories might die with them. Operating mainly as a volunteer organization, ALHI set out to conduct comprehensive interviews with working people from a variety of backgrounds throughout the province. ALHI has also sponsored and recorded events in which key players discuss major working-class historical issues, and its website (www.labourhistory.ca) includes a labour history chronology of the province and excerpts from its many interviews. ALHI's annual labour history calendar is popular with trade unions throughout the province.

ALHI played a key role in the evolution of this book. In 2008, the institute formed a partnership with the AFL in order to produce materials to mark the centennial of the federation in 2012. This collaborative project, named Project 2012, was largely funded by the AFL and its affiliates, with ALHI and AFL staff sharing the work. The two groups have been working together to produce booklets, DVDs, posters, and a conference so that the centennial will be a means to reflect on the labour movement's past and provoke discussion about future directions. Both groups agreed that a new book detailing labour history in the province should be produced, and I was asked to coordinate this effort. Discussions between ALHI and the AFL revealed a common interest in ensuring that the book be more than simply a history of the labour movement; it was also to be a social history of working people, including both unorganized workers and the trade unions.

Unlike the Caragata book, which begins with the arrival of white settlers in Alberta and the creation of a classic paid labour force, *Working People in Alberta: A History* begins with the history of work in Alberta during the 98 percent of its history when only First Nations lived there. Chapter 1, "Millennia of Native Work," tells the story of the period of First Nations' control over the areas that constitute today's Alberta and the sophisticated ways in which they organized their work and their lives. This chapter provides a glimpse into how people distributed necessary work tasks and benefited from labour before European domination of Alberta ushered in organizational inequality with respect to work and distribution of social benefits. But it is indeed just a glimpse. The history of Native work in Alberta deserves a book of its own: this book only traces the outlines of what such a book might detail.

Chapter 2, "The Fur Trade and Early European Settlement," deals with the period in which the commercial fur trade, organized by Europeans, was superimposed on the traditional economies and societies of First Nations in what is now Alberta, assessing the fur trade's impact on the lives of Aboriginals. It also explores the effect on the First Nations of the decline of the fur trade and the advance of European settlement into the region. Overall, we see that the fur trade was a partnership among two peoples in which Native peoples retained most features of their traditional cultures while absorbing European ideas and goods to the extent that they deemed appropriate. In contrast, the settlement period was marked by dispossession and marginalization of

Native peoples, a ruthless attack on their traditional cultures, and heavy-handed efforts to assimilate them to European ways.

Chapters 3 to 8 detail a chronological history of working people in Alberta from the settlement period onward. In each chapter, an effort is made to explore the political economy that underpinned labour issues. Chapter 3, "One Step Forward: Alberta Workers, 1885–1914," deals with the period of initial European settlement in the region, a period in which Alberta was mainly a burgeoning agricultural province. Industry and a concomitant industrial working class developed to meet the needs of the farmers for goods and services. While the farmers were mainly independent commodity producers, they felt subordinated to the power of shippers, buyers, and bankers, and could sometimes make common cause with industrial workers to restrain the power of such big capitalists. But as employers of farm labourers, whom they often exploited, farmers were cool to labour's calls for shorter work days, better pay, and more worker control within workplaces. They were often ambivalent about advocacy for social insurance programs and for nationalization of industry. The early labour movement that developed in this period had both conservative elements, particularly within the trades unions that emphasized craft exclusivity, and radical elements, exemplified by the miners who sympathized with Marxist calls for the elimination of capitalists and the creation of a workers' state in which exploitation would disappear.

The first three chapters are based almost exclusively on the existing secondary literature on early Alberta history. The remaining chapters rely very heavily on the documentary record and, in particular, on the ALHI interviews. Chapter 4, "War, Repression, and Depression, 1914–39," with its focus on World War I and the interwar period, traces an era of relative economic stagnation and major political changes. The farmers' movement took power provincially in 1921 from the bourgeois elements that controlled the Liberal Party government from 1905 to 1921, and it remained in power until the finance-obsessed Social Credit party won the provincial election in 1935. Independent labour politics emerged after World War I, and labour had electoral victories at all levels of government, reflecting a growing class consciousness among Alberta workers, particularly in urban and industrial areas. The mainstream of the labour movement attempted to work closely with the United Farmers of Alberta (UFA) during its period in government, but the wisdom of that decision was called into question when the Great Depression arrived in late 1929 and the UFA proved to have only anemic strategies for helping its victims. While a Communist movement, originating in the 1920s in Alberta, played an important role in organizing the unemployed in the 1930s, other new forces emerged during the Depression including the Co-operative Commonwealth Federation (CCF), the forerunner of the New Democratic Party (NDP), and a reinvigorated industrial union movement with American roots.

Chapter 5, "Alberta Labour and Working-Class Life, 1940–59," assesses the impact on workers of a major reshaping of Alberta's political economy, particularly after the chain of discoveries of large oil and gas deposits, beginning with the oil strike in Leduc in 1947. Alberta changed from a predominantly rural, agrarian province dependent on prices for agricultural products to a province dependent on the fortunes of "black gold." Most of the coal mines closed, farming became a poor cousin to oil and gas exploration and exploitation, and dizzying economic growth replaced the stagnation of the interwar period. Workers' efforts to benefit from the new wealth were limited by the Social Credit government's alliance with big capital in the oil and gas industry and the determination of these two partners to keep unions out of the energy fields. Labour managed some gains despite this anti-union alliance, but in the context of the Cold War, a right-wing provincial government that passed anti-labour laws, and economic growth, Alberta workers lost much of their class consciousness and their interwar economic and political power. Large-scale migration of workers from other provinces and abroad meant that some of the province's former labour struggles were unknown to many workers in Alberta.

Chapter 6, "The Boomers Become the Workers: Alberta, 1960–80," examines the impact of international movements of anti-colonialism and youth rebellion on class consciousness in a province where the power of the energy industry was increasing dramatically. Although the Social Credit government was finally defeated in 1971, the successor Progressive Conservative regime was no more sympathetic to workers' efforts to gain a greater share of the province's wealth and to have safer workplaces and better provincial social programs. The fledgling New Democratic Party received some support from the provincial labour movement, but conservative elements within the movement continued to be apolitical and to see labour's job in the narrow terms of dealing with individual employers. State employees were increasingly restive, however, and rebelled against the paternalism of their employers to build fighting unions during this period.

Chapter 7, "Alberta Labour in the 1980s," deals with what may have been the most radical period of labour history in Alberta to date. As international energy prices collapsed in the context of a global recession that began in late 1981, the weaknesses of having the province's economic strength based on one industry became apparent. Labour and its allies called for greater government involvement to diversify the Alberta economy. But this was the era in which neo-liberalism was emerging worldwide, with employers and governments calling for a return to the policies of the pre-Depression era in which the marketplace made most economic decisions. It meant that governments would severely cut the social benefits that workers had achieved since 1945 and that the laws governing the operation of unions would render them almost toothless so that capital could regain the profit levels that it had enjoyed in earlier periods. Workers and their unions resisted employers' efforts to make workers pay for the recession that capitalists had caused, and strike waves and worker protests of various kinds marked this period. The NDP became the provincial official opposition in 1986 and again in 1989.

Chapter 8 concludes the chronological history of Alberta's working people. "Revolution, Retrenchment, and the New Normal: The 1990s and Beyond" examines the eventual triumph of neo-liberalism as well as continuing working-class efforts to mitigate its effects and to discredit its ideological assumptions. This was a period in which the energy industry, now focused on the northern oil sands, went beyond dominating the provincial economy to become its almost exclusive focus. The province's manufacturing base crumbled,

leaving the Alberta economy less diversified than at almost any other time in its history. Politically, the so-called Klein Revolution, referring to the period when Progressive Conservative Premier Ralph Klein decimated the civil service and provincial programs, challenged the idea that citizens had a right to basic health, educational, and social services, and that such services could be provided efficiently by the state. The labour movement, more divided than in the 1970s, scrambled to unite its members behind campaigns to protect public services, while efforts to organize in the private sector yielded only a few key victories.

Chapter 9 elaborates on a theme that runs throughout this book but requires a synthesis and evaluation of its own. "Women, Labour, and the Labour Movement" looks at both the factors that have held women back within the labour force in Alberta and their determined efforts to use both trade unions and pressure upon governments to create more gender justice. It argues that the unions, while laggards on issues of gender rights before the 1970s, have made considerable progress since that time in fighting for the interests of working women.

Finally, Chapter 10, "Racialization and Work," looks at the continuing struggle of minority workers of colour to achieve social justice in Alberta. As was the case for gender struggles, the trade union movement was rife with prejudice in earlier periods. Since the 1960s, however, the labour movement has played an increasingly important role in the struggle for social equality and human rights, both in the workplace and the broader community.

1 MILLENNIA OF NATIVE WORK

ALVIN FINKEL

The world is round and each society has been given the right to exist in this world within its territory. This is how the Creator had arranged it. Therefore, the traditional territory of the Blackfoot Nation was given to our people by our Creator. We respected and protected this traditional territory with our minds and our hearts and we depended on it for what it encompasses for our survival. Everything that we ever needed for our way of life and survival existed in our traditional territory, such as herbs for medicine, roots, rivers, game animals, berries, vegetables, the buffalo.[1]

Elder Adam Delaney's description of the Blackfoot people's views of their lives in the millennia before the arrival of Europeans is largely echoed by the other First Nations people of Alberta, though in each natural region the resources allegedly bestowed by the Creator differed. Any history of Alberta that accurately reflects historical time should devote 98 percent of its space to Native peoples, who, according to the most conservative estimates, have lived within what is now called

Alberta for at least thirteen thousand years. The post-contact period (the period in which both Natives and newcomers have lived in Alberta) is less than three hundred years old, a blip in historical time.

The Native view of their traditional past emphasizes the role of the Creator and the importance to Native people of following the Creator's teachings. Like Christianity, Islam, and Judaism, Native religions are monotheistic. The great religions of the Old World, however, have creation stories in which God gave dominion to humans over all other animals as well as plants. In contrast, according to Aboriginal religions, the Creator gave spirits to all animals and plants, and humans, while they needed to consume other living things, were instructed to do so in ways that respected them as God's creations. If they failed to do so, the Creator would punish them by depriving them of game and plants. In their view, the Creator expected them to take only what they needed and to demonstrate respect for non-humans via elaborate rituals.[2]

Humans were also expected to respect one another,

particularly within their primary affinity group, which was also their work group. Cree communities in the parklands region gathered regularly in circles to collectively pray, talk, heal, and reconcile, and to make supreme efforts to treat one another as equal children of the Creator. The Dene or Athabascan in the North, the Cree in the north-central region, and Blackfoot peoples in the centre and south of the province had similar beliefs and ceremonies. Although it is important to emphasize that each Native culture had its own language, its own story of how the Earth was created, and its own social structures, for all of these cultural groups, land was the property of the Creator, not of individuals, and everyone had to work together to use, share, and conserve the land and resources that the Creator had bestowed upon the group.[3]

On the surface, then, it might seem that Native peoples in Alberta experienced no historical development during the thirteen thousand years before they began contact through the fur trade with strangers from Europe. Some people, particularly during the period of colonial conquest of the Americas, used the word *primitive* to describe pre-contact Native societies in Alberta and the rest of Canada and the Americas. (The term *pre-contact* generally refers to the period before an Aboriginal society developed regular contact with Europeans.) They suggested that Natives hunted and gathered using never-changing, almost intuitive, techniques. In this view, Native societies in 1700 AD were no different than they had been in 9000 BC. To some, this meant that they were uncivilized and needed to be swept away by the Europeans, who were supposedly more advanced in areas such as technology and religion. Others argued for leaving them alone and treating the

Americas much like a game preserve for early humans. While the latter, minority point of view would have benefited the Natives more over the long term, it was, like the former view, based on a completely incorrect dichotomy of allegedly "civilized" societies — European cultures — and "savage" societies — virtually all other cultures. In fact, Native societies changed dramatically over time as they constantly tried to find ways to better shape the resources that the Creator had given them to ensure that their material and spiritual needs were met.

The view that Native societies in the Americas were less advanced technologically than European societies was based largely on the superiority of European weapons and on the "logic" of conquerors that those whom they are conquering are inferiors. That view was reinforced in the Americas by the conquerors' destruction of many Native societies and the burying of the Natives' achievements. Archaeology and the oral histories that have been passed on from generation to generation of Aboriginal survivors have challenged the "cowboys and Indians" caricatures of the European–Aboriginal conflicts. We now know that the knowledge of various Native groups was immense and that terms such as *Stone Age* and *primitive*, once used to denigrate these societies, cover up the complexities and ever-changing character of the cultures of the Americas. The pre-contact Native peoples had long histories of interacting with a changing environment, and though the names of individual inventors and developers are largely unknown, the collective knowledge of these peoples that developed over time was impressive. Some of it may never be recovered because colonial germs and violence resulted in millions of deaths over a short period of time.

The Inca Empire centred in Peru, for example, synthesized the architectural, mathematical, astronomical, agricultural, and religious knowledge of the various Andean peoples whom the Inca conquered. Among the achievements of these peoples, who used stone and not metals, was the construction of earthquake-proof buildings and flood-proof roads. Their understanding of how stones could be chiseled to fit together so as not to be dismantled by natural forces was one application of their sophisticated mathematical and geological knowledge. In contrast, the Spanish conquerors and their successors deprecated the people they conquered and never bothered to learn anything from them about survival in the Andes region; instead, they applied their "developed" European technologies to build lovely edifices that were frequently ruined by earthquakes and ambitious roadway projects that stood covered in water and mud when flooding occurred. The sophisticated irrigation systems that the Andean peoples had developed in the desert conditions of their region remained unmatched for at least the first three hundred years of Spanish occupation.[4]

On the surface, the achievements of the peoples of pre-contact Alberta may seem modest compared to those of cultures such as the Inca, Maya, and Aztec, who built huge temples and thousands of miles of roads and irrigation canals. But this is only true if one measures societies in terms of what one can see on the surface. Prairie Native cultures also had complex technologies that resulted from the collective labour of their peoples. As archaeologist Jack Brink, who led the team that reconstructed Head-Smashed-In Buffalo Jump, now a UNESCO World Heritage Site, in southwestern Alberta, concluded:

Alone in that basin that day, I knew that I stood among the remains of a huge construction project involving the collection and careful placement of thousands of individual rocks. Each one was selected for certain size and weight and placed in a spot deemed just right by a team of people who must have discussed and debated how the map was to be made. What started off as simple clusters of stone had morphed into a mental blueprint of complex, group-based decision-making on a scale and for a purpose that had mostly eluded consideration by archaeologists, anthropologists, animal ecologists, and pretty much everyone else.[5]

Brink argues that the Europeans first in contact with the prairie Natives, wanting to minimize the achievements of the First Peoples, assumed that it must be easy to herd buffalo over cliffs and then crudely cut up their bodies to get food and clothing. In fact, it took years of invention and experimenting to determine where and by what means buffalo, which were wary animals, could be herded to cliffs from which a fall would kill them, with the least risk to humans in the process.

Equal ingenuity was needed in knowing what to do once the buffalo had jumped. Natives could only cut up and process the meat of a small number of buffalo, and not just any buffalo would do. They needed buffalo that had sufficient fat at that time of year to ensure a nutritious food supply for the people who had conducted the kill. To determine which animals were worth taking from a herd, they searched for hair over the eyes and on the horn, and for stripes on the spine. In addition to using buffalo meat for food, the people learned over time which parts of buffalo could

FIG 1-2 Dig from below Old Women's Buffalo Jump near Cayley, Alberta. Glenbow Archives, B20-B-1.

suited to killing big game as well as smaller animals, but the mammoths and mastodons that they hunted soon disappeared, perhaps because of overhunting.[6]

The First Peoples of Alberta adapted by turning their attention to the bison of southern Alberta, developing bone and antler tools and experimenting with and perfecting their projectiles. Sturdier projectiles were needed since there was limited access to stone for resharpening and for changing broken segments. Archaeologist Trevor Peck explains the importance of the development of "Folsom points," some 12,800 to 12,200 years ago:

> The regularity and exquisite form of Folsom points suggests that knowledge transmission within tight kingroups or working with designated craft specialists was an intricate part of an individual's upbringing. Practices of stone conservation, the use of biface cores, multifunction stone tools, and Folsom point preforms as tools were all elegant adaptive responses to a highly mobile lifeway focused on hunting bison in stone-poor areas.[7]

be used to make such items as clothing, toboggans, cutlery, and powder flasks.

Such knowledge, along with prairie, parklands, and northern peoples' more general hunting expertise — as well as their understanding of horticulture, natural medicines, and social relations — did not develop overnight. Archaeological evidence shows that small groups of hunters lived on the prairies of Alberta at least thirteen thousand years ago when the glaciers of a long ice age were beginning to retreat. It is likely that they crossed an ice-free corridor from British Columbia through a section of the Rocky Mountains. By that time, they had developed projectiles with large fluted points

Over time, there were more inventions and more adaptations. For example, archaeological remains suggest that sometime between 7200 and 6500 BC, Native peoples began fine-tuning darts to fit the spear thrower. The melting of glaciers brought greater population movements within Alberta and between that territory and other parts of North America. For example, an unearthed burial complex dating back to the period from 4900 to 4400 BP (2950 to 2450 BC) included copper and evidence of the use of stone boiling, which suggest the migration of peoples from elsewhere, probably the Great Lakes region, where stone boiling to extract bone grease had become common by the third millennium BC. The bone grease was used to preserve meat, reducing dependence on fresh meat and allowing communities to grow. Subsequently, there was a migration of Indigenous peoples from today's American Midwest, as evidenced by discoveries of iron and copper projectile points as well as a style of pottery that was clearly introduced rather than developed locally.[8]

New technologies and techniques, whether brought by newcomers or developed locally, helped to make hunting more successful. The successive adoptions of the atlatl (spear thrower), the bow and arrow, and finally the buffalo pound were particularly important in enabling the growth of more and larger communities, first in southern Alberta and later in the northern reaches of the province. The buffalo pound was an enclosure that Native peoples built with logs and hides, generally at the bottom of a hill, to trap buffalo. Even though the animals were strong enough to crash through the wall that suddenly appeared before them, their instincts told them to stop in their tracks when confronted by a barrier. Thus trapped, they were speared by hunters who aimed through holes in the walls of the enclosure. The success of this method encouraged the bolder concept of the buffalo jump, in which Natives steered the buffalo along a path that ended not with a barrier but with a high cliff from which the stampeding buffalo fell to their death. Beginning in the first millennium BC, encampments of more than a hundred people were established at repeatedly used buffalo jump sites.[9]

Over time, the various Native peoples developed beliefs sacred to themselves about their origins and about the values that the Creator expected them to embody. They also developed a variety of rituals to appease the Creator and the spirits that the Creator had given to all living things. The Sun Dance, though its features varied among different peoples, was especially critical to prairie Aboriginals. It brought together related communities, allowed for the renewing of relationships, and offered young men the opportunity to demonstrate their bravery through a ceremony involving self-inflicted pain.[10] Among the Blackfoot peoples, it was a multi-day event. An all-male warrior society chose the site, but the event was presided over by a holy woman. The highly ritualized Sun Dance was actually a series of religious ceremonies involving feasting, dancing, and singing. Each person carried a Sun Dance bundle in a rawhide bag filled with objects bestowed upon them at birth or for special achievements. Every item in the bag was made sacred by carrying it on vision fasts — fasts meant to induce a connection with the relevant spirits — and by learning special songs associated with that item. Individuals' performances at a Sun Dance had to conform both with the special gifts bestowed upon them in their medicine bundle and with the rituals of the First Nation overall. Unsurprisingly, given the importance of the buffalo to the Plains peoples, the rituals of sacrifice and thanks to the buffalo spirits occupied as much time during the Sun Dance as the ceremonies devoted to the Sun Spirit.[11]

Labour was organized along lines that reflected the Aboriginal communities' need to carefully balance the spirit world's demands on the collective and on individuals. Everyone played a role in providing the community's essential material goods, especially its food supply, but not everyone made the same contribution or received the same share of the total product. By the 1500s, the further south one might have travelled in Alberta, the more inequality one might have found, though compared to European societies of the time, all of the First Nations of Alberta were relatively egalitarian. The rigid divisions between European nobles and peasants, merchants and day labourers, and owners and slaves that had developed in Europe had some echoes among the Aztec, Maya, and Inca, but they were not replicated anywhere in Alberta.

Among the Dene peoples of northern Alberta, a class system did not develop in the pre-contact period. The Dene lived in small communities, usually of about twenty or thirty people, and harvested local resources including fish, small game, caribou, trees, and berries. They co-operated in the tasks necessary to maintain their communities, which relocated on a seasonal basis according to food sources. While these communities were largely self-sufficient and minimally involved in trade with other communities, they were generous to other Athabascan-speaking communities who came to them for help because nature had temporarily failed to provide their needs. In turn, they expected that when they were in trouble, aid would be reciprocated.

Intermarriage occurred among the communities within a region, and women and men took on different social roles. While men hunted the caribou, which often meant working at a distance from their homes, the women, who had the primary child care responsibility, stayed close to home, hunted smaller game, and harvested berries and other edible plants. Men manufactured boats and hunting tools, while women produced all the household goods and clothing. Though women played important social roles in Dene society, it appears that men sometimes exchanged or shared wives without their consent. When famine struck, it was female babies and only rarely male ones who might be subjected to infanticide. Still, as historian Kerry Abel notes, missionary and fur trader reports of women's subordination to men as beasts of burden reflected European prejudices about the proper division of labour between the sexes rather than real exploitation. The European view that women were the "weaker sex" was not shared by the Dene, who regarded women as naturally stronger than men. In the sexual division of labour, women hauled to camp the carcasses of animals hunted by the men, butchered the meat, and transported all of the camp members' possessions when camp was moved. "The available evidence suggests that the Dene considered men's and women's work to be different," writes Abel, "but not of relatively higher or lower value." [12]

The Cree of the parklands were similarly egalitarian despite the fact that the somewhat milder environment in which they lived allowed them to form communities of fifty to a hundred people. The women constructed tipis from caribou or moose hides, which the family set up and dismantled as they followed the seasonal paths of moose, caribou, beaver, and bear. Sturdy birchbark canoes made by the men provided the major means of transport. Cree communities, like those of the Dene, shared their wealth with sister communities who had suffered a bad year. The bonds among social groups were strengthened each summer when large numbers of communities gathered in a central location to renew ties of friendship that might also be called upon to gather forces against perceived enemies. [13]

While the Sioux and the Blackfoot of southern Alberta were once egalitarian as well, their societies became somewhat less equal as they became buffalo-hunting peoples. The intricacies of planning a buffalo hunt and the need for prompt selection of buffalo, quick storage of meat, and longer-term preparation of the many products that could be made from buffalo led to at least some specialization of labour and some rewards for those seen to have higher status within the buffalo society. Chiefs of the hunt and of warfare, along with shamans (the religious leaders or diviners), were at the apex of the social hierarchy. Their superior position within the society was reflected in their dwellings, which were larger than those of other families, and in their having more than one wife. Among the Blackfoot, however, the chief positions were not hereditary; furthermore, the chief's credibility depended upon his ability to ensure that all members of the tribe were taken care of.[14]

The Plains people learned to be flexible in order to ensure their survival. As Plains scholar Frances Kaye observes, they "countered climate variability with geographic mobility." She adds, "Indigenous people did not follow the buffalo herds — rather they anticipated buffalo movement and stationed themselves where experience told them the bison would be moving. Or, if their forecast was wrong, they moved towards alternate or supplementary food sources such as deer, elk, berries, or prairie turnip."[15]

Just as work and the products of labour were largely shared within the pre-contact societies of Alberta, looking after those who fell on misfortune was viewed as the responsibility of the whole community. Fur trader and explorer David Thompson, writing about the Cree, noted:

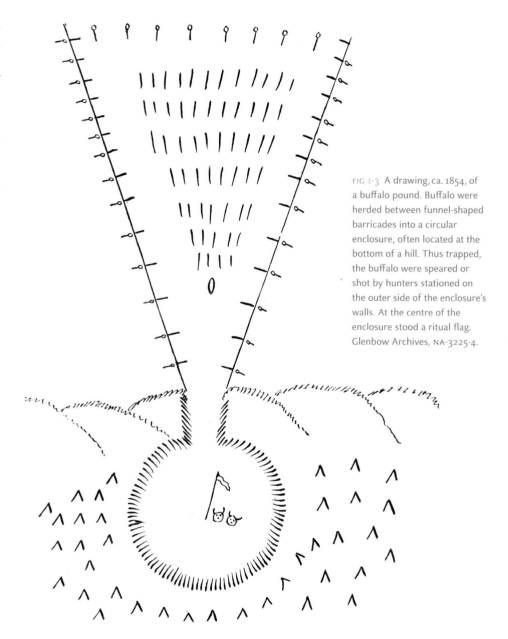

FIG 1-3 A drawing, ca. 1854, of a buffalo pound. Buffalo were herded between funnel-shaped barricades into a circular enclosure, often located at the bottom of a hill. Thus trapped, the buffalo were speared or shot by hunters stationed on the outer side of the enclosure's walls. At the centre of the enclosure stood a ritual flag. Glenbow Archives, NA-3225-4.

These acts that pass between man and man for generous charity and kind compassion in civilized society are no more than what is every day practiced by these Savages as acts of common duty; is any one unsuccessful in the chase, has he lost his little all by some accident, he is sure to be relieved by the others to the utmost of their power.[16]

Although Thompson used the common racist epithet "Savages" to describe Aboriginal people, he had a great deal of respect for their society, as did many of the fur traders. He was hardly alone in raising doubts about the idea of European societies representing a higher form of civilization. American photographer Walter McClintock, living among the Blackfeet in Montana, who shared an ancestral culture with the Blackfoot of southern Alberta, wrote: "Their unselfish and patriotic lives, devoted to the welfare of their tribe, rise before me in strange and painful contrast with the rich and powerful of my race."[17]

Sharing with those who had suffered misfortune applied not only within a community but across all social groups within a First Nation. Among the Dene, for example, while each community had its designated hunting grounds, there was an understanding that any group that had been unable in a given year to meet its needs from within its customary hunting areas could hunt in another tribe's territory. It had to request the right to hunt outside its traditional territory, but such requests were ritual and were always granted as long as the solicited tribe was not also short of food.[18]

Some European commentators presented northern peoples as callous regarding old people and the sick, since the survival of a community sometimes required them to leave an old or sick person behind as they changed camp with the seasons in search of food. But oral tradition, backed by evidence from European observers, stresses that abandonment occurred only after heroic efforts to preserve the life of someone who could not contribute to the common good. "When the explorer Ross met the Netsilik people a century and a half ago," writes Keith J. Crowe, "he saw Iliktat, an old man who was being pulled on a sleigh by his family across a difficult land. Early in this century Chief Robuscan of Abitibi carried his very heavy crippled wife on his back in their travels for almost twenty years."[19]

Sharing was also the norm for the Cree and the Blackfoot. While each Cree community had some territories under its control, each region also contained common hunting, trapping, and gathering areas, as well as "medicinal lands that we shared [sacred lands], peace territorial lands that we designated for the shelter and safety of all people."[20] The Blackfoot societies also practised reciprocity in the annual Sun Dance. Though a chief might have more material goods than others within the group, "a man aspiring to become a leader sought to outshine his competitors by his feasts and presents given to others, even at the cost of self-impoverishment. . . . Care of the poor was one of the recognized responsibilities of the band chief. Should he fail in this duty, his leadership position was severely jeopardized."[21]

◆ ◆ ◆

During the First Nations period in Alberta, the organization of work and the distribution of the products of work were based on sophisticated and ever-evolving social relations that were undergirded by Native spirituality. Natives carved out communities in which each individual contributed to the collective's well-being and which could in turn count on related groups for support in hard times. This achievement is evidenced in the fact that these communities proved able right to the end of the pre-contact period to govern themselves without developing formal state-level institutions of governance. Ironically, the governments and settlers who looked down on the Natives interpreted the lack of formal state institutions and formal churches as revealing "primitivism" among Canada's First Peoples. We now recognize how ethnocentric their views were. But many of the earliest Europeans in contact with Native peoples came to respect them and to recognize the complexities of their societies and their organization of work. Our next chapter, which deals with both the fur-trading period and the early settlement of Alberta, demonstrates that the European fur traders found much to admire in First Nations societies and that the fur trade represented a partnership, though not always an equal one, of Natives and Europeans. In contrast, the settlement period, though superficially a negotiated partnership, was for the most part simply an example of European imperialism that resulted in the dispossession of Aboriginal peoples and the attempted erasure of their cultures, which had evolved over millennia.

FIG 2-1 It was customary for Plains Native women to carry a baby in a cradle board, or *papoose*, on their shoulders or back, which allowed women to perform their many chores inside and outside the home while also attending to their babies. Provincial Archives of Alberta, P149.

2 THE FUR TRADE AND EARLY EUROPEAN SETTLEMENT

ALVIN FINKEL

Charles the Second establish confirme and declare by these Presentes and that by the same name of Governor & Company of Adventurers of England Tradeing into Hudsons Bay they shall have perpetuall succession And that they and theire successors by the name of Governor and Company of Adventurers of England Tradeing into Hudsons Bay bee and at all tymes hereafter shall bee persons able and capable in Law to have purchase receive possesse enjoy and reteyne Landes Rentes priviledges libertyes Jurisdiccions Franchyses and hereditamentes of what kinde nature and quality soever they bee to them and theire Successors. . . .

Doe give grant and confirme unto the said Governor and Company and theire successors the sole Trade and Commerce of all those Seas Streightes Bayes Rivers Lakes Creekes and Soundes in whatsoever Latitude they shall bee that lie within the entrance of the Streightes commonly called Hudsons Streightes together with all the Landes and Terriroryes upon the Countryes Coastes and confynes of the Seas Bayes Lakes Rivers Creekes and Soundes aforesaid that are not already actually possessed by or granted to any of our Subjectes or possessed by the Subjectes of any other Christian Prince or State . . . and all Mynes Royall as well discovered as not discovered of Gold Silver Gemms and pretious Stones to bee found or discovered within the Territoryes Lymittes and Places aforesaid And that the said Land bee from henceforth reckoned and reputed as one of our Plantacions or Colonyes in America called Rupert's Land.[1]

In such flowery language, King Charles II declared in 1670, with a stroke of the pen, that all the lands draining into Hudson Bay — a vast expanse the extent of which he could hardly have imagined — belonged to his cousin Prince Rupert and the prince's associates. He called these unknown lands Rupert's Land in honour of his first cousin. In this manner, the British, who would have no direct contact with anyone who lived in what is now Alberta for almost another century, claimed the land and resources that ancient peoples had cultivated for thirteen thousand years. It was just one example of the colonial mentality that resulted in Europeans seizing control of the Americas in the name of Christianity and civilization, though mostly to indulge an insatiable desire for the riches of what they called "the New World."[2] The Company of Adventurers — or, as it eventually became known, the Hudson's Bay Company (HBC) — was destined to become the first capitalist venture in the province of Alberta. Its rival, the North West Company (NWC), would emerge later, operating from 1779 to 1821.

Initial relations between Native peoples and the Europeans who came to the Americas from the sixteenth century onwards varied. Many of the peoples of the Americas faced enslavement by European conquerors, who wanted captive labour to exploit mines and cultivable lands. The Portuguese, who had pioneered the European slave trade in Africa in the sixteenth century, enslaved the Native peoples of today's Brazil, slaughtering those who rose up in resistance. When Native deaths from exhaustion reduced the colonial labour force, the Portuguese simply replaced them with African slaves.[3] The Spanish made slave labour in the mines and in the *encomiendas* (plantations) the key to their riches, with devastating consequences for the survival of the conquered Aboriginal populations. Writer Edouardo Galeano, describing the exhausting work of the Bolivian miners in Potosí, the largest silver mine in the world, notes that they were forced to live within the mine for months at a time while working exhausting hours with toxic substances, and that "eight million Indian corpses" were the product. "The bleeding of the New World became an act of charity, an argument for the faith."[4]

By the 1540s, the Spanish had wiped out the Arawak of the Caribbean. They went on to reduce the Native population of Mexico from about 27 million in 1519 to 1 million in 1600; in the same period, they decimated the Peruvian Natives, whose population dropped from 7 million to 1.75 million.[5] Historian G.V. Scammell observes: "In short, in an unequalled record of genocide, the Spaniards had destroyed about 90 per cent of their new subjects in the course of a century. This they had in part accomplished, as a wide body of testimony confirms, by what a royal official described as 'unheard of cruelties and tortures.'"[6]

As British colonies were established in what is now the United States, the African slave trade came to provide most of the labour required by plantation owners in the South, though some Natives were enslaved as well. In New England, Kentucky, and Tennessee, among other areas of settlement where the British newcomers did not practise labour-intensive agriculture, Natives were viewed as nuisances rather than a potential labour force. They were chased from their traditional lands, which caused many bloody wars as they attempted to assert their sovereignty and either disperse the newcomers or compel them to respect Native control.[7] Throughout this period of conquest, for all Native peoples in contact with the Europeans, European diseases to which they had no immunities proved devastating.[8] But it is important to note that disease as such does not explain the longer-term decimation of the original peoples. Comparative studies of the impact of disease on Native groups demonstrate that when a Native group remained able to control its food supply and to negotiate its relations with the Europeans, a short-term demographic upset was turned around in several generations.

European exploitation and robbery of resources, not European germs, were responsible for genocides and near-genocides of Native peoples in the Americas.[9]

Initially, the experiences of the Natives with Europeans in much of what became Canada were somewhat more positive than those of Natives in the rest of the Americas. There were no early discoveries of gold and silver in Canada, and the climate was not suited to plantation crops or, in most areas, to extensive single-family farming, given the European technology of the period. The main riches of interest to the French, the first Europeans to establish permanent settlements in Canada, came from ocean fishing, which they did themselves without conflict with Native fishers, and the fur trade. The HBC was similarly interested only in furs and not in settlement.

The fur traders had neither option of ignoring or enslaving Native peoples. The Europeans in the small fur-trade posts and settlements lacked the labour power and the geographic knowledge required to trap and prepare furs for the lucrative European markets. For the same reason that the Spanish enslaved Natives — the need of their labour power — the French and the British involved in the fur trade formed partnerships with First Peoples in lands rich in furs. The Natives quickly learned to bargain shrewdly for the European goods that they wanted in trade for their furs. Samuel de Champlain, the fur trader responsible for the establishment of Quebec in 1608, complained three years later that the Natives "waited until several ships had arrived in order to get our wares more cheaply. Thus those people are mistaken who think that by coming first they can do better business; for the Indians are now too sharp and crafty."[10]

FIG 2-2 Painting by Frederic Remington showing the interior of one of the Hudson's Bay Company's fur-trading posts, 1886. Glenbow Archives, NA-77-1.

Generally, the fur trade in a region followed a predictable pattern. First, while furs remained abundant, mutual respect characterized relations between European fur buyers, on the one hand, and Native trappers and Natives who served as trade intermediaries between trapper and buyer, on the other. The Native peoples drove as hard a bargain as they could for the products of their labour, incorporating the goods that they received in trade from the Europeans into their traditional material and spiritual lives.[11] While some Natives succumbed to the blandishments of the Roman Catholic missionaries and became Christians, most remained skeptical of a religion that contradicted their own and offered no guidance for trapping animals or gathering plants.[12] Eventually, though, supplies of furs diminished, sometimes along with game, which had been sufficient for the Natives but could not supply the needs of both Natives and Europeans in an area. As their resources dwindled, Natives could no longer negotiate the terms of trade with Europeans; thus, some of them became dependent on fur buyers and on government officials for credit and for goods. A return to old ways of living was possible for some groups when fur supplies or distant markets collapsed: Natives in northern Canada, for example, seemed to simply return to the *status quo ante* for several generations after the fur trade in their region declined. But usually European agricultural settlements were established in the wake of a shattered fur trade, and pressure was put on Native peoples to settle on small reserves while white settlers took over their former lands.

With respect to the Prairie region, historical geographer Arthur Ray notes:

> In spite of the fact that necessity for cooperation prevented any deliberate attempts to destroy the Indians and their cultures by hostile reactions, their traditional ways were transformed nonetheless. The fur trade favoured economic specialization. . . . Ultimately the resource bases upon which these specialized economies developed were destroyed due to over-exploitation. Significantly for Western Canada, this occurred before extensive European settlement began. Therefore, out of economic necessity, the Indians agreed to settle on reserves with the promise that the government would look after their welfare and help them make yet another adjustment to changing economic conditions.[13]

Such a sad result would not have been predictable when Alberta Natives first began to trade with Europeans since their initial involvement was indirect. As various areas in eastern Canada became overtrapped, Native intermediaries searched for furs in areas further west and north. By the early eighteenth century, furs that Alberta-based Natives traded with intermediaries had become part of the international fur-trading industry. But Alberta Natives had yet to encounter any Europeans; according to archaeologist Trevor Peck, the European goods that Plains peoples acquired before their direct contact with Europeans, including guns, were simply made use of alongside their traditional goods in ways that had minimal impact on their existing cultural practices.[14] Sometime between 1725 and 1750, the Blackfoot acquired horses from First Nations in the United States who traded with the Spanish.[15] Horses became incorporated into the buffalo hunt and the social and religious practices of the Blackfoot.[16] The Cree, who were allies of the Blackfoot in pre–fur trade days, also acquired horses.

By the mid-1700s, both the French fur traders, headquartered in Montreal, and the English, based in York Factory on Hudson Bay, were attempting to establish relations with Natives in the West so as to reduce the role of the intermediaries in the trade and thus increase their potential profits. The first European known to have set foot in Alberta was Anthony Henday, a labourer with the HBC at York Factory. Accompanied by Cree guides, he came west in the hope of establishing relations with the Blackfoot and to encourage them to bring furs to York Factory or other HBC forts. The Natives were largely indifferent to his efforts since having more European goods hardly seemed worth the risk of lengthy treacherous voyages, a view generally shared by all Alberta Native communities.[17]

But after the British defeated the French in the Seven Years War (1756–63) and the French ceded control of Canada to the British, Anglo-American fur traders who settled in Montreal, in alliance with Anglo-American traders on the frontier, began establishing fur-trading posts throughout the West, including what is today Alberta. The allies formed the North West Company (NWC) in 1779, uniting the efforts of most of the free traders who defied the HBC's monopoly. Native groups for whom a visit to a fur-trading post was only days away down river were generally happy to become part of the trade. While the Blackfoot continued for some time to reject any role as trappers, they proved quite willing to prepare and sell pemmican — dried buffalo meat seasoned with berries — to the traders who lacked their own sources of food. The ability of Native peoples in the interior to trade with the Montreal-based firms forced the HBC, which was enraged that Britain would not enforce the monopoly granted to the company in 1670 over the western trade, to also establish western posts. The result was not only a series of competing posts, often close together, across the West, but also frequent violence between HBC and NWC traders.

FUR-TRADING COMPANIES AND THEIR WORKFORCES

The first fur-trading post in Alberta was Pond's Fort, established by Peter Pond in 1778 on Lake Athabasca. Fort Chipewyan followed in 1788. Soon there were also posts in today's Edmonton region. Two posts, Fort Augustus, built by the NWC, and Edmonton House (also known as Fort Edmonton), the HBC response, were constructed in 1795 near what is today Fort Saskatchewan.

FIG 2-3 A sketch by Frederic Remington of a Canadian voyageur, with rifle and axe. The sketch appeared in *Harper's New Weekly* in March of 1892. Glenbow Archives, NA-1406-5.

Fort Edmonton was moved to the site of today's Rossdale Flats, just south of downtown Edmonton, in 1801, then briefly to Smoky Lake in 1810. Returned to Rossdale Flats in 1812, the fort was moved to the higher ground of the site of today's legislature in the 1830s because of the constant threat of floods on the Flats. In total, about sixty forts were built in Alberta between 1778 and Confederation in 1867, though some only lasted a few years.

The presence of fur-trading posts in their region gave an incentive to large numbers of Alberta Native communities to participate in the fur trade. By the 1790s, even the Blackfoot, once so reluctant to trade with the Europeans, brought wolf and fox skins to trading posts on the northern fringe of their hunting territories. Before the HBC and NWC merged in 1821, Natives took advantage of the companies' competition to get the best prices possible for their products. Even after the merger, Natives traded with American free traders when they could not get better prices from the Canadian monopoly fur-trading company. The change from a subsistence to a trading economy impacted all of the First Nations, though throughout the years of the fur trade, they were social actors, not victims like Natives elsewhere in the Americas who had become slaves or landless and confined to small reserves. The Alberta First Nations retained many of their core beliefs. Even when smallpox, diphtheria, and other diseases killed thousands at a time, they continued to have faith in the medicine of their traditional healers.[18]

Social work professor and Blackfoot scholar Betty Bastien, a member of the Piikani First Nation, writes that the Blackfoot, during the fur-trade period, adopted some of the Europeans' materialistic values. "The relationship with the bison," she writes, "shifted from a ceremonial and subsistence relationship to one of commercial use."[19] American demand for buffalo robes fuelled large buffalo kills in the Canadian West early in the nineteenth century. But a bigger threat to maintaining buffalo herds arose in the 1860s when industrialists discovered that buffalo hides provided excellent belts for power-transmission systems.[20] While Native peoples participated in the slaughter of the buffalo, by the 1860s their refusal would have made little difference since white American buffalo hunters were also engaged in the lucrative hunt for buffalo hides.

Initially, the Native peoples who took part in the trade participated mainly as independent providers of furs or pemmican, or as middlemen. The NWC and HBC employed mainly whites to operate their trading posts, to build boats, and to ship furs to Montreal and York Factory, respectively. The NWC used primarily French-Canadian voyageurs, following in the footsteps of the French companies that had been forced out of the fur trade after France was routed from Canada. In 1802, the company employed about fifteen hundred French-Canadians, mainly as seasonal contract workers.[21] In response, the HBC, beginning in the 1770s, hired a large group of experienced boatmen from the Orkney Islands off the north coast of Scotland.

Though the "servants" of the company accepted the right of their masters to rule, they expected their bosses to demonstrate both compassion and common sense. When they felt that instead their supervisors had been cruel and stupid, they occasionally revolted, often as individuals but sometimes collectively. Some forms of protest involved working slowly or inefficiently, deliberately mistranslating what their master was trying to convey to a Native or vice versa, or, if there seemed few alternatives, deserting their master, though that violated the terms of their contract. In turn, masters often responded with intimidation and threats, and the withholding of alcohol and feasts. Occasionally, despite the tight job market, a company would fire a worker. The NWC, for example, faced with a strike in Rainy Lake in 1794, managed to persuade a number of the workers to return to work. The company then promptly fired the strike leaders.[22]

The Orkneymen of the HBC collectively demanded higher wages in 1805, and the company, following accepted capitalist principles of the period, fired the instigators and replaced them with another group of workers.[23] They turned to Natives, mostly mixed-bloods, whom they paid the existing wage but hired on purely seasonal contracts.[24] The lack of Native worker solidarity with the Orkney workers was unsurprising since the Orkneymen, like other Europeans in the region, made no effort to treat Natives as equals or to insist that the company hire them on the same terms as whites.

While the fur trade may have been a partnership of Europeans and Natives, there was never any doubt in the minds of the whites in charge of the HBC about who should rule the roost. The company, as reorganized in 1821, had a clear social class structure, which, in turn, was based on race and gender. At the apex of the company was the governor appointed by the leading shareholders in Britain. Then came the chief factors, who supervised trade districts, and beneath them, the chief traders, who ran the main trading posts. These individuals were incorporated into the company as partners and received, between them, 40 percent of company profits, with the non-working investors receiving the remaining profits. From 1821 to 1833, chief factors earned average profits of 800 pounds a year while the chief traders earned 400 pounds. Clerks, who earned salaries of about 100 pounds a year, were next in the hierarchy, followed by assistant clerks earning half that amount. No First Nations person was ever appointed to a position of clerk or higher. Only a few mixed-bloods with influential fathers broke the racial barrier. In 1821, none of the 25 chief factors of the company were individuals known to have Native blood, while only two chief traders of 28 and 16 clerks of 140 were mixed-blood.[25]

NATIVE-EUROPEAN INTERACTION AND THE ORIGINS OF THE MÉTIS

From the earliest days of interaction between European fur traders and Native peoples, some of the former lived among the latter and, to a degree, adopted their ways. Many European men chose to live with or marry Native women. For Native women, the decision to live with a European man was fraught with dangers, including abandonment. But to some, it offered the opportunity to live a somewhat easier, sedentary life with more material goods. Though the HBC, during its first century, attempted to prevent its servants from having intercourse with Native women and having mixed-race families, the NWC recognized early on that such marriages cemented the bonds between the company and particular Native communities. By the time Alberta Natives were drawn into the fur trade, marriages of European-origin traders and Native women were the rule rather than the exception. Until the churches had established themselves firmly in western Canada, such marriages followed Native customary practices.

FIG 2-4 Métis family, Fort Vermilion, 1900. Provincial Archives of Alberta, B7256.

Racist sentiment pervaded European-Native relations, including those within the HBC. While marriages in the early period of the trade in western Canada were between European men and First Nations women, a prejudice eventually developed against women who had only "Indian" blood. Mixed-race (Métis) women became the valued marriage partners because they had some white blood, and, according to historian Sylvia Van Kirk, "with the emergence of the mixed-blood wife, the trend was the formation of lasting and devoted marital relationships."[26] Although traders viewed life at the remote trading posts as too rough to appeal to white women, that view changed as communities such as Manitoba's Red River Settlement developed agriculture and expanded their populations and institutions. Once the traders and settlers believed that the West had become "settled" enough to bring white women there, they decided that mixed-race women were not good enough for them. In short, a hardening of racial lines occurred as the fur trade became more established, and those lines became even more rigid as the fur trade gave way to agricultural and urban settlements.[27]

Whether First Nations or Métis, Native women played an essential, unpaid, and largely unmentioned role in ensuring the profitability of the fur-trade companies. Arthur Ray summarizes some of those contributions: "They produced and repaired essential footwear (mocassins and snowshoes), chopped wood, collected canoe-birch supplies, made canoe sails, provided tanned hides and pack cords, re-dressed furs for shipment to London, grew vegetables, snared hare, and caught and preserved fish."[28]

The offspring of marriages of European men and Native women sometimes found a home in the First Nations societies of their mothers, and a few integrated themselves, with many difficulties, into the European societies of their fathers. Many, however, viewed themselves as a distinct people because they had ties as individuals to two very different social groups. The French-speaking Métis — who had served as boatmen, guides, and interpreters for the French as they ventured west of Quebec and served similar roles for the North West Company — developed their own clothes, Red River carts for the buffalo hunt, and their own language, a mix of Cree and French, which they called *michif*. While they contracted their labour to the fur-trading companies, the limited careers that

the companies offered them encouraged them to remain freelancers, copying the Plains Natives in filling many of their subsistence needs with the buffalo. The Métis began to see themselves as a "nation" when the first leaders of the Red River Settlement, a settlement associated with the HBC's efforts to provision their posts more cheaply, attempted to interfere with their access to buffalo.[29] Though their resistance to the settlers was encouraged by the NWC rivals of the HBC, the Métis acted in their own rather than company interests as they challenged the rights of the settlers to limit Métis livelihoods. In 1816, a standoff at Seven Oaks, an area now part of the City of Winnipeg, resulted in the Métis forcing the dispersal of the first settlement in the area. Though outnumbered three to one, the Métis lost only one of their warriors while the HBC forces lost twenty-one.[30]

The sense of Métis nationhood strengthened in the 1840s when the HBC tried to enforce its monopoly over furs and pemmican, and to control supplies and prices for both by penalizing Métis and First Nations people who traded with free traders. A showdown came in 1849, when the HBC — which ran everything in the Red River Colony, including the courts — jailed and charged four Métis with illegal trading. As three hundred armed Métis gathered outside the company court, Guillaume Sayer, the first of the four to be tried, pleaded guilty but argued that he had traded with a relative and believed that he was exercising his customary rights. The jury recommended clemency and the judge, concerned about potential violence, imposed no sentence. The other three prisoners were released without a trial. The Métis interpreted these events as a vindication of their right to trade with whom they pleased, and the HBC subsequently made few efforts to prove them wrong.[31]

English-speaking mixed-bloods often intermarried with the Métis, but also often formed communities separate from the Métis as well as from their English fathers and First Nations mothers. *Bungi*, the mix of English, Gaelic, and Cree spoken by this group of mixed-bloods, marked them off from other groups. These communities often felt caught in the middle of European-Métis clashes since English-speaking mixed-bloods seemed pulled between identification with other English-speaking people versus other mixed-bloods.[32]

Native (First Nations and Métis) people formed an important part of the working class in the fur trade. We have already noted the significant unpaid contributions of Native wives to the functioning of trading posts and the trade more broadly. Native men — apart from being free-enterprising providers of furs and pemmican, for which they received a negotiated rate per pound rather than a wage — also did many of the "grunt" jobs within the fur-trading companies. Foreshadowing the future of capitalism in Alberta from that time to the present day, only a small group of workers, almost exclusively white, had any job security. Clerks and surgeons, and a small group of tradespeople had contracts of three to five years, which were often renewed; this provided guaranteed wages for set periods. But boatmen, guides, interpreters, and canoe builders, who over time were increasingly mainly Native, had only seasonal contracts and could be barred from future contracts if they proved militant.

That did not always prevent militancy, however. In the 1850s, Native transport workers, led by Métis, organized a number of mutinies in an effort to force the HBC to provide better working conditions. While wages were at issue, more important demands were that the company provide sturdier, easier-to-navigate boats, along with smaller loads and better food on the boats. The boatmen were tired of dealing with dangerous currents in worn-out, overloaded boats. The company, unwilling to yield to such demands but aware that it could not easily replace its Native workforce, gradually switched to steam-powered boats to reduce the number of transport workers required.[33]

THE SETTLEMENT ERA

The Natives' successes as both entrepreneurs and workers contributed to a growing sense in the Hudson's Bay Company by the early 1860s that fur trading in western Canada had become unprofitable. Demand for the company's product had fallen, and many areas previously rich in furs had been tapped out. Showing little concern for the fate of its Native "partners," this capitalist enterprise sold out in 1863 to new London financial owners, who focused not on the fur trade but on the company's alleged control of western Canada's land base. Based on the original charter and Britain's colonial view that Aboriginals had no legal control over land except for partial control over lands that Britain reserved for their use, the HBC became a land speculation machine first and a fur-trading operation a distant second.[34]

The HBC view of western Canada was shared by the Fathers of Confederation, mainly capitalists in Ontario, Quebec, and the Atlantic colonies who viewed the Canada that they created as a potential commercial giant. They wanted it to follow the US model in which the original states in the east captured lands further

Design, Title, Picture and Matter Copyrighted by ERNEST BROWN

Published by The Art League Publishing Co., 10131 Jasper Avenue, Edmonton, Alberta, Canada.

1885 THE BONES OF THOUSANDS OF BUFFALOES STACKED FOR SHIPMENT

BUFFALO BONES AT MEDICINE HAT 1885

"THE BUFFALO" (NATURAL HISTORY)

Teaching Pictures

The Art League EDMONTON

FIG 2-5 Buffalo bones awaiting shipment at Medicine Hat, 1885. Bones were gathered then loaded onto railroad cars and shipped to factories in the east. There, the bones were ground and used in refining sugar or for fertilizer. Provincial Archives of Alberta, B10102.

west from Natives and Mexicans alike and turned them into successful commercial farming areas that became the market for the goods produced by eastern manufacturers. In this model, traditional Native societies based on hunting, trapping, and fishing stood in the way of social progress.[35]

In 1869, the HBC ceded political control over the lands that it had been granted by Britain one year short of two centuries earlier. The Government of Canada paid the company 300,000 pounds (about 1.5 million dollars) for its land, the same price that the HBC owners had paid to buy the company in 1863. But more

FIG 2-6 The 1870 execution of Thomas Scott by the provisional government of Louis Riel in the Red River colony, as depicted in a painting done in 1879. Known for his hostility to the Métis, Scott was charged with plotting against Riel's government. Glenbow Archives, NA-20-8.

importantly, the government, as part of the bargain, gave the HBC control over 5 percent of Rupert's Land, which, after the building of the CPR, would yield the HBC a profit of almost 200 million dollars.[36] The Government of Canada — maintaining the fiction that the Government of Britain, not the people who had lived in western Canada for thirteen thousand years, was the owner — did not at the time offer the First Peoples one penny for their lands.

The Canadian government also ignored the concerns of the Métis and English-speaking mixed-bloods that they receive assurances of title to lands that they farmed: at that time, they had no title since the HBC, although a quasi-government, had followed rather informal rules regarding farms and hunting territories. This resulted in a Métis-led armed resistance in 1869–70 against efforts by Canada to establish its sovereignty in Red River. Though the federal government negotiated with representatives of the provisional government at Red River, led by Louis Riel, and agreed on paper to many of their demands, it subsequently sent a twelve-hundred–man military expedition to take control of the new province of Manitoba until a provincial government was elected. The leader was Colonel Garnet Wolseley, who had already achieved some colonial notoriety for putting down an uprising in India and who would subsequently play similar roles against opponents of British imperialism in southern Africa and Egypt. Murders and beatings of rebellion supporters persuaded many Métis to flee Red River and to establish new settlements in areas of today's Saskatchewan and Alberta. Riel and other leaders of the provisional government fled the colony.[37]

Efforts to oblige the federal government to furnish the land promised to the Métis in Manitoba in 1870 and to recognize Métis title to lands that they had settled further west, in present-day Alberta and Saskatchewan, came to naught. Euro-Canadian farmers received titles to Red River lands that the Métis regarded as their own, and Métis leaders worried that the same fate would befall them in their new settlements to the west. Unable to persuade the federal government to communicate with them, they brought Louis Riel out of his American

FIG 2-7 Militia camp near Batoche, in present-day Saskatchewan, during the North-West Resistance of 1885. Provincial Archives of Alberta, A5569.

FIG 2-8 The Battle of Cut Knife Creek, 2 May 1885, near Battleford, in what is today Saskatchewan, during the North-West Resistance. Cree and Assiniboine warriors repelled an attack by Canadian government forces. Provincial Archives of Alberta, B1732.

exile and deputized him to pressure Ottawa on their behalf. Since this changed nothing, they began a second armed resistance in 1885, this time in the Northwest. (Until they became provinces in 1905, the area that is today Alberta and Saskatchewan was divided into districts that were administered as parts of the Northwest Territories.) The federal government crushed this resistance, which had been joined by a small number of the First Nations communities in northern Saskatchewan and Alberta. The government also hanged Riel and eight of the First Nations rebel leaders, six Cree and two Assiniboine, and jailed other participants, some of whom died during their imprisonment or just after their release.[38]

Shortly after the first of the two Métis-led armed resistances, the federal government began to respond to demands from the Plains First Nations for the negotiation of treaties prior to any further European settlement within their lands. Seven treaties were negotiated from 1871 to 1877, covering all of the territory of the southern regions of the eventual Prairie provinces, the areas that the Canadian authorities regarded as having agricultural potential.

The two sides had different agendas in the negotiations. For the federal government, the important objective was to ensure that the Native peoples' defence of their traditional territories did not stand in the way of plans to create a European commercial agricultural economy and society in what they called western Canada. To ensure the success of such plans, the Natives themselves would have to be assimilated to European culture, and traditional Native societies would disappear.[39] The Natives had a contrasting goal: to preserve their communities and as much as possible of their traditional economic pursuits and culture, while adding agriculture to the economic mix to compensate for the loss of food resources that the thinning of the buffalo population had occasioned.

During treaty negotiations, the spokespersons for Native people emphasized their willingness to share land and resources with the newcomers in return for federal help in making a partial move from a hunting and fishing society to one that included agriculture as well. They wanted their traditional hunting and fishing rights protected. In the case of what became Treaty Six in 1876, the First Nations of central Alberta and Saskatchewan also asked for and received guarantees for a free "medicine chest": European doctors and medicines to supplement Native doctors and traditional treatments, government aid during famines, and free agricultural implements. Speaking at Fort Carlton, Saskatchewan, Chiefs Mistawasis and Ahtahkakoop emphasized that the Natives and Europeans must agree at one and the same time to share resources and not to interfere with each other's lifestyles. Chief Sweetgrass at Fort Pitt focused on similar themes.

Though historians often suggest that there was a failure of the two sides to communicate during the negotiations, Euro-Canadian eyewitnesses, including journalists who covered the discussions, claimed that the government commissioners responded to the Native side by suggesting that the government was also interested in sharing resources, not in dispossessing Aboriginal peoples. While the government viewed the whole purpose of treaties as the surrender of most Native lands, the negotiators were careful to avoid talk of land surrenders and emphasized instead that the government did not need all the land for white settlers and that there would be plenty of land left over for Natives to carry on their traditional economy. Referring to Treaty Six negotiations, historian Sheldon Krasowski observes that the negotiators failed to raise the issue of land surrenders: "the eyewitness accounts also revealed that the treaty commissioners neglected to mention the surrender clause during the discussions, which was also the case at Treaties Three, Four and Five."[40] Some historians, noting the discrepancies between what the Aboriginal negotiators reported regarding the contents of discussions and what the commissioners wrote down, give the latter the benefit of the doubt, claiming that a wide cultural gulf made it impossible for the two sides to understand one another. Krasowski,

From the Aboriginal point of view, the notion of ownership and surrender of lands held little meaning since the Creator was the only owner of lands; communities simply contracted with the Creator to make use in a given area of what the Creator had granted them, in return for which they would behave in a way that demonstrated their respect for the Creator's gifts. In a practical sense, they wished to avoid copying their fellow First Nations to the south in the United States in going to war with a ruthless enemy who would despoil them of their lands. While they were not keen on hordes of white agricultural settlers becoming established on their traditional territories, they hoped that at worst, the treaties would give them some state protection from these settlers, and at best, they would provide for a kind of co-management of the lands and resources of the region.[42] Important leaders of the Cree, such as Mistahimaskwa (Big Bear) lobbied the Department of Indian Affairs for large reserves in which the Native peoples would not be surrounded by European settlers. But Indian Commissioner Edgar Dewdney persisted with plans to have small reserves scattered throughout the western provinces to prevent Natives having a geographical homeland and a base for resisting assimilation and marginalization.[43]

The Natives' disappointment began almost immediately after signing the treaties. The government never made a serious effort to live up to the letter of the treaties, much less the spirit of the negotiations. It ignored its pledge in Treaty Six to fill the nutritional gap during lean times when famine struck in the winter of 1883–84; it cut back on rations for Native peoples as a government cost-cutting measure, saving its money instead to generously subsidize the private owners who

however, suggests, based on both the reports of the Natives involved in negotiations and the European eye-witness reports, that "during the treaty making period, Euro-Canadians understood the expectations of Indigenous peoples in the treaty relationship."[41] In plain English, the commissioners deliberately misled their Native counterparts and produced treaties that they understood very well did not replicate the agreements that they had reached with the First Nations in the actual negotiations.

were building the CPR; and it looked aside as Indian agents, farm instructors, and civilians mistreated Native peoples in ways that violated treaty understandings.[44] The attitude to Native starvation was similar to the British attitude that had permitted a million Irish people to die during the Great Famine of 1845 to 1852.[45] Though in both cases, the precarious circumstances of the people who were dying had largely been created by imperialist dispossession of their land base, the imperial power argued that the people's inherent laziness was the cause. The agent-general of Indian Affairs made clear that this inverted view of reality was at the base of the government's relief policy: "So long as they can rely, or believe they can rely, on any source whatever for their food they make no effort to support themselves. We have to guard against this, and the only way to guard against it is by being rigid, even stingy in the distribution of food, and require absolute proof of starvation before distributing it."[46] So, contrary to treaty provisions, there was no general distribution of food during famines in Treaty Six territories, and rations were distributed only for labourers on Indian Agency farms. But the farms provided fewer jobs than were needed to meet the demand of starving Aboriginal peoples, and farm labourers were paid with rations that were too small to feed large families.[47]

From the government's point of view, regardless of what lies their representatives might have told to get them, they had the signatures of Native leaders guaranteeing that Native peoples would not interfere with Canadian and European immigrants to the West who settled on traditional Native hunting and gathering lands. The government also established the North West Mounted Police in 1873, nominally to protect Aboriginal people from ruthless whites, but in practice to enforce a new status quo to restrict Native peoples' mobility and to prevent them making demands on the new settlers in their midst.[48]

Aboriginals' mobility was further restricted by the provisions of the *Indian Act* of 1876 and various subsequent amendments, as well as by administrative practices. In 1885, for example, the act banned the potlatch, the key ritual of the Pacific Coastal peoples. The next year, the government of John A. Macdonald implemented a passbook system, which required Prairie Natives to receive written permission to travel off reserve. While the pass system was never legislated, it remained in place until the 1940s, though its enforcement was not always rigorous. It was used to discourage Sun Dances and other Native practices involving First Nations gatherings that united people from many reserves.[49] In another colonial gesture, Euro-Canadian laws regarding polygamy and divorce were used to call Native marriages into question and to restrict the rights of Native women.[50]

Perhaps the most damaging interference in Native family lives was the forced attendance of children from reserves at schools well away from the reserves. With roots in earlier efforts by governments in the colonies of what became Canada to impose European languages and cultural values on Native children, the residential school system enforced mandatory attendance of reserve children in the Prairie provinces from the 1870s to 1948. The schools were run by mainstream churches, and staff members punished children who spoke their own language and taught them not only that traditional Native religions were sinful but that they must embrace Christianity if they wanted to go to heaven when

FIG 2-10 Cree students, suitably clad in European-style clothing, pictured with their Methodist Church teacher at Hobbema, Alberta, ca. 1890s. Glenbow Archives, NA-682-5.

they died. Most died quite young. In the early years, the underfunded schools made the children perform hard physical labour, fed them poorly, and did little to provide proper sanitation. The medical superintendent for the Department of Indian Affairs, which was responsible for the schools, reported that for the years between 1894 and 1908, 30 to 60 percent of all children who had been placed in a residential school died within five years of first attending. While the department suppressed the report, Native parents had become aware of the high mortality rate associated with their children being kidnapped by the faraway schools and frequently resisted having their children taken away from them. But Indian agents often used the pass system as a way of forcing recalcitrant parents to send their children to residential schools. They would deny uncooperative parents a pass allowing them to hunt off reserve, without which the family might starve.[51]

The state's desire to assimilate Native children to Christian values was not accompanied by a belief that Natives should have the same economic rights as other western Canadians, any more than it was by a willingness to grant them human rights. White settlers who moved to the Canadian West, cleared ten acres of land, and built a home within three years received 160 acres of land and therefore the ability to farm commercially. But Native families on reserves received only ten acres of land. Whereas the government was convinced that white "pioneers" could become part of the commercial economy that would make western Canada the linchpin of economic development for the entire country, Natives were regarded as people who could never do more than become subsistence farmers. So not only were they given smaller plots of land, but the government also resisted making good on promises, laid out in the treaties, of material aid intended to help

Native peoples become successful farmers, arguing that Natives were not serious about farming. The Natives responded by assuring the government that they *were* serious but could not get started without seed or farm implements.[52]

In short, Native peoples, in the government's view, were to become the equivalent of peasant farmers in Europe who had only enough land to grow what their families needed to subsist. This also meant that Natives, short of income and wanting to supplement it, would be conveniently available to help white farmers who needed help getting their farms operational or harvesting crops.

◆ ◆ ◆

The unequal treatment of Natives and whites with respect to farming was the most salient characteristic of the division of labour in early western Canada. But as other industries became established in the region and as successful farmers began hiring temporary labour, it became clear that exploitation and class divisions, as well as resistance by oppressed workers and minorities, would mark work life for many years to come in the area that in 1905 became the Province of Alberta.

FIG 3-1 Chinese workers building the CPR main line, 1884.
Library and Archives Canada, C-6686 B.

3 ONE STEP FORWARD
ALBERTA WORKERS, 1885–1914

JIM SELBY

Although there was scarcely a recognizable workforce in 1885 in the southwestern half of the Northwest Territories, which would later become Alberta, all the essential elements that would shape the experiences and conditions of the early working class were already in place. The suppression of First Nations' land rights after the treaties were signed and the military defeat of Métis aspirations of autonomy at Batoche cleared the last obstacles in the way of exploitation of the land and resources of the Northwest Territories by the federal government. Both the Canadian Pacific Railway — which, through its initial federal grant of twenty-five million acres of land "fairly fit for settlement," had instantly become the largest corporate enterprise, employer, and private landowner on the prairies — and the federal government were actively promoting the settlement of the prairies by immigrant farmers.

The first significant coal development in Alberta was at Coal Banks (soon to be renamed Lethbridge after William Lethbridge, the company's first president), where Alexander Galt, Canada's first finance minister, and his son procured extensive coal leases for the company Galt had begun selling to British investors while he was Canada's High Commissioner in London.[1] The Galts then secured further land and coal grants at special low rates to construct a railway connecting Lethbridge to the CPR mainline near Medicine Hat. Once the Galts had secured a coal contract with the CPR, their North Western Coal and Navigation Company began producing coal in 1883 for the railway and the local house heating market.[2] Another new mine at Anthracite near Banff began to produce high-quality bituminous "steam coal."

The railways themselves were the other main providers of employment. Calgary, which became the site of a European settlement when the North West Mounted Police (NWMP) established a fort there in 1875, was in the midst of an early real estate and housing boom as a result of railway construction, creating work for skilled craftsmen in the building trades. That boom and continued railway construction provided the demand for the area's largest manufacturing outfits, two sawmills.

FIG 3-2 Galt family mine and rail link to CPR, Lethbridge, 1904. Glenbow Archives, PD-310-72.

temporary construction camps. Single-industry coal towns, which offered a mixture of skilled and unskilled jobs, constituted a second environment for workers. A third was the growing urban centres, in which skilled workers in the construction industry, the railway running trades, and other skilled crafts lived and worked alongside unskilled and semi-skilled workers employed in the retail trade, transportation, manufacturing, domestic service, and the public sector. Finally, there were waged farmworkers, the largest component of paid labour in this period. Within each of these four distinct environments, workers struggled to improve their lives in their workplaces and within their homes and communities. They confronted contradictions and prejudices and engaged in debates over ideology, tactics, and strategies that continue to this day.

Was it possible to extract a living wage and acceptable working conditions during this period? If so, how could that best be accomplished? What was the relationship between unions and social class? What did worker solidarity mean? Was political action advisable, and if so, how could workers best participate? What role did the state play? Could or should the capitalist system be reformed? How could a socialist alternative be achieved? These were some of the questions faced by workers moving into the evolving area of European settlement that had dispossessed the Aboriginal residents. Unsurprisingly, the different answers that workers arrived at depended upon their experiences with employers, labour organizations, governments and police, and their own diverse communities. Cumulatively, their experiences created a diverse yet vibrant workers' movement capable of responding to the economic, political, and social conflicts ahead.

For workers arriving in Alberta over the next thirty years, job opportunities were available in four quite distinct environments. First, massive railway construction projects employed tens of thousands of unskilled and semi-skilled workers, who were housed in isolated

THE RAILWAY CONSTRUCTION WORKERS

"Why were the recognized leaders of union labour in Canada so long indifferent to the wage conditions of the navvy?" wondered Edmund Bradwin, using the name given to railway construction labourers.[3] Given the low wages and poor working conditions they endured, navvies should have been fertile ground for union organizers. Their work was brutally labour intensive. Throughout the spring, summer, and fall, navvies cleared the railway right-of-ways, largely by hand. Using picks, shovels, axes, and wheelbarrows, they worked ten hours or more each day shoveling clay and gravel, breaking rocks, and clearing bush.

Between 1883 and 1914, three transcontinental railways were constructed across Alberta, along with lines to coalfields in Lethbridge, the Crowsnest Pass, Drumheller, Nordegg, and the Coal Branch south of Hinton. One line connected Calgary to Edmonton, another ran between Edmonton and Peace River, and both Canadian Pacific and Canadian Northern built branch lines into the farmlands. At the peak of railway construction, between 1907 and 1914, when both the Canadian Northern and the Grand Trunk Pacific were completing their transcontinental lines and the CPR was building branch lines, the railways employed between fifty thousand and seventy thousand workers annually.[4]

FIG 3-3 Slavic workers laying track for the Canadian Northern Railway. Library and Archives Canada, C-46156.

ALBERTA AND "IMMIGRANT" LABOUR

The population of the District of Alberta in 1885 was 15,533 persons, of whom 9,418 were listed as Indian and 1,237 as Métis. With a provincial population of 374,663 persons reported in the 1911 census, the vast majority of Alberta workers during this period were migrants to the province.[1] Canada's political elite, having created a new country in 1867 in the hope of copying the American success story of establishing an expanding marketplace by moving the country's borders ever further west, were disappointed that the British settlers whom they had recruited proved less than enamoured of their new homes. Between 1881 and 1901, despite government efforts to attract new immigrants, Canada experienced a net out-migration, with 1,229,000 people entering the country and 1,615,000 emigrating, mostly to the United States. Only natural increase saved the country from a net decline in population.[2]

The picture began to change dramatically in 1897. The best land in the American West had been taken, and the Canadian government, while closing the door to non-whites except for very specific work, relaxed its former prejudice against potential southern and eastern European immigrants. Between 1901 and 1911, 1,782,000 newcomers arrived in Canada.[3] The majority were not of British descent.

From 1901 to 1905, the federal government actively recruited peasant farmers from eastern Europe. Simultaneously, the railways and industrial employers sought immigrants from southern Europe and the Balkans, particularly from 1907 to 1914. Between 1896 and 1914, approximately one million immigrant farmers arrived in Canada, along with two million other immigrants.[4] Most of the non-farmers found their way into wage labour in the manufacturing centres in central Canada and in railway camps, mines, factories, and logging enterprises in the West.

In central and eastern Canada, the western, eastern, and southern European immigrants remained a minority within the dominant Anglo-Celtic (English, Scots, Irish, and Welsh) majority, or, in the case of Quebec, the French-speaking majority. However, in Alberta, the British held a bare 51 percent majority by 1911. The largest other groups were, in order of size, Germans, Scandinavians, Ukrainians, French, First Nations, and Russians. Even among Albertans of Anglo-Celtic origin, the majority were newcomers to the province, with migrants from other provinces outnumbering English speakers from the British Isles.

In his seminal work, *The Bunkhouse Man*, Edmund W. Bradwin notes that workers on the railways were divided into "whites" and "foreigners."[5] Canadian-born English- and French-speaking workers, new arrivals from Britain and the United States, Scandinavians, and sometimes Finns were included in the "white" category. "Whites" got the better jobs on the railway construction gangs while the "foreign" navvies — Ukrainians, Poles, Czechs, Slovaks, Serbs, Hungarians, Croats, Bulgarians, Macedonians, Turks, Orientals, and Sikhs — got the "mucker" jobs.

Ethnic stereotypes regarding temperament, work habits, abilities, and intelligence abounded. Even Bradwin freely painted the various ethnic groups' "characteristics" with a broad brush, despite his observation regarding their skill:

Not that the man from Central and Southern Europe is un-acquainted with the art of bridging great rivers by huge spans of steel, for he is prone to criticize the seeming haste with which, in Canada, the long trusses are soon girded into great arches and tracked with level crossings, but too frequently at a sacrifice of the solidity and finish of workmanship which characterize those in his own land. Many newcomers to the

Dominion from Central Europe would prove useful on structural work, but have not the requisite knowledge of English so essential in the conduct of these hazardous tasks.[6]

The negative response of the British elite to the incoming ethnic immigrants is typified by a *Calgary Herald* article from 2 February 1899:

What is this country coming to? Doukhobours pouring in by the thousands on the eastern slope, Galicians [Ukrainians] swarming over the central portions, and rats taking possession of Dawson City, one would imagine that Canada had become a veritable dumping ground for the refuse of civilization.[7]

The equating of rats that accompanied the Yukon gold rush with certain ethnic groups reflected the deep racism of many British-origin Albertans. Their careless stereotypes also ignored the fact that Alberta's ethnic workers included many who were skilled, literate, and politically sophisticated. For example, a study of the Polish community in the Crowsnest Pass found that young Polish immigrants, although coming from farming communities, had experience as carpenters, bricklayers, brewery workers, and tailors. They could read and write Polish. These were not the strong-of-body and weak-of-mind Eastern Europeans stereotyped by English Canadians.[8]

---

2 Gerald Friesen, *The Canadian Prairies: A History*, 248–49.

3 Ibid., 248.

4 Donald Avery, *"Dangerous Foreigners": European Immigrant Workers and Labour Radicalism in Canada 1896–1932*, 16–20.

5 Edmund W. Bradwin, *The Bunkhouse Man: A Study of the Work and Pay in the Camps of Canada, 1903–1914*.

6 Ibid., 101–2.

7 Quoted in Helen Potrebenko, *No Streets of Gold: A Social History of Ukrainians in Alberta*, 39–40.

8 Krystyna Lukasiewicz, "Polish Community in the Crowsnest Pass."

1 The 1885 Census boundaries for the District of Alberta excluded the northern third of the current province and a narrow band on the east, including Medicine Hat. The populations of First Nations are therefore understated, and the numbers elsewhere, while representative, are not exact. *Census of the Three Provisional Districts of the North-West Territories: 1884–5*, and *Census of Canada, 1911*, Vol. 1, *Areas and Population by Provinces, Districts and Subdistricts*.

Although labour for the CPR mainline in the early 1880s was originally recruited from central and eastern Canada, some fifteen thousand indentured Chinese labourers were given the most dangerous jobs in the construction through the mountains in British Columbia. More than fifteen hundred died on the job, a rate of attrition more akin to a war than to a construction project. Exhaustion and scurvy claimed many lives since the employer provided no medical services and the state placed no limits on exploitation of labour.[5] The sacrifices of the Chinese workers, however, did not dispel racism against Orientals. During the construction of the Crowsnest Pass line from Lethbridge to Nelson, BC, in the late 1890s, which involved about forty-five hundred navvies, Prime Minister Wilfrid Laurier's government made the hiring of only British subjects as construction labourers one condition for government financial support. They may later have regretted that decision because many of the one thousand Welsh workers complained in the newspapers about their treatment rather than tolerating the low wages and inhuman working and living conditions in the camps. Navvies recruited in eastern and central Canada were equally critical.

The criticism caused enormous embarrassment for the Canadian government, which feared that such complaints would choke off desired immigrants from Britain. In response, the government appointed two Royal Commissions to investigate wages and working and living conditions. The CPR, unhappy with the bad publicity that the newspapers and Royal Commissions gave to their employment practices, turned to immigrant labour from eastern and southern Europe on future construction projects, a strategy subsequently copied by other railways and industrialists.

The findings of the commissioners, along with reports by the North West Mounted Police, provide vivid glimpses of the life of a navvy. Most had been misled about the terms and conditions of work when they signed their contracts. For example, they were not told that they would have to pay their fare from Ottawa to the worksite. Charged a penny a mile, they owed the employer $22.49 before they began their first day's work. They had to purchase blankets, boots, work clothes, candles, and other necessities from the company store, which often doubled the normal price of goods. Food was supplied at a fixed rate of $5.00 per worker each week. There were also deductions for sending mail and for receiving medical care. Considering that the men were paid $1.50 per day for a ten-hour workday and received no payment for days when they were too sick to work or when the weather did not allow work, it is not surprising that after working for two months, men could find themselves either with no money coming in or in debt to the contractor.

Living conditions in the camps ranged from bad to appalling, depending upon the particular contractor. One group was housed in tents without stoves in the middle of winter. Groups of fifty or sixty men were crowded into tiny, unventilated bunkhouses with leaking roofs, mud floors, and seven-foot ceilings. Blankets and bedding were generally infested with lice, and the unsanitary bunkhouses were home to vermin. The meat and other food sent to feed the workers was frequently spoiled and rancid by the time it reached the camps. The workers had to find and transport water for personal use, and privies were badly constructed and often contaminated local water supplies.

Unsurprisingly, such conditions caused rampant

illness among navvies on the Crowsnest line, including colds, flus, diphtheria, mountain fever, and rheumatism. Despite workers being charged for medical care, only five doctors served thousands of workers strung out along hundreds of miles of track. The deaths of two sick workers who received no medical care prompted the second Royal Commission. During the hearings, there was testimony that men too sick to work were fired and ejected from the camps.

On the Crowsnest line, as with most other railway construction during this time, workers were not allowed to quit. Bound by the *Master and Servant Act*, the men were compelled to work unless permitted to leave by the employer. The North West Mounted Police enforced work contracts. If the police caught a worker who had left an employer before his labour contract

had ended, he was forced back to work or jailed for desertion. By contrast, there were few repercussions for a contractor who violated the contract. According to Warren Caragata:

> A frequent cause of dispute was, as it had been on the mainline, the failure of contractors to pay the workers wages owed. In some cases examined by the commission, contractors just abandoned the camps and the men in them. At Wardner, just inside the B.C. border, several complaints were heard from men in a camp that they had not been paid for two months. . . . In such cases, the options open for the workers were few. The Mounties could come and arrest a navvie for deserting his contractor but there is no reference in the Dugas commission report of any contractor, having deserted a camp full of men and leaving them one hundred miles from Macleod with dwindling food supplies, being arrested and tossed into the guard house.[6]

One option always open to working people when individual protest proves futile is collective action. During early railway construction in the region, two major confrontations with bosses occurred, one to the east and one to the west of what would become Alberta's borders. In 1883 at Maple Creek, not far from Medicine Hat, and in 1885 at Beaver Creek, near the Rogers Pass, navvies collectively put down their tools and refused to work. Both strikes were suppressed by the North West Mounted Police, under the leadership of Inspector Sam Steele. At Maple Creek, the strike leader was arrested and imprisoned and the men forced back to work, but at Beaver Creek a pitched battle between five hundred navvies and the Mounties ended only when one of the strike leaders was shot by a policeman and further gunfire appeared imminent. Strike leaders were arrested and either fined or sentenced to six months of hard labour. The North West Mounted Police had the authority of magistrates at the time: they could arrest, charge, convict, and sentence offenders at will.

One barrier the navvies faced in struggles to assert their rights was the disinterest of the labour movement in organizing them. There were many reasons for this. Most early trade unions were craft-based and not interested in unskilled workers. For unions that might have been interested, the isolation of the camps made them difficult for outsiders to reach. Furthermore, the work was seasonal and workers frequently moved locations and changed contractors, which made sustained union involvement difficult. Probably the most significant barrier to organizing, though, particularly after 1900, was the fact that most of these workers were non-British immigrants. Edmund Bradwin calculated that in the early 1920s, 32 percent of the railway construction workers were Slavs (Ukrainians, Czechs and Slovaks, Yugoslavs, and Poles), 24.7 percent Scandinavians (Finns, Swedes, Norwegians, and Danes), 7 percent Italians, and 3.8 percent other non-British (other European, Orientals, Blacks, and East Indians). Once the 11.3 percent made up of French-Canadians was factored in, only 20 percent of the workers had English as a first language, and 40 percent of those were new arrivals from Great Britain.[7]

The language barrier to organizing these new immigrants was secondary in many cases to the problem of nativism on the part of the dominant Anglo leadership and membership of existing unions. The one union that welcomed railway navvies was the Industrial Workers of the World (IWW). After its founding in 1905, the IWW focused on the masses of unskilled workers whom other unions were unwilling to organize, including textile-factory workers in the east of the continent and migrant labourers who worked the farms, railway construction camps, and logging camps in the west. Historian Greg Hall, in his study of the IWW and agricultural workers in the American West during this period, describes the bond shared by IWW members, who were often referred to as "wobblies":

> During the first few decades of the twentieth century, the vast majority of migrant and seasonal laborers working in western agriculture were white, native-born men. Among these predominantly unmarried workers, travelling by rail from job to job and living in "jungles," harvest wobblies developed a distinctive culture of work and life on the road, which I have termed their "worklife culture." They shared much of this culture with other migrant and seasonal agricultural laborers of the day. Yet the wobblies embodied a unique camaraderie in the jungles, worksites, union halls, skid rows, jails, and freight cars of the American west. Their common experiences forged a sociocultural bond that was further strengthened by aggressive opposition to employers, law enforcement officers, and "hi-jacks, the robbers and confidence men who preyed on migrant harvest workers."[8]

In the Canadian West, these observations were equally true for the "navvies": single white males working in camps in the summer, riding the rails to jobs, and

FIG 3-5 Industrial Workers of the World song book. Courtesy of the Alberta Labour History Institute.

spending winters in the skid rows of cities like Calgary, Edmonton, and Vancouver. With the added shared experience of being immigrants standing outside the Anglo-dominant mainstream in terms of both language and custom, the immigrant navvies were a unique part of Alberta's early labour history.

This worklife culture of the navvies predisposed them to the IWW message. Shunned by the crafts unions and the dominant Anglo society, exploited at work and routinely cheated by employers and labour agents, and discarded when no longer needed, migrant workers believed that employers and the government would always treat them unjustly. Few could fulfill the residency and citizenship requirements to vote, so the IWW disdain for the electoral process found fertile ground. Furthermore, the lack of a permanent community left most migrant workers without the mechanisms so essential for the survival of the working class during this period. Single men on the move had no families to provide the critical waged and non-waged contributions by women and children that helped workers make ends meet.[9] For them, taking on the employer in IWW-organized job actions with other immigrant workers, regardless of ethnic background or language, was the only way forward.

THE ALBERTA COAL MINERS

In the absence of another fuel supply for home heating, coal was essential to both the settlement of the southern prairies and the operations of the railways that made settlement economically possible. From the beginning, coal mining was one of the most important industries of the province — with softer, heating lignite coal found at Drumheller, Lethbridge, Taber, and Edmonton, and the harder bituminous steam coal found in the mountains of the Crowsnest Pass, Canmore, the Yellowhead, and the Coal Branch. However, Alberta coal mining was both physically dangerous and economically precarious, a volatile mixture that produced increasingly bitter confrontations between workers and owners, establishing the province as one of the bastions of radical labour activity in Canada.

All underground coal mines were dangerous, but employers refused to reduce those dangers because safe explosives, safety gear, ventilation equipment, and safety measures involving timbers for shoring diverted money from profits. Miners complained that the ponies used to haul coal carts inside the mines were treated better than the men; mine ponies cost money to replace; men were replaced for free.[10]

Coal production was financially precarious because of the economic power of the railways. Data from 1920 to 1945 indicate that the railways commonly purchased over 90 percent of Alberta's annual bituminous coal production.[11] In addition, the CPR's ownership of "captive mines" gave the company even more influence over the market price of coal. The CPR effectively controlled the Hillcrest mine in Alberta and in 1908 launched the Hosmer mine across the BC border in the Crowsnest Pass. In 1905, the railway's capacity to depress coal prices led to profit margins being half of what original investors in the coal mines expected. Finally, the coal producers were absolutely dependent on the railways to transport their product to markets outside the province; the freight rate structure of both the CPR and CNR discouraged export of coal.[12]

INDUSTRIAL WORKERS OF THE WORLD

The Industrial Workers of the World (IWW) was a revolutionary union created to address the inability of the labour movement, as it was then constituted, to free workers from the economic suffering they experienced in the early twentieth century. The back of the manifesto sent out before the 1905 founding conference in Chicago articulated what a labour organization must do to properly represent the working class:

> First — It must combine the wage earners in such a way that it can most successfully fight the battles and protect the interests of the working people of today in their struggle for fewer hours, more wages and better conditions. Second — It must offer a final solution of the labor problem — an emancipation from strikes, injunctions and bull-pens [labour concentration camps then in use in America].[1]

Unlike the craft-based unions of the American Federation of Labor, the IWW welcomed women, black workers, and immigrants (the union printed literature in many languages). One of the harshest criticisms of the existing labour movement was that it ignored the need for labour solidarity. The American Federation of Labor had only limited interest in workers beyond the "aristocracy of labour" represented by skilled workers, who were almost invariably white males. Even within skilled ranks there was little solidarity. Crafts-based unions routinely ordered their members to cross other craft-union picket lines on the grounds that their own contracts with the employer in question were still in force.[2]

The IWW rejected signed contracts in its constitution because contracts prevented workers from striking when the time was best, restricted the calling of sympathetic strikes, and encouraged the crossing of picket lines (union scabbing). The IWW constitution bore the motto "An Injury to One is an Injury to All," and all IWW workers in an industry belonged to the same branch of the union regardless of skill or occupation.[3]

Although initially tolerant of Socialist Party members being active within the union, in 1908, the Wobblies (as IWW members were called) explicitly removed all references to electoral politics from their constitution, claiming that political action presented no danger to the economic elite and wasted labour's efforts on futile struggles.[4] The new preamble read:

> The working class and the employing class have nothing in common. There can be no peace so long as hunger and want are found among the millions of working people and the few, who make up the employing class, have all the good things of life.
>
> Between these two classes a struggle must go on until the workers of the world organize as a class, take possession of the earth and the machinery of production, abolish the wage system and live in harmony with the Earth.
>
> Instead of the conservative motto, "a fair day's wage for a fair day's work," we must inscribe on our banner the revolutionary watchword, "abolition of the wage system."
>
> It is the historic mission of the working-class to do away with capitalism. The army of production must be organized, not only for the everyday struggle with capitalists, but also to carry on production when capitalism shall have been overthrown. By organizing industrially we are forming the structure of the new society within the shell of the old.[5]

The Wobblies were famous for their creative strike strategies, and they encouraged their members to strike at will. They pioneered the idea of mobilizing strikers in mass actions in order to keep morale up. Since the union refused to produce a "war chest," IWW strikes were purposefully very short. If there was no immediate victory, they simply returned to work and announced that they were "taking the strike to the job" by harrying employers through slowdowns and delays at the worksite.[6]

From the beginning, the IWW had strong Canadian and Albertan connections. A key union involved in founding the IWW, the Western Federation of Miners, was strong in British Columbia and was active until 1905 in the coal mines in Lethbridge and the Crowsnest Pass. The United Brotherhood of Railway Employees, which had led workers in a Winnipeg-to-Calgary-to-Vancouver strike against the CPR in 1903, was directly linked to another IWW founder, the American Labor Union.

With its militant, revolutionary message and its focus on unskilled factory workers and transient labourers, mostly new immigrants, the IWW gained a strong following among railway construction workers, miners, loggers, and farm workers in Alberta. With the exception of the miners, the IWW was the only union that tried to organize these groups of workers.

Despite attacks by more conservative labour leaders and organizations, and despite savage repression by governments in Canada and the United States during World War I and its aftermath, the IWW maintained a presence in lumber camps and other settings during the 1920s and 1930s, and its ideas influenced the campaign in 1919–20 to get existing unions in western Canada to join the One Big Union.[7]

1 Philip S. Foner, *The History of the Labor Movement in the United States*, vol. 4, *The Industrial Workers of the World, 1905–1917*, 2nd ed., 18.

2 Ibid., 32–33.

3 Ibid., 37.

4 Ibid., 109.

5 Ibid., 33, 111.

6 Ibid., 134–38.

7 Greg Hall, *Harvest Wobblies: The Industrial Workers of the World and Agricultural Laborers in the American West, 1905–1930*; Nigel Anthony Sellers, *Oil, Wheat, and Wobblies: The Industrial Workers of the Work in Oklahoma, 1905–1930*; Charles Allen Seager, "A Proletariat in Wild Rose Country: The Alberta Coal Miners, 1905–1945"; Donald Avery, *"Dangerous Foreigners": European Immigrant Workers and Labour Radicalism in Canada 1896–1932*; Cecilia Danysk, *Hired Hands: Labour and the Development of Prairie Agriculture, 1880–1930*; Martin Robin, *Radical Politics and Canadian Labour, 1880–1930*; Mark Leier, *Where the Fraser River Flows: The Industrial Workers of the World in British Columbia*; and A. Ross McCormack, *Reformers, Rebels and Revolutionaries: The Western Canadian Radical Movement, 1899–1919*.

In an era when all North American workers, even those in mighty craft unions, faced savage attacks that increased work hours, speeded up production, and reduced wages, Alberta coal mine owners needed little encouragement to grind their workers.[13] However, the chronic downward pressure on coal prices orchestrated by the railways meant that the mine owners had little capacity to secure industrial peace by meeting even the most basic needs of their workforce. Even the Galts were no match for the CPR. In early 1886, the CPR demanded, and received, a price reduction in coal from $5.00 per ton to $2.50 by threatening to otherwise hand the CPR's coal contract to Pennsylvania producers. In response, Galt ordered coal to be stockpiled at the Medicine Hat terminal and then laid off all his miners, giving the unmarried men one-way tickets to Medicine Hat and offering the married miners their jobs back with a 75 percent reduction in pay.[14]

Alberta's First Coal Strike

Within a year, the bitterness created in the mining community at Lethbridge by company lay-offs and wage cuts simmered over into a strike for higher wages in April 1887. Surprisingly, the workers won because the CPR was short of coal and the North Western Coal and Navigation Company was short of money. However, when the men struck again two months later, the coal shortage had eased and the company imported strikebreakers from eastern Canada and Ohio, using the NWMP to escort them across the picket lines. The strike was lost.[15] This pattern of massive layoffs whenever demand for coal fell became a repeated theme for heating-coal producers in Lethbridge and elsewhere.

The cyclical suffering of miners and their families during these sudden, temporary layoffs had lasting effects on the social fabric of coal towns. Although the railway needed coal year round, heating coal was only needed in the winter, so mines were only busy during early and mid-winter.

When the North Western Coal and Navigation Company again fired its 518 workers in early 1894 and offered to rehire only 150 married workers if they agreed to a 17 percent wage cut, the miners rebelled. Although 150 miners immediately left town to look for work elsewhere, the remaining workers went on a strike organized by local leaders since they had no union affiliation yet. The Mounties placed a guard on company property and attempted to mediate the strike. Finally, the company broke the strike by threatening to evict all the workers from the company-owned houses despite the winter weather.[16]

Three years later, protesting the company's installation of larger coal screens (the men only got paid for coal that did not fall through the screen) and demanding higher wages, the Lethbridge workers struck again. This time, a large group of miners left to work on the rail line being constructed in the nearby Crowsnest Pass, but the CPR would not hire the strikers despite its need for labour. With the local NWMP captain constantly coercing the men back to work, the strike again failed.[17]

Following these three successive defeats, Lethbridge miners proved receptive when a representative of the militant Western Federation of Miners (WFM) visited Lethbridge in October 1897, bringing a message of the need for collective action. The WFM had been involved in bitter struggles in the hard-rock mines in Idaho, Montana, and Washington, often confronting gun-wielding company forces and state troops with armed resistance. By 1898, the Lethbridge local boasted about two hundred members. However, when tested in 1899, the new union failed to gain either recognition or better terms from the employer, and it was disbanded in 1902. But the union did establish viable locals in the Crowsnest Pass mines at Fernie, BC (1899), and at Frank, Alberta (1903).[18] The WFM also officially endorsed the Socialist Party of America in 1902, and its Canadian locals backed the Socialist Party of Canada.

In 1903, at the same time that an allied union, the United Brotherhood of Railway Employees (UBRE), was striking the CPR in western Canada, a crucial strike by the WFM coal miners in the Crowsnest Pass and on Vancouver Island brought first a federal Royal Commission and then the threat of punitive and restrictive legislation against the union.[19] The deputy minister of Labour for the governing federal Liberals, Mackenzie King, threatened to pass legislation declaring both unions illegal organizations.[20] Seeing the handwriting on the wall, Frank Sherman, the leader of Crowsnest Pass miners organized in District 7 of the WFM, changed his allegiance to the United Mine Workers of America (UMWA) in late 1903, reorganizing the locals into a new District 18.[21]

Although some criticized Sherman for abandoning the WFM, the UMWA, with its larger membership, offered a better chance to gain real improvements for rank-and-file coal miners. Unlike the embattled and battered WFM, the UMWA had emerged as a major national union in the United States by winning an interstate coal contract in 1898, in the process bringing out on strike the whole American Midwest. They won the eight-hour day, the union check-off, and a process of collective bargaining. Their subsequent leader, John Mitchell, led a strike of 100,000 hard-coal miners in Pennsylvania in 1902, and the subsequent government intervention in the dispute forced an arbitration that awarded significant gains to the workers.[22] The new organization swept up the miners in the Pass; by 1906, it had a membership of four thousand and had negotiated contracts with Crow's Nest Pass Coal, West Canadian Collieries, the Hillcrest Coal and Coke Company, and Coleman International; later contracts included Canmore and Taber.[23]

The Lethbridge Strike of 1906

The first real test for Frank Sherman and District 18 took place at the Galt mine in Lethbridge in 1906. Control of the company had passed to Toronto financiers, with A.M. Nanton of Winnipeg being the new managing director. The new management was no more sympathetic to unions than the Galts, who had beaten back four strikes and the Western Federation of Miners. Nanton specifically instructed mine officials not to meet with any union representatives.

On 8 March 1906, the newly organized local went on strike in support of demands for union recognition, an eight-hour day underground, some wage adjustments, dues check-off, a checkweighman to monitor the weighing of coal for the workers, and a pit committee to handle grievances and supervise safety. With only thirty of the six hundred peak-season miners scabbing (crossing the lines to go to work), the strike got off to a strong start. The nine-month strike, which ended on 2 December 1906, was marked by the dynamiting of strikebreakers' houses, confrontations between the NWMP and strikers, the exposing of an agent-provocateur, and the intervention of Mackenzie King on behalf of the federal government.

The NWMP were heavily involved in this strike, as in every strike in Lethbridge. Thirty-four men were assigned to the strike, and a further eleven company men were sworn in as special constables; reinforcements later increased the number of men available to fifty-four. An undercover policeman was planted as a spy among the foreign miners. Company officials warned the police about potential violence by the strikers, particularly the non-Anglo element, and even suggested that the strikers were armed with guns, which no evidence has supported.[24]

Despite police claims of neutrality in the strike, the force was boarded in railway cars on company property and fed and housed at company expense. Police escorted a company official through miners' houses as he urged them to return to work. In their attempt to stop strikers and their families from verbally abusing scabs whom they were escorting home, six Mounties drew their revolvers and pointed them at the crowd of men, women, and children. The strikers later relaxed their harassment of the scabs because of both the insufficiency of scab numbers to operate the mine and the dangers of police repression.[25] But the strike dragged on through the summer with sporadic outbursts of violence, including the dynamiting of a house that the union claimed was an attempt to discredit the union by a company-employed agent from the Thiel Detective Agency in Chicago (an offshoot of the Pinkerton Detective Agency).

By May, most of the single miners had left to seek work elsewhere, leaving the married miners and their families on the picket lines.[26] In July, the company prematurely announced that the strike was over; by October, two hundred men, mostly inexperienced, were living in bunk cars on company property and working the mine, but the amount of coal actually produced was disputed. In the fall, Mackenzie King concluded that the green workforce would need much more training to be productive and noted that no new miners were coming to Lethbridge to work during the strike.[27]

Because of the sudden and deep onset of an early winter on the prairies that year, a public panic over the coal crisis caused the premier of Saskatchewan to plead with Ottawa to end the strike. Although there were heating-coal shortages in the West in the winter of 1906–7, it is doubtful that the striking miners were primarily responsible, despite the claims of media and politicians. The Lethbridge strike affected only one-third of Alberta's coal capacity; Saskatchewan, despite the cries of its premier, depended on Pennsylvania, not Alberta, for its normal supply of heating coal; and finally, the operators of Alberta's bituminous mines claimed that they would have been happy to supply the shortfall, but the CPR would not provide them with coal cars. Regardless of the reason for the coal shortage, it convinced the federal government to send Mackenzie King to mediate the strike at Lethbridge.[28]

After King travelled twice to confer with John Mitchell, international president of the United Mine Workers of America, he cobbled together a compromise that the company accepted and the union agreed to on behalf of the miners. During the mediation, King insisted that the workers make the greater concessions and treated the union spokesmen with contempt and fits of temper.[29] Instead of union recognition, the miners got a non-discrimination clause claiming that union and non-union workers would be treated equally. Given the imbalance of employer and worker power, such a clause allowed the operators to discriminate against union militants. The union lost the check-off, and the men had to apply to get their old jobs back. They did, however, get a 10 percent wage increase and a cumbersome grievance procedure.[30]

The Industrial Disputes Investigation Act

Based on his experience in Lethbridge, King prepared legislation that the Laurier government tabled in 1907. The *Industrial Disputes Investigation Act (IDIA)* mandated compulsory arbitration in all disputes in public utilities (e.g., coal mines, railways). During investigation by a three-person board appointed by the government, neither side could stop work through a strike or lockout; the resolution recommended by the board was not binding on either party. The act did not prohibit employers from firing or intimidating union supporters, arbitrarily altering wages and work-time, hiring anti-union workers and agents, or stockpiling to serve markets during a strike. Essentially, King was disarming the union and leaving the company free to act.[31]

Another significant development from the Lethbridge strike was the creation of the Western Canada Coal Operators Association (WCCOA), an employers' bargaining agent designed specifically to deal with the United Mine Workers of America from a position of strength. In 1907, negotiations foundered between the union and the WCCOA. The union wanted an across-the-board wage increase and had a 90 percent strike mandate behind them. With the *IDIA* just put into effect, the operators instituted a wage reduction, confident that the workers could not legally strike until the mandatory conciliation process had run its course. Despite the silence of union leaders, the rank-and-file miners walked off the job in the Crowsnest Pass. On 15 April, fourteen hundred miners walked off on the BC side, followed by a thousand more on the Alberta side and then by six hundred more in mines along the CPR mainline.[32] When Mackenzie King and influential union and government leaders urged the striking miners to accept the *IDIA* conciliation process, every local but one small one voted him down.[33] Although a deal was hammered out on 28 April, it was not the result of conciliation but rather a negotiated settlement forced by the striking miners.

District 18 went through two more rounds of negotiations with the WCCOA in 1909 and 1911. During the recession of 1909, the negotiations ultimately resulted in a three-month strike that gained little and split the membership.[34] The 1911 negotiations foundered on wage rates because inflation had accompanied a new economic boom and made it impossible for miners to live on the old wage scale. Despite recognition from the union that the CPR stranglehold on the bituminous operators severely restricted their ability to pay a living wage, the miners could not accept the wage freeze and rate equalization proposed by the WCCOA, nor the employers' demand for a return to the non-discrimination clause, which negated union security. On 1 April, the strike began with six thousand miners leaving the job. Evictions and attempted evictions of strikers from company housing ensued, with gunshots

heard near Frank. When the miners turned down a conciliation award that mirrored the employers' position, the operators declared on 18 August that mines in District 18 were now "open shop" (that is, the miners were not required to join or financially support the union). In the end, the miners voted 58 percent in favour of a four-year contract containing the employer wage positions but retaining the union check-off. The strike had been thoroughly lost.[35]

The Miners and Socialism

Despite extensive courting by the Conservative and (especially) the Liberal parties, western coal miners from Vancouver Island to Alberta became more and more solidly entrenched in the socialist movement between 1900 and 1914. Both English-speaking and ethnic miners supported the Marxist Socialist Party of Canada (SPC) electorally, fighting for an end to a social and economic system that blighted their lives. But the first coal miner elected to the Alberta legislature, Donald McNab, was an independent labour candidate elected by acclamation in Lethbridge in January 1909 in a by-election held a mere month ahead of a general provincial election. Despite allying himself with the ruling Liberals in the legislature, he lost his deposit in the February election as the local Liberals rejected him in favour of a businessman.[36]

However much the Liberal party schemed to enfold the organized miners in their party structure, the miners rejected the idea. The Liberals in 1909 endorsed a mine union leader, John Angus McDonald, in the coal-town–dominated Rocky Mountain constituency, which included both the Crowsnest Pass communities and the mines near Banff. However, the winner of the election was the SPC candidate, Charles McNamara O'Brien. O'Brien ran without official union support despite the fact that District 18 president Frank Sherman had run under the SPC banner himself in the 1908 federal election. According to historian Allen Seager:

O'Brien's win certainly did serve notice of a popular political ferment which went well beyond the demands of the Province's labour reformers, who really were, in

Marx's famous phrase, just the tail of the great Liberal Party. For one thing O'Brien, unlike the Gladstonians, never claimed to be the guardian of the miners' special interests. He spoke for all workers, in the name of the "working class."[37]

A native of Ontario, O'Brien came west as a navvy on the Crowsnest line and worked as both a miner and logger. He was a gifted speaker and a committed socialist who rejected the idea of social democratic reforms as unworkable.

O'Brien's election reflected a growing radicalization among Alberta coal miners. For example, at the 1909 UMWA western Canadian convention, the members passed resolutions calling for public ownership and democratic management of coal mines, welcoming Chinese and Japanese workers to the union, and supporting potential realignment with the Western Federation of Miners.

O'Brien served only one term in the legislature. In the 1913 elections, the Liberals ran two coal miners as Liberal-Labour candidates in the mining constituencies of Lethbridge and Rocky Mountain, both endorsed by prominent UMWA leaders. The Conservatives won both seats and O'Brien, despite increasing his vote from 37.5 percent to 39 percent, was defeated. The union executive members who had cooked up the Liberal-Labour alliance were kicked out of office at the first opportunity after the election.[38]

In 1914, District 18 officially endorsed the Socialist Party of Canada with its revolutionary platform. Although undoubtedly many miners still supported social-democratic, independent labour, Liberal, and even Conservative strategies, the majority of the coal miners had rejected the possibility of reform.

Life in Coal Towns

The mining workforce comprised 50 percent experienced miners, 40 percent unskilled labour, and 10 percent skilled tradesmen.[39] Alberta miners came from across Canada, the United States, Great Britain, and Europe. Since both miners and mine labourers moved frequently in search of work and wages, they were hard to track. The 1911 Canada census provides a good example. Since the census was taken beginning 1 June, it would have significantly underestimated coal workers in the heating-coal industry, which was at its lowest ebb of production during the warm months. Miners, and particularly single miners, simply left to look for other work during the down times. Even the bituminous miners were busier in the fall to accommodate the harvest rail shipments.[40]

Despite the limitations, however, the census provides valuable insight into the broad ethnic diversity of the coal communities, as a quick look at table 3.1 shows. Of the Europeans counted, there were 821 Austro-Hungarians (composed of Ukrainians, Czechs, Slovaks, and Hungarians), 637 Italians, 258 Belgians, 167 Russians, 114 Germans, and a scattering of Poles, Scandinavians, Jews, Dutch, and Greeks. There were also 58 Chinese and a small number of Japanese.[41]

The UMWA worked diligently to build solidarity across ethnic and linguistic barriers. Between 1911 and 1915, the District 18 union publication, the *District Ledger*, ran foreign-language news, socialist political manifestos, letters, and other local contributions in French, Italian, Finnish, and Slavic languages. By 1914, ethnic union leaders had begun to emerge, including Jean Legace, Nick Tkachuk, John Lauttamus, Frank

TABLE 3.1 **ETHNIC COMPOSITION OF CROWSNEST COAL TOWNS, 1911**

	Anglo-Celtic	French	European	Oriental	Unknown
Bellevue	217	7	230	3	6
Blairmore	593	105	395	40	4
Coleman	797	47	696	14	3
Frank	261	150	389	2	4
Hillcrest	261	39	181	0	0
Lille	111	26	164	2	0
Total	**2,240**	**374**	**2,055**	**61**	**17**

Bonacci, and Alex Susnar, all of whom became officers of the union.[42] There is little evidence of ethnic stratification into the miner/mine-labourer jobs except for a British/Italian domination in the skilled trades group, which made up about 8 percent of the workforce.[43] The broad presence of both skilled miners and committed socialists among the ethnic miners was attested to by one observer lamenting the ideology of the miners:

> Many of the miners in Canada came from mining areas in Europe where injustice and poor conditions had promoted communism, anti-clericalism, and general disaffection. Very few of them, except the Slovaks, practiced their religion. [Bellevue's] Father Donovan reported in 1927: "We have 750 European Catholics in this parish; only 50 of them attend Mass."[44]

A random sampling of 515 European workers employed from 1907 to 1909 at the Crows Nest Pass Coal Company showed that the men had an average of 4.5 years of experience in mining.[45] Within the coal towns, the various ethnic groups constructed halls, co-operatives, and mutual aid societies for their own particular groups while at the same time joining together as a larger collective within the union and in the mines. Another important factor in Alberta coal towns was the number of married women and families. According to the 1911 census, the Crowsnest coal towns had a greater proportion of married men than the Alberta average (see table 3.2).[46]

The fact that married miners and their families were settled in the coal towns in far greater proportion than was the provincial norm belies the idea that the coal towns were simply a harsh, alienating environment occupied by an extremely transient population. Rather, it indicates a commitment to both the job and the towns themselves. Single miners may have voted with their feet when labour disputes or seasonal layoffs occurred, but the married miners clearly had a greater stake in the community. In the Lethbridge strike of 1906, it was the married non-British miners living in the mine town of Stafford next to the mine who stayed for the duration of the strike, and their wives caused as much grief for the strikebreakers and NWMP as the miners.[47]

The coal towns in the Pass were open towns with independent merchants and town councils. That meant that the miners, particularly the married miners and their families, were integral parts of communities in which they had both influence and ownership. Working-class families in the coal towns used the same survival strategies as their urban counterparts. They raised livestock, sometimes as small farm owners and sometimes simply turning their livestock loose in the wild. They took in boarders and did laundry and housekeeping, and family members earned money where they could.[48]

Death and Danger in the Mines

Working in Alberta coal mines was extremely dangerous. Deaths per million tons of coal mined between 1907 and 1916 in British Columbia and Alberta were more than double the comparable figures for Nova Scotia and the United States.[49] However shocking the major mine disasters were (the Bellevue disaster of 1910 took 31 lives and the Hillcrest disaster of 1914 killed 189 miners), weekly accidents in the mines were a fact of life for several reasons. The Crowsnest coal had an unusually high amount of methane gas, which produced a high risk of both major explosions and minor "bumps" (sudden shifts in a mine that can lead to the collapse of walls or ceilings). Furthermore, the coal seams inclined an average of thirteen to twenty-six degrees, resulting in many haulage accidents. In addition to these natural risks, however, cost-cutting by the mine operators

TABLE 3.2 **MARRIED MEN IN ALBERTA AND IN CROWSNEST COAL TOWNS, 1911**

	Married	As % of total men	Married men per 100 single men	Single
Alberta	70,706	31.6	47.9	147,587
Crowsnest	1,189	39.9	67.4	1,765
Bellevue	1,147	40.0	67.9	168
Blairmore	291	39.6	68.1	427
Coleman	403	41.3	70.6	571
Frank	173	36.2	56.9	304
Hillcrest	117	37.9	61.9	189
Lille	91	46.0	85.8	106

was a huge factor in mine accidents. To cut back on expenses, the operators routinely coerced the men to use less shoring timbers than required for safe operations. Poor shoring caused more cave-ins, seriously injuring and killing mine workers. The use of cheap, dangerous explosives was another factor: since miners had to buy their own explosives, their low wages put the safer but more expensive explosives out of reach. This bare-bones operation of the mines produced 1,435 serious accidents (not counting fatalities) in the Crowsnest between 1904 and 1928. When "slight" accidents are added, the overall accident rate rises to an average of two per week between 1906 and 1928.[50]

FIG 3-7 Graves of several of the 189 victims of the Hillcrest mine explosion, 1914. Library and Archives Canada, A-1780.

Alberta Coal Miners and Socialist Politics

Many factors played a role in creating the lasting Marxist socialist tradition of the coal miners in Alberta between 1885 and 1914, a tradition that remained a powerful influence on coal miners and the labour movement for the next twenty-five years. The incorporation of non-English European immigrants, many with pronounced radical leanings learned back home, into the British workforce in the mines, mining communities, and union created a broad class solidarity that transcended ethnic, linguistic, and religious differences. The lack of a British majority probably defused the nativist reaction found among the British community elsewhere. Shared dangers of the work — made worse by the actions of the owners, layoffs, chronic unemployment, low wages, and the inability of government to reform or regulate the mining corporations — all influenced miners toward a radical socialist position. Certainly, there was no universal agreement on politics: reformist liberals, labourites, and the anarcho-syndicalists of the IWW all had significant support in the mining community. However, unlike the navvies and migrant workers, many coal miners put down roots in communities and could exercise their franchise. Frustrated by the state interventions on the part of the NWMP and Mackenzie King's collaborationist legal processes that always seemed to benefit the owners, many miners adopted a political strategy of putting the state in the hands of the workers. When District 18 officially endorsed the Socialist Party of Canada, it indicated that the majority of miners were willing to formalize a relationship that had been growing for a decade.

THE URBAN WORKING CLASS

The early development of Alberta's urban centres was determined largely by the railways. When the CPR decided in the early 1880s to build its mainline through Medicine Hat, Calgary, and Rogers Pass instead of through the previously planned Battlefords, Edmonton, and Yellowhead Pass, the centres along the northern route went into decline as land speculation died down. Speculative land investment moved to Medicine Hat and, particularly, Calgary. It was not until a Calgary-to-Strathcona rail link was built in 1891 that Edmonton and Red Deer began to grow.

Railways brought the settlers, and the railways' location played a large role in determining where settlement occurred: proximity to a transportation corridor was essential for moving goods economically to and from the farms and rural towns. Calgary's first boom in the 1880s was mercantile, largely based on supplying goods to the CPR, its contractors, and their employees, and on building homes for the burgeoning population. By 1891, Calgary's population had grown to four thousand. There were 28 manufacturing firms, employing 170 workers, much of their production directed at supplying the local construction industry.[51]

The First Unions

The twin pillars of the railway and the construction industry provided the focus of early union organizing attempts. The first unions in Alberta represented skilled railway workers: the engineers, brakemen, and firemen without whose skill the trains would not run. The running trades, as they were known, were

FIG 3-9 CPR workers, including engineers, conductors, yardmasters, linemen, brakemen, baggage men, firemen, and trackmen, at a banquet in Medicine Hat, 1895. Glenbow Archives, NA-21-5.

considered an elite group because their skills gave them a relatively strong bargaining position with the employer. They were essential to the operation of the railroad and hard to replace quickly in a work stoppage. Without organization, however, they were vulnerable. In 1883, the unorganized Alberta-based locomotive engineers and firemen joined a national work stoppage to protest an arbitrary wage cut by the CPR. However, the workers were forced to accept the wage cut after the NWMP intervened not only to guard company property, but also to operate the trains themselves when necessary.[52] In September 1886, three years later, the Brotherhood of Locomotive Engineers chartered the first union in Alberta in Medicine Hat, and the Brotherhood of Locomotive Firemen and Enginemen followed them within months. Two other railway running trades locals were established shortly thereafter, and by 1900, with a few short-lived exceptions, these four railway locals were the only organized workers in what is now Alberta.[53]

There had been other efforts to unionize in the region, as indicated by the arrival in Calgary in December 1886 of the Knights of Labor, which had already organized some twelve thousand Canadian workers, mainly in Ontario's industrial heartland and in Montreal. The result was Calgary's Local Assembly 9787, of the Knights of Labor. In 1888, the local attempted to organize the miners of bitumen at the Canmore mines west of Calgary but by the 1890s the group had disbanded.[54] The Knights — with their willingness to organize across craft divisions, combine skilled and unskilled workers, and welcome women into the union — offered an alternative to the unfettered capitalism of the late nineteenth century in North America and a major challenge to the narrower crafts-based unions that were affiliated with the American Federation of Labor. However, suppression by the state and a growing, organized antagonism by employers and the craft unions finally extinguished the Knights' vision of a more egalitarian workers' society.

Craft Versus Industrial Unions

With large-scale immigration beginning around 1897, Edmonton and Calgary began to grow rapidly, and the population boom triggered a construction boom. In 1901, Calgary's population was 4,398 and Edmonton's was 4,176 (including Strathcona, also known as South Edmonton). By 1906, the populations had tripled, with Calgary at 11,967 and Edmonton at 14,088. Five years later, Calgary was home to 43,704 and Edmonton to 30,479.[55]

With the construction boom came a demand for construction workers in both cities and the first major expansion of union organizing in the urban centres. Although a short-lived local of the United Brotherhood of Carpenters and Joiners of America (UBCJA Local 95) was founded in Calgary in 1892, it did not last through the recession that gripped the city in the following years. In 1902, however, the booming construction industry triggered a wave of union organizing among the building trades, with the carpenters' union organizing Local 1055 in Calgary and Local 1325 in Edmonton. The stonemasons organized in both cities in 1903, as did the bricklayers, and the plumbers and pipefitters followed in 1904. In the decade from 1900 to 1910, local branches of American-based craft unions proliferated in Alberta's cities. Among the skilled trades organized were confectioners, blacksmiths, brewers, lathers, bakers, retail clerks, barbers, tailors, teamsters, and brewers. In 1905, 30 percent of the adult male workforce in Calgary was organized into a craft union, and by 1913, there were 44 union locals in the city, representing over 3,000 workers. The province contained 171 locals with a combined membership of 11,500, of whom half were coal miners. Edmonton was in a similar position to Calgary with the coming of the two transcontinentals (the CN in 1905 and the Grand Trunk Pacific in 1909) and the addition of new locals of key railway workers: carmen, locomotive engineers and firemen, machinists, and maintenance-of-way workers. An influential group among the organized workers were the printing trades, represented by the International Typographers Union, which had locals in both cities.[56]

Even at their best, however, the craft unions of the day represented no more than one-third of the workforce, and they largely resisted notions of organizing the majority of other workers: the unskilled and women. Craft unions were exclusionary by nature. Their strength depended upon restricting membership and controlling the apprenticeship process — and with it, access to the knowledge and skills of the craft. The fewer skilled workers available in each craft, the more job security and bargaining power the union members had. That exclusionary underpinning provided fertile ground for nativist tendencies among the skilled workers. Most skilled tradesmen at the time were of British descent, as was the leadership of the craft unions. Through hiring hall practices and apprenticeship selection, the craft unions could remain largely British male preserves, leaving the less desirable work for women, children, and ethnic groups. In Calgary, for example, where over 80 percent of the citizens claimed a British heritage, maintaining a homogeneous union membership would have been relatively easy. Province-wide, the British were a much smaller majority.[57]

Another problem with craft union organizing was the splintering of the workforce of the same employer into discrete units, each with its own contracts. At the CPR, for example, each trade had its own bargaining unit and contract. When the trackmen went on strike in 1901, all their co-workers — the engineers, firemen, shop workers, machinists, clerks, and freight handlers — stayed on the job, ensuring that the company continued to operate easily and won the conflict. Craft union insistence that their members honour their contracts meant that during a dispute by any one union in a plant or industry, other unionists would consistently be crossing picket lines, weakening the strike and breaking down solidarity.

FIG 3-10 United Association of Plumbers and Pipefitters Local Union 488, created in Edmonton in 1904. Provincial Archives of Alberta, A19670.

By the close of the nineteenth century, the craft unions were under attack. The ongoing evolution of industrial capitalism was steadily eroding the craft unions' base of support. Scientific management techniques promoted by engineers like Frederick Winslow Taylor and Harrington Emerson were assimilating skilled crafts and breaking them down to subsets of skills and processes that allowed semi-skilled workers to do them with less training, a process often referred to as deskilling. Technological change produced machines that replaced workers' skills. The concentration of capital into larger monopolies and trusts tipped the balance of bargaining power between union and employer. Factories became larger and larger, as did the machines inside them, and employers became more aggressive in their opposition to unions.[58] Unions affected by deskilling, mechanization, and loss of job autonomy represented crafts in crisis.

Although all crafts unions developed various strategies to maintain their traditional control over work and the labour market, those most deeply affected by the changing workplace were more likely to engage in more radical strategies. In Vancouver between 1900 and 1919, the crafts in crisis — the machinists, boilermakers, bakers, tailors, and carpenters — amalgamated and broadened their organizations to include less skilled workers, building solidarity beyond their craft boundaries, and participated in sympathy strikes.[59]

The problem confronted by the crafts unions was that as the deskilling process continued through both new technologies and scientific management initiatives, their members' numbers and job autonomy decreased within an industry, while the numbers of semi-skilled and unskilled workers increased. The obvious solution was to adopt an industrial union strategy to meet the new employer attacks. Industrial unionism stressed organizing all workers in an industry into a single bargaining unit, regardless of craft or skill.

Two industrial unions in Alberta, the Western Federation of Miners and the United Mine Workers of America, took everyone — miners, unskilled muckers, and the 10 percent of their workforce made up of skilled craftspersons like stonemasons and carpenters — into the same bargaining unit. However, despite the fact that at least one of its affiliates, the UMWA, was clearly an industrial union, the American Federation of Labor (AFL) officially rejected industrial organizing and reaffirmed its commitment to organizing by craft in 1901.[60]

The 1903 UBRE Strike Against the CPR

The AFL's declaration against industrial unions soon had consequences for Alberta workers. The United Brotherhood of Railway Employees (UBRE) was an industrial union from the United States associated with a socialist labour central, the American Labor Union, which had been formed by the Western Federation of Miners and would merge into the Industrial Workers of the World in 1905. By 1903, the UBRE had a thousand unskilled workers organized in locals at Vancouver, Revelstoke, Nelson, Calgary, and Winnipeg. Although it initially represented the freight and baggage handlers and freight and ticket clerks, the UBRE made no secret of their intention to organize all CPR employees, both skilled and unskilled, into one union. The CPR began a systematic campaign against the Vancouver local in January 1903, with extensive use of intimidation, dismissals, and the insertion of company spies into virtually every union meeting. By the end of February, the UBRE members in Vancouver were forced to go on strike demanding only the protection of their union. The union called out its other members in support.

Workers across western Canada supported the strike, and strike support funds were received from every major western city. Victoria sailors, teamsters in Vancouver and Calgary, and Vancouver longshoremen went on strike in sympathy, refusing to handle CPR freight. In late May, labour councils in Winnipeg and Calgary began organizing a campaign to declare the CPR "unfair," boycotting any goods handled by the railway.

In contrast to the strong local support from many craft and industrial unions in the strike region, at the national and international levels, the Trades and Labour Congress (TLC), the Canadian equivalent of the American Federation of Labor, was determined to defeat the UBRE strike in the name of crafts unionism protection. TLC's western organizer, J.H Watson, worked with the CPR to organize a union of scab metal-trades helpers to replace the strikers. He also ordered boilermakers who had joined the strike back to work, an act replicated with the machinists by the Canadian vice-president of their craft union. The president of the boilermakers' union in the United States threatened to revoke the membership card of any member who supported the strike. The railway running trades would not support the strike and kept the trains running throughout.

In the meantime, the CPR recruited strikebreakers from central Canada and the United States, and infiltrated the union with spies. The railway police murdered popular socialist labour leader Frank Rogers on a picket line in Vancouver. The company even subverted and bought off the UBRE's Canadian organizer, who turned over all the union's inside information to the CPR. By the beginning of June, the CPR had hired enough strikebreakers to return to normal operations, and the strike was lost. Most strikers were blacklisted and never got their jobs back.[61]

The Limits of Solidarity: Calgary Carpenters' Strikes, 1902–3

Three labour disputes within one year involving Calgary carpenters illustrate both the strengths and weaknesses of craft union organizing. The new United Brotherhood of Carpenters and Joiners of America Local 1055 was formed on 12 April 1902, and went on strike for three weeks in July that year, winning a reduction in daily work hours to nine and an increase in daily wages to $2.50. During the strike, which by its end had reduced work for plasterers and plumbers, the carpenters enjoyed support from the other construction unions in the city, as witnessed by the organizing of a successful mass rally by the Calgary Trades and Labour Council. The next year, the carpenters again went on strike, this time to protest the use of non-union labour by Calgary contractors in violation of the 1902 agreement. The strike ended when the contractors dismissed all non-union men and signed a new agreement.

Almost immediately following their successful second strike, the Calgary carpenters decided to hold a sympathy strike in support of a newly organized teamsters local. The teamsters had gone on strike to get a raise to $50 per month. The carpenters decided to stop handling any lumber delivered by strikebreakers. The employers pre-empted the conflict by locking out the carpenters on 4 June 1903, but the construction labourers' union subsequently refused to handle any lime or sandstone delivered by strikebreakers. Soon, however, the general shutdown of construction in the city that resulted from the strike created rifts within the craft unions. Leading construction unions refused to participate in the actions, the stonemasons denounced the carpenters and refused to support them, and the bricklayers also refused to support the strike.

With the unskilled teamsters and labourers on side but the other trades opposed, the carpenters lost the strike and, in the settlement eventually mediated by Mackenzie King, lost their right to have only union carpenters on job sites. The local went bankrupt and was dissolved. When the carpenters had struck to defend their own skilled trade, the other craft unions had supported them, but when they struck in support of the rights of unskilled workers like the teamsters or labourers, that support was withdrawn.[62]

Life in the Cities

The divide between the skilled workers in the craft unions and the rest of the workforce was reflected in more than wages and social status. Both Calgary and Edmonton were victims of constant land and real estate speculation during the boom years from 1900 through 1912. While skilled male workers could perhaps earn enough to purchase small wood-frame houses (kitchen, living room, several small bedrooms, and a dirt basement), other workers rented even smaller three-room

FIG 3-11 United Brotherhood of Carpenters and Joiners Local 1779
parade, Calgary, 1912. Glenbow Archives, NA-1791-9.

houses, boarded with other working-class families, or took rooms in boarding houses or downtown hotels. The worst off put up tents or thrown-together shacks in Edmonton's river valley, along the railway tracks, or in areas like Calgary's Hillhurst district.[63]

Across Canada, wages were extremely low during this period. From 1900 to 1905, workers' wages increased slightly in real terms, but high inflation reduced real earnings.[64] Wage levels in Calgary failed to meet the federal government's minimum figure for meeting the monthly needs of workers with a family of four: $127. At the end of 1911, none of Calgary's skilled trades earned that much. The closest were bricklayers, who could have earned about 90 percent of that amount in the unlikely event they had a full month of continuous employment. The unskilled and unorganized were lucky to earn half that amount.[65]

Making Ends Meet: Women and Children at Work

Given the poor wages for unionized crafts workers and the even lower rates for unskilled and semi-skilled non-union workers, despite the relatively buoyant economy in Alberta in the 1900 to 1912 period, family survival clearly required more than any single wage earner could provide. One obvious strategy was for women and children to enter wage labour to add to family income, yet the 1911 census indicates modest employment of Alberta women and children. Only 7.9 percent of women were employed in wage labour compared with 66.8 percent of men. The key occupations for the women with paid jobs were domestic and personal service (46%), the professional occupations of teaching and nursing (20.7%), employment in the retail and merchandising sector (10.4%), and manufacturing jobs (8.7%). With few exceptions, the work that women found was low paid and non-union. For children aged 10 to 14, only 540 boys and 259 girls were listed as employed in wage labour. Of the girls, over 85 percent worked as domestic servants, and the boys mainly worked on farms (40.4%), in the retail industry (17.4%), and in manufacturing (10.9%).[66]

Clearly, working-class families found other ways to cope than depending upon second salaries from women and children, although even the smallest amount of income could make a huge difference in standard of living. Historian Bettina Bradbury's study of late-nineteenth-century Montreal workers shows the importance of relatively modest differences in income for working-class families. A difference of twenty-five cents per day in average pay for each of four levels of workers — new industrial skilled workers (engineers, moulders, machinists), the more seasonally affected skilled workers in the construction trades, workers in trades undergoing rapid deskilling (shoemakers), and unskilled workers — had substantial implications for families. The most skilled had a better chance of eating and living at a level that helped ward off diseases common in working-class neighbourhoods and were less likely to be forced to send young children out to work.[67]

Like families in coal towns, urban working-class families adopted various strategies to augment family income. Keeping cows, pigs, and chickens gave them products to sell (eggs, milk, butter, livestock), as did small garden plots. A common strategy was to take in other workers as boarders. Children could also be sent to scavenge such goods as coal near railway tracks or to

work as unlicensed street vendors, selling papers and shining shoes.[68] For women, prostitution was another way to fend off destitution. Most prostitutes arrested in Calgary during this era claimed employment in other low-wage women's occupations like waitressing, dressmaking, and laundry work.[69] Women's and children's petty capitalism involving the barter and sale of homemade products of all kinds — activities that would not have been captured by the census questions regarding "employment" — probably also contributed to fulfilling family needs.

Urban Workers and Politics

One of the main activities of the early labour councils involved mobilizing the strength of labour politically. Initially, that meant lobbying government over issues like the number of working hours and working days and the payment of fair or union-scale wages on all city contracts. Increasingly frustrated with the almost universal failure of such lobbying efforts, the municipal unions moved toward a more class-oriented position near the end of the decade. In 1911, the Calgary Trades and Labour Council amended the preamble to its constitution to make political action a priority. The craft unions that made up the leadership and the majority of membership of the municipal labour councils at the time were never as radical as the miners, with their adoption of revolutionary socialist parties, or as the migrant navvies, with their affinity to the anarcho-syndicalism of the IWW. Instead, they promoted a labourist policy whereby councils only endorsed candidates who were trade union members.

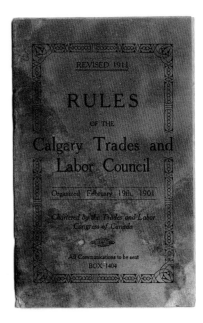

FIG 3-13 Rule book of the Calgary Trades and Labor Council, 1911. Glenbow Archives, M-4743-14.

THE FOUNDING OF THE ALBERTA FEDERATION OF LABOUR

A labour central is an alliance of two or more independent unions in a voluntary association for the purpose of pursuing common goals. In Canada, there are labour centrals at the local or municipal level, the provincial level, and the national level. The first labour centrals in Alberta were municipal labour councils. The Calgary Trades and Labour Council (CTLC) first met on 19 February 1901. Less than two years later, the Edmonton Trades and Labour Council was formed on 16 January 1903. These early labour councils were voluntary associations of skilled trades unions and were created as independent bodies to meet perceived needs at the local level. Although both Calgary and Edmonton received charters from the American Federation of Labor, they did not even bother to apply for them from the American parent body of craft unions until 1905 and 1906, respectively.

The municipal or local labour councils provided a ready and useful means for unions to communicate with each other and to keep each other informed about upcoming issues and events. The councils encouraged cooperation among unions on many fronts and gave labour a recognizable voice in the community. They presented labour's political demands in the municipal arena and made representations to provincial governments on such issues as reduced work time and job safety. Another concern of the councils was promotion of the social status of labour — the respectability of the craft workers — through events like the Labour Day parades that publicly displayed workers' pride in their crafts.

The early CTLC included in its charter a commitment to organize men and women in both skilled and unskilled occupations into unions. Following its founders' intent, the CTLC helped organize unskilled railway workers into the United Brotherhood of Railway Employees,

the Allied Mechanics Union, the General Labourers Union, and the Retail Clerks Union. It is questionable whether this commitment to organize unskilled workers survived official affiliation of the CTLC to the American Federation of Labor, with the latter's active dislike of industrial unions like the UBRE and its focus on skilled rather than unskilled workers.

Labour councils were loose federal structures that exercised only moral authority over the union locals that voluntarily agreed to join. Although there is some validity to the argument that this was a consequence of the nature of the craft unions that dominated the early councils, where each union's strength lay in its ability to control the work rules and protect the jurisdiction and knowledge of its singular craft (especially from other craft unions), it is also true that a loose federal structure was a method of control.[1] All meaningful labour authority within any council would always trace back through each craft union to its headquarters in the United States. Essentially, this control provided councils with the autonomy to act only on those issues where there was no debate, while constraining them to proceed only at the pace of the most conservative member.

Labour councils, even when successfully initiated, had no guarantee of survival. For example, labour councils were formed in Medicine Hat in 1905 and in Lethbridge in 1906, but neither remained viable, with Medicine Hat's council disappearing after a year and Lethbridge losing its charter in 1908.

Although Alberta officially became a province in 1905, it was seven years before a provincial labour central was formed. On 14 June 1912, at the instigation of District 18 of the United Mine Workers of America, forty labour delegates met in the Lethbridge Trades Hall and founded a new provincial labour central. District 18 had pursued the creation of the Alberta Federation of Labour (AFL) since their 1911 convention, which had mandated both a provincial federation and closer ties and co-operation with the new and growing United Farmers of Alberta (UFA).

The miners tried to kill two birds with one stone by reserving two vice-presidential positions on the AFL executive for UFA representatives. The initial response from the UFA was positive. UFA president W.J. Tregillus told the delegates at the AFL founding convention, "The farmers are as much labourers as the miners or any other workers."[2] Donald McNabb, who had been a Labour MLA, agreed. "If organized," he said, workers and farmers "could go to the legislators as a united band and cooperate in demanding legislation for the farmers, the city toiler, and the miner."[3] But the UFA quickly soured on the idea of having official ties with the labour movement. The founding convention of the AFL supported the unions' calls for minimum wages and maximum hours of work. While the farmers had been anxious to work with labour in opposing the power of large, monopolistic corporations, they were employers too and were unenthusiastic about any suggestion that they needed to pay their workers more. So, by the time of the second convention of the AFL in 1913, the farmers had broken all ties to the organization.

District 18 itself was in the middle of a sectarian political struggle between the Socialist Party of Canada and the liberal and labourist tendencies. As the dominant voice in the new federation (the miners supplied the majority of members and 60 percent of the dues of the organization), the miners' internal differences surfaced at the first convention. On the one hand, the liberal miners supplied both the chairperson of the founding convention and the first president of the organization, John O. Jones. On the other, radical miners' voices were

also present at the convention. Clem Stubbs, the leader of District 18 of the UMWA, informed the delegates that he would support the federation if it would work to abolish the wage system.

Despite the wishes of the more radical miners, the new AFL confined itself to lobbying government for the next few years. With the miners themselves divided on political action, any attempt to create a unified political stand was seen as too divisive. Instead, the work of the AFL's first years related to easily supportable resolutions calling for a workers' compensation system, a fair-wage clause for government contracts, better health and safety regulations, an end to child labour, and banning of employment agencies.[4]

---

1   See Mark Leier, *Red Flags and Red Tape,* 54, 55.
2   *Lethbridge Daily Herald,* 15 June 1912.
3   Ibid.
4   See Warren Caragata, *Alberta Labour: A Heritage Untold,* 35, 36; and Charles Allen Seager, "A Proletariat in Wild Rose Country: The Alberta Coal Miners, 1905–1945," 254.

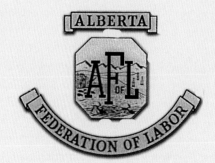

FIG 3-14 The original logo of the Alberta Federation of Labour. Courtesy of the Alberta Federation of Labour.

The cities had always provided a substantial base of support for candidates with a labour background. When he was elected to Calgary City Council in 1902, the president of the carpenters' local, R.A. Brockelbank, became the province's first labour candidate ever elected to public office. Another carpenter, J.A. Kinney, president of the Edmonton local, became that city's first labour alderman in 1914. The weakness of the labourist tactic of making union membership the critical condition for labour support is illustrated in the case of Brockelbank, who by 1907 had moved his allegiance to the Conservative party.[70] One critique of the labourist position of the craft-dominated urban labour councils was related to their exclusivity. It was difficult to develop and maintain a class position that spoke to the needs and issues of all working men and women when the councils themselves never represented the two-thirds of working people in the cities who were either unskilled, unorganized, or both.

THE 1913–14 DEPRESSION

During the Canadian economic boom from 1897 through 1913, the Canadian and Albertan economies expanded at a phenomenal rate. Investment in massive railway construction, port expansion, extension of telegraph and telephone systems, and increased power-generating capacity was accompanied by sustained growth in population and land settlement in the West, and by the growth of cities. Driven first by the Klondike gold rush and then by the prairie wheat exports, economic growth was construction-led. The construction boom in the farms, towns, and cities of the West was financed with foreign (largely British) capital. British capital financed railway construction,

farm development, house-building, and land speculation across the prairies. The construction boom in the West stimulated consumer goods industries in central Canada and iron and steel manufacture in Nova Scotia.

In 1913, the boom came to a sudden halt when the Balkan wars created a financial panic that turned off the tap on British capital investments in Canada. In 1914, the Canadian economy collapsed, nowhere more drastically than in the West. Railway construction stalled, and the building boom ended as urban centres actually began to shrink. Land speculators forfeited property back to cities by refusing to pay property taxes. Unemployment hit 25 percent in the manufacturing centres of Ontario even before the normal winter slowdown. In Alberta, Calgary and Edmonton were suddenly inundated with unemployed workers.[71]

The influx of thousands of unemployed railway navvies and other migrant labourers added to already burgeoning numbers of unemployed citizens from construction, retail, and railroad operations. The federal government refused to act on the unemployment crisis, simply fobbing it back onto municipalities ill-prepared to deal with the scope of the crisis. Union membership plummeted in the cities, local charities were incapable of coping, and the unemployed, lacking even the most basic social safety net, were desperately destitute.

The Industrial Workers of the World (IWW) intervened and became instrumental in mobilizing the unemployed. The Wobblies pioneered work with the unemployed, a logical step since so many of their members were migrant workers who suffered repeated bouts of unemployment. Rejecting the charitable and often demeaning "relief" at the municipal level — generally just enough help to fend off starvation in exchange for menial make-work — the IWW had a different message and tactic. Its message to unemployed workers in Edmonton and Calgary was that the depression was not the fault of workers, but rather a failure of the capitalist system; therefore, workers had the right to work at fair wages and should not have to beg for charity. The Wobblies mobilized the unemployed to occupy local churches demanding places to sleep and encouraged penniless workers to order and eat meals at restaurants and then instruct the restaurant to "bill the mayor." They held marches demanding work and wages, and even contemplated a march of the unemployed to Ottawa. On several occasions, police in the cities clashed with militant unemployed workers.[72]

Things were no better in the coal fields. Workers at the mines in Taber averaged one day of work per week throughout 1914. Coal miners across Alberta were working short time and suffering from loss of income. The western boom had ended, and with it, many workers' belief in the social and economic system.

FARMHANDS AND SEASONAL AGRICULTURAL LABOUR

Farmers and farm labourers also suffered as the boom ended and markets for wheat shrank. Beginning in 1897, the pace of westward migration had accelerated. Lured by the promise of free homesteads, the rising international price of wheat, and government propaganda, tens of thousands of would-be farmers from central and eastern Canada and from Europe moved to the Canadian prairies. Many of these newcomers, however, lacked the capital necessary to establish themselves on the land and were forced to turn to wage labour to survive. In fact, it was assumed that agricultural immigrants would provide a cheap source of seasonal labour both for established prairie farmers and for the developing industries in the west. On several occasions, the government even amended homesteading requirements so as to allow cash-poor farmers to gain clear title to their land even though they spent long periods away from their farms working for others.[73]

Newcomers were thus encouraged to take up waged farm work as a path to eventual independent land ownership. In fact, without the steady flow of new immigrant homesteaders to replenish the agricultural workforce, established prairie farmers could not have survived. At the same time, the low wages, irregular seasonal employment, and poor accommodations they offered provided little incentive for most workers to take employment with them. Thus, despite the incoming labour supply, farmers were left constantly complaining about labour shortages.[74]

The two main sources of year-round labour for farmers were full-time permanent farmhands and homesteaders in need of cash. For a time in the pre–World War I period, even the full-time farmhands could aspire to eventually become farm owners. In 1900, homesteading costs were approximately $500, which could be accumulated in three to five years of farm labour. By 1911, homesteading costs had risen to about $1,500 — representing six years of steady farm work. And by the beginning of the war years, this "agricultural ladder" (from farm worker to homesteader to independent farmer) had disappeared altogether. Most of the good homesteading land was gone, and the price of purchasable land had risen rapidly as a consequence of the steep inflation of the war years.[75]

The ambiguous relationship among established farmers, poor homesteaders, and full-time farmhands during the prewar era created a peculiar work culture. On the one hand, the farmer was both aspiring capitalist and employer. On the other, his employees were either already small landowners on their own or else aspiring young landowners. An employer in a given season might someday find himself taking work from a former employee. Furthermore, the farmer and his family worked alongside the hired hands, generally doing the same work in the same conditions. Farmhands usually lived and ate with the family, with room and board provided on top of the wages.

Historian Cecilia Danysk likens the farmer-farmworker interaction in this period to an apprenticeship. Employer and employee alike expected the farmworker to become a farmer — to graduate from apprentice to master. The farmworker accepted what would otherwise have been unacceptably poor wages and working conditions as the cost of gaining an education in the craft of prairie grain farming.[76] Even once a homestead was established, paid farm work enabled the homesteader to earn badly needed cash while remaining in the vicinity of his own land, to which he could return when his short-term employment ended.

Farmworkers also typically traded job tenure for wages. If a farmhand worked during the winter months, he generally did so for room and board only, with the occasional five dollars of "tobacco" money tossed in each month. The seven-month summer job covered the working year of the farm and was considered full-time for a hired hand, but the pay was less per month than that of the most common hires for one to three months during seeding or harvest. Workers could also be hired for specific jobs like rock-picking that paid by the day. Farm workers' wages in Alberta varied according to weather, crops, the personal experience of the worker, and labour supply in a given district. In 1909, the average annual farm wage (not counting room and board) was $242. That fell to $168 during the recession in 1914 but rose steadily as the manpower shortage grew during the war: in 1920, it was $690.[77]

Farmhands seldom engaged in collective action to better their wages or working conditions, nor in the early period were any unions active among farmworkers. Normally, if dissatisfied, they would "vote with their feet" by simply leaving the current employer and finding a new job at another farm. Several factors contributed to the apparent inability of farmworkers to act collectively like other wage labourers in pursuit of better treatment. First, farmhands were isolated. There was seldom more than one hired hand per farm, and often one farmhand worked for several farmers in a district. The farms were far apart and there was little opportunity for farmworkers to meet. As well, farmworkers' perception of their class position was often at odds with their subordinate status in the labour force. Although they were undoubtedly wage earners, they did not intend to remain in that position: they saw themselves as future farmers and employers of labour. Their ideology was directed by their ambitions rather than their current conditions, and their lack of radicalism was often reinforced when farmers treated them as part of the family and encouraged their participation in social, recreational, and religious events within the community.[78]

This ambivalent social and class position for permanent farm labour faded as land costs skyrocketed and farmhands lost the dream of becoming independent commodity producers. By the mid 1920s, the prairie communities characterized hired men more as shiftless drifters and unambitious failures than as future farmers and community men.[79] Canada was still recruiting agricultural immigrants on the promise of eventual land ownership in the 1920s, but after 1914, newcomers arriving without capital had little chance of ever reaching that goal.

The Harvest Excursionists

Although full-time farmhands and poor homesteaders provided prairie farmers with the labour they needed for spring planting and other seasonal work, they represented less than half the labour required to bring in the wheat harvest in the fall. That critical harvest work on the Canadian prairies was provided by migrant workers from eastern and central Canada, who were transported west by special reduced-fare trains for the harvest in August and returned east in October or November the same way.

Begun by the Canadian Pacific Railway (CPR) at the request of the Manitoba government in 1892, the "harvest excursions" expanded as western agriculture expanded. In 1925, the peak year, 54,850 agricultural labourers were delivered to the West. Between 1901 and 1914, over a quarter million farm labourers, an average of about twenty thousand per year, took part in the harvest excursions.[80]

The process was simple. After the provincial governments provided the railway with an estimate of total labour that would be needed that year, the CPR (and later the Soo Line, Grand Trunk Pacific, Canadian Northern, and Canadian National as well) advertised the jobs and offered extremely low-priced tickets west. Originally, the tickets were to specific stops on the prairies, but after 1912, all harvesters stopped first in Winnipeg, where they were recruited at a job fair with representatives from each province and many farming districts present to extol the virtues of their specific area. The harvesters then purchased a second ticket to their final destination at a price of half a cent per mile. To get the same reduced fare to return home, a harvest worker had to produce his ticket stub signed by a farmer verifying that the harvester had worked at least thirty days in his employ. There was also a time limit: excursionists had to return home before 30 November.[81]

Unlike the permanent farmhands and homesteaders, the harvest excursionists were unambiguously wage labour and were treated that way. While farmhands either lived in the farmer's house or in proper quarters, harvest workers took whatever shelter was available — granaries, unused chicken coops, haylofts, and even derelict boxcars. Accommodations were never good and frequently terrible. Sanitary facilities were generally an outhouse and a bucket for well water. Harvesters worked from sunrise to sunset, stopping only for the typical five meals per day provided by the employer.[82]

The work was brutally hard and unvaried. The farmer (or his son or a permanent farmhand) drove the binder that cut the slightly green wheat and tied it into sheaves. The harvesters lifted and carried two sheaves at a time, stacked eight to ten of them into a stook, and then repeated that exercise all day while racing to keep up to the binder. After harvesting, threshing was slightly less onerous but also provided fewer jobs for the excursionists, who generally got jobs pitching the ripened sheaves onto wagons that transported them to the threshing machine. Threshing paid slightly higher wages per day, but the day was longer because it could be done by moonlight or lamplight. Work was six days a week unless it rained, and harvesters were not paid on days they didn't work.[83]

To continue to attract the massive amounts of labour required at harvest time every year, farmers had to pay wages that balanced the back-breaking labour, long hours, and poor living conditions. Harvest excursionists were paid at least double the going daily rate for agricultural labour in Quebec, Ontario, and the Maritimes, and one-third more than unskilled urban construction workers in the eastern cities. The daily wage rates varied depending on labour supply and demand, the weather, the experience and skill of workers, and their negotiating ability. In 1901, the rate was $1.88 per day; in 1914, it was $2.55, but between those years it fluctuated, going as high as $3.13 and as low as $2.00. Harvesters typically worked about forty-two days each season.[84]

Although the Industrial Workers of the World was very successful at organizing migrant harvest workers in the United States during this period (the wobblies claimed eighteen thousand members in their agricultural component), there was little union presence among the Canadian harvest excursionists before 1919. When the IWW did begin organizing farmworkers in Canada, it faced a hostile police and government action that effectively suppressed the organization. IWW organizers were often jailed for "vagrancy" or simply deported to the United States. In addition, the RCMP and railway police kept a close eye on trains that were carrying migrant workers, and once the harvesters were dispersed to farms, it was all but impossible for the IWW to contact them.[85]

Although easily the largest, most important part of Alberta's workforce between 1900 and 1914, migrant harvest workers, poor homesteaders working for wages, and full-time permanent farmhands have left little mark on the face of labour history. Never successfully unionized on the Canadian prairies, homesteaders and farmhands were isolated from each other and largely at the mercy of their employers. Eventually, they either successfully made the transition to farm ownership or left the farming industry completely.[86] For migrant workers, the farm work was a short-term promise of quick cash, not a vocation. The Great Depression of the 1930s put a temporary end to the demand for harvest excursionists, while the introduction of gas tractors, combines, and ever-larger farm equipment essentially eliminated the need for such workers altogether.

◆ ◆ ◆

Between 1885 and 1914, Alberta was transformed from a territory of dispersed First Nations and Métis peoples, and the outsiders who earned a living from their endeavours, to a densely populated farming economy with significant urban centres. The early workers whose labour transformed the terrain came from diverse ethnic, linguistic, and cultural backgrounds. The massive influx of immigrants who settled the homesteads, constructed the railroads, mined the coal, and built the cities created union structures and communities that reflected their struggle for a new life in an economy very much shaped and governed by foreign investment interests and the needs of the central Canadian state and its economic elite.

In the railway construction camps, single male European immigrant workers toiled under working and living conditions that were stark even by the standards of the times. Their isolated working conditions and spells of winter unemployment in the skid rows of western cities, and their constant migrations in search of work that moved them across provincial boundaries and the Canada–US border, caused them to view the IWW as their natural ally. The union's message of a world without bosses made sense to them.

The mine workers, though also facing precarious lives, lived in permanent communities, and many had families to help anchor them in place. Despite their ethnic diversity, they developed a solidarity that allowed them to withstand employers who freely employed strikebreakers and agents who, in turn, were aided by the police. That unity across ethnicities was mirrored in a unity across skill and craft lines in their industrially organized union. Between 1904 and 1914, they transformed the United Mine Workers of America District 18 from a business union into an openly socialist fighting organization.

In the urban centres, the craft unions associated with the American Federation of Labor were incredibly successful at organizing the elite skilled trades essential to the operation of the construction, railway, and printing industries. They formed labour councils and pursued a political program of labourist reform to protect their interests as workers. However, although the urban labour movement was very good at protecting the interests of elite workers, it did not speak for the majority of workers in the cities since it disdained to organize the semi-skilled and unskilled workers in the manufacturing, service, retail, and public sectors.

FIG 3-15 Camrose farmers and farmhands, 1908. Provincial Archives of Alberta, PAA 2443.

By 1914, Alberta workers had developed competing socialist, labourist, and syndicalist political programs. Sometimes they remained divided by ethnicity while at other times they overcame their divisions to fight and win both strikes and elections. When World War I began in 1914, the state and employers demanded that workers respond as "Canadians" confronting enemies of Canada and Britain rather than as members of an international working-class confronting exploitative and competing national capitalist groupings. In the face of these demands, Alberta workers' different approaches to fighting exploitation would continue to produce both victories and setbacks for the working class as a whole and for its various subclasses.

FIG 4-1 Determined to have their voices heard, approximately 12,000 farmers, farm labourers, and town workers gathered in Edmonton's Market Square for the Hunger March of 1932. Provincial Archives of Alberta, NC-6-13014.

4 WAR, REPRESSION, AND DEPRESSION, 1914–39

ERIC STRIKWERDA AND ALVIN FINKEL

Whereas, holding the belief in the ultimate supremacy of the working class in matters economic and political, and that the light of modern developments have proved that the legitimate aspirations of the labor movement are repeatedly obstructed by the existing political forms, clearly showing the capitalistic nature of the parliamentary machinery;

This convention expresses its open conviction that the system of industrial Soviet control by selection of representatives from industries is more efficient and of greater political value than the present system of government by selection from district.

This convention declares its full acceptance of this principle of "Proletarian Dictatorship" as being absolute and efficient for the transformation of capitalist private property to public or communal wealth;

The convention sends fraternal greetings to the Russian Soviet government, the Spartacans in Germany and all definite working class movements in Europe and the world, recognizing they have won first place in the history of the class struggle.[1]

This resolution, passed overwhelmingly by delegates to the Western Labour Conference in Calgary in 1919, indicated the extent to which workers across the Prairie provinces and British Columbia had become radicalized by their experiences during wartime. Eighty-nine of the 239 conference delegates were from Alberta, giving Alberta the largest contingent.[2] This chapter traces the events that led to this radicalism and documents its gradual decline under an employer onslaught in the 1920s, followed by a revival of radicalism during the Great Depression.

It was a turbulent time for Alberta workers. The onset of the Great War in mid-summer 1914 coincided with the province's most serious bout of unemployment and depressed conditions in its short history. The depression would linger on to 1915, prompting, in part, thousands of Alberta workers to early sign up for paid military service overseas. As Alberta's wartime economy improved, thousands more found work in the province's resource extraction industries, particularly in southern Alberta's abundant coalfields or as wage labourers on growing farms. For those workers remaining in the cities, opportunity abounded as jobs in factories and other businesses vacated by young soldiers off to war needed to be filled. But one year into the war, labour surpluses had turned to labour shortages. "Everything stopped," Calgary's city commissioner recalled later, "and hundreds of single men — they were carpenters and bricklayers and so on — went off to war."[3]

Through the war years, Alberta workers secured important concessions, both from their employers and from the state, flexing labour's muscle during a time of labour scarcity. But at the same time, they encountered new legislation, shifting employer organizational strategies, and inflationary prices that challenged their autonomy both on and off the job. When the guns fell silent on 11 November 1918, hard times returned to Alberta, and the province's workers struggled once more against high unemployment and recalcitrant employers determined to claw back concessions made during the prosperous war years. This produced a wave of strikes that swept across the province in 1919.

A measure of prosperity had returned to Alberta by the middle of the 1920s. Wheat, a commodity so central to Alberta's economic well-being, fetched more reliable prices through the last years of the decade, buoyed in part by higher international demand, higher yields, and technological innovations.[4] Newcomers, too, arrived in larger numbers than earlier in the decade, some fleeing political upheavals or persecution in Europe, and many winding up in Alberta cities and on Alberta farms. Young women, many lately arrived from Great Britain, found work as domestics, while (primarily) central and eastern European men arrived

as unskilled workers, artisans, and tradespeople. All of these newcomers added distinct ethnic and cultural dynamics to the growing province.

The relative prosperity through the late 1920s was dashed again at the end of the decade, this time on the shoals of a worldwide economic depression. Nearly ten years passed before Alberta workers again found economic security. Nevertheless, many workers banded together under newly organized Communist-inspired groups to advance ideologically radical agendas with varying degrees of success. Their efforts were met and restrained in different ways and for different reasons by employers, the state, and organized labour. The organized labour movement itself underwent serious and difficult ideological divisions throughout the economic downturn, and emerged from the 1930s with different goals and organizational strategies.

Through these years, Alberta workers consistently challenged their employers, their governments, and their society more generally to think about (and respond to) the "labour question." Some continued to work for alternatives to the conservative craft-dominated labour movement. Others entered formal politics at the local, provincial, and national levels. Still others confronted their employers and the state with radical new ideas on how their society ought to be organized. Overall, they created important forums for building solidarity and collective activities that sometimes crossed ethnic and gender lines.

Some of the most dynamic contributions to Canada's labour history emerged in Alberta through the interwar years: the Western Labour Conference of 1919; the One Big Union (OBU), formed the same year; and the Co-operative Commonwealth Federation (CCF),

The Morning Bulletin

FINANCIAL AGENTS
Stocks and Bonds
Fire Insurance, Etc.
Real Estate and Farm Lands
The Alberta Trust Co.
Union Bank Building   Limited

VOL. X, No. 22   TWELVE PAGES   EDMONTON, ALBERTA, MONDAY, MAY 26, 1919   CITY EDITION   PRICE FIVE CENTS

GENERAL STRIKE IN CITY AT 11 A.M. TODAY

Labor Unions Vote Three to One for Walk Out--Definite Order of Strike to Develop

RIGORS OF 'PEG STRIKE RULES ARE LESSENED

Free Press Now Issuing Daily Paper Under Very Great Difficulties

NEWS BY WIRELESS

No Mail Received and No Soldiers' Pay Forthcoming-- Utilities Work

Copies of the Winnipeg Free Press morning and evening editions dated Thursday May 22nd reached Edmonton on Saturday, brought by travel from Winnipeg. They contain the latest authentic news of the strike situation up to the hour of writing. There was also received by the same hand a copy of the Winnipeg citizen of Wednesday, May 21st, and copies of the Western Labor News of May 20th and 22nd. The latest Vancouver Province received carries despatches of the 22nd.

Printers Not On Strike

The Free Press evening edition is of eight pages and the morning edition of only two. The Free Press explains that the printers did not strike, but the pressmen and stereotypers did, although all three had sometimes...

At eleven o'clock this morning, unless news has been received before that time that the Winnipeg strike is settled, or from some accredited source that it is about to be settled, business in Edmonton will be tied up by a walkout of members of local trade unions in sympathetic support of the Winnipeg strike.

This decision was arrived at as the result of the strike vote taken among the local unions during the week-end, and which was counted on Sunday afternoon. According to figures handed out by the propaganda committee subsequently appointed, the vote in favor of a strike was 34 unions for and 4 against, with some others yet to send in their votes. Some 49 unions were supposed to record their vote. Although not given out officially, it is understood that the individual voting was about 1670 in favor of a strike to 500 against.

The Edmonton strike will automatically cease with the conclusion of hostilities in Winnipeg. Workers have been warned not to pay any attention to news of the cessation that might be given out by the newspapers, but to wait until direct word is given out by the central strike committee, or through the government at Ottawa.

The Trades and Labor hall in the Purvis block on 101st street was a beehive on Sunday afternoon. The results of the strike vote taken by the local unions was supposed to be handed in for counting between the hours of 3 and 5 p.m., and during that time the hall was thronged with labor men, all anxious to know how the vote had gone.

Business Done Secretly

The votes were received by a special committee consisting of J. J. McCormick, assistant secretary of the Trades and Labor Council, J. Findley, representing the machinists and Carl Berg of the

BOLSHEVIK IN TIGHT CORNER AFTER REVERSES

Paris Peace Conference Circles Take Interest in Russian Situation

NO ARMISTICE—KOLCHAK

Lenine and Trotsky Facing Most Critical Period in Bolshevik Regime

Paris, May 25—Interest in the Russian problem which the council of four is considering at every session is intensified by the despatches from Finland, announcing that explosions and fires have occurred in Petrograd. This is interpreted as meaning that the Bolsheviki are destroying their superfluous ammunition supplies preparatory to retreating northward. Helsingfors despatches declare that the Bolshevik demand for an armistice from Admiral Kolchak has been refused. This coupled with the reports of anti-Bolshevik advance upon Petrograd from the north and west as well as Kolchak's successes along the trans-Siberian, and General Deniline's advances from The Don district toward the Volga, is regarded in conference circles as proof that the Bolshevik ministers, Lenine and Trotsky are facing the worst crisis the Bolshevik government has encountered.

Finday in Russia.

Omsk, (Saturday)—Reports to the general staff of the Siberian army indicate disintegration of the morale of the Bolsheviki, mobilised working men and peasants are deserting at the first opportunity, and even the Bolshevik commissaries are reported to be disheartened, many of them declaring openly that they are ready to flee from Russia. Siberian newspapers print resolutions adopted at recent meetings of peasants in the district of Samara. Peasants decided to expell all those with Bolshevik sympathies to organise special peasant detachments to fight the Bolshevik and to arm all men between 18 and 50 for this purpose.

PREMIER BACK

Missing Airmen Safe

Petrograd Is Closely Invested By Success Of The Estonians

LONDON, May 24.—(Bulletin)—Great fires and loud explosions have occurred in and around Petrograd, according to reports forwarded by the Daily Mail correspondent at Helsingfors under date of Thursday. It is believed the Bolsheviki, pressed by the Esthonian advance, are destroying the munitions in Petrograd. Machine gun firing also has been heard in Petrograd, and it is reported that the population has risen against the Bolsheviki.

LONDON, May 24.—Polish troops have captured the important town of Lutak, Involhynia, northeast of Lemberg, from the Ukrainians, according to a Central News dispatch from Berlin. The Poles also took 2,000 prisoners and a large number of guns.

Austrian Treaty Almost Ready For Submission To Delegates; German Counter Draft Complete

CALGARY TO STRIKE

CALGARY, May 25.—A general strike has been called in Calgary to take effect at 11 o'clock tomorrow morning. Practically all unions affiliated with the Trades Council will be affected, the vote being four to one in favor. Essential activities, such as police and fire protection, delivery of milk, bread and other necessities will be carried on. Hotel and restaurant employees have also been requested to stay

Reported That Counter Proposals Will Demand German Administration for Rhineland — Also Claim Right to Keep Border Coal Districts

PARIS, May 25.—The council of four has completed the Austrian treaty with the exception of financial clauses and the southern boundary on which some details remain to be straightened out. Chinese and Japanese delegates were before the council yesterday afternoon in connection with the Russian question which continues to occupy much of the council's attention owing to the proposal to recognise Admiral Kolchak, anti-Bolshevik leader in Russia.

COPENHAGEN, May 25—Accord-

Hawker and Grieve Have Been Found

Daring Aviators Given up for Dead After Failure to Arrive from the Trans-Atlantic Attempt Picked up by Danish Steamer— Sopwith Plane Is Lost

LONDON, May 25.—(Bulletin)—Harry G. Hawker and Lieut. Commander Mackenzie Grieve, the two airmen who started last Sunday in an attempt to fly across the Atlantic from St. John's, Nfld., have been picked up at sea and landed in Scotland. Both men were in perfect health.

It is officially announced by the Admiralty that the aviators were picked up in latitude 80.20 and longitude 29.30, having alighted close to the little Danish steamer Mary, owing to a stoppage of circulation in the water pipes between the radiator and the water pump. The

FIG 4-2 In May of 1919, the *Edmonton Bulletin* announces that Edmonton workers would begin general strikes in show of solidarity with the Winnipeg General Strike. Edmonton Archives 267 138.

whose founding meeting took place in Calgary in 1932. Though these interventions proved to have larger implications outside the province than within it, they nevertheless reveal a vibrancy that challenges Alberta's one-party, one-ideology, one-class reputation. Alberta labour prior to the Second World War grappled with many of the same problems and challenges that workers elsewhere in Canada struggled with, including how to organize the labour movement effectively, how to accommodate new ethnic and gender dynamics, what goals to pursue, and what strategies to use to achieve those goals.

WAR

Tension had been building for some time, and war was widely expected. After Yugoslav nationalist Gavrilo Princip assassinated Archduke Franz Ferdinand, heir to the Austro-Hungarian throne in July 1914, the world watched and waited. In rapid succession, the paving stones of the road to war fell into place, and by 4 August, when Britain declared war on Germany, Austria-Hungary, Serbia, the Russian Empire, and France had already taken sides as a result of prior alliances, agreements, and treaties. In those days, when Britain was at war, so were her dominions, including Canada. It may have seemed a complicated business to people thousands of miles and an ocean away, but for many Albertans, the idea of war was exciting. It represented adventure, romance, and a little danger. For some, it was a chance to distinguish themselves and to defend the honour and glory of the British Empire. Alberta's religious, political, and business leaders, who led the charge in beating the imperialist drum, were not alone in their enthusiasm for the war. Many urban-dwellers got caught up in the excitement. Edmonton's streets "thronged with excited crowds and patriotic demonstrations" almost as soon as the war began.[5] Calgary, the *Daily Herald* reported on 8 August, had never seen "such an imposing military parade," as hundreds of new recruits marched through city streets cheered on by onlookers.[6] Within days, some two thousand Calgary men had enlisted for overseas service; prominent among them were members of Calgary's wage-earning class. Nineteen of the city's firefighters signed up almost immediately, most of whom became stretcher-bearers, medics, and combatants.[7] Their departure affected

firefighting services in the city: "I have lost so many good men through enlistment," complained fire chief James Smart. By August 1915, Calgary's bricklayers and stonemasons had joined the war effort in force, followed by all of the city's painters, decorators, and paper hangers a year later.[8] Historian David Bright suggests that, by war's end, some 60 percent of Calgary tradesmen had enlisted.[9] Similar patterns emerged in Edmonton and Lethbridge, in Drumheller and Red Deer.

Many of the province's labour leaders were more skeptical about the whole business. To them, militaristic nationalism and allegiance to empire, king, and country undermined the wider class struggle. It seemed clear to socialists that the war was a "miserable muddle," of benefit only to a wealthy international elite. "Capitalists of the world cause all war," delegates to the 1911 Trades and Labour Congress (TLC) meeting in Calgary declared. And though the TLC had become more conservative and softened its anti-war stance by 1914, western radical labour leaders maintained that the war was of little interest to workers. Why, leaders like Edmonton's Joe Knight asked, should workers fight — and maybe die — for capitalist interests? What quarrel did Albertan workers have with German or Austrian workers? The state repression of workers' efforts to seek economic justice, discussed in chapter 3, caused class-conscious workers to guffaw at government and corporate propaganda stating that the war was meant to spread democracy. Anti-militarism and pacifism were fed by the obvious lies of the pro-imperialists.[10]

Rank-and-file workers across the prairies largely set aside labour leaders' pacifist exhortations early in the war. Most of the first recruits rushing to hastily organized recruitment centres were recent arrivals from

Britain, anxious to defend the mother country.[11] Others, French and Belgian immigrant miners from the Crowsnest Pass among them, found that their own ethnic and national loyalties coincided with those of their new homeland, and either signed up as members of the Canadian Expeditionary Force or returned home to fight for their mother countries directly.[12] French reservists from Edmonton, that city's *Bulletin* reported in early August 1914, were leaving daily for Calgary, where they would shortly join their counterparts from the southern parts of the province travelling to France.[13] Others still viewed the war as a way to prove their loyalty to their adopted home.[14] "Thousands of our Ukrainian boys have enlisted with the Canadian overseas force," Winnipeg Ukrainian leaders boasted in 1916, "and many have already lost their lives fighting beside their British brethren on the battlefields in France."[15]

For more than a few, however, military service represented mainly steady, full-time work during a time of uncertain and precarious jobs and high unemployment.[16] Though the war would eventually provide a short-term lift for Alberta's economy from the depression that had lasted more than a year, the downturn's true end still lay some months into the future. Not until the summer of 1915 would more prosperous economic times arrive in Alberta. Thus, Alberta's unskilled and migrant workers faced bleak problems through the winter of 1914–15. Continuing low prices for coal meant little work in the mines of southern Alberta, and disappointingly small harvests in 1914 and 1915 left little seasonal work for migrant farm workers. Meanwhile, the bulk of the work associated with railway construction begun earlier in the century also disappeared as projects reached completion in 1913. More generally, the great boom that had fuelled the rapid urbanization and modest industrialization of the prairies went bust after that year. To make matters worse, British capital, on which prairie dreams had largely been built, dissipated fast in the wake of a worldwide industrial slowdown, leaving an overheated prairie economy to freeze.[17]

Unemployment soared in the cities as well. Edmonton, the *Labour Gazette* reported in 1915, was one of the "five great labour reservoirs in Canada, the cities to which the unemployed chiefly gravitate."[18] This was certainly true for some one thousand unemployed men — cold, hungry, and tired — who descended on that city in December 1913 seeking work or relief. In the end, Edmonton relief officials were able to offer meals, beds, and a little relief work to only a third of them.[19] Jobless numbers would only get worse, reaching on average between three thousand and six thousand men for each of the years 1914, 1915, and 1916. The city instituted work relief projects and opened a camp and dining hall on the city's fair grounds. But relief authorities ordered the camp closed after they discovered Industrial Workers of the World (IWW) efforts to organize the campers.[20]

At Calgary and Lethbridge, the numbers of unemployed were equally higher than normal, putting a severe strain on local relief efforts. Calgary's Associated Charities Association reported in June 1914 that it was "overtaxed in caring for the destitute." Nearly a year later, conditions had not improved: in March 1915, Associated Charities was spending some $8,000 per month on relief.[21] "All charitable institutions were strained to the utmost to assist families who would otherwise have starved," a Lethbridge social worker recalled of the prewar recession.[22] In this context, many jobless workers joined the Canadian Expeditionary Force. As if to underline the relationship between enlistment and food, new Edmonton recruits received a meal following successful medical examinations.[23] For some, the prospect of regular pay and regular meals was alluring. "To such the war proved a veritable safety valve, and many enlisted," the Lethbridge social worker continued. "I heard one man say he might as well be shot as starve to death."[24]

Many were shot on the fields of France at places like Vimy, Amiens, and Paschendaele, and of the over 45,000 Albertans who eventually served overseas, 6,140 never came home. Despite the often harsh and unimaginably dangerous conditions at the front, some kept up their spirits. Calgary fireman Private Jim Carswell had been in the trenches for five days in August 1915 when he wrote home: "Tell them it's fine out here, and that I wouldn't have missed this experience for Rockefeller's fortune. We have a bear of a time — get fed good, have concerts every night when resting, and have football and baseball matches, too. Beats training all to pieces."[25] Others, like Donald Bannerman, an electrician from Banff, described the difficult and uncomfortable trench conditions in starker terms: "We went into the trenches the night before and, as it was raining cats and dogs, our rations for the next day were spoiled and we had nothing with which to break our fast."[26] Bannerman was wounded the following year while trying to aid a comrade. He returned to Banff in August 1916. Thousands more were not so lucky.

Alberta's workers contributed to the war effort at home as well. They bought war bonds, both to help defeat "Kaiserism" in Europe and as an investment in their own futures. They also sent their sons off to Europe to fight, no small contribution given the critical roles young men played in many working-class family survival strategies. Some labour leaders, however, counselled workers against buying war bonds or supporting so-called Patriotic Funds, warning that the bankers and war munitions profiteers would be the real beneficiaries of their sacrifices.

After the recession lifted in 1915, nominal wages generally rose for those workers who stayed behind. Farm workers' wages, for instance, stood at $27 per month in 1915 and rose to as high as $60 per month by 1918. Monthly earnings for female farm wage workers were much lower, but they enjoyed a faster average rise, nearly tripling from $10 to $28 over the same period.[27] By the late summer of 1916, farm workers in southern Alberta were refusing to work for anything less than $3.50 per day.[28] Wages paid to manufacturing workers in the province remained steady through the early years of the war. While manufacturers paid out a total of just over $5 million in 1916 and more than $10 million the following year, this increase reflected a doubling of the number of factories operating in the province over the same period.[29] Nevertheless, compared to the immediate prewar years, work was plentiful, as is also illustrated by Alberta coal production. Production fell between 1913 and 1915 from 4.3 million tons to 3.4 million tons. But it increased rapidly thereafter, to more than 6 million tons by 1918, and as a result, work at the mines was more regular and generally better paid than it had been during the recession.

But the wage increases often did not even keep up with soaring wartime inflation.[30] Food and fuel costs, for instance, had doubled by war's end. And while rents changed little during the war, they jumped dramatically with the return of overseas soldiers in 1919.[31] Calgary's firefighters viewed the situation as dire enough to organize for the first time and demand better pay. Married men especially, they pointed out, could not live on the wages they earned in the inflationary climate.[32] In mid-November 1916, miners in the Crowsnest Pass region threatened to strike if wages did not rise 25 percent to help them make ends meet. The miners had secured an 8 percent increase the previous August, but food costs at the camp stores had risen 30 percent.[33] The coal operators' refusal to bargain with the miners resulted in a much wider strike near the end of November, reaching Lethbridge and Drumheller miners, as well as miners in the Crowsnest Pass.[34] Over the next five months, miners in southern British Columbia and southern Alberta — members of District 18, which covered all of western Canada — struck often, defying agreements made in 1915 by the United Mine Workers of America to maintain industrial peace in the region for the duration of the war.[35]

The miners were striking from a position of relative strength, given the imperative need for reliable coal supplies to fuel the nation's war-related railway and manufacturing needs.[36] Equally important for their solidarity, the miners, through shared experiences, maintained a strong sense of unity, as well as class- and ethnic-based solidarity. For the most part, they made their homes in coal towns that, according to historian Gerald Friesen, had a "depressing sameness to them, whether situated in the stark landscape of southern Saskatchewan, the badlands of central Alberta, or the majestic valleys of the Rockies." Their work was hard and dangerous, resulting in an average of thirty deaths per year on the job through the interwar years. Off the job, they were "brought together by sporting teams, cultural events, reading groups, benevolent funds, and especially by political action and strikes."[37]

THE WARTIME POOR

Not all Alberta workers enjoyed high wages, good working conditions, or strength in numbers during World War I. In the spring of 1916, the Alberta and Great Waterways Railway advertised work at wages of $1.50 per day laying steel near Fort McMurray. Recent European immigrant men took the company up on its offer and arrived at the work camp in June.

Once there, however, they discovered that the railway company charged each man one dollar per day for room and board, and a further dollar per month for "doctor's fees." On Sundays and other days when the weather was rainy, the men did not work and did not get paid, but the company still required them to pay for their food and lodging. The ten-hour workdays were hard, but this was not altogether unexpected. What the workers probably did not anticipate were the hordes of mosquitoes and sawflies that harassed them day and night.

The men demanded a raise of 25 cents per day, and the company agreed. Soon thereafter, however, conditions deteriorated even further when the railway company refused any additional wage increases. In the end, the workers felt they had little choice but to walk off the job. They asked for their last pay, determined to make it back to Edmonton with a little money in their pockets. The foreman, however, said the men could retrieve their pay in Edmonton. They walked, hungry and tired, to Lac la Biche, some 175 miles to the south, where they rested a few days before making the rest of their journey to Edmonton.

SOURCE: Ann Woywitka, "Strike at Waterways."

Inflation and poor working conditions caused serious problems, but many Alberta workers were also angry at the obvious disconnect between wartime rhetoric and apparent wartime profiteering and cronyism, first evident in contracts that Minister of Militia Sam Hughes awarded to his friends and later during businessman Joseph Flavelle's tenure as head of the Imperial Munitions Board.[39] A Unitarian minister and labour activist in Calgary, William Irvine, reflected the frustration of many in the pages of his *Nutcracker* newspaper: "No other country in the world," he claimed in 1916, "has permitted capitalists to pile up fortunes at the expense of the soldiers in the trenches — 200 million dollars in the profit extracted by our army contractors since the war began."[40] Workers also opposed the federal government's extension of the *Industrial Disputes Investigation Act* to war production work. According to legal scholars Judy Fudge and Eric Tucker, "the extension of the IDIA favoured employers because it required strikes and lockouts to be postponed until after the conciliation process was completed."[41]

The war exacerbated existing prejudices against "enemy" aliens — workers principally from the Austro-Hungarian Empire who had earlier in the century been recruited to solve labour shortages during the great boom by serving as a temporary, industrial workforce. These migrant workers, many of them single men from Galicia and Bukovyna, made for an attractive, largely unskilled workforce because they would work cheaply under difficult conditions in isolated places. Once the two new transcontinental railways were nearly completed and other work requiring unskilled labour dried up after 1913, many of these workers made for western Canadian cities in search of work or relief. There, historian

In July 1917, the federal government intervened in the District 18 strike, establishing a "de facto nationalization of the interior coal mines." For the remainder of the war, prices, wages, and supplies would be set under the dual authority of a Dominion Fuel Controller and a Director of Coal Operations. Wages rose shortly thereafter, reaching as high as five dollars per shift by 1918. Province-wide, more than eleven thousand workers were involved in some seventeen industrial actions in 1917, mostly in the mining communities in the south, up from some five hundred workers the year before.[38]

Bill Waiser says, "they were received coolly — if not with revulsion — and forced to eke out a miserable existence in crowded, filthy, urban ghettos." They initially attracted little interest or attention, save for disdain by the Anglo-Protestant majority, many of whom considered them "ignorant foreigners," the "scum of Europe."[42] Through the war years, however, many were regarded as "enemy aliens," especially if they had been born in the Austro-Hungarian Empire. The federal government moved swiftly due to business pressure and widespread public prejudice to establish internment camps for thousands of destitute and unemployed "enemies."

Edmonton's city commissioners were similarly concerned about masses of unemployed "enemy aliens" arriving in their city. The city authorities conducted a survey of city workers in February 1916 with a view to dismissing German and Austrian workers. The commissioners found five street-railway workers who had been born in Germany or Austria. Although all five had been naturalized, they were nevertheless suspended until they could produce their naturalization papers. Another man who had arrived in Canada from Germany some twenty years earlier and had worked at the city's power plant for twelve years was likewise dismissed from his job, despite his assertion that he had been born in Russia.[43] Four more men of Austrian birth were suspended from their jobs in the waterworks department until they became naturalized British subjects. More covert operations were also launched specifically to keep an eye on migrant workers of enemy nationalities. The Royal North West Mounted Police hired "high-priced Secret Service Agents" to infiltrate immigrant communities throughout the war, including an undercover barber in Edmonton.[44]

Given such outright hostility, it is unsurprising that many recent-immigrant workers banded together, both to assert their own interests and to protect themselves from nativist hiring practices and policies. At Coleman, Polish immigrant workers established the Polish Society of Brotherly Aid in 1916. John Liss-Pozarzycki later noted:

> I was one of the co-founders of this Society. I prepared the constitution for them, taking as a model, the constitution of the National Union of Poles in Chicago . . . . In addition to helping its compatriots in distress, the Society issued each member an identity card stating that he was not an Austrian or a German, but a Pole. These documents were recognized by the authorities in Alberta and saved their bearers much grief.[45]

But perhaps the biggest issue and object of suspicion among workers during the war was the looming threat of conscription, state-enforced service in the Canadian Expeditionary Force. As voluntary recruitment fell after 1916 and earlier recruits continued to die on the battlefields of Europe in high numbers, Canada found it increasingly difficult to make good on its promises to Britain regarding soldier numbers for the war effort. Even the release of "enemy aliens" from internment camps through 1916 and the expected entry of the Americans into the war on the Allied side by 1917 could not sate the need for more soldiers at the front. Early in 1916, Prime Minister Robert Borden floated the idea of registering men, supposedly to use the nation's manpower as efficiently as possible. The business community, especially in central Canada where labour shortages abounded, applauded the prime minister's initiative. "Has the time not come for Canada," Canadian Manufacturers Association president J.H. Sherrard asked rhetorically in 1916, "to register her men so that those who can be most useful to the war by remaining at the work they are necessary to, shall not be recruited?"[46]

Many labour leaders interpreted the registration of men differently. The Trades and Labour Congress, for example, opposed registration on the grounds that it was a precursor to military conscription. In Calgary, trade unionists were cautious, accepting "a National Service Scheme which has for its Object the mobilization and use of the Natural Resources and Utilities of this Country for the direct benefit of the State," but stopping short of endorsing the registration of men as part of the plan.[47] By the summer of 1916, some Calgary labour leaders were poised to accept what the *Albertan* called "conscription in the fullest meaning of the word" but were hesitant to do so until there was "first a conscription of wealth." In the end, the Borden administration introduced a conscription bill in June 1917, a measure that became law after the election in December of a "Union" government: the Conservatives joined by the pro-conscription elements of the Liberal Party. Labour's call for conscription of wealth — that is, a ban on profits for capitalists during wartime — went unheeded.

Alberta workers did secure limited labour-friendly provincial legislation during the war years. The Liberal government passed the *Factory Act, 1917*. Among other provisions, the act established a minimum wage of $1.50 per day for men, except for apprentices, who would receive $1.00 per day. (Women, however, who were included in other provinces' minimum wage legislation, would not be incorporated into the Alberta legislative scheme until 1920.) The 1917 changes also included a joint industrial council program that provided for a "chief inspector" in any city or town with a population greater than five thousand. On the recommendation of a local advisory committee representing employers and employees, the inspector was allowed to "make regulations respecting the hours of labour per day or per week in any local factory, shop, office, or office building," so long as such regulations did not abridge the 1917 *Factory Act*.[48]

Low levels of unemployment during the war emboldened many workers to unionize, including government workers. Edmonton city labourers received a charter from the Trades and Labour Congress of Canada in 1917, and municipal workers in Calgary, Lethbridge, and Medicine Hat had also organized by war's end. In the early postwar period, more government workers unionized. By 1919, in Calgary, both inside and outside city workers, along with police and firefighters, street-railway workers, and city hospital workers, had joined unions.[49]

The Civil Service Association (CSA), predecessor of the Alberta Union of Provincial Employees, also formed in 1919. Before the war, the prevailing philosophy had been that employees of the federal or provincial governments were servants of the public rather than workers and that they therefore should not seek the rights that unionists demanded. Alberta's *Civil Service Act* forbade government employees from asking for a salary increase (such a request was considered equivalent to resignation), meaning that wages could only be increased if the government decided to increase them. Given that the provincial government decided to save money during the war by ignoring the impact of inflation on its employees' wages, it was only natural that its workers would rebel and demand the right to negotiate wages and working conditions. Although the CSA joined the Alberta Federation of Labour in 1927, in its early years it behaved more like an advisory body to the government than a trade union.[50]

REVOLT

When the war ended in November 1918, Alberta's labour market shifted once again. The labour shortages that had characterized the last years of fighting in Europe quickly became labour surpluses once again as thousands of veterans returned home. Making matters worse was the federal government's promise, as part of its demobilization program, to resettle veterans anywhere they chose in the country. Veterans from all over Canada descended on western cities like Edmonton and Calgary seeking work. Adding tension to an already tense work situation were increasingly sharp ethnic divides. Through much of the war, employers had relied on (and benefited from) recent-immigrant workers who were often willing to work for less pay to fill vacated jobs in mines, factories, and lumber camps. Many returning veterans focused their hostility in the recessionary climate on these workers. Furthermore, women who had participated in the wage labour market during the war years were encouraged — both by society and public policy — to return home to non-wage labour following the war.

Workers in Alberta, as across the nation, had a substantial list of grievances, some left over from the war years and others associated with the postwar

demobilization process. Inflation, wartime profiteering, and conscription had left a bitter taste in workers' mouths. Walter Smitten, president of the Alberta Federation of Labour, expressed a fairly common view of workers' postwar expectations: "We have been told that this was a war for democracy, and I think we should make sure that democracy attains a decent standard of living."[51]

In an effort to head off worker militancy, and in response to deteriorating relations between workers and employers, the federal government appointed a Royal Commission with directions to "make a survey and classification of existing Canadian industries . . . with a view to improving conditions in the future." In reality, the Mathers Commission (so named after its chair, Justice Thomas Graham Mathers of Manitoba) sought evidence of existing worker-employer councils designed to lessen industrial conflict. Perhaps more importantly, the commission promoted such councils (modelled on the so-called Whitley councils in Britain, named for the politician who first proposed the idea) as a means of solving industrial disputes in future. In any event, in carrying out its work, the Mathers Commission visited cities across the country, taking testimony from workers and employers about the state of industrial relations at that time. The commission also inspected industrial plants and workplaces with, as its final report pointed out, "the object of visualizing for ourselves the operations of the plant and the working conditions of the men employed in it."[52] In the end, the commission summarized its findings that the "chief causes of unrest" nation-wide were unemployment and the fear of unemployment, and the high cost of living.

FIG 4-4 Logo of the Civil Service Association, predecessor of the Alberta Union of Provincial Employees. Courtesy of the Alberta Labour History Institute.

The calm procedures associated with the Mathers Commisson's work belied a more militant and radical strain in the labour movement running through especially the province's coal seams. Alberta's miners, together with their counterparts in British Columbia, had for some time been growing increasingly disillusioned with the association of the United Mine Workers of America (UMWA) and with conservative and craft-dominated international trade unions. There was dissension regarding the UMWA's cautious paths throughout the war, which even included agreeing to guarantee industrial peace for its duration. This position was taken despite longstanding and unanswered grievances from the miners themselves. By 1918, a majority of western workers had determined to shake off conservative approaches in favour of more radical ones. They increasingly argued that organizing industrially and adding the general strike to their arsenal were necessary innovations that would together usher in a new, more equitable industrial order: a "syndicalist" economy in which worker-operated co-operatives would replace privately owned profit-seeking corporations. History, too, was on their side, they believed. After all, the successful Bolshevik Revolution in Russia the year before had clearly illustrated the possibilities of more militant approaches to industrial relations.

A critical first step toward fashioning changes along industrial lines, western workers believed, was to convince the Trades and Labour Congress at the annual convention of the immediate and pressing need for industrial (as opposed to craft) unionism and for the adoption of the general strike as an industrial tactic. But although central Canada and Atlantic Canada would later experience an upsurge of postwar radicalism, the balance of both conservative and radical delegates from east of Manitoba favoured the conservative sufficiently to vote down the western proposals in favour of maintaining the business unionist status quo that characterized the American Federation of Labor.

Undeterred, western workers returned home from the convention determined to fashion a workable industrial alternative to "Gomperism." That pejorative term referenced Samuel Gompers, president of the American Federation of Labor from 1886 to 1924 and chief spokesperson for the view that unions should be organized only to protect particular crafts and should ignore other workers as well as socialist movements. Leaders of the Socialist Party of Canada (SPC), operating out of its Vancouver headquarters, organized a wholly western labour conference to take place at Calgary in March 1919. The SPC initiative had a good deal of support among western labour leaders, winning endorsement from such leading figures as Joseph Knight and Carl Berg in Edmonton, for example. The 239 delegates representing workers across the Prairies and British Columbia met in Calgary's Paget Hall and voted unanimously to form what they called the One Big Union (OBU). It was, the *Calgary Daily Herald* reported on 14 March, a "momentous . . . pronouncement in the annals of the labor movement in Canada."[53] Through the course of the morning and early afternoon, delegates adopted the radical program mentioned at the opening of this chapter.

The OBU, formed at a second conference in June 1919, insisted that workers needed to achieve change in their working conditions by uniting their efforts in combat with employers. It called on workers to turn each strike against a specific employer into a general strike of all workers in order to put maximum pressure on a struck employer and to demonstrate worker power that would eventually allow workers to seize control of their workplaces and dispense with capitalists altogether. Unsurprisingly, the federal government sided with employers to ruthlessly suppress the OBU via arrests of leaders and brutal suppression of their strikes.[54]

It would be misleading to suggest that Alberta workers were suddenly united in their embrace either of industrial unionism or of the general strike. Certainly, the fledgling Alberta Federation of Labour was caught between the radicals and the more cautious elements within the labour movement. Before the radical program was adopted at the Western Labour Conference, the federation had moved a resolution that better reflected the positions that it would take politically over the next fifteen years than did the conference's resolution. They called for the "formation of a political party with the object in view of uniting labour and kindred organizations into a homogeneous political party; believing that a united political labour party is a necessary adjustment to the development of our industrial organizations and to the attainment of our national ideals."[55] The resolution was soundly defeated.

Labour leaders like Alex Ross, future cabinet minister in the United Farmers of Alberta government, and Edmonton's Alf Farmilo vigorously opposed what they viewed as radical solutions to labour's problems, frequently pointing out the OBU's shortcomings in the pages of the *Alberta Labour News*, the official newspaper of the Alberta Federation of Labour from 1919 to 1935, edited throughout that time by Elmer Roper.[56] Nevertheless, as historians Tom Mitchell and James Naylor point out, "local after local in the West passed motions in favor of joining general strikes."[57]

FIG 4-5 The One Big Union, founded in 1919, soon became the target of government suppression. Courtesy of the Alberta Labour History Institute.

In its most visible illustration of workers' anger, the Winnipeg General Strike, which preceded the OBU conference, finds few matches. It all began, perhaps, ordinarily enough: workers in the building trades demanded higher wages to offset the ever-increasing cost of living. Employers, speaking through the Building Trades Council, refused. The city's metal-trades workers, meantime, had been demanding higher wages and a forty-four-hour work week through much of the spring. Again, workers' demands were rejected.

Through the first two weeks of May, other organized workers met with determined employer resistance to wage increases, shorter working days, and better workplace conditions. On 13 May, the city's Trades Council overwhelmingly endorsed a general strike. Two days later, on 15 May, more than twenty-two thousand Winnipeg workers set down their tools and walked off the job. Participant numbers would eventually reach as high as thirty-five thousand. The story coming out of Winnipeg was impressive. Workers in that city had literally shut down the town. Acting, for the most part, as one, workers from a wide variety of political and ideological persuasions joined forces to challenge their bosses and the status quo.[58]

The strike's end was equally impressive, though for different reasons. Following six weeks of national and even international attention, the Royal North West Mounted Police (RNWMP) descended on the city charged with restoring order to what authorities had taken to calling a "Bolshevik Revolution" run by "crazy idealists" and "ordinary thieves."[59] Joining the RNWMP were eighteen hundred "special" constables hired by the so-called Committee of 1000, which represented the city's business interests. The RNWMP began its work in earnest in the third week of June, bursting through the doors of the city's labour halls and the strike leaders' homes, and arresting and jailing twelve key strikers. Finally, the RNWMP charged a large, open-air gathering of strikers at Portage and Main on 21 June — Bloody Saturday — killing one and wounding scores more. The strikers returned to work four days later, their demands unmet.[60]

The Winnipeg General Strike, though dramatic, was only the most visible sign of what historian Craig Heron has called a much broader national "workers' revolt" that had begun as early as 1917 and would last until the mid-1920s. In the spring of 1919, many Calgary workers supported a sympathy strike with workers in Winnipeg. Some fifteen hundred workers walked off the job at 11:00 a.m. on 26 May 1919 and would not return for four weeks. They included postal workers, flour and cereal workers, and workers at the CPR's Ogden railway shops, the latter constituting two-thirds of the strikers.[61] In Edmonton, thirty-four Trades and Labour Council locals supported a sympathy strike, and only four opposed one (though eleven locals abstained from voting).[62] As in Calgary, the Edmonton general strike lasted four weeks, and in both cities, the strikes were preludes to mass parades and picnics sponsored for another fifteen years by the local trades and labour councils on May Day and Labour Day.[63] In Lethbridge, too, workers voted to join the general strike in sympathy. The general strikes appeared to close some of the fissures that had been developing in the province's labour movement, as strident anti-OBUers like Edmonton's and Calgary's trades councils supported the Winnipeg workers. Nor was the strike wave limited to the West. Workers in Hamilton and Toronto, Halifax, and Montreal all engaged in sympathy strikes.[64]

RECESSION AND ORGANIZATION

But a deep recession in the early 1920s and a ham-fisted employer and state counter-offensive stemmed the growth of this class-conscious working-class movement. Alberta workers' wages in most industries fell precipitously through the early 1920s as the province, along with the rest of North America, entered a severe postwar recession, the result of a failure of governments to devise policies to cushion the blow of postwar unemployment. Farm wage labourers' annual wages fell rapidly through the early 1920s, from a high of $697 per year in 1920, to $463 in 1921, to a new low of $367 in 1922.[65] Falling wages, unfortunately, was only half the problem. Job losses were huge. In 1920, nearly eleven thousand men earned manufacturing wages in the province, mostly in small firms. By the following year, that number had fallen to fewer than seven thousand. The number of women employed in manufacturing rose slightly over the same period, from eleven hundred to sixteen hundred.[66]

In 1919, only 2 percent of trade unionists in the province were out of work. Two years later, that number jumped to nearly 8 percent. And while unemployment figures for trade unionists fell to almost zero for each of 1922 and 1923, thereafter unemployment hovered around 6 percent until the end of the decade.[67] The new United Farmers of Alberta government, elected in 1921, regarded the situation as serious enough to call a special conference in Edmonton on 20 July 1921, to deal with the matter. At the meeting, representatives of various municipal governments, labour organizations, and veterans' groups agreed that the provincial government should help finance some form of relief work throughout the province.[68] The bulk of unemployed wage earners lived in either Edmonton or Calgary, with smaller numbers living in Lethbridge, Medicine Hat, and villages like Redcliff, in Cypress County. Redcliff, like other farm-service centres, played host to a number of small manufacturers. Redcliff's high-grade shale and abundant natural gas deposits combined to entice a

shoe factory, a cigar factory, and a rolling mill and bolt factory, as well as brick, glass, iron, and clay works.[69] The recession caused most of these firms to go under, while jobs in the farm-service sector disappeared as farmers, facing low prices for their crops, limited their purchases.

The recession also affected coal-mining areas. While Alberta miners pulled nearly seven million tons of coal from the mines in 1920 worth a total of nearly $30 million, the largest output of any province, output fell to six million tons in each of 1921 and 1922.

By war's end, almost 230 union locals represented Alberta workers although most workers remained unorganized. But despite the radical displays of worker solidarity and strength in the spring of 1919, the dramatic end to the Winnipeg General Strike had dealt the "workers' revolt" a crushing blow. After that event, most of the province's organized workers were associated with the American Federation of Labor and the rest with national unions, totalling a trade union membership of more than fifteen thousand in 1920.

Although the One Big Union (OBU) had an enthusiastic beginning, state suppression, sometimes supported by established unions, halted its advance. In 1920, 90 percent of the Crowsnest miners voted to leave the United Mine Workers of America (UMWA) and join the OBU. Recognition of their new union became one of the goals of the miners' strike that year, along with a rescinding of pay cuts announced by the coal companies as a response to the recession. The coal operators opposed all of the workers' demands. They had friends in both the government and the UMWA. The former approved a cabinet order requiring the miners to belong to the UMWA, thus ignoring their democratic choice of the OBU. As journalist Allan Chambers notes, "In a semi-official history years later, UMWA District 18 acknowledged the arrangement to be 'one of the few instances in history providing such solid evidence of employer-union collaboration.'"[70] That alliance allowed the UMWA to prevail over the OBU in mines across the province despite majority support for their upstart opponent.

But Alberta's unionized miners continued to complain that the American head offices of the union took their dues but did not provide sufficient strike relief when they required it. In 1922, for example, Slim Evans, secretary of the UMWA local in Drumheller, withheld union dues from the international union so that starving miners and their families could eat while on strike. For his troubles, he was charged by the UMWA with "fraudulent conversion" and spent three years in prison. By 1925, most miners had had enough of the UMWA and a wave of organization for an independent union, the Mine Workers' Union of Canada (MWUC), beginning with District 18, began. Though the Communist Party initially opposed secession from the UMWA, it decided that worker opposition to the existing union was too strong for the party to continue its line of supporting the achievement of change within the international union. Communists took the leadership of the MWUC, which, with four thousand members by 1926, was larger than the UMWA in Alberta.[71] Since the Alberta Federation of Labour, like the Trades and Labour Congress, was dominated by branches of American unions, the MWUC joined the rival All-Canadian Congress of Labour, a small but feisty organization of unions independent of American unions.

ELECTORAL POLITICS

While the OBU organized workers for an eventual collective takeover by workers of their workplaces, more moderate unionists turned to the electoral politics favoured by the Alberta Federation of Labour to advance the labour agenda. In 1919, trade unionists from the province's cities and towns formed the Alberta branch of the Dominion Labour Party (DLP). Its program, largely based on the British Labour Party's principles, included the gradual socialization of industry and financial institutions, the allotment of surplus wealth for programs for the common good, and the guarantee of a minimum income for all citizens. This emphasis on systemic change, however gradual, represented a leftward shift from prewar labour politics in which labour candidates focused narrowly on specific social reforms. In the lead-up to the 1921 provincial election, the Alberta DLP formed a sometimes uneasy alliance with farmers disillusioned by the old-line political parties.

There was room for discussion between the United Farmers of Alberta (UFA) and the DLP, given UFA president Henry Wise Wood's philosophy of group government in which occupational groups, including both farmers and workers, rather than geographical constituencies, ought to control the legislature. Wise Wood had long been hesitant to support the idea of the farmers' movement running candidates for office, preferring to pressure the Liberal government into enacting farmer-friendly legislation instead. But he caved in to rank-and-file pressure for the UFA to run candidates.[72]

The group government idea offered a second chance for labour-farmer co-operation, which the founding meeting of the Alberta Federation of Labour had promised but could not deliver. The Calgary trades council opted not to join forces with the UFA in 1918, arguing that there was "too much at variance between the aims of farmers and workers."[73] By 1921, however, a coterie of UFA and DLP activists were advocating joint labour-farmer support for candidates in sprawling federal ridings where one or the other seemed most likely to succeed. A long-time labour activist in both Calgary and Edmonton, Elmer Roper, later explained the pragmatic promise of co-operation:

> If it is seen to be advisable to cooperate in elections . . . such cooperation should not compromise the position of either group. It should be freely admitted that in East Calgary the farmers had no candidates because they doubted their ability to elect one, and their support was given to Labor as the group that more nearly represented the economic position of the farmers. The same applies to the reverse situation in Medicine Hat.[74]

Indeed, in Medicine Hat, the UFA recognized that to encourage the type of co-operation that Roper envisaged, it needed to nominate a candidate acceptable to the city's railway workers; it therefore opted for Robert Gardiner, a left-leaning farmer who ran on a Farmer-Labour ticket and openly endorsed the DLP.

In the provincial seats, which rarely combined both urban and rural areas, the need for rural-urban co-operation in the selection of candidates was less evident, and the UFA candidates were generally prosperous farmers with little affinity for the labour movement. Still, the election of the UFA in 1921 raised some hopes among workers in the province. Premier

Herbert Greenfield, who appeared to support the ideas and philosophy behind group government, appointed newly elected MLA and DLP member Alex Ross as minister of Public Works. In addition to Ross, three other DLP candidates had won election to the provincial legislature: William Johnson in Medicine Hat, P.M. Christophers in Rocky Mountain, and Calgary's Fred White. Christophers, a coal miner, stood out from the others as a strong supporter of both the OBU and the Soviet Union.[75]

FIG 4-6 Political cartoon by the American socialist Art Young, whose work appeared frequently in the left-wing publications *The Masses* and *The Liberator*. Courtesy of the Alberta Labour History Institute.

Later that year, the DLP rebranded itself as the Alberta section of the Canadian Labour Party (CLP), though its membership remained largely the same. The CLP was the product of a decision by the Trades and Labour Congress in 1917 to establish a broadly based labour party to unite under one umbrella organization reform-minded socialists, communists, and other groups that held political opinions then current in the labour movement. The shaky early alliance between the communists and socialists made some electoral gains, electing six council members in Calgary in 1926 and a majority of Edmonton aldermen in 1928. Its goals remained the social ownership of the means of wealth production and distribution, and employment for all. The CLP also argued for higher taxes on larger incomes, a corporations profit tax, public ownership and control of financial institutions, and public operation of hospitals.[76]

Many socialists had welcomed the Russian Revolution. By April 1919, Communists had staked out a position on the radical left with the publication of a seven-point program calling for, among other things, "the forcible seizure of the governmental power and the establishment of the dictatorship of the proletariat."[77] Following a formal, though secret, convention in a barn just outside of Guelph in 1921, the Communists established the Communist Party of Canada and set to work bringing the message of communist ideals to "the masses." Shortly thereafter, the Communist International ordered the party's underground apparatus dissolved and replaced with the legal Workers Party of Canada (WPC). In Alberta, as elsewhere, the WPC co-operated with the CLP on municipal and provincial political campaigns. CLP leaders, like party president and machinist George Latham, declared anti-communism a tool of the bosses.

But the non-Communist and Communist wings of the CLP had major disagreements with each other. The trade union leaders, who dominated the party, regarded their alliance with the UFA as useful. It had led, they argued, to improvements in workers' compensation legislation, minimum wage and maximum hours (54) for most workers, improved widows' pensions, and relief projects for the unemployed.[78] The Communists, by contrast, pointed to the UFA government's poor enforcement of the *Mines Act* and its use of provincial police to disperse strikers to argue for labour independence from the UFA government, which would have meant that Alex Ross would have to leave the cabinet.[79] The Communist leadership of the secessionist Mine Workers' Union of Canada, though it had been reluctant, also created resentment among the leaders of American-dominated unions within the Alberta Federation of Labour.

Ordinary workers appeared to want Labour to take a more independent stance in dealing with the UFA. Continuing its agreement with the UFA not to divide the progressive vote, Labour only ran twelve candidates in the 1926 provincial election, all in urban and industrial constituencies. Five were elected, along with socialist Robert Parkyn, who ran as an independent labour candidate in Calgary. Significantly Alex Ross decisively lost his Calgary seat. At the time, Calgary and Edmonton each constituted a multi-member seat, with representation provided through an alternative voting system that allowed voters to rank their choices. So workers' decision to support Parkyn over Ross spoke volumes regarding their views about whether Labour should play second fiddle to the UFA government. The UFA did not offer any Labour member a place in the cabinet as Ross's replacement.

FIG 4-7 The *Alberta Labor News,* the official organ of the AFL from 1920 to 1935. It was edited throughout that period by printer Elmer Roper, later the leader of the Alberta CCF, from 1942 to 1955, and then the mayor of Edmonton, from 1959 to 1963. Courtesy of the Alberta Labour History Institute.

The rift between the reformists and the Communists continued. In 1928, the Comintern, the organization that united the official Communist parties around the world, reversed its former stance requiring co-operation of Communists with social democrats electorally and within unions. Now the Comintern called on Communists to expose social democrats as "social fascists" and "labour fakirs." Alberta's Communists, in line with the Communist Party of Canada, adopted this ultra-left and destructive position. This made it easy for the reformists within the CLP, who might have succeeded anyway in removing Communists from their party, to win the support of individuals and unions who had earlier argued that labour unity required the CLP to include all elements within the labour movement.[80]

With the Communists gone, the voices in the CLP calling for a more nuanced relationship with the UFA government were muffled. The CLP continued its support of the UFA during the provincial election of 1930, and even its loss of a seat did not cause a reconsideration of its political stance. When the UFA responded in a conservative manner to the mass destitution of the Depression, the CLP was tainted with guilt by association.

DEPRESSION

The Depression hit Alberta hard, and all levels of government had trouble knowing how to respond to the devastation. By 1933, 15 percent of Edmontonians, 13 percent of Calgarians, and 13 percent of Lethbridge residents were receiving modest municipal relief, for which only the most destitute qualified. Recipients were households headed by married men, the only group for whom federal and provincial funds were made available. Destitute single women were expected to receive aid from relatives; governments showed little concern that for those who were unable or unwilling to depend on family or friends, prostitution, begging, and theft were the only alternatives. Initially, single men could receive relief, but in 1932, the federal government established relief camps for single men under the control of the Department of National Defence as the only source of relief for men without wives or children to support. Overworked, poorly fed, living in austere bunkhouses, and paid only twenty cents a day beyond their room and board, they built roads and public projects, and faced a grim future. While "family men" remained in the cities and towns, relief could barely feed their families, and a voucher system that limited potential

FIG 4-8 Many of the unemployed rode the rails in the 1930s in hopes of finding work somewhere in the country. Glenbow Archives, NC-6-12955(b).

purchases meant that their wives were stigmatized as they shopped for the family.[81]

Working people did not accept Depression conditions and government callousness lying down. The Communists organized a union of relief workers across the country, and there were many relief camp strikes. This culminated in the On-to-Ottawa trek in 1935, which began with relief camp workers from British Columbia climbing into railway boxcars and picking up more protesters as they moved from city to city across western Canada. They demanded improvements in camp conditions and the payment of living wages to camp inmates. Their rebellion was ruthlessly suppressed by R.B. Bennett in Regina on 1 July 1935. Later that year, Mackenzie King's Liberals were re-elected, and the following year, his government closed the camps. This did not, however, lead to just treatment of the single unemployed. Rather than aggregate them in camps or cities, where they had opportunities for collective protest, governments attempted to use them as cheap labour for farmers.[82]

Meanwhile, married relief workers protested both the low rates of relief and the work rules that cities imposed in order for them to collect the pittance offered to those unable to find private sector jobs. Unemployed relief workers in Calgary called a series of strikes between 1932 and 1935, leading them into several serious confrontations with local police.[83] Unemployed organizations made representations before city councils and relief boards, wrote letters of complaint and suggestions to relief policy-makers, and generally advocated on behalf of the unemployed.

No protest more signified both the militancy of the unemployed and the unwillingness of the authorities to improve workers' conditions than the Hunger March of 20 December 1932. Farmers, farm labourers, and town workers converged on Edmonton from rural points for days. Travelling determinedly by car, truck, rail, and sleigh in mid-winter, the hunger marchers wanted Premier Brownlee to protect "their farms and their living," and they intended to make their situation clear to him at the legislature.[84] The farmers had had a rough go of it through the growing seasons of 1931 and 1932. Owing to dust storms, grasshopper infestations, severe drought in the south, and chronically low grain prices in the north, Alberta farmers, like prairie farmers generally, were in danger of losing their farms and their means of livelihood. Many already had.[85] But not only rural workers were struggling. Edmonton's unemployed workers also faced hard times that December; many were equally intent on registering their dissatisfaction with the province's relief systems.

The idea was to amass thousands of hunger marchers — both farmers and unemployed urban workers — at Edmonton's Market Square on 20 December and then conduct an orderly parade westward toward the provincial legislative building some nine blocks away. Organizing the march on the ground was the Hunger March Committee (HMC), a Communist-inspired group representing both the Farmers' and Workers' Unity Leagues, which had been organized in the wake of the Comintern call in 1928 for new Communist-led organizations of workers and farmers to replace Communist participation in existing non-Communist institutions. From its headquarters at the Ukrainian Labour Temple, the HMC had for months been busy making the

event known among struggling rural farmers and unemployed urban workers alike, plotting the parade route, arranging accommodation for out-of-towners, and stockpiling food for the marchers.[86]

FIG 4-9 The On-to-Ottawa Trek, 1935, makes a stop in Medicine Hat. Provincial Archives of Alberta, A5149.

City officials, too, had been busy. Having learned of the planned march well in advance, Labour Mayor Dan Knott — pressured by UFA Premier John Brownlee, who in turn was under pressure from Prime Minister Bennett — ordered Chief of Police A.J. Shute to deny the marchers a permit to parade. Shute clearly expected trouble, despite the mayor's ruling. In short order, he assembled special police squads to meet the marchers, made arrangements to call on further reinforcements as needed to restore order, and secured assurances from Premier Brownlee that the province would make available to the city an extra detachment of the RCMP.[87]

By 18 December, just two days before the planned march, the HMC made clear that it had no intention of cancelling. An undercover officer, posing as one of the prospective marchers, attended a six-hundred–person rally at the Gem Theatre that night, where unemployed organizers insisted that the parade would go ahead as planned. The morning of 20 December — parade day — opened badly. Shortly before noon, city police raided the HMC headquarters, arresting one man on the charge of assaulting a police officer and searching the place for rumoured revolvers and rifles. They found none; instead, they discovered a small group of women busy in the kitchen preparing turkey dinners for the marchers. Moving from the Labour Temple to Market Square, police ensured that hardware storeowners had removed all pickaxes and grub hooks from their storefront displays, lest they find their way into the hands of the marchers. Finally, and under the personal direction of Chief Shute, eighty city policemen lined up on the north side of the square. Flanking the city police to the west were twenty-four armed and mounted RCMP officers. Another contingent of police guarded the square's east side.

Milling about the growing crowd of prospective marchers inside the square itself were dozens of plainclothes police bearing revolvers. The police set-up left open only the south end of the square, facing the steep river valley, for anyone to exit the area. One can only assume that this strategic tactic was meant to force the marchers toward the nearest geographic barrier, the North Saskatchewan River. City police, it seemed, were taking no chances.

Out on the square, minutes before the parade was set to begin, march organizers dispatched a small delegation to the legislature in a last-ditch effort to get the premier to overrule the mayor's ban and allow the demonstration. Word soon returned to the square that the premier had refused even to see the delegation. With that, according to an *Edmonton Bulletin* report filed the next day, "hoots, jeers for the police and the government and cries of 'All right Comrades, let's go'" filled the square. "Immediately a parade formed up . . . banners which had been concealed sprang up along the march to reinforce those which had been prominently displayed during the speech-making and in a slow shuffle with a number of youths in the lead wearing red badges, the parade moved off."[88]

The mounted police moved fast, cutting south and intercepting the parade as it tried to leave the square. Blocking any escape from the rear was the city's foot patrol, batons in hand, marching steadily toward the back of the parade. The *Bulletin* described the clash: "Batons rose and fell, yells and jeers filled the air as here and there a rioter went down before the police clubs. Women among the marchers screamed imprecations at the police, charging them with being cowards who were riding down their class, but the steady police pressure continued and the back of the parade was broken."[89]

AN ACTIVIST'S STORY

Clare Botsford, a lifelong social and political activist in Edmonton, was shaped by her experiences of poverty and state oppression during the Depression era.

> North Edmonton, there was a place called the Martell Block. It was Cold Water Flats. Very poor people lived there. Everybody on welfare. There were wood stoves. You actually had to haul your wood up. The Hope Mission brought us food. . . .
>
> Really dark days. And we went out to the dump, we kids, and we found a bunch of wheels. We had four different wheels and we made up a wagon. We went all through the city and picked up wood boxes and broke them down and made kindling and sold it.

Stories of this kind of childhood entrepreneurship have sometimes caused individuals who did well enough in later life to become somewhat right-wing, excoriating the poor of a later generation as lazy people who did not follow their predecessors' example of making a buck the hard way. But Botsford, who did not come from a left-wing home, had an experience as a nine-year-old petty entrepreneur that influenced her leftwards. She was picking up boxes in Edmonton's downtown on 20 December 1932 and searching for her dad, who was supposed to meet her, when she encountered the Hunger March that the Communists and their allies had organized. She heard some speeches and then witnessed the RCMP suppressing the demonstration:

> You never forget the sound of heads being clubbed. . . . Suddenly this happened. Then the police got down off their horses as well. People ran for shelter in the pyramids of Christmas trees that were on sale. The clubbing went on. The heads were being clubbed inside the shelter of these trees. Some of it you saw, some of it you heard. But certainly a lot of people were injured.

Botsford's workforce experiences reinforced her sense of social injustice. Too poor to afford clothes for school, she entered the workforce at age twelve or thirteen as a waitress. She worked twelve-hour days for a mere dollar. But restaurateurs were often not content to simply exploit the labour of the young women they employed.

> Oh, quite often you had to quit because your employer just took it for granted that you'd be his next sexual victim. Oh many, many times I walked off a job. I knew how to walk. I walked fast. There really was no protection. Who could you go to?

SOURCE: Interview with Clare Botsford, Edmonton, August 2001, ALHI.

THE MAKING OF A COMMUNIST

A farm boy of eighteen, adrift after completing high school during the Depression, Ben Swankey was in despair that his family's farm was virtually bankrupt and his opportunities of finding steady work negligible. But although he was rebellious, he was largely apolitical. Staying with a cousin in Vancouver, however, he joined a demonstration of the unemployed in 1931 attended by ten to twelve thousand people, about the same number who were part of the Edmonton Hunger March that Swankey, by then politicized, helped to organize. When the police on horseback and on foot attacked the demonstrators, leaving many people bloodied and even baby carriages knocked over, "I was just astounded and shocked that such a thing could happen in the Canada I knew." Swankey began attending meetings of left-wing organizations and before long had become a committed Communist. As a farm kid, he was particularly impressed by the fact that while "we wanted relief, we wanted work, we wanted food," food was being destroyed because of the irrationalities of the international capitalist marketplace. "I knew that in the 1930s in California, they were throwing oranges into the ocean. In Brazil, they were burning coffee. In the Okanagan, they poured gasoline on apples."

SOURCE: Interview with Ben Swankey, Burnaby, July 2003, ALHI. Swankey also gives his account of the Hunger March in Ben Swankey, "Reflections of a Communist: The Hungry Thirties."

The *Bulletin* reported that following the initial charge, some paraders regrouped at the northwest corner of the square but were quickly put down by both the RCMP troopers and city police constables. Most paraders had quit the square for good by around 5:00 p.m. The large number of unemployed and farmer participants — as many as twelve thousand — speaks to the evident unpopularity of city and farm relief policies and provisions. The march was directed at both the provincial and the municipal governments, indicating that despite government efforts to minimize their responsibility for unemployment, the marchers clearly held them principally accountable for their aid. The march also showed a high level of organization on the part of the marchers. This was no spontaneous "mass" rally lacking in specific goals and precise discipline. It was instead a highly organized and controlled protest against the governments' relief policies. Furthermore, the marchers were determined to voice their opinions in their own way, even though it meant defying direct city orders. Despite the participants' determination, however, government officials were prepared to meet their defiance with force to control threats to the existing social order.

THE RISE OF THE CCF AND SOCIAL CREDIT

The view that governments' response to the Depression implied a defence of the interests of the wealthy rather than the working people, both urban and rural, sparked the formation of new political forces in the 1930s in Canada. The willingness to support third parties actually began in the 1921 federal election with the success of the national Progressive Party of Canada, the farmers' protest party for which the UFA at the time was the Alberta wing. The Progressives formed the Official Opposition. Neither the Progressive Party nor the UFA had much ideological cohesion: they simply represented disappointment with what farmers regarded as the old-line parties' dismissiveness regarding their interests. Two Labour MPs were also elected in 1921: J.S. Woodsworth from Winnipeg and William Irvine from Calgary. The Labour MPs were non-communist socialists and they formed an alliance, often called the Ginger Group, with the more radical Progressive members, most of whom were from Alberta.[90]

It was the small Ginger Group of MPs who decided at a meeting on 1 August 1932, in Calgary that the time had come to create a Canadian national version of the British Labour Party and other social-democratic parties in Europe, but with a name that would reflect the party's commitment to both farmers and workers. The founding convention of the party, which adopted the name Co-operative Commonwealth Federation (CCF), occurred in Regina in July 1933. It adopted a program of emergency measures needed to get people back to work and to give them income if no work was available. But its long-term aim was more revolutionary. The "Regina Manifesto" promised: "No C.C.F. Government will rest content until it has eradicated capitalism and put into operation the full programme of socialized planning which will lead to the establishment in Canada of the Cooperative Commonwealth."[91]

Attempting to get organized nationally and provincially as soon as possible, the CCF did not initially focus on grassroots organizing. Instead, it tried to coalesce existing labour and farmer parties and political lobby groups in each province. This worked quite well

FIG 4-10 Child poverty was widespread during the Depression. Provincial Archives of Alberta, 6-1.

in several provinces. In Saskatchewan, for example, the CCF brought together the United Farmers of Saskatchewan (UFC-SS) and the Independent Labour Party, while in British Columbia, it brought a truce among rival socialist and labour parties. In Alberta, though, the attempt resulted in a disaster that should have been predictable.

The UFA and the Canadian Labour Party (CLP) together became the Alberta CCF, an inauspicious and confusing beginning for a new party. After all, the UFA was the governing party of Alberta and by 1933 had demonstrated that, under Depression conditions, it was more of a friend to the bankers and businesspeople than workers or farmers. Premier John Brownlee had no use for CCF socialism, and R.G. Reid, who replaced him in 1934 when Brownlee was forced from office as a result of a sex scandal that still remains controversial, was equally conservative. So why would anyone think that this organization could offer the people of Alberta hope? The confusion occurred because while the UFA government moved to the right, the UFA organization, dominated by federal MPs, moved significantly to the left. It did so, however, without getting rid of conservative UFA MLAs. Much of this party chaos occurred because of a degree of naiveté in the thinking that had shaped the UFA's move into politics in the first place: believing that farmers had common interests and world views, the UFA had no real platform, and farmers simply picked a successful local member of their profession to represent them in Edmonton. Those individuals ranged across the political map but were generally conservatives who wanted to limit government spending and therefore farmers' taxes. The larger presence of radicals among the UFA MPs occurred because the farmers were more restricted in their choices of MP candidates in mixed urban-rural ridings, where they had to appease labour interests in their choice of a farmer as a successful candidate.[92]

By the time the UFA organization, responding to the Depression, decided that the capitalist system was a disaster for farmers, they lacked the will to throw out their conservative provincial representatives and instead focused largely on federal politics. But the conservatism of the provincial UFA discredited the entire UFA organization. The CCF's decision to hitch its cart to this woebegone provincial organization rather than start something from the grassroots doomed the CCF in Alberta in its early years. The CLP's adhesion was also no gift to the CCF: the party that had joined the UFA in beating up Hunger Marchers hardly resembled a party that would not rest until capitalist exploitation had disappeared.

Enter Social Credit. Led by the popular radio preacher, William Aberhart, Social Credit was based on a loony monetary ideology, but, in fairness, it may have been no more loony than the capitalist system itself, which Social Credit only challenged tangentially. Social Credit theory — originated by C.H. Douglas, a British engineer who was extremely paranoid and anti-Semitic — rejected the socialist notion that depressions occur because of a maldistribution of wealth between capitalists and workers. Instead, argued Douglas, the problem was that the combination of wages and dividends (the distribution between the two, he claimed, did not matter) in a given firm was less than the value of the product produced because of the need for a firm to buy inputs. So, he claimed, money was leaking out of the economy. In truth, since firms were buying from other firms, there was no leakage across an entire economy except in terms of what might be lost through unfavourable international trade balances. Nonetheless, Douglas's solution — a bonus to every adult to make up for the alleged leakage — caught many people's attention. Aberhart promised twenty-five dollars for every adult in the province each month and a smaller amount for care of their children. This was a great deal of money at a time when the average worker earned less than a thousand dollars a year and when farmers were often spending more to produce a crop than they could possibly earn from it.[93]

Social Credit swept the province in the provincial election of 1935. Both the UFA and the CLP lost all their seats; indeed the CLP candidates received only a negligible vote despite the fact that the labour movement firmly opposed Social Credit, viewing it as a demagogic movement, and continued to support the CLP. The era of direct labour representation in the legislature under its own name had ended in the province. Efforts were made to dissociate the new CCF from the past errors of both the UFA and the CLP. But before World War II, the CCF in Alberta had only a tiny audience. Anti-socialists, of course, rejected their message, but even pro-socialists regarded the party as inauthentic because of its past association with the UFA and CLP. Social Credit, though it was ideologically amorphous, was given more slack.[94]

In its early years, while William Aberhart was the premier (until his death in 1943), Social Credit was something of an anomaly. Though this party would gradually become rather business-friendly, particularly once Ernest Manning became premier upon Aberhart's death, it was hated by the business community during its first term of office. Belligerent and authoritarian, Aberhart had no use for the leaders of either business or labour. He struggled to produce a legislative program, realizing once he came into office that there was no money for his ambitious Social Credit schemes and that, under the terms of the *British North America Act,* provincial control over banks was negligible.[95]

But it was not until the 1940s that Social Credit took a firm stance in favour of capitalists over labour; it did pass some pro-labour legislation in its first term. In 1936, Aberhart, himself a former teacher and school principal, made it compulsory for all teachers to be members of the Alberta Teachers' Association, and the following year, he gave teachers a form of tenure, with any dismissal requiring a ruling from an independent tribunal. Also, in 1936, the government restricted most trades to licensed individuals, which won Social Credit kudos from many crafts unions. In 1937, Alberta became only the second Canadian province, just a few

months after Nova Scotia, to give legal status to collective bargaining. The *Freedom of Trade Union Association Act* established the process for certification of unions as collective bargaining agents for specific groups of workers and prohibited employers from interfering in workers' efforts to sign up enough members to force a vote on whether a union should be recognized for a particular group of workers.[96]

Social Credit was, however, hardly an unqualified friend of workers or the labour movement. Though it had promised to treat the unemployed with greater humanity than the UFA had, it largely failed to change regressive policies. It did not follow the federal government in closing down all relief camps and provided relief to those whom it classified as transient only if they went to the camps. Unemployed single men who remained in the cities were not given food vouchers like married men were; instead they were expected to eat at municipal soup kitchens. The province also forced single relief workers to work as farm labourers during the growing season for five dollars a month, the same rate of pay that they received in the work camps.[97]

Although the Aberhart government received hundreds of complaints about the mistreatment of the unemployed, it was largely intransigent. It was equally unsympathetic to complaints about a hardening of attitudes on the part of the Workmen's Compensation Board. And within a year of legalizing collective bargaining, it passed the *Industrial Conciliation and Arbitration Act* of 1938, which imposed a fourteen-day delay before a strike could begin, time enough for an employer to hire scabs and otherwise take steps to limit potential losses of profit from a withdrawal of work by a unionized labour force.[98]

DEPRESSION-ERA STRIKES

Though the strikes of the unemployed captured the most public attention during the Depression, workers who had not lost their jobs sometimes risked everything to protest wage cuts, speed-ups, and dangerous working conditions. Three-quarters of the strikes were miners' strikes and, in Depression conditions, the bosses usually won. Most miners had only a few days' work per month as the mines cut back production, and working conditions, always dangerous because of company efforts to cut costs, deteriorated further. On 9 December 1935, for example, sixteen miners died in a CPR mine at Coalhurst, near Lethbridge, because the company had not sealed off old sections of the about-to-be-closed mine, which allowed gas to accumulate. As Harvey Murphy, a Mine Workers Union of Canada (MWUC) official, later recalled: "They were getting out all the cheap coal they could and turned the mine into a death trap. Sixteen of our brothers have been destroyed, 23 orphans and 11 widows remain, because the CPR wanted cheaper coal."[99]

The MWUC joined the Communist-controlled Workers' Unity League and did its best to lead the miners in their fights against the coal bosses. But the companies responded ruthlessly, forcing workers out of their homes in company towns and blacklisting them from further mine employment. With work so scarce, there were always enough miners who were too desperate to work to join the strikes, and the companies could encourage divisions among the miners by taking advantage of the desire of the United Mine Workers of America (UMWA) to take back mines from the MWUC. Indeed, in most areas, the UMWA slowly regained its former prominence.

The MWUC held out most effectively in the coal mines in the Crowsnest Pass. In 1932, it struck the mines in Coleman, Blairmore, and Bellevue for a variety of reforms, including an equal sharing of work among all the miners rather than leaving workers subject to the will of bosses, with some getting almost no work at all. The companies tried to starve the workers into submission, and the mainly Anglo-Canadian Coleman workers did give up the strike and leave the MWUC to form a "home local," which they maintained for several years before rejoining the UMWA. But the largely eastern European workers of Blairmore and Bellevue, who had experienced intense ethnic discrimination from their employers, held out for seven months, after which the provincial government, concerned about fuel supplies in the province, forced the companies to make major concessions. The jubilant Blairmore workers promptly elected a "red" city council, which, among other things, renamed the main street Tim Buck Boulevard after the leader of the Communist Party of Canada. But after the Comintern line on Communists going it alone shifted in 1934, the Canadian Communists dissolved the Workers' Unity League in 1935 and the MWUC rejoined forces with the UMWA.[100]

While the very existence of coal mining in Alberta would soon be threatened, the expanding meat-packing houses became a major site of unionization and strikes in the late 1930s. The Committee for Industrial Organization had formed in the United States in 1935 to focus on industrial organization as opposed to the craft unionism favoured by the American Federation of Labor (AFL). The AFL suspended the ten Committee unions in 1936, but the unions continued their efforts to extend the industrial union movement. In

VERONICA FONTANA'S REMINISCENCES OF BLAIRMORE

We grew up through the thirties when the big strike was on. That's when all the parades and everything were going on, the union was pretty strong. The men were fighting for better working conditions and shorter work time. When they won the strike, they were working five days a week and they got eight-hour shifts. During the strike time, we were all kids going into the parades. We had Violet Manakay and George Peer, they were the leaders of organizing the kids for concerts, which kept the people occupied during their idle times. We'd go on these parades, they'd take us out on the parades, and we'd sing these songs. But there was a separate community. There was West Blairmore and East Blairmore. East Blairmore was all the foreigners and all the big families, whereas in West Blairmore all the pit bosses and that had company houses. . . .

They used to make these concerts, silver collection, that used to help pay for some of the relief for the people. We used to have wonderful concerts. There was the Campeau sisters: Vickie, Mary, Dorothy, and Rosie. They used to sing, they were beautiful singers. And we had all the accordion players. There was Mike Mohalski, Aldo Binoni, John Sekina, and the concerts were wonderful. The people used to just pack into the hall. People just put five cents in, and it added up. That helped provide food and clothes for some of the people who really needed it the most.

Then the big strike was on in Corbin. A lot of the union people from Blairmore all got onto a truck and went to Corbin to help them fight their strike. That's where the big battle started. The RCMP were on their horses and they had a whip. They used to chase the women off the parade with the whip. A fellow with a tractor from the mine used to come and try to scare the women off with his tractor, and used to chase them right off the road. However, nobody got hurt on that, and then they shut the Corbin mine down. So that was the end of that issue in there. But the one in Blairmore continued. There was Sam Paterson, Eric Tyburg, Harvey Murphy, they were the big organizers for the Pass. They all wound up on the councils and the school boards, which made it good for the working-class kids. They provided free books and pencils for school.

SOURCE: Interview with Veronica Fontana, Coleman, 10 November 2005, ALHI.

FIG 4-12 Mine Workers' Union of Canada strike in Coleman, 1932. Crowsnest Museum Archives, C.M.P.86.323.8.

1938, they created the Congress of Industrial Organizations (CIO) as a rival federation to the AFL. The CIO's militant organizing tactics included sit-down strikes in which workers refused to leave factories until the employer agreed to bargain collectively and accede to various union demands. The first group of unorganized workers to get the CIO bug in Alberta before the CIO itself lay down roots in the province were the packing-house workers. In 1935, Alberta's fifteen hundred slaughterhouse employees accounted for more than one in five of workers in manufacturing in the province. Like the miners, they had no guarantee of employment and no seniority provisions from employers. They lined up daily in the hope of being assigned work, without pay for their time in the line-up. In addition, speed-ups on the job led to numerous accidents.

In 1937, the Canadian Victuallers and Caterers Union, an affiliate of the All-Canadian Congress of Labour, made heroic efforts to organize the packing-house workers of Edmonton and Calgary. In Calgary, workers occupied the building of the misnamed Union Packing, only leaving when the company agreed to conciliation and not to discipline strikers. But the company ignored the conciliator's report and fired union leaders. Edmonton slaughterhouse employees at Swift, Gainers, and Burns staged sit-down strikes as well, but the companies waited them out and fired many of the strikers. In 1938 and 1939, however, the companies accepted a union that was a direct affiliate of the Trades and Labour Congress and that had been established by Alberta Federation of Labor executive member Carl Berg. By all accounts, the union, under Berg's direction, behaved almost like a company union, and unsurprisingly, it would be swept away by a CIO union during the war.[101]

◆ ◆ ◆

During the quarter century between the beginning of World War I and the beginning of World War II, Alberta workers experienced a roller-coaster economy that moved from boom to recession and back again every few years. The insecurities that the marketplace economy brought with it and the suspicion that capitalism and war-making were closely linked caused many Alberta workers, along with compatriots in other provinces, to embrace socialist ideas. While the revolutionary ideas of the One Big Union proved short-lived in the face of unrelenting state suppression, the postwar workers' revolt left a legacy in terms of union militancy even during the worst days of the Depression. Social-democratic "labourite" politics remained important in Alberta until the mid-thirties, when Alberta workers, confused by the disconnect between CCF socialist rhetoric and the pitiful performances of the UFA government and the short-lived CLP municipal government in Edmonton, largely tuned out. Many embraced Social Credit as the only other game in town outside the conventional bourgeois parties. As the Depression decade ended, it appeared that the Alberta Federation of Labour's dream of creating a permanent social-democratic labour party with a chance of eventually forming the provincial government had been dashed to pieces.

FIG 5-1 The campaign to keep "rats" out of Alberta launched in the 1950s. Provincial Archives of Alberta, PA 1579/2.

5 ALBERTA LABOUR AND WORKING-CLASS LIFE, 1940–59

JAMES MUIR

In 1949, the Government of Alberta launched a crusade to rid the province of the Norwegian rat. Flyers and posters exhorted people to buy the rat-poison warfarin. A 1950 poster featured the headline "You Can't Ignore the Rat" and urged the population, "Kill Him! Let's Keep Alberta Rat-Free." On the back cover of a 1956 pamphlet titled "Kill Rats with Warfarin," a map of North America was stamped in red, with only an empty white block for Alberta. Poised on the province's borders lay rats, ready to invade.

Clearly, this campaign was about rodents. And yet, perhaps unintentionally, the campaign also seemed to be about organized labour: unions who allegedly destroyed property and caused waste in industry, "Reds" who sat on the borders waiting for a chance to pounce on capitalist Alberta so as to wreak havoc and bring everything down from within. The state's warfarin for radicals was legislation and administrative procedures to restrict the formation and activity of trade unions. This was aided by a labour movement that, throughout Canada, sought to purge its Communist elements

and that, at least in part, acquiesced to conservative state policies. The two decades between 1940 and 1960 were revolutionary for Alberta workers. Many began the 1940s by leaving fields and mines for the even more dangerous workplace of war in Europe and Asia. Workers closed these decades having moved in ever larger numbers from farm to city or from extracting coal to extracting oil. In the same years, the home and family changed radically. The war also gave Canada its unique system of compulsory collective bargaining, which the Alberta government later attempted to neuter. Within this new environment, the labour movement faced two internal crises: the expulsion of communists that accompanied the Cold War and the merger in 1956 of its two major organizations, the Alberta Federation of Labour and the Industrial Federation of Labour of Alberta.

WARTIME ALBERTA

During the war years, the Army, Navy, and Air Force together became Alberta's largest employer: seventy-eight

FIG 5-2 The *Edmonton Bulletin* announces the outbreak
of World War II. Edmonton Archives 267 138.

thousand men and forty-five hundred women joined, about 10 percent of the population. It was a dangerous workplace: 9 percent of Canadians who served during the war were killed or wounded. Many who survived without physical wounds were nonetheless scarred by the experience.[1]

Soldiers' Work

For many, military work began with training: drill, often for several hours a day, combined with arms training and related work. In the early years of the war, rifles were scarce, so the recruits to the South Alberta Regiment trained with one platoon using the regiment's rifles, who then handed them to the next platoon up for training. The regiment's minister and doctor provided a limited sex education, a mix of conventional morality and the very real threats of disease.[2] All the training aimed to condition soldiers to give up their freedom: military thinking equated effective soldiering with strict adherence at all times to the commands of superiors.

When Canadians entered the battlefields, their capacity to meet the expectations of their commanders was put to the test. In his memoir *And No Birds Sang*, author Farley Mowat describes one night-time battle in the Italian campaign:

What followed was the kind of night men dream about in afteryears, waking in a cold sweat to a surge of gratitude that it is but a dream. It was a delirium of sustained violence. Small pockets of Germans that had been cut off throughout our bridgehead fired their automatic weapons in hysterical dismay at every shadow. The grind of enemy tanks and self-propelled guns working their way along the crest was multiplied by echoes until it sounded like an entire Panzer army. Illuminating flares flamed in darkness with a sick radiance. The snap and scream of high-velocity tank shells pierced the brutal guttural of an endless cannonade from both German and Canadian artillery. Moaning Minnie projectiles whumped down like thunderbolts, searching for our hurriedly dug foxholes. Soldiers of both sides, blundering through the vineyards, fired with panicky impartiality in all directions. And it began to rain again, a bitter, penetrating winter rain.[3]

After such battles, the soldiers had to deal with their dead. South Alberta Regiment padre Albert Silcox observed, "We laid each on a blanket, wrapped him in its folds, and lowered him, under the Union Jack where possible, into the earth." When fighting had ceased, the padres divided the possessions of the dead between those to be sent home and those that could be used by others. Finally they "wrote letters to mothers and fathers, wives or sweethearts, to brothers in other regiments, to close friends, and casual acquaintances of whom we knew."[4]

The desire to serve, while widespread, was hardly universal. In 1940, the *National Resources Mobilization Act* made military training and serving in home defence compulsory for men who were called up. Trainees could, however, petition to postpone their training for such reasons as their work in farming or mining, and conscientious objection to war. The Edmonton district granted 47,773 postponements of orders for compulsory military training: this constituted 97 percent of requests, a higher percentage than in any other province.[5]

Women's Work

Women's labour changed drastically during the war years. Though Alberta's munitions industry was modest, wartime demand for uniforms created numerous jobs at the Great Western Garment (GWG) plant in Edmonton. By 1940, seventeen-year-old Norah Hook had left school for a full-time babysitting job, but she wanted something better. She first tried responding to an ad in the newspaper calling for saleswomen at Woolworths, but "the line up of girls looking for work was . . . out the door and down the street. So that didn't work out." Instead, through a friend, she got a job at GWG making army fatigues. Assunta Dotto, a young Italian immigrant, also found GWG appealing: "I was quite interested because all I could do was clean houses for a dollar a day."[6]

The GWG plant was organized so that each woman along a line did the same task over and over. Dotto's line comprised about twenty women. As she described it, "the shirt department, it was like a horseshoe. . . . And the girl over here would start right from the first operation. When it came to me [inserting the sleeves], the cuffs were already on the sleeves and so the collars were already on the shirt. So all I did was that and then it went to the next girl. The next girl would sew this like this [indicating underarm and side seam], then it went to the next girl."

Dotto did "hear some grumbling about hard work and little pay . . . but to me it was just good." But not everyone agreed. Hook recalled: "I hated it, it was an awful place. I was an outdoors person and I just couldn't be shut up like that, it was like being in jail almost." Getting out of the factory during the work day was important. Dotto and several friends left the GWG plant every lunch hour for the confectionary store across the street, rather than eat in the noisy plant cafeteria.

In the summer of 1945, as war work was dwindling, the appeal of leaving during working hours became too great. One day, Dotto was at lunch with four other women:

> We started to talk about the exhibition, and I said, "Gee I've never been to the exhibition." I'd already given my notice that I was going home to be married. I thought, well, why not now? So three of the girls said yes. Juliet, Anne, and Elsie. . . . So I was sitting to the front by the window, or the doors, there was all glass there and I saw the streetcar or the bus, whatever, is coming, and I said, "Come on girls, let's go." . . . So anyway, we had a good time. . . . We were all on special machines, but the line would stop without us being there. . . . The next morning, we reported for work, we had to wait downstairs. The bell went and everybody stood up. . . . Mrs. Nufer said, "You, you, you, and you, in the cafeteria." She said, "I hope you had a good time. Now you can go back to the exhibition." She handed us the pay envelope. . . . "You can't fire me," I said, "I've already quit," but she ignored me. So we left and I felt horrible because the other girls had lost their jobs. But shortly after that I heard that they were all rehired, and they didn't rehire me because they knew I'd already quit.

Even as wartime production wound down, GWG needed to keep its staff. It might threaten free-spirited workers with dismissal, but then it took them back. Earlier in the war, the company had been even more insistent on keeping its employees. After a few weeks at GWG, Nora Hook, along with a workmate, Wanda, applied at Aircraft Repair, which was also hiring women. Indicative of the need, even in Edmonton, for women labourers, "the next thing was GWG wouldn't let me quit because it was wartime and . . . we were considered . . . essential services . . . so you couldn't move around in jobs. So they weren't going to let me quit. . . . My mother got involved and because I was under eighteen, I could quit, so I went to Aircraft Repair."

At GWG, Hook seamed the backs of jeans. At Aircraft Repair, she was a sheet-metal worker. She preferred that job: "I could move around. There was light, there were people you could talk to, the work was never the same two days in a row. One day you might be working on whatever, next time you might be riveting on an airplane, it was interesting, it was exciting. There was a war on. You were helping, you weren't sitting." The responsibility and freedom this work offered, in contrast to the work at GWG, provided a positive experience for many working-class women during the war. But at war's end, though paid work at GWG and Woolworths remained available, skilled blue-collar jobs at places like Aircraft Repair disappeared for most working women.

Internment

Wartime disruption of people's work lives took different forms. Tets Kitaguchi worked in pulp mills in Vancouver in the late 1930s and the early war years. When the Canadian government interned all Japanese-Canadians in British Columbia in 1942, he and his wife were required to register. The authorities seized most of their possessions, including his accordion and many books, and they received no compensation. Given the option of internment or voluntary relocation to an in-land agricultural community, the Kitaguchis moved to Raymond, where a sister of Tets lived. Assigned to a sugar beet farm, the Kitaguchis were given charge of twenty-five acres, which they cultivated for the owner in exchange for a portion of the return on the crop and a place to live. The accommodations were meagre: "A one-room shack. . . . We had one bed and a stove. You could sit on the bed and cook on the stove. It must've been an old granary at one time. It was filthy." The work was hard:

> From the time it was planted, we waited until they sprouted up two leaves. Then you go out there with a hoe and separate all the beets to about twelve inches apart. It was a backbreaking job, especially for my wife. Never been on a farm or anything. I used to break in the heart when I see her work. . . . During the fall, around September, "this is very nice weather," I says to the farmer, "why don't you harvest it? The weather's great." He said, "Oh, we can't do that. We wait for the first frost to bring up the content of the sugar." So that was harder still. We got to pull those things out of the ground, bang them together, get all the mud off them. It was tough work, but we got it all harvested. After harvest, we were paid our share. The wife and I, we ended up with ninety dollars to live on through the winter. But we were kind of lucky. He was one of those kind of guys that took in the cattle or sheep during the winter months from the stockyard and fattened them up, then sent to the packers. So he hired me on for twenty-five dollars a month through the winter. It was good. We managed.[7]

The Kitaguchis were not alone; as many as twenty-six hundred Japanese internees worked on sugar beet farms in Alberta at any one time during the war. In addition, prisoners of war were hired on a daily or term basis from camps: by 1945, four hundred German prisoners were permanently on loan to beet farmers.[8]

Some non-Japanese were interned too. In the late 1930s, Patrick Lenihan served as an alderman in Calgary, having won election as a coalition "people's candidate" without hiding his Communist Party membership. When war was declared in the fall of 1939, the Soviet Union remained neutral, Stalin having signed a pact with Hitler. On 3 December 1939, Lenihan spoke at a meeting in the Calgary Labour Temple denouncing the war and labelling some of the Canadian government's actions as fascist. Soon after, he was arrested, charged with sedition and causing "disaffection to His Majesty's forces." A jury exonerated him.

The fall of France and the rest of Western Europe prompted a second arrest in June 1940, but this time Lenihan was interned at a camp in the Kananaskis under provisions of the *War Measures Act* that gave him no right to a trial. The following year, he was moved to another camp at Petawawa and then finally to a new jail in Hull, Quebec. Only in September 1942, was Lenihan released, more than a year after the Soviets became Canadian allies against Nazi Germany.[9]

Trade Unions During the War

Wartime full employment emboldened workers to join unions, but when the war started, some alleged unions were employer lapdogs, as Patrick Lenihan learned. Though after the Soviet Union was invaded by Germany, Communists largely opposed strikes until Germany was defeated, many employers still refused to hire individuals whom they feared would later "agitate" workers to fight for better wages and conditions. Lenihan used his connections, as an ex-alderman, to Calgary Mayor Andy Davison to get a job in the city's transit system. The Street Railway Union in Calgary was passive and elitist. Railway employees could only apply for membership in the union after working for the company for a year; the union members then voted on whether to accept the application. During the war, the president of the Street Railway Union was Sam Sligo, president of the Calgary Labour Council and future president of the Alberta Federation of Labour (AFL). As Lenihan recalled, Sligo "was an anti-communist, left-wing hater. . . . His politics were cooperation 100 per cent with management and accept anything. There was no struggle really for improvement in the lives of the people. The union meeting was a matter of reading the minutes, new business and good and welfare and that was it." Unsurprisingly, Lenihan's application for membership was rejected several times.[10]

Many unions were more open, encouraging all workers in a plant to join, but it was challenging to collect dues. Nellie Engley started working at GWG in 1938 and volunteered to work with the union; she became the financial secretary. Collecting dues required "somebody that would sit at the top of the stairs and as you got your pay we'd want your fifty cents . . . for the union and you'd be surprised how they wouldn't give it to you." As the women collected their pay, Engley "was right there with all the names all down and how much money they would give me and then I knew exactly if they were paid up to date or how far behind

they were." Anne Ozipko remembers, "At lunch time you'd go to the treasurer and pay your dues then. Well I guess they'd get after you and come to your machine and ask you to pay." This weekly or bi-weekly direct contact between union and worker, as Engley says, "was a horrible job, nobody wanted it."[11] But it had advantages: in an era when many of the unions were international unions with headquarters in the United States, the need to collect dues in person meant that rank-and-file workers had regular contact with a steward or other member of the local union executive. The dues collector, in turn, had to be prepared to convince, cajole, or harangue the reluctant worker into paying up, which meant regularly reminding workers what the union was doing and achieving at the local level.

Origins of Compulsory Collective Bargaining

Though landlocked and some distance from the supply routes for most of the forces, Alberta workers were deeply affected by the war. The clearest example was in coal mining, which employed as many as eight thousand men at one time in more than three hundred mines during the war. Many still lived in company towns and lost ground under wartime restrictions. Wages trailed rising costs, especially in company towns, and rationing further limited access to basic necessities.

Workers across Canada engaged in a strike wave from 1941 through 1943. For the federal government, maintaining wartime production was essential, and measures were adopted to prevent strikes or limit their impact. Coal mining production, though on the rise until mid-1942, failed to keep pace with wartime demand. As more young miners left for the front or for better wages in other work, production started to decline. In response, in June 1943, the federal government ordered all existing coal miners to remain in their jobs while miners who had taken other jobs were ordered to return to the mines. Nevertheless, nationally there were more coal mine strikes in 1943 than ever before. On 14 October, with Privy Council Order (PC) 8021, the federal government banned strikes and lockouts in coal mines for the duration of the war. But on 1 November, 9,850 miners of UMWA District 18 struck for higher wages, two weeks paid vacation, and time and a half for the sixth day out of seven they were required to work. The strike lasted fifteen days and culminated in the appointment of a Royal Commission on Mining as well as a wage increase and the requested vacation time.[12]

As with World War I, the Second World War presented workers with an opportunity to wrestle significant advances from their employers. As prices rose and the availability of workers fell, unions — particularly industrial unions — successfully organized many workers and pressed for better wages. Strikes like the November 1943 mining strike led the federal government on 17 February 1944, to issue PC 1003, the Wartime Labour Relations Order. This order introduced a legislative scheme for union recognition, defined unfair labour practices to restrict employer interference with union activity, and mandated compulsory collective bargaining in war-related industries.[13] PC 1003 had a relatively limited effect in Alberta since it applied only to industries that the federal government regulated constitutionally or that fell under the *War Measures Act*. Coal mining was one of the few inclusions.

The federal government also encouraged provinces to opt into its provisions for the duration of the war and then model their own legislation on them. The AFL had begun pressuring the government for similar legislation a year before PC 1003. In February 1943, it asked the provincial government to amend Alberta's labour legislation to introduce compulsory collective bargaining, arguing that workers had a *right* to join a union and have it bargain on their behalf; it should not be left to the employer to decide if, when, how, and for whom such bargaining would happen. In addition, the AFL expressed concern that the current legal regime in Alberta was too lenient on employers who engaged in unfair practices. The province, for example, declared legal an employer's notice to its employees that unionization would result in shutting the shop and relocating.[14]

Alberta, led by Premier Ernest Manning, Aberhart's successor, did not opt in, but in 1944, amendments to Alberta's *Industrial Conciliation and Arbitration Act* paralleled much of PC 1003. The most significant difference was that employees under the Alberta act could only unionize following a secret ballot election, regardless of how many had already signed union membership cards.[15]

THE DECLINE OF RURAL ALBERTA
Farms

The war years witnessed major changes in agriculture: farm income rose considerably and mechanization quickened.[16] At war's end, veterans could apply for land grants in the Peace River country. Changes in income and mechanization were unevenly distributed, however, and land grants in remote areas proved less appealing and profitable than many had hoped. Many

farmers, new and old, owners of their own means of production, were pushed off the land into the growing regional centres and cities, and into paid labour. Even still-prosperous farmers could not persuade their children to remain as farmers. In previous generations, farmers' children typically took up paid labour only until they either inherited the family farm or were able to buy one of their own. Now a majority turned to paid labour permanently. By the beginning of the 1950s, a slim majority of Albertans were urban dwellers.[17]

Though farmers had no legal right to unionize, the Alberta Farmers' Union (AFU) made one last attempt at continuing 1930s' radicalism into the Manning era. In 1946, the AFU joined its Saskatchewan counterpart to try to force the federal government to introduce pricing parity for farm products: that is, the tying of farm product prices to the increases in farmers' production costs and to the overall improvement in incomes within Canadian society. This was seen as the only hope for the small family farm. After a one-day farmers' holiday in June and the balloting of members of the AFU and the Saskatchewan Farmers' Union in August, on 6 September 1946, more than sixty thousand farmers in the two provinces began to refuse to deliver any produce. The strikers organized as industrial workers did, with pickets at depots to prevent strike-breaking farmers from making deliveries of grain, meat, eggs, or dairy. In both towns and cities, the stocks of produce declined considerably. At Beaver Siding on 27 September, more than two hundred farmers attempted to stop a cattle buyer from getting a hundred steers to the railway. The confrontation ended in violence, with agricultural labourers, the police, and spooked cows physically breaking the farmers' line.[18]

The striking farmers received support from unionized workers. Walter Makowecki recalled an attempt by strike-breaking farmers to make a delivery to the trains: "My uncle . . . John Zukarko and his son Bill . . . would come with their truck and pick up the picketers at the Ukrainian [Farmer] Labour Temple, drive fifteen miles to St. Paul, and picket to see that the farmers didn't ship the cream to Smoky Lake or wherever on the trains." The picketers lined up on both sides of the tracks. If a delivering farmer got through the lines, unionized rail workers received his cream:

> The railway guys would open up the doors in the cars, the cream can would go through this door. The farmer thinks his cream has gone to market, and it went out on the other side [passed by the rail workers to the picketers on that side of the train]. The train is gone, his cream is sitting on the other side of the train.[19]

Even before the strike began, both provincial and federal governments denounced it, with Manning telling farmers that the strike would be too small to effect change, while hurting those whose produce went unsold. When the thirty-day period originally agreed to by the strikers ended, so did the strike. The governments and the organizations of large farms like the Canadian Federation of Agriculture and its provincial counterparts offered the strikers nothing of value, and the strike marked a last gasp both to organize farmers as workers and to try to protect the small farm. Legislated parity did not materialize, and more farmers and their children left for other work, their land usually bought out by farmers who were surviving by expanding their holdings.[20]

FIG 5-4 Mine rescue team.
EA 748-1

The remaining farmers generally reduced labour costs through mechanization. They employed fewer hired hands. For some crops, however, such as sugar beets, the effect of machines was less notable. Workers were still needed to thin and trim the fields by hand. But attracting cheap labour to those farms still requiring extra workers was difficult in the postwar environment, when overall employment rates were high. The federal government responded by recruiting displaced persons as well as recent and poor European immigrants to work in the fields. When this pool dwindled, the farmers, aided by the government, turned to First Nations people, mainly from northern Saskatchewan and northern Alberta. The Dominion-Provincial Farm Labour Committee (and its successor), in conjunction with the Department of Indian Affairs, paid the costs of recruiting First Nations and Métis people to work on farms. Farmers were required to provide (low) wages and accommodations for their workers during the growing season, while the government subsidized transport from reserves or communities to the farms,

and even trips to some of the regional rodeos paid for by the Sugar Beet Growers' Association. By the late 1960s, this proved insufficient to meet labour demands, so the Department of Indian Affairs began cutting welfare payments in May and June to encourage Aboriginal migration to farms. This was matched by provincial cuts to non-status Indians and Métis people.[21]

Coal

The drain from the farms was significant, but the postwar collapse of coal mining — and with it, working-class communities — across the south-central part of the province was even more severe. There were 8,865 coal miners in Alberta in 1948 but only 3,443 in 1956.[22] Western Canadian Collieries in the Crowsnest produced 906,000 tonnes of coal in 1945 and 1,279,000 tonnes in 1951, but only 130,000 tonnes in 1958.[23] The miners and their families survived as best they could. Bill Skura, a farmer's son from Manitoba, for example, trekked west intending to reach Yellowknife's gold mines but ended up at the McGillivray Mine in the Crowsnest in November 1945. "The wages were very low," he recalled. "They were $7.55 a day for coalminers, and $8.02 for rock mining. That's what I got a day. There were no holidays, no nothing. When we did get vacation time, you had to work so many days. If you were sick or so, you would lose that month."[24] When Clara Marconi and her coal-miner husband married in 1945, "things were so rough, [my husband] had a little Model A, and he sold it to buy a stove. We lived in three rooms, and eventually we had three kids. Three rooms, three kids, two great big stoves. We used to walk around the tracks to pick up the coal so we could keep the fires burning."[25]

By the end of the 1950s, the remaining work in the mines was often intermittent. Joyce Avramenko described her husband's experience in the mines near Drumheller:

The way it usually worked is once they started to cut down, it would always seem to be after Christmas or January. At first they'd be missing one day a week. Then pretty soon they'd work one day, miss a day, work a day, miss a day, work a day. So now they're getting three days in a week. Then the next thing you'd see they're only getting two days in a week. Then pretty soon they'd only be getting one day a week. Then, if they got a large order they might get weeks of work, but then they'd be back again to one day or two days a week. . . . The weather's getting nicer in May, people aren't burning the coal, so by that time the mine would be completely at a standstill. September — women are canning again, they need more coal again. October — the weather's getting cold so people are burning more coal, so now the days are picking up and they're getting more. Now the cold weather's really socked in, so now they're all back working full time again.[26]

When work was uncertain, the miners "had to listen to the whistle. If it was three, you stayed home. If it was one, you went to work next morning. . . . There were times that we got laid off for two or three weeks. . . . So it was tough."[27]

By the late 1950s and early 1960s, the towns had few children or working-age people. Avramenko noted:

I think the first hard part of it was when you seen the first family move away to another coalmine. Everybody talked about it at great lengths. The next thing you knew there was a couple more families going, then a couple more families going. It left these empty houses. . . . We left, but my father-in-law didn't leave. He was one of the ones that was here right to the end. We came back to visit, and you drive down the street and here's all these empty houses that used to be full of mothers and fathers and children. All of a sudden there's nothing. Then the sad part about it was there started to be a lot of fires. These houses somehow started to burn. That made it look worse yet. There's nothing worse than a pile of burnt rubbish, it's worse than an empty house.[28]

For many mining families, Avramenko's included, moving meant going to another mine. Sometimes just the workers moved, and sometimes the whole family.

For others, the move came only after tragedy. Pauline Grigel's husband, Frank, was killed, along with two other men, by a bump (a sudden shift leading to a collapse) in the McGillivray Mine in 1953. A widow at thirty-two with five children, Grigel received $175 a month in compensation. To keep her family surviving, Grigel planted a large garden. "And I had a cow and chickens and rabbits. . . . When the girls got old enough to go to school, then I'd go out and work a bit. A little bit here, a little bit there." The money she received was through Workmen's Compensation: fifty dollars for her and twenty-five for each of her children. "I'll say one thing," she recalled. "Coleman Collieries didn't give me anything. They didn't even let me know that my husband was killed. I found out by the grapevine that my husband had been killed." Like many women in similar positions, Grigel's work life was precarious: "My first job was in the hospital, but that was temporary just to fill in for a couple of weeks. But after that I went out cleaning houses, washing walls, painting, wallpapering, whatever I could do to make a few dollars, eighty-five cents an hour. After that I started working at different stores."[29]

The threat of accidents was omnipresent in mining communities. In the weeks that followed Frank Grigel's death, two more incidents and four more deaths occurred. Bill Skura observed, "That year there was nine killed in Alberta and seven of them were killed in McGillivray."[30]

Many mines were unionized, often by the United Mine Workers of America (UMWA). In an era of declining demand, however, the unions had limited success. As Bill Skura said, "We got the conditions improved, but slowly."[31] But there were flashpoints. The first big, multi-mine strike in the Crowsnest after the war was from 27 September to 22 October 1945. Still faced with strict meat rationing, the workers of UMWA District 18 demanded that rations either be doubled (for fresh meat) or removed altogether (for prepared meat, like sausage). The strike ended with only minor concessions;[32] it marked to a great degree the end of the previous era of union activism in the Crowsnest and Alberta generally. Here was a strike across several workplaces and employers against the policies of the Wartime Prices and Trade Board. In the post-PC 1003 era, this was clearly an illegal strike, and such political strikes subsequently became rare.

A year later, the UMWA mines started their first organized pension plan. In October 1946, the operators of the unionized mines in District 18 began putting into a trust fund three cents for every tonne of coal moved out of their mines. The two trustees, representing the unions and the employers, invested the money in Dominion Savings Bonds while further details for the plan were developed.[33]

The next district-wide strike occurred in 1948, this time in demand of a new collective agreement with a raise. From mid-January until mid-February, when demand for coal was highest, the miners walked the line. They secured a significant victory, including a two-dollar (22 percent) increase to their minimum daily pay and an improved pension fund.[34] At first, the pension fund only provided death benefits to surviving families, but over the next several months, it began to provide a disability pension and then a retirement pension for workers after twenty years of service.[35] By this point, the UMWA was a modern union engaging in few wildcat strikes and mostly concerned with incremental advances in its agreements and in looking after the welfare of its members.[36]

RURAL LIVING PERSISTS

The declining agricultural population and the collapse of traditional extractive industries did not mean there was no work in rural Alberta, which continued to draw some workers even as its relative decline intensified.

Nursing

Jean Shafto trained in Toronto as a nurse, graduating in 1944. The following year, she came west in search of skiing and began work at the Banff Mineral Springs Hospital, a small hospital of thirty or forty beds and two wards. Helen Krizan, a nurse from Port Arthur (later Thunder Bay), came west to Canmore ten years later to join her new husband.

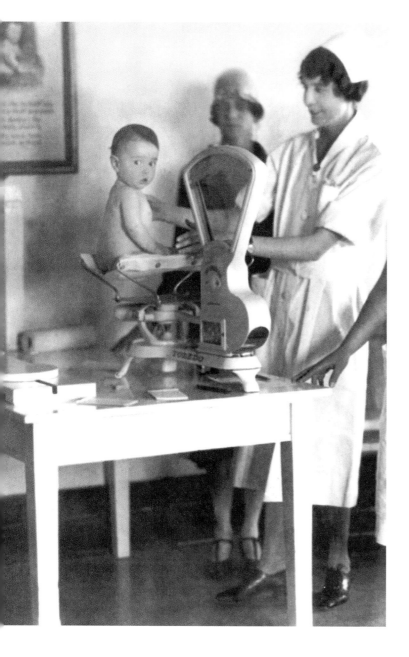

These working women faced significant challenges. Nurses worked day or night shifts in groups of four or five to a ward. In the early years, the Banff Mineral Springs Hospital was both a general service hospital and, because of the mineral springs, a rehabilitative hospital for people suffering from polio and arthritis. As Shafto recalls, there was much less supervision in the hospital in those days: "[I] had to deliver a baby about six months after I came, and that was terrifying." Krizan described her first shift at the Canmore hospital, which began at eight in the morning:

I believe there were six or eight patients at the time. [The night nurse and matron] gave me a report and said, "Okay, here's a few things about where things are. That's it. I'm going to bed." That was my report. I had no orientation or anything like that. . . . You were on shift by yourself. . . . I remember that day was utter chaos. I didn't know where things were. I didn't know the patients. One lady passed away on my shift. They brought in an accident victim from Lafarge, the cement plant down the highway. Then we had office hours and I was helping the doctor. Then about two o'clock a pregnant lady walked in. I had never done a delivery before in my life. I thought to myself, "All that I remember is that if it's her first baby, it takes longer." So that was what I asked her, and she said, "No, it's my fourth." So I proceeded to do all the things I was supposed to do, and I remembered. But anyway, she delivered the baby in the bedpan. I went hollering for the doctor, and he said, "Get the mat bundle." I had no clue to where all these things were that I needed. That's the day I went home at eight o'clock and thought, "I don't ever want to go back." It was very scary for me, the rural nursing, because I had not had any time to do that prior to coming here.

The Canmore nurses, working without an elevator, "carried patients up to a surgery on a stretcher up the stairs." Outside there were "bats at the back door of the hospital" that would "swoop down" at the nurses. One nurse was so afraid of bats that she refused to work nights.[37]

In addition to her paid work, Shafto, with the other nurses, formed a nurses' chapter in Banff, which took on the tasks in the mid-1950s of distributing the polio vaccine and running public health clinics for townsfolk. Nurses were not the only working-class professionals moving to rural areas; teachers and some civil servants also took jobs in rural Alberta. The biggest growth in rural employment in the 1940s and 1950s, however, was in the oil industry.

Leduc No. 1 and the Oil Industry

By the end of the 1920s, Alberta had the most significant oil industry in Canada, surpassing Ontario's older wells around Sarnia. In 1940, the province produced more than ten million barrels of oil, mainly from the Turner Valley area. A peak was reached in 1942 before the Turner Valley wells started to dry up. Throughout the war years and after, geologists, geophysicists, and other wildcatters searched for new sources. The discovery of oil at Leduc #1 in February 1947 marked a major shift in the location of oil from the foothills to the great plains, and with it, the potential to access far more oil. By 1948, Alberta's annual production was over ten million barrels again. In 1950, petroleum overtook liquor as the largest source of revenue for the provincial government, and in 1957, oil production in Alberta equalled Canada's annual con-sumption; two years later, the billionth barrel of oil was produced.[38]

Oil represented a major shift in resource extraction in Alberta, and Leduc #1 is a good example of this. According to oil-industry historians, "located on a weak seismic anomaly and 80 kilometres from the closest attempt to find oil, it was a 'rank wildcat.'"[39] Coal mining relied on large numbers of men digging for years at a seam. Towns built up around the mines, and the workers and their families worked and lived beside each other for years. For them, wildcatting meant striking without notice. Oil was found by small crews of workers who would roam the province away from their homes in small towns or cities; for them, wildcatting was the frontier exploration for oil. Once a well was dug and running, it was left largely to work on its own and the men moved on. The opportunities to organize these workers were limited, and their own self-image as rebel explorers likewise made organizing difficult.

In 1949, Tom McCloy tried to organize drill workers around Leduc into the Oil Workers International Union (OWIU). Having signed up enough workers to get a vote, McCloy was faced with the employers transferring all the drillers to either the Northwest Territories or British Columbia and hiring a new, anti-union crew. This defeat followed earlier failed attempts at organizing oil field workers in the Turner Valley area in 1942 and 1947.[40]

The Roughneck, a magazine for drillers and managers in Alberta that began publishing in 1952, reflected the attitudes that made unionization difficult. It reported on social activities, sports competitions among the drillmen, and safety information, along with humorous items. An early issue provided "An Alberta Schoolboy's History of Oil":

Oil which lives under the ground was discovered by the Social Credit Company. The oil would not come up for the Liberals because they lived in Ottawa and it would not come up for the United Farmers because they liked wheat better. The president of the Social Credit Company lived in Calgary and he knew the oil was there so he got a driller named Douglas to come over from England but Douglas drilled in the wrong places and he went home. The Social Credit did not give up but kept drilling and by and by the oil decided to come up near Edmonton. That was in 1947 and everyone is rich and happy because the Social Credit Company knew where to drill. And that is the history of oil.[41]

Clearly satirical, the piece nevertheless capitalizes on stereotypes of the political parties and celebrates Social Credit's role. To the extent that *The Roughneck* was representative of wildcatter opinion, it is little wonder the union movement found it difficult to organize the extraction industry.

But Alberta's oil and gas created more jobs than just extractive ones. Petrochemical plants and refineries that processed fossil fuels opened around Edmonton and elsewhere in Alberta. These urban factories offered ideal prospects for organizing. In 1951, the OWIU moved Neil Reimer from Saskatchewan to Alberta to organize the oil workers. It was never easy. As he recalled:

> I learned that there was an undertaking between the Manning government and the industry that they would try to keep our union out. Certainly I wouldn't say that we were welcomed by open arms. When a lot of our neighbours found out that I was a union representative,

I was looked upon as the guy that came here to kill the goose that laid the golden egg.[42]

Reimer faced organized opposition as he attempted to unionize the bigger plants and refineries. He managed to secure support from two-thirds or more of the workforce in the British American (BA) refinery, and he took his cards and list to the Board of Industrial Relations to secure recognition. The board stalled, and then, recalled Reimer, "for some reason or other the whole board of directors of BA came out from Toronto to the board hearing. They didn't have enough chairs or a table big enough. Just them all coming was a message for the board." When Reimer and the pro-union workers held rallies to keep support strong, company officials attended and recorded the names of those present. When the board finally called a vote, the pro-union side lost by ten votes. Many pro-union men were appalled by the outcome. Reimer recounted that

> all my supporters . . . quit their jobs and went to Celanese and CIL. . . . There was enough workers quit the BA plant that they had to shut the plant down. It's an organizing strike. I tried to persuade them not to. [BA] had to then bring in people from other plants, a foreman and what not, to run it until they hired other people. I was against [the workers] quitting, but I couldn't persuade them. They weren't going to work for those bastards. I knew if they quit it would be a long time, the anti-union guys would have to die off. They finally did and we got the plant, years later.[43]

In the months that followed, Reimer was able to organize both CIL and Celanese.

WORKING-CLASS LIFE IN POSTWAR URBAN CENTRES

As the government gradually loosened wartime price controls, the costs of consumer goods started to rise precipitously. Workers responded in various ways. In early 1947, Calgary barbers collectively raised their rates to match inflation. By late spring, women from Calgary and Edmonton had joined a national consumer boycott to protest the rapid rise in food prices. Their efforts culminated in June with an in-person appeal to the minister of Finance in Ottawa to reimpose price controls. He flatly refused.

In Calgary, children joined the boycott in late spring to protest the sudden 60 percent increase in the cost of chocolate bars. Perhaps partly in response, two chocolate manufacturers announced a one-cent price reduction for their bars in July 1947.[44] The concepts of the strike and the boycott, key weapons for trade unions, had permeated the consciousness of many working- and even middle-class Albertans.

The Struggle for Better Wages

Some in the Alberta labour movement, like Carl Berg, now vice-president of the Trades and Labour Congress (TLC), opposed worker agitation. He told the Calgary TLC:

> In spite of many blunders made by Governments, the many inequalities and injustices that do now exist, and while not in any way condemning those who have been forced to resort to strike action, I cannot, now any more than I did in War-time, agree that this is the time to throw our industrial machine and economy out of gear, and into complete chaos through strikes. . . . Strikes will only further retard our building, housing and reconstruction programs, increase scarcity of commodities, and thus increase prices as well as decrease the flow of supplies to a suffering world.[45]

Such "statesmanlike" views served to keep workers compliant rather than seek their share of the prosperity just becoming obvious in Alberta and throughout the Western world.

The more serious response to rising consumer prices came in the form of a national strike by meat-packing workers. Beginning in August 1947, the United Packinghouse Workers of America (UPWA) struck all of the unionized Alberta packing plants. During the war, in 1944, the UPWA had begun to pattern bargain across Canada. When the three largest firms — Canada Packers, Swift, and Burns — balked at pattern bargaining, the union held strike votes at all of its plants in an effort to get the federal government's attention. They were successful, and an industrial disputes inquiry commission was appointed in October. It did not, however, recommend national standards for wages or conditions, although the three employers agreed to the basic principles of collective bargaining.

In 1947, the union tried again. It issued the same bargaining positions for all employers: a wage increase of fifteen cents an hour, a work week of forty-four hours, dues check-off, and a single national wage scale. Swift workers took strike votes that were illegal under provincial laws, and after 98 percent of workers voted to strike, they began to walk out illegally across the country in late August and early September 1947. The strikes soon spread to the other big packers and then the independent and smaller packers. At its peak, 14,150 workers from 47 plants across Canada were out.[46]

As it did during the Farmers' Union strike, the provincial government lashed out at the workers and the union. Premier Manning accused the strikers of trying to sabotage the economy and foment revolution. Other Social Credit leaders red-baited the union leaders. Ignoring the membership votes for a strike, the minister for Public Works accused the union leadership of trying to "impose labour totalitarianism" by browbeating the "helpless men and women" who worked for a living.

UPWA members and their federation, the Canadian Congress of Labour (CCL), responded defensively. They lamented the typical Social Credit line that "all labour unions are wrapped up in one inseparable parcel and led by professional fomenters of industrial unrest, and by inference take their orders from foreign countries — even as far distant as Moscow." In fact, they pointed out, the CCL had "denounced Communism in all its forms." In addition, strikes were not imposed on workers; rather, they were called by "democratic means." This was a tepid response from an association representing twelve thousand Albertans at the time.[47]

An agreement was reached at the Swift plants in October, and then the Burns and Canada Packers workers went back with an agreement to go to binding arbitration. The arbitrator, C.P. McTague, followed the Swift agreement, thus effectively establishing national pattern bargaining for packing workers.[48]

In the 1950s, GWG still offered employment opportunities for young women. Mary Romanuk, newly married, moved to Edmonton from Vancouver Island to find work. The only job available for a "twenty one year old girl with no education" past grade 12 was

doing piecework sewing at GWG. Within five years, Romanuk, who had been secretary of the local for the International Ladies Garment Workers Union (ILGWU), was made a floor supervisor. Romanuk was born in Canada, but many women she worked with in the 1950s were postwar immigrants from Europe. This remained true throughout the decade; when Hungarian immigrant Elizabeth Kozma began working at the plant in 1957, workers included other Hungarian women, as well as "Yugoslavian and uh, Romanian, and Chinese, Korean, what else, Polish, German, Hungarian, Italian, Portuguese . . . not many Canadian though." The factory could be frightening at first, and there were too few translators, according to Kozma.[49]

Romanuk suggested that several of the immigrant women "had [a] hard life and they would try and get every cent they could; so a lot of them would want to work through the lunch hour if they could, just to make extra money. . . . And of course the unions would say no, you've to stop at twelve." At the end of the day, however, "young sisters were sewing and they always quit at quarter to the hour and they would clean up their machine, they'd go to the washroom and put on their makeup and clean their hair up and [get] ready to go home and I'd try to make them work until at least five to. Well, they brought a grievance against me and they won [laughs]. So that's all right. It was the boss wanted the machinery and the space used up for the most pieces they can get."[50] Even with this victory, the ILGWU and the women at GWG were still treated like second-class workers. When the union attempted to bargain for better wages or for benefits like a pension, the employer replied that the women had husbands to support them, so benefits were unnecessary.[51]

FIG 5-6 Women from the Medalta Potteries assembly line play baseball in Medicine Hat, 1943. Provincial Archives of Alberta, BL 596-2.

Working-Class Aspirations

Anne Ozipko arrived in Canada along with the rest of her family in 1930, when she was three years old. She moved to Edmonton on her own in 1943 and found work at the Royal Alexandra Hospital, "in the kitchen setting up trays and serving trays to the patients. And sweeping the floors, mopping the floors on [the] maternity ward." By the 1940s and 1950s, courtship and recreation for the urban working class took place in public and often without family chaperones. Anne and her women friends would often go to the Ukrainian hall to attend concerts, eat, or dance to live bands. Her future husband worked during the day at Woodland Dairies and played in a band at night. "They played

polkas, waltzes, square dances, fox trots. . . . My husband played the violin, and he played drums. Two of his brothers played as well in the same band. One played banjo and one played guitar." She first met her husband after one of these evening dances when she and a friend, along with other people from the dance, went to the Puritan Cafe to cool down and socialize before heading back to work.[52]

As the 1940s and 1950s progressed, working-class people and families developed aspirations similar to those of the middle class. Most important were cars and homes. By 1951, more than 250,000 motor vehicles were registered in Alberta: one for every four people. This was a higher rate of vehicle ownership than in many other parts of Canada.[53] Of course, for many working-class families, owning a car was still an un-reachable goal, but as incomes grew faster than the cost of cars, more and more families were able to afford at least a used car.

Even more marked was the boom in housing that began after the war. By 1951, 144,000 lots had been opened up for new homes. The houses were around twelve hundred square feet and were often bungalows.[54] Workers in slaughterhouses, railways, and oil and chem-ical plants began earning enough to buy a home, and working-class families began to populate the new sub-urbs of Calgary and Edmonton, as well as smaller cities. These new working-class neighbourhoods were further away from work and from any form of public transit, forcing workers to also invest in a car.

Even so, home ownership came only after a time. Before owning a home, many people had to find a place to rent, and that could be difficult. When Lorne and Ag-nes Wiley moved to Medicine Hat to work as teachers in 1952, Lorne made $2,700 a year and Agnes earned between $2,000 and $2,400. Despite a respectable com-bined income, they found few affordable suites; they lived first in a two-room basement apartment and later in an upstairs suite in a house.[55]

Social Welfare

There were, of course, some who could not work, among them the elderly. In 1930, the federal government in-troduced a shared federal-provincial pension program for people over the age of seventy with an annual in-come under $125. The maximum that a destitute old person could receive was $20 a month, but most prov-inces paid less. Alberta agreed to match the federal

contribution, so its destitute elderly did receive $20 a month. During the war, the maximum federal pension was raised to $25 a month. In 1942, the Alberta govern-ment began supplementing the means-tested pension by $5 a month, raising the supplement to $10 a month by 1950. This policy led the way in Canada. Over the same decade, societies of elderly people, led by prairie feminist Violet McNaughton, began petitioning the federal government for a universal pension without a means test. They were joined by the national labour organizations and other national groups. Finally, in 1951, a universal pension for people over seventy was instituted at $40 a month, an "outrageous pittance" according to the Canadian Congress of Labour.[56] The $10 supplement in Alberta helped, but not a lot.

However small their pensions in the 1950s, the el-derly were among the best served by social programs in the province. In addition to their pensions, after 1947 the province provided them with free hospital care and other medical treatment. Municipalities that provided care for the elderly soon also received half the cost of care from the province.[57]

Two other federal programs significantly affected Alberta's working families in the 1940s and 1950s. In 1940, national Unemployment Insurance (UI), a long-time union demand, was finally introduced, but with significant restrictions on eligibility. As with so much labour and employment legislation, farm workers and domestics were excluded, along with fishers, forestry workers, and other seasonal workers. Other workers who had worked for 180 days in the previous two years and were "capable and available for work" were eligible. The program administrators decided, curiously, that married women were neither capable nor available for work and excluded them from 1950 to 1957. Payouts were based on employment wages, so the more poorly paid received less. Again, this disproportionately hurt women workers. Nevertheless, UI offered real protections for many workers: even in the post-1947 boom in Alberta, many workers who lost their jobs could now rely temporarily on the program to help them make ends meet until they found their next job.[58]

The second federal program, the family allowance, was designed in large part to weaken unions and remove women from the workforce. Introduced in 1945, the allowance provided mothers from five to eight dollars a month per child for their first four children, with less for each additional child. It served two special functions. First, because it provided a supplement to families based on the number of young children they had, it allowed employers to argue that they only needed to pay a wage that supported a male worker, and not the worker's wife and children. The second function was to give married women some financial incentive not to seek paid work. With the monthly cheques made out to the mothers, the family allowance effectively became a little wage for mothers independent of their husband's wages and thus, at least in theory, theirs alone to spend. To emphasize the point that the government wanted married women at home, the family allowance was coupled with large reductions in the wartime income tax deductions available to men whose wives worked.[59] The allowance made a difference for poor families, but the government never raised the payouts, and by the end of the 1950s, if not earlier, it was no competition for a good job.

The provision of medical services remained in private hands throughout the 1940s and 1950s. Just after the war, the provincial government made available some funding to municipalities that instituted local hospital insurance schemes. Under the act, if 60 percent of the electorate in a municipality agreed to set up a local, user-pay medical insurance plan, then the province would pay for half the cost of all hospitalizations over and above a one-dollar flat fee that had to be paid by the patient (allegedly to prevent people from abusing the system).[60] It was not a particularly generous plan, and it placed health care costs on either the local governments (which could not rely on oil or liquor revenue like the province could) or the patient. However, the federal *Hospital Insurance and Diagnostic Services Act* of 1957 offered provinces significant grants in return for provinces providing free hospital care. Premier Manning and the Social Credit government resisted both this interference with provincial responsibilities and the removal of user-pay provisions, choosing to endure reductions in the province's federal hospital insurance grant rather than get rid of "co-insurance" payments by hospital patients. In the 1960s, these would double to $2.00 a day for active patients and increase to $1.50 for chronic patients.[61]

POSTWAR LABOUR LAW AND ORGANIZING

At war's end, Alberta workers could organize and operate unions of either a general or craft-specific nature with some security. In 1945, the Alberta Federation of Labour congratulated the Social Credit government as "leaders in social legislation." But not everyone was satisfied: the Communists demanded significant pro-labour changes, while the Canadian Manufacturers Association continually accused the government of

FIG 5-7 A pensioner delivers papers in the 1950s in an effort to make ends meet. Provincial Archives of Alberta, J1370.

giving too much to workers.[62] Neither PC 1003 nor the Alberta legislation that followed, however, were designed to *encourage* unionization. In both cases, the purpose of the legislation was to limit or even prevent workplace conflicts that would interfere with production.

By according unions certain legal rights, the legislation effectively forced unions to buy into the new regime of bureaucratized organizing and bargaining. Along with creating opportunities for unions to secure recognition and challenge unfair anti-union activities by employers, the legislation created a system to decertify unions and entrenched the view that a variety of labour practices were unfair, significantly restricting the scope of union activities. For instance, the legislation made unions liable for wildcat strikes during the life of a collective agreement. Conflicts over the enforcement and application of a contract had to be handled through a grievance procedure and eventually arbitration; workers could not simply put down their tools on the spot in an effort to get immediate relief. If they did, the employer could use the courts to get injunctions that might lead to fines against the union and its leaders, and to imprisonment of leaders. Even when an agreement had ended, workers could not strike if an employer had requested conciliation or arbitration in an effort to get ready for a possible strike, at least until the board of conciliation or arbitration had issued a report. The delay gave many employers the opportunity to stockpile goods and sit out a strike. Throughout the war, Alberta legislation allowed ad hoc groups or employee associations — that is, company unions — to be legitimate workers' representatives in collective bargaining.

The government's anti-union bias became crystal clear in 1947 as labour legislation was amended again. That year, the government consolidated its employment and labour legislation into one law, the *Alberta Labour Act*. The government's desire to limit the growth of unions was evidenced in a provision that certification of a union required not just a majority of those voting, as in other provinces, but a majority of all workers in the bargaining unit. The act also gave the Board of Industrial Relations the right to more oversight of the certification process. The legislation continued to allow company unions and employer-friendly worker organizations.[63]

Following a major strike at Medalta Potteries in Medicine Hat, the minister of Labour successfully sought further changes to the *Labour Act* in 1948, imposing new burdens on unions and their officers that made the legislation patently anti-union rather than just pro–industrial peace. Some changes superficially achieved balance: for example, unions and employees would join employers in being liable to penalties should they refuse to bargain collectively or to live up to the conditions of an agreement in force. But even getting a union organized became more difficult. The 1947 act had barred employers from interfering in efforts to organize a trade union — for example, by firing activists. Now, however, organizers could only organize on the work site during work hours with employer consent. Conversations encouraging people to join a union occur mainly on the job, so this legislative change undermined earlier protection from firing given to organizers.

New procedures were also introduced for strikes and lockouts. The minister could refer any strike or lockout to a judge to determine its legality. Penalties against unions were draconian, while employers faced a tap on the wrist. If a strike was declared illegal, any collective agreement in force was immediately declared null and void, though the minister of Labour had the discretion to reinstate the collective agreement once the strike ended. Once the collective agreement was null and void, protections in the agreement regarding hiring, firing, promoting, or demoting employees were likewise nullified, and the employer could fire or otherwise punish strikers. By contrast, when a lockout was declared illegal, the employer had three days to let the workers back. After that point, it *could* face a fine of *up to* a dollar a day for each locked-out employee while the lockout persisted.[64]

The Canadian Congress of Labour denounced the 1948 amendments for weakening workers' rights, but Alberta Federation of Labour secretary Carl Berg defended the government.[65] A year later, though, the AFL responded to the amendments by using twisted logic to support limits on the right to strike. Since the legislation made striking precarious for unions, the AFL asked that when disputes went to arbitration, the arbitrators' award be binding. The AFL was prepared to give up any right to strike in exchange for compulsory binding arbitration. Employers, generally favourable toward the act, did not want to be bound by arbitrators' decisions and argued against any such amendment. The Manning government supported the employer view.[66] In fact, when Norman Bezanson started organizing for the International Association of Machinists and Aerospace Workers in 1955, he encountered a system that supported employers at every turn:

Employers committed what would even under weak legislation be considered unfair labour practices, but you had to prove beyond any kind of a doubt that this had been done, and that was often almost impossible to do. So personally, I got to the point that if I was making an application to certify, before I took that in to the Labour Relations Board, I'd take a letter to the employer telling him that this was being done. So there was none of this, "Well, I didn't know this happened when I fired so many people. I didn't know there was a union on the scene." And if a campaign was going to be a lengthy one, sometime early in the campaign I'd notify the employer. This may seem very stupid to many committed trade unionists, but I know it saved a number of people from being fired.[67]

In some instances, though, organizing proved relatively easy. Tets Kitaguchi worked for Lime Works in Coleman following the war. Many of his fellow workers were new immigrants from Yugoslavia, but the foreman was a much earlier Balkan immigrant who controlled the workers with threats of deportation. One worker approached Kitaguchi for help, and he in turn met with Jack Evans of the Chemical Workers Union. As Kitaguchi recalls:

[Evans] came to visit us and said, "You want a union?" I said, "Yeah, these fellows here want a union. They want better living conditions." "Yeah, I can see that right now, the minute I come in here I was wondering what those shacks were." I said, "They're homes." It was all company owned. Jack said, "You've got to have 51 percent to sign up to get a union in here." So I said, "Okay." I had a problem there, because

these people come from Croatia, Bosnia, and that has a history of people that never got along for years. . . . But we managed to sign everybody but two of them. We still needed the 51 percent for next morning. Jack was coming back to get this signed petition. During the night I said, "We gotta get hold of those two guys somehow." Almost midnight I went to their home and said, "You gotta sign this." He was a real grump. He wouldn't sign anything. Young fellow and his wife. But he finally signed it. I guess that bothered him for a couple of days at work. One night at work, he didn't like me at all, he was going to clobber me with an iron pipe. But I had a friend with a black belt behind me, grabbed him and threw him against the wall. Kinda shook him out and straightened him out a bit. He said, "We're not going to get anywhere, you just make trouble for us." "Never mind," I said, "we'll find out what's going to happen." So he signed it, we got a union.[68]

Other organizing efforts faced a variety of impediments, including the craft unions' desire for respectability. Neil Reimer kept office hours in downtown Edmonton after his arrival in the city in 1951 because "in those days the people came downtown to shop on Saturday. The men would drive their wives to the stores. It might take all morning, so many of them came up to my office and we would talk union." One morning, Ole Nelson Wigger, a powerhouse engineer from McGavin's Bakery, came to the office and indicated that the company's maintenance workers wanted a union. Wigger asked Reimer to come to the back of the bakery, and Wigger introduced him to the men. The bakery had been organized by the Bakers and Confectioners Union, but the maintenance men had been left out. Reimer learned "that [the] John Howard [Society] had placed them there. They all had records of some kind." The bakers' union did not want a group of ex-convicts in its local. So the maintenance workers became members of the Oil Workers International Union (OWIU) instead.

Certification came quickly, and a collective agreement had to be negotiated. At first the bakery workers wanted Reimer to negotiate for them, but he refused, arguing that some of them had to join the negotiating committee for their own collective agreement. "So two of them decided they would come with me," said Reimer. "I never realized how important that was." By directly involving them in that first negotiation,

Reimer showed that he was not another person who saw these workers as people requiring assistance or charity; rather, he was helping them assert their own rights. Interestingly, management was afraid of these ex-convicts. "It only took us a couple hours to negotiate a whole new agreement, because the employer was afraid of them." [69]

In some of the bigger plants, Reimer's greatest competition came from other unionists with different politics. The labour legislation allowed employers to voluntarily recognize unions or employee associations for their workers. Inevitably, these associations, even company unions, would be weak. They might secure minor advances for the workers, but their most important role was to keep more radical unions out. When he attempted to organize Building Products, a plant that made shingles and other asphalt products with oil provided from the Imperial Oil refinery, Reimer was "handing out leaflets in front and Carl Berg came out the front door and he waved a piece of paper and told the guys they had a collective agreement." Berg had organized the company, not the workers: without consulting the workers, he had negotiated a collective agreement that the company would like. But at both Building Products and Husky Oil, Reimer persevered to organize the workers, comparing for them their union's sweetheart deals with what workers at other plants organized by the OWIU were getting. Finally, he persuaded workers in both plants to switch to the OWIU. [70]

Being organized was no guarantee of continued success. In 1954, beer parlour and other hotel workers across the province won a conciliation report recommendation that Alberta Hotel Association (AHA)

FIG 5-8 Striking bartenders in front of a shop in Edmonton, 1954. Glenbow Archives, NA-1312-5.

members reduce the workers' work week to forty hours without a reduction in pay. The AHA refused, and the Hotel and Restaurant Employees Union business agent led the workers in a legal strike. They shut down hotels in Calgary, Edmonton, Lethbridge, and Medicine Hat. In response, the AHA brought in scabs who crossed the picket lines. When picketers at one site tried to prevent their replacements from crossing, they were charged with assault. At that point, the AHA effectively won: their new employees faced no effective interference by the strikers, and thus the parlours stayed open. When the strike ended, the employers refused to rehire strikers: the strike-breakers kept their jobs and the union was broken. In Edmonton alone, the union lost seventeen hotels, and seven to eight hundred workers lost their jobs.[71]

In the aftermath of this loss, Doug Tomlinson — once an organizer and by now working in a Legion — and others tried to rebuild the union. He continued to face strong opposition from the employers:

> The Hotelman's Association and the rotten bunch that they are, they just held an iron grip. . . . I became an organizer. . . . But we couldn't get an agreement. [The association] brought a lawyer by the name of Dave Ross in. As soon as we organized, he'd come in there and decimate the staff. The Board of Industrial Relations was useless. [It] was a rubber stamp for the hotelmen. . . . We fought and organized and won and lost and lost and lost certifications. When we did get certified, [we] couldn't get an agreement. There was no unity in the union. "Oh, they're a bunch of Reds you know, leave them on their own."[72]

UNION POLITICS: THE MERGER OF THE AFL AND IFLA

In 1939, the Alberta Federation of Labour, in line with the Trades and Labour Congress, expelled industrial unions associated with the American Congress of Industrial Organizations (CIO). The following year, the Canadian Congress of Labour (CCL) formed as an industrial federation representing Canada's CIO unions and unions that were former members of the All-Canadian Congress of Labour. Alberta locals of CCL unions came together in local councils in both Calgary and Edmonton during the war and later worked together in a planning council. Finally, in 1949, they formed the Industrial Federation of Labour of Alberta (IFLA) as a union central. Alberta's CCL unions at the time included the United Mine Workers of America, the United Packinghouse Workers of America, the Mine, Mill, and Smelter Workers (Mine Mill), and the Canadian Brotherhood of Railway Employees. But there were strains within the fledgling IFLA. Should they follow the CCL and endorse the CCF politically, or should they follow the suggestion of Mine Mill and endorse the Communist Party? In a tense showdown that led to a brief walkout from the founding convention by Mine Mill delegates, the IFLA decided by a one-vote margin to support the CCF. By the end of the year, the CCL had expelled Mine Mill nationally, and the IFLA had moved back closer to the AFL.[73]

Within union politics, the most important event of the 1950s was the unification of the rival federations. Nationally, the TLC and the CCL united in 1956 to form the Canadian Labour Congress (CLC). Not long after, the AFL and the IFLA came together in a reformulated AFL. The new AFL was to be affiliated with the CLC,

FIG 5-9 The Medalta union charter from the International Union of Mine, Mill, and Smelter Workers (commonly known as Mine Mill). Courtesy of the Alberta Labour History Institute.

but it took a while for the AFL to break conservative habits from the Social Credit period.

Throughout the 1940s and 1950s, many AFL leaders were members or sympathizers of the Social Credit party, or at least accommodating to it in an effort to gain some traction or advantage. But their efforts yielded nothing of value to working people. Neil Reimer remembered:

> When the federation had a convention, [the provincial Department of Labour] would shut down the offices and everyone would come to the convention. They used to have it at a building on 100th Ave., the Lodge Building. . . . They all sat in the front row. I got on the floor and said, "It looks to me this is like what Caesar had, whether they'll turn their thumbs down or whether they'll [put] their thumbs up."[74]

Government interference was generally even more direct. Someone from the Department of Labour — often the deputy minister, the highest ranking bureaucrat — would be on the resolutions committee for the convention, effectively vetoing resolutions before the convention delegates could even vote.

The merger of the AFL and IFLA did not initially change these habits. On the October 1957 weekend of the founding convention, Donald Macdonald, the secretary-treasurer of the newly founded CLC, was in town, yet the AFL invited Premier Manning to give the address at the opening banquet. Macdonald, not surprisingly, declined to attend the banquet, though he attended the convention itself. In his profoundly conservative speech at the banquet, Manning commented that in Alberta there was a horn of plenty from which everyone could receive a fair share; Alberta workers received what they deserved and it was inappropriate to ask for more.

The next morning, Reimer, speaking to a resolution, commented: "I come from the farm. One time we had a sow that had thirteen piglets and twelve tits. . . . We're that thirteenth piglet, as far as Manning is concerned."[75] Many delegates chastised Reimer: "You can't talk that way in Alberta. . . . They [the government] won't do you any favours." Reimer replied, "I'm not getting any anyways."[76]

THE REDS

Unsurprisingly, many labour organizers and militants were leftists. In the 1940s and 1950s, many on the left remained Communists or Communist sympathizers, but within the unions, the Communists were always a minority.

For some, especially Social Crediters, all unionists and leftists were communists. In 1951, two cabinet ministers raised the communist bogeyman. First, Municipal Affairs Minister C.F. Gerhart told the Canadian Manufacturers Association that there were between five and six hundred communist spies among Alberta's workers. He urged employers to scrutinize job applicants more closely, to fingerprint all employees, and to report suspicious behaviour to the RCMP. Later that year, Minister of Labour J.L. Robinson commented that communists intended "to mislead rather than lead, the workers. Their purpose is to use and seduce their fellow-travellers in the CCF and their purpose is finally to confuse and befuddle everyone."[77] The newsletter *The Canadian Social Crediter* in 1955 described the platform

of the CCF (the forerunner to the NDP) as "Communism . . . in Short Pants" and asserted that "one does not have to have a Communist membership card to follow the communist line."[78] In his weekly radio show and in other places, Premier Manning thundered against communists and called for vigilance: "There is happening in this world today a whole chain of events that is paving the way for the ultimate world government of the Anti-Christ and his ruthless communistic dictatorship."[79] Nationally, the federal government took an active role in purging the civil service of communists, communist sympathizers, and others, such as gays, whom only a distorted logic linked with communism.[80]

The defection of Igor Gouzenko, a Soviet embassy employee in Ottawa, and his revelation of Soviet spies in Canada and beyond marked the first of a series of anti-communist spectacles in the postwar period. Ben Swankey, a prominent Edmonton communist, was interviewed by an *Edmonton Journal* reporter when Gouzenko's defection and claims were revealed, several months after the actual defection:

> The *Edmonton Journal* came to me and said, "Were you involved with Gouzenko?" Of course I said no. I didn't know anything about Gouzenko at that time. So they had a big article in the *Journal:* "Swankey denies any support or connection with Gouzenko." So people would say, "Well, it might be true or it might not be true. They must've asked the question for a reason."[81]

Such public exposure had serious ramifications. Swankey noted, "The children of communists were harassed in school, which is a terrible thing. Even in the public school, never mind high school. They were harassed because their parents were communists."[82]

This public exposure was paralleled by intensive RCMP surveillance of suspected communists, a continuation of the surveillance that had begun long before the war and never stopped. When Patrick Lenihan was released from internment, he remained a member of the Labour Progressive Party (LPP), the party that grew out of the reorganization of the Communist Party after it was banned by the government in 1941. The LPP assigned Lenihan to organize in the Calgary city unions. Soon after he started in the Calgary street-railway shops, he was visited on the job by RCMP officers:

> They said, "Look, Pat, we want to talk to you. We have information that you are back in the Communist movement and that you are in charge of trade union work. You know you're not supposed to do this. You could be interned again."
>
> I knew they wouldn't answer me, but I asked, "Where did you get your information? I'm working here like a working man and that's all and I'm minding my own business."
>
> "Well, we came down to let you know that we know what's going on. Goodbye."

The public nature of the interview was aimed at identifying him as a problem to the other workers on the shop floor as well as to intimidate him directly. In this case, they did not succeed on either score.[83]

The surveillance and harassment only intensified after the war. After Walter Makowecki's farmer father opened a new account at the Bank of Montreal in Vegreville:

the RCMP were in our yard. "How's things? We were in the neighbourhood, thought we'd drop in. You're a newcomer here. How are things going? Do you know about this neighbour has some kind of trouble with his wife?" Dad said, "I don't know, I'm new here." "Oh yeah, by the way, why did you change the spelling of your name [from *cki* to *ski*]?" . . . Dad said, "That's to accommodate you Englishmen." It happened over and over again.[84]

When Walter and others bought property on Gordon's Lake to set up a summer camp for the Association of United Ukrainian Canadians, a Soviet-sympathetic Ukrainian association, the RCMP returned to the farm, asking many questions about the family's farms and incomes.[85] And the RCMP went beyond interviewing individuals whose loyalty to Canada they suspected. Swankey comments, "What the RCMP would do where I lived, they went to see all my neighbours and said, 'You've got a very dangerous man living here, did you know that? You'd better be careful what you talk about to him. If he says anything that's wrong, let us know.'"[86]

Labour officialdom, national and provincial, co-operated with the RCMP spies. Jack Phillips describes one of the key early moments in the purges:

> Come 1950 we had the convention of the Trades and Labour Congress of Canada meeting in Montreal. That was where the cold war in the labour movement was officially launched. Don Guys [from Lethbridge] and I were refused admittance to the convention. I forget the number, but a number of other prominent trade unionists were also refused admittance. . . . "You just can't come in, you're communists." There

was no legislation on the books of the Trades and Labour Congress of Canada. But they assumed that there was, or they assumed they could act as if there [were] sufficient policy resolutions to justify what they were doing. . . . I remember the red squad walking up and down in the aisles. I can remember Johnny Hines getting up and saying something that got him thrown out. He pointed out that there was somebody on the floor from the American FBI. Whether it was true or not, I don't know, but he said so. At any rate, Don Guys and I decided that we would go before the executive of the Trades and Labour Congress of Canada. We came into this room. Claude Jodoin was presiding; he was the president. There were all sorts of documents on the table. They were petitions. We weren't allowed to look at them. Petitions from members of the rank and file of the union asking that we be kicked out because we were communists. They had a minority support, but they had some support. . . . They knew more about my background than I did. I figured it out that the RCMP had filled them in. . . . Jodoin . . . looked at me and said, "Mr. Phillips, you work for Joe Stalin." I said, "No, I'm working for peace." He said, "Don't give me your propaganda." I just listened to him without saying a word after that. At the end of it we had our hearing. Then they sent a chap by the name of Carl Berg out here [to Vancouver] to take over the union.[87]

Doug Tomlinson recalls how the Edmonton business agent for the hotel union in the early 1950s "went into a rampager. In fact he reminded me of Goebbels. He'd work himself up into such a fury at union meetings." In 1954, the year of the disastrous strike, Tomlinson "got put on trial in the union for being a Red. They

removed me from the executive." As part of this, "I got expelled from the Edmonton District Labour Council for being a Red. Carl Berg did it. Old Carl Berg, the reactionary."[88] Berg had graduated from being a One Big Union supporter to a left Labourite before becoming a well-paid union leader and Social Credit apologist, an embodiment of the shift to conservatism in Alberta labour circles from the end of the First World War to the end of World War II.

Although many communists were removed from leadership ranks in unions, not all were. Patrick Lenihan, for example, remained in leadership positions in Calgary and then nationally in the public employee unions throughout the period. At the same time, he never lost his personal feelings of sympathy for communist ideals. Fortunately, for him, he had been purged from the party itself in 1945 because of his drinking problems, allowing him to escape the union purges of communists in the postwar period.

Employers also engaged in purges. Many required employees to fill out security questionnaires that asked them about their political persuasion, their church, whether they had ever been union members, and the like.[89] The purpose was to root out potential troublemakers, which might include anyone who favoured a more equitable division of resources or having a union in the workplace.

The anti-communist rhetoric was sometimes used in union contests as well. In the aforementioned AFL/TLC battles with IFLA/CCL unions to represent workers, the red-baiting temptation often cropped up. For example, when Neil Reimer was trying to organize the Celanese plant in Edmonton for the OWIU, he was competing against the International Chemical Workers

FIG 5-10 The convention in Toronto that created the Canadian Labour Congress, April 1956. Courtesy of the Alberta Federation of Labour.

(ICW). In an effort to swing the vote their way, the ICW released a pamphlet calling the OWIU a communist union. Reimer, later the head of the Alberta NDP, was no communist, but would not dignify the accusations with a rebuttal. Instead, he said, "We don't call names, we're not against things. Here is what we're for." Reimer believes that this approach swayed many workers: "To be called communists was just something they weren't going to accept. So they voted for us more against them."[90]

Anti-communism was a destructive force not because the communists had all the answers or because the extremely authoritarian Soviet Union was an attractive model for workers. Instead, its destructive character came in the closing down of discussion about workers' rights, which communists raised consistently, as

did many social democrats like Reimer. The desire for respectability on the part of some unionists and the fear of being tarred as communists too often led to them becoming apologists for capitalist greed rather than defenders of workers' interests. While the IFLA was somewhat better than the AFL in this regard, it also purged communists and showed undeserved respect to the anti-labour premier. For example, after being invited to a state dinner in 1952 in honour of the British king and queen, the IFLA president and secretary-treasurer thanked the premier for inviting them, claiming that it showed that "your government recognizes this labour organization as a responsible, loyal and essential part of our society."[91]

Despite the purges, Communists remained active and communist ideas continued to be brought up in union strategy, even if from a minority position. Dave Werlin recalls being hired by the City of Calgary in the late 1950s:

> First day I started, a fellow by the name of Gordie Mitchell, who was the shop steward, comes up to me and says, "Hey, you have to join the union." I had no problem with that. My parents had been socialists and I understood a little bit about it. I said, "That's fine, but I have no money." He said, "Don't worry about it. The initiation fee is a dollar; they'll take it off your pay cheque." Fine, I signed up.

When he got to his first meeting, he realized they were right in the middle of negotiating a new contract. Lenihan had reached an agreement with the employer, but at the meeting he faced off against Art Roberts, who argued that they could get more from the city. When the offer came to a vote, the majority voted it down. At the end of the meeting, Werlin went and sat down beside Roberts:

> I said, "You kind of remind me of my dad. He used to talk like you do." I said, "He was in the farmers' union. But I can remember whenever he talked like that people used to call him a communist." Art Roberts says, "And what the hell's the matter with that?"[92]

◆ ◆ ◆

As Alberta working people marched off to war from 1939 to 1945 or into jobs in an economy mobilized above all for the war effort, most had dreams of a postwar era from which both the destitution of the Depression and the horrors of war would be eradicated. Many never came back from the battlefields to see whether such hopes would be realized. For many who did, the new oil wealth of the province delivered more economic prosperity than they had ever known. But that wealth was poorly distributed, and the Social Credit government, which had come to power in 1935 with radical-sounding promises, had become a shameless tool of the bosses. The trade union movement might have been expected to serve as a fighting force against both employers and the government that kept workers from getting their share of the province's new wealth. Some unions, particularly those in the IFLA, did mobilize workers and achieve some victories. But the pre-1956 AFL had lost its status as a fighting force and behaved much of the time like an extension of the Social Credit government. The "labour statesmen" in charge of the AFL ignored the anti-union, anti-worker character of the province's labour law and its enforcement, and turned their fire on workers and unions that did demand better wages and working conditions for workers. The merger would gradually change that as the industrial unions and unions of public servants became the AFL's strongest voice in the period after 1960. While the Cold War gave Social Credit and conservatives within the labour movement alike an opportunity to add reds and radicals to rats on Alberta's list of eradicable pests, many Alberta working people struggled to retain a radical purpose for their unions and fought for a better deal for their families and communities.

FIG 6-1 Social service workers, members of the Civil Service Association, strike in 1974. Provincial Archives of Alberta, J2070-2.

6 THE BOOMERS BECOME THE WORKERS
ALBERTA, 1960–80

ALVIN FINKEL

Then in 1968 I ran for the negotiating committee and came 1969, we got what we called the 1969 collective agreement. It was a very progressive agreement. That's when we really moved ahead on the health and welfare and pension. We introduced the seven-and-a-half-hour day into the construction industry. That came in during the term of that agreement. The supplementary benefit fund, which now is a big thing in the local union and provides bursaries for members' children, donations to United Way, charities, and those kind of things. The inception was then. Travel time, rotation leave, and things like that were all introduced in that 1969 agreement. . . .

In the latter part of 1969, I was working on a job in the southern part of the jurisdiction of Local 48 in the Red Deer area. I crushed my heel. I was off work for pretty close to a year. It's never been the same since, but I learned to get around and live with it. When I came back to the workforce, I ended up in warehousing and things like that.[1]

Pipefitter Jack Hubler's experiences in 1969 encapsulate the two sides of the typical male Alberta worker's narrative during the on-and-off energy boom of the 1960s and 1970s. On the one hand, the construction companies, faced with labour shortages and huge contracts that they did not want to see interrupted, made significant short-term concessions to the trades on wages and benefits. On the other hand, in their search for profits, they organized the work process in such a way that accidents were inevitable and plentiful.

The typical female worker's narrative was somewhat different. Women workers, whose numbers jumped from 26.1 percent of the provincial labour force in 1961 to 42.2 percent in 1981, were rarely well paid, and while they were less likely to die on the job, they faced gruelling pressures.[2] Daycare worker Susan Keeley described her work at a private daycare in Calgary in the early 1970s: "My first job was a non-union private daycare centre, horrible conditions. I actually got fired after six weeks because I complained about the conditions. The boss overheard me, so I was out the door. I was

FIG 6-2 Slogan of the first province-wide nurses' strike, 1980. Provincial Archives of Alberta, J 5024-4.

basically responsible for ten infants from the age of six weeks to eighteen months, by myself. If I needed a break there was nobody to go in and watch them when I left. Any time that I would take a break, we'd have to leave the door open and hope we'd hear if there was a problem."[3] Fortunately for Keeley, her next job was with a non-profit City of Calgary daycare, where both she and the children she cared for benefited from the City of Calgary's socially responsible attitude to child care, and where she was a member of the Canadian Union of Public Employees, thanks to being a city employee.

Most women workers were less fortunate, enjoying neither a socially responsible employer nor a union to protect their interests.

This chapter attempts to capture various narratives, both male and female, of workers' lives in Alberta from 1960 to 1980. It was a period of great prosperity overall in the province, but prosperity poorly shared between employers and workers, men and women, urban and rural residents, the employed and the unemployed; nor was it shared with the working class generally. During this period, the population of Alberta almost doubled, jumping from 1,265,572 in 1960 to 2,094,212 in 1980.[4] Though fertility rates were falling, Alberta's energy economy benefited from migration to the province of mainly young workers, both from other provinces and other countries. The result was a province where the median age in 1971 was 24.9, the lowest of any Canadian province, and where there were 5.1 children under the age of 15 years for every 10 people in the 15- to 64-year age group.[5] A young workforce with no memories of the Great Depression or World War II had different attitudes than their parents. Though Alberta remained in the main a conservative province with conservative governments, the younger generation absorbed many of the values of its counterparts throughout North America and western Europe. In part, that simply meant an embrace of the consumerism that the media trumpeted in ever-more sophisticated ways as the only way to have a happy life. But it also meant the counter-movement of 1960s and 1970s protest values, which included feminism, anti-racism, acceptance of sexual difference, environmentalism, and opposition to American imperialism. Governments, employers, and the trade union movement alike attempted to co-opt youth by harnessing their anti-authoritarianism in ways that benefited entrenched interests. However, although only cautiously at first, the labour movement blended the issues of the younger generation with labour's earlier equality-seeking goals. In the Alberta Federation of Labour and in many unions, that meant a stronger embrace of the human rights orientation of youth groups and a greater focus on non-wage issues, both in collective bargaining and in political life.

Some of the changes that occurred in the workforce and in the labour movement in Alberta during these two decades reflected changes that were occurring nationally. Beginning in 1962, the federal government, anticipating labour shortages and recognizing that western Europeans were less eager to migrate to Canada now that their own economies had fully recovered from wartime ruin, began to allow non-Europeans to immigrate to Canada. Whereas almost all immigrants arriving in 1960 had European origins, half of those arriving in 1970 came from Asia, South America, or the Caribbean.[6] The workforce became more polyglot. It also became more unionized, with 37.2 percent of all non-agricultural workers represented by a trade union in 1980 compared to only 32.3 percent in 1960.[7] Growing unionization in the public sector was bringing more women into the labour movement, but in 1977, 47 percent of male workers were unionized compared to only 10 percent of women.[8]

Increased nationalism in Canada was reflected in the trade union movement. In 1960, about 72 percent of unionized workers were enrolled in unions headquartered in the United States. By 1980, that figure had dropped to just under 50 percent. Breakaways from so-called international unions — that is, American unions

with Canadian sections — accounted for some of the decline. The Communications Workers of Canada founded in 1972, the Canadian Paperworkers Union and the Brewery Workers Union in 1974, and the Energy and Chemical Workers Union in 1980 were new unions with significant memberships in Alberta that resulted from the Canadian sections of international unions cutting their umbilical cord from the American sections.[9] But it was the major unions that represented public sector workers and were under Canadian control that accounted for most of the Canadianization occurring in the Canadian trade union movement.

THE GROWTH OF THE STATE AND PUBLIC WORKERS' MILITANCY

The growth of the state in Alberta at all levels reflected the demands of a young population for better services and of industry for subsidies of every kind. Though the Social Credit government, which remained in office until 1971, often gave in reluctantly to demands from below for additional services and attempted to provide such services in ways that penalized low-income Albertans, it could not fully hold back the tide. Neither could the Progressive Conservative government led by Peter Lougheed, which defeated Social Credit in 1971 after that party had held office for thirty-six uninterrupted years, but which shared many of its predecessor's social values. Indeed, Lougheed, while uninterested in using the state to redistribute wealth among Albertans, did see a positive role for the state in encouraging economic diversification. Although his overreliance on subsidies to companies that created jobs in the province — at least in the short term — helped to frustrate his diversification aims, Lougheed did preside over a continued growth in state employment.[10]

The government wanted docile employees, but the workers often proved to have their own ideas. Changing attitudes among civil servants and nurses indicate the evolution that occurred from 1960 to 1980. In 1960, the civil service was still a compact collection of appointees whom the government's director of personnel regarded as mainly friends and relatives of government officials: the province had yet to hire a social worker with a social work degree as opposed to a Social Credit membership card.[11] Unsurprisingly, the Alberta Federation of Labor (AFL) regarded the Civil Service Association (CSA) — the representative of these workers who owed their positions to nepotism and a 1958 AFL dropout — not only as a company union but also as virtually a mouthpiece for the government and its anti-labour policies. In 1968, AFL president Roy Jamha accused "the state-controlled Civil Service Association" of spearheading an organization of company unions in the province.[12] The CSA included both managers and workers, and throughout the 1960s, remained largely under management control.

Six years later, however, the CSA was an affiliate of the AFL, and its members had staged their first strikes ever. A formal hiring process initiated in 1959, as well as extensive hirings throughout the civil service, had gradually turned the old Social Credit hires into an insignificant minority relative to the young, better-educated, and more demanding workers who filled the new government employee ranks. In 1969, Social Credit, responding to other provinces having granted their direct employees union rights, rewrote the *Public Service Act* to give the CSA bargaining rights as opposed to simply advisory rights. But, in line with Social Credit labour legislation generally, the new act gave the minister of Labour the right to determine what issues were negotiable and gave the cabinet, not an arbitrator, the right to impose an agreement if the two sides could not find a consensus.[13]

The members of the CSA chafed under such a pseudo–collective-bargaining regime, and in 1972, they elected T.W. (Bill) Broad as their leader. Broad, a machinist, had been a union activist in both Britain and Canada. He had joined the public service in Alberta as a NAIT instructor in the early 1960s and was not impressed with the cozy relationship between the CSA and the government. Broad insisted that the new Conservative government remove management figures from the CSA and provide government workers with the same rights as unionized private sector workers.[14] In 1974, for the first time, provincial workers went on strike to back up their demands. In the spring, three hundred Alberta Liquor Control Board workers hit the bricks for increased wages; in October, 12,500 civil servants struck for two days, causing the government, which had attempted to unilaterally impose a wage settlement, to negotiate with the union. In 1976, the CSA shed the last remnants of its company union past, changing its name to the Alberta Union of Provincial Employees (AUPE) and removing its registration under the *Societies Act* to register as an unincorporated union. At a founding convention in Edmonton in November, the new AUPE chose Bill Broad as its first leader.

The Alberta government, unhappy with the new militancy of some of its employees, moved to limit the ability of their unions to represent them. The 1977 *Public Service Employee Relations Act (PSERA)* created

FIG 6-3 Bill Broad, the first president of AUPE. Courtesy of the Alberta Union of Provincial Employees.

FIG 6-4 Members of AUPE rally during their "illegal" strike, 1980. Provincial Archives of Alberta, J 5056-1.

a Public Sector Employees Relations Board, which was empowered to serve as a counterpart for provincial employees to the Alberta Labour Relations Board. But the act banned strikes in favour of arbitration and removed from the scope of arbitration such issues as work organization, promotion, training, and termination of employment. The legislation covered not only direct employees of the state but also the teaching staff of universities and colleges. Professors were barred from following the lead of their counterparts in other provinces who had unionized under the *Labour Act* and were limited instead to representation under the *Universities Act* and the *Colleges Act*. While the International Labour Organization ruled that the wholesale ban on striking violated the Freedom of Association and Protection of the Right to Organize Convention,

which Canada had signed, the Lougheed government proved immoveable.[15]

Although such a ban might have been respected by the Depression-born workers of the Social Credit era, it was treated with contempt by the members of AUPE, a union that represented about forty-one thousand workers in 1980. Faced that year with rampant inflation and an employer determined not to let public sector wage settlements match those in an overheated provincial private sector, three thousand government employees, mainly corrections workers, struck for almost a month in a successful effort to get the government to concede better wages.[16] Corrections worker David William Potter recalled: "We went into the strike very much knowing that we were in a strike that was illegal. We more or less said, to hell with it. Illegal or not, we're not paid properly, not taken care of properly, so we're in it for the long haul. We defied it."[17] Potter and fellow guard Walter Watt noted that the strike yielded not only better wages for the corrections workers but also the appointment of a labour relations coordinator, to whom the guards could bring complaints about the ways in which prisons and juvenile homes were organized. The managers, they noted, often had no experience as guards and did a poor job of classifying prisoners, with grave consequences for the guards.

About half the AUPE members in 1980 were women, but the union was largely led and staffed by men in the early years. That was not the case with the United Nurses of Alberta (UNA), and the transformation of attitudes among nurses between 1960 and 1980 was even more dramatic than the transformation among the CSA/AUPE members. Despite their training and responsibilities, nurses, like many other women workers in 1960, were not regarded as either real workers or professionals.[18] Their wages were determined by their employers, though the Alberta Association of Registered Nurses (AARN), their sole organization, attempted to have an impact on nurses' pay and working conditions through its efforts to regulate membership in the profession. Despite such efforts, the wages of Alberta nurses lagged behind those in several other provinces.

Working conditions in the pre-union period were terrible. Medicine Hat nurse Barb Charles, a founding member of the UNA, recalls:

> You had to work thirteen shifts in a row to get a weekend off. There was no such thing as overtime. If you missed your break, you missed your break. Days off were few and far between. You would know

your schedule one week or two weeks ahead of time. If you wanted to plan going to a wedding or anything, it just didn't happen, because you didn't know when you were going to be working. So as we've come through and things that we've got, we've got overtime, we have scheduling twelve weeks in advance, stat holidays off, you get paid for your stats. It's amazing how it's changed. Maternity leave, pensions. Married women never used to be able to belong to the pension plan, you could only be single.[19]

Efforts to win better wages and working conditions for nurses began with baby steps. From 1964 to 1966, staff nurses' associations formed in various hospitals: by the end of 1966, fifty had received recognition from either a hospital or the Board of Industrial Relations. Within the AARN, the Provincial Staff Nurse Committee (PSNC) formed as a bargaining group and excluded nurse managers from its ambit. But the nurse managers' control over the provincial council of the AARN limited the PSNC's ability to act as a union. In June 1977, the nurses, who had decided that they needed a negotiating body independent of the AARN, formed the UNA, an independent trade union organization. Angry about low wages and understaffing, the nurses in seven urban hospitals undertook the first-ever strike of nurses in the province one month later. The government, making use of back-to-work provisions that had been added to the Labour Relations Code in 1960 (sections 112 and 113), ordered the 2,349 striking nurses back to work in four days, forcing binding arbitration.[20] Though nationwide wage controls were in effect from 1975 to 1978, the arbitrator gave an award that was slightly higher than the mandated wage-control maximum.[21]

The UNA's first full-scale negotiations with the hospitals in 1978 produced a contract that the nurses regarded as successful, but negotiations for a second contract stalled. In April 1980, the UNA struck at seventy-nine hospitals. "We are not Florence Nightingales," UNA president Marg Ethier told the media proudly. The days when nurses were akin to self-sacrificing missionaries rather than proud workers demanding humane working conditions and wages that recognized their education and responsibilities had passed. The trade union movement eagerly took up the nurses' cause, creating huge picket lines at all the hospitals. When the government ordered the six thousand striking nurses back to work after three days, the union challenged the order in court while resuming negotiations.[22] Faced with public opinion that sympathized with the nurses' grievances and with the threat that a militant UNA would resume the strike despite the back-to-work order, the government agreed to a 29.8 percent wage increase over two years, a large award even at a time of 10 percent annual inflation. It also agreed to better work schedules and a number of improvements in working conditions, along with a professional responsibility clause that gave nurses more power to demand better standards of care and increased staffing on hospital wards.[23]

Teachers, no less militant than nurses during the 1970s, learned that militancy paid off in better wages and working conditions despite the Alberta government's propensity to limit workers' efforts to achieve gains by invoking the egregious back-to-work clause. In the teachers' case, the government relied on the alleged "unreasonable hardship" that a strike imposed on third parties. There had been only one teachers'

MARG ETHIER, NURSING UNION MILITANT

Marg Ethier was an unlikely candidate to bring a measure of both feminism and union militancy to the nursing profession in Alberta. Born into a right-wing Baptist family in Nova Scotia's Annapolis Valley, she entered a hospital nursing program when she was seventeen. She worked in Nova Scotia and then in Flin Flon, Manitoba, where she married a miner, later moving to Winnipeg and eventually to Edmonton, where her husband had found work as a fireman. Continuing her nursing career, she became involved in the UNA in its earliest days and served as its president from 1980 to 1988. In her view, creating a separate union of working nurses was a crucial first step in advancing nurses' rights as workers. "We saw the Alberta Association of Registered Nurses as being mostly managers and academics who had no interest in the needs of the actual working-class people, which we were." She emphasized that nurses were fighting for themselves as workers every bit as much as they fought for their patients, and that the two struggles were closely related. Explaining the 1977 strike, she noted:

> We were really ticked off at work. Whenever you want to talk about the shortage of nurses, that was about the time they phased out the students. So we were working very short of nurses. Our wages were poor. You could hardly get your work done. I know everybody says nurses go on strike because they're concerned about the patients, but that's not really true. That's a secondary concern. If you don't have enough nurses, it's not good for the patients either. We could see that. When you're working as a nurse, that's a very difficult thing to see. You don't have enough bodies to go around. But mainly you're going for broke. You're doing everything you should be doing, and you still can't get your work done. Maybe people just about died, or you're missing stuff. So it's very frustrating to go home from work. So we're bargaining, and we figured with the more money, if we got more money there'd be more nurses so at least you could work better. I would say the first strike was more a concern of you're going on strike so you can get more money so you can give better patient care.

SOURCE: Interview with Marg Ethier, Edmonton, September 2003, ALHI.

strike in the province in the 1940s and four each in the 1950s and 1960s, none involving the large urban school boards. That changed in the 1970s, when nine strikes occurred, including one each by the Calgary and Edmonton public school teachers: the former involved 4,113 teachers and the latter, 1,978. The Calgary teachers struck again in 1980, this time with 4,644 teachers on strike. In each case, the government ordered the teachers back to work, fairly quickly in the 1971 Calgary and 1978 Edmonton strikes, but only after forty-one days in the Calgary strike of 1980.[24]

During this period, the Alberta Teachers' Association (ATA) had only cautious relations with the Alberta Federation of Labor (AFL). Since 1936, by legislation, all teachers in the province had to become members of the ATA, which set standards for their work, judged their competence, and bargained for them. Because of these sometimes contradictory roles, the ATA was cautious about the extent to which they wanted their organization identified as a trade union. Nonetheless, from 1968 to 1987, ATA chief executive officer Bernie Keeler, a socialist, did encourage ATA-AFL co-operation on public issues. Keeler had come to Edmonton to become the principal of Jasper Place High School in 1961 and served as ATA president in 1967–68.[25] But most ATA leaders were more conservative: for example, Halvar C. Johnson, the 1976–77 president, later became a Progressive Conservative cabinet minister, and K. Mac Kryzanowski, president from 1977 to 1982, was also quite visible at PC conventions.

In 1960, some of the representatives of municipal employees were also quite conservative. Gil Levine was hounded by Cold Warriors in the leadership of the

National Union of Public Employees (NUPE) because he had once been a card-carrying Communist and remained a committed socialist. Fortunately for him, one NUPE leader, Patrick Lenihan, also a former Communist, defended him from the establishment-oriented leaders. NUPE had been part of the Trades and Labour Congress (TLC) before the merger of the TLC and the Canadian Congress of Labour (CCL) in 1956. Its CCL counterpart was NUPSE, the National Union of Public Sector Employees. The merger of NUPE and NUPSE in 1963 produced the Canadian Union of Public Employees (CUPE), for which Levine became the founding research director.[26] By the 1970s, to Levine's delight, his union, and the Canadian union movement more generally, had moved beyond the business unionism of an earlier period and was actively involved in efforts to promote social and economic change in Canada. CUPE's national membership shot up from 80,000 in 1963 to 294,000 in 1983.[27] In Alberta, CUPE organized a broad array of municipal workers and non-ATA school employees, including social service workers in both the public and private sectors.

A colourful character in CUPE's early Alberta history was Fred Pyke, a wartime munitions plant worker who later took a job as a custodian for the London Board of Education while studying nights to become a priest. His union involvement caused him to decide that organizing workers rather than serving as a priest was his life's mission. Appointed a full-time Alberta representative for the union in the 1970s, he was labelled "Strike Pyke" by the right-wing weekly magazine *Alberta Report* when the magazine did a feature on him shortly after a strike by Royal Alexandra Hospital employees, the first CUPE strike in the province.

Ironically, his role in that strike was minimal, but the label stuck. Pyke was a great believer in strikes and received much publicity for his role in a number of strikes in the 1970s, such as those of hospital workers in Grande Prairie and Fort Saskatchewan. Years later, he defended the early resort to strikes in collective bargaining, noting, "The workers, I don't believe they've ever lost a strike. Because if you don't stand when you're pushed to the wall, and mark your place by letting the employer know they can only go so far, you're going to be pushed further the next time. You must stand at some point in time and defend what you believe are principles that should be supported. When workers will do that and stick together, they can accomplish a lot."[28]

That militant philosophy did not appeal to all CUPE locals in conservative Alberta. There was a longstanding feud between the leaders of the inside workers for the City of Edmonton (Local 52) and CUPE National over issues ranging from per capita dues to be given to the national office, to the quality of CUPE's training programs, to CUPE membership in the Canadian Labour Congress. In 1975, urged on by "Strike Pyke," the local had struck the city for two weeks to get an additional 1.5 percent increase in wages. Although the city capitulated, the increase was rolled back by the province because it violated the wage-and-price controls that the province had implemented at the request of the federal government. Some workers therefore thought the ten-day strike had been "useless," blaming their union for taking them out on strike rather than the provincial government for reversing the increase.[29]

In 1978, Local 52 broke away from CUPE altogether,

renaming itself the Civic Service Union. CSU 52, a true business union of the pre-1960 type, was determined to be independent from national and international unions and from involvement in political life. It was proud of the very low union dues that it assessed for its members.[30] The Edmonton inside workers were not alone among public service workers who decided not to join the larger public service unions. The University of Alberta's non-academic staff, who had long beeen members of a company union, were courted by several unions during the 1970s but decided in 1978 to turn the Non-Academic Staff Association into a certified union.[31]

Militancy among public employees in Alberta echoed the growing willingness of public sector workers across the country to resort to strikes, and within the province, employees of the federal government were among those who demonstrated the greatest militancy in the 1960s. Although federal employees lacked the legal right to strike before 1967, Alberta's inside postal workers participated in a national postal workers' strike in 1965, in which rank-and-file workers defied their association's leadership and won wage concessions from the federal government. This success emboldened the postal workers to create a union, the Canadian Union of Postal Workers, to replace an association that was little more than a company union. In 1967, about 120,000 other federal workers, who had also previously been represented only by company unions, created the Public Service Alliance of Canada. That same year, the federal government, faced with militant-sounding unions who demanded the same rights as other Canadian workers, granted its employees the right to strike in the *Public Service Staff Relations Act* while trying

AN ALBERTA CUPE PIONEER REMEMBERS

Frank McGregor had been a blacksmith in Scotland and continued in his trade when he came to Canada. He began working for the City of Edmonton in 1954 and became active in the Edmonton Civic Outside Employees union, which became Local 30 of CUPE in 1963. He was especially proud of the union's ability to find accommodation for injured members and to provide decent retirement pensions.

> I think back then we had about thirty-three hundred employees. Quite a lot did heavy hard work, and they would sustain injuries where they couldn't return to their former job. Between us and the city, we established a program where we'd try and find a job for these disabled — well, not disabled, but not able to return to their old job. There was one particular lady in the city, she was quite good and I had found quite a lot of jobs for these people. But the biggest problem was again the heads of these departments. I don't know if it was justifiable, but they said, "We've only got so many jobs. And if we can't get so-and-so to do the work that's required, we can't have her." Of course, our position was, perhaps you can adjust that position somewhat so that it can meet that condition. There were quite a few managers that was helpful. But then again there was quite a few that were not. They'd fight you tooth and nail. . . .
>
> At private blacksmiths' shops, of course, there was no pension. But when I came to the city, the city had a pension plan. It wasn't a great one, but it was a start. Then we had a coalition of unions that used to negotiate fringe benefits. That's all kinds of benefits. We determined that we could do better under the Alberta Local Authorities Pension Plan. . . . It reached a stage that we've got quite a good pension plan.

McGregor retired in 1990, and, looking back, he believed that Local 30 was stronger in the 1970s than in the late 1990s, as neo-liberalism reached into every corner of governance. "The city used to do most of its road work and all the curbs and gutters. That's all gone practically, that's all privatized. That has lost a lot of jobs for Local 30 employees."

SOURCE: Interview with Frank McGregor, Edmonton, n.d., ALHI.

to limit both negotiable issues and the right to strike. But the die had been cast, and federal civil servants clearly wanted to be seen as workers and to have wages and working conditions matching those that unionized private sector workers had been able to win as a result of organizing.[32]

Most public service members appreciated the benefits and services that the unions provided, but some did so only begrudgingly. Andre Van Schaik, a development control officer who was a member of CSU 52 in the late 1970s, complained that "as a supervisor, I always had the union against me when I was trying to discipline employees or change the way they operated." Yet this conservative supervisor did appreciate that the union had fought to get his position reclassified from zoning analyst to the better-paid development control officer position. He also admitted that the unions "are good at protecting employees that need protection from tyrant bosses, the old-style managers," though he clearly viewed himself as not being one of them:

> With the City of Edmonton, I think employees take it for granted that they get health coverage and they get sick days and they get short-term sick and long-term sick at fairly good percentage of wages as compared to private industry. With the city, you can earn up to six weeks vacation a year, which isn't something that's normal in private industry. So yes, there were a lot of benefits, but when you become a city employee you kind of take it for granted that that comes with the job. You don't really recognize or realize that that probably got there due to some unions and hard-working people in the past in those unions.[33]

ANTI-LABOUR LEGISLATION AND THE PRIVATE SECTOR

Privatization was always a threat for many government workers during the 1960s and 1970s. Alberta Government Telephone workers, for example, were concerned in the late 1970s about discussions within the Lougheed government about possibly privatizing the company. But while government revenues remained high and the attraction of getting short-term revenues from the sale of Crown corporations was therefore weak, except for ideological reasons, few major privatizations occurred in the province. Indeed, the Lougheed government, in carrying out its plan to expand the Alberta-based bourgeoisie within the North American energy economy, pursued some nationalizations and public-private investment partnerships. The government bought Pacific Western Airlines in 1974 when it appeared that the airline might go out of business, which would have had a negative impact on energy development in the north of the province. One year earlier, it created the Alberta Energy Company — in which it retained half the stocks — as the government's investment arm in energy developments, including Syncrude's oil sands project and the Suffield natural gas field.[34]

On the whole, then, it seems easy to explain why government workers proved defiant as the Social Credit and then Conservative governments passed anti-labour legislation. Their jobs were secure. Public demand for more and more services meant expanding government payrolls and only a marginal threat that wage gains and better working conditions would lead to massive layoffs. The government workers of the pre-1960 period, mainly people who had lived through the Great

Depression and often Social Credit devotees, made few demands for their fair share of the growing oil and gas wealth of Alberta. Their children and immigrants to the province, however, who were younger and not haunted by Depression memories, unionized and made use of their unions to better their lot.

How did the private sector workers fare during the energy boom, and how successful were unions in ensuring that these workers had collective representation? As the Alberta Federation of Labor recognized at the time, the government's anti-labour legislation had its greatest impact on the private sector, though some unions in that sector continued to thrive, their workers demonstrating as much defiance of government and employer intimidation as state workers. But anti-labour legislation and enforcement of legislation continued to limit union successes in collective bargaining and in campaigns for better safety legislation and better enforcement of that legislation.

In 1960, the Manning government amended the *Alberta Labour Act* in a major way for the first time since 1948. All the changes that were implemented met with disapproval from the labour movement, which viewed Manning's intent as the weakening of labour and the strengthening of capital in Alberta, especially but not exclusively in the prized energy sector. The amendments included a prohibition on information picketing outside a workplace: any union that defied this prohibition could not be certified as a bargaining unit even if it signed up every eligible worker. The government gave the Board of Industrial Relations the power to remove from union membership all those whom it considered to be supervisors or employees with a confidential relationship to management. Another amendment provided a sweeping ban against professional unions, specifying architectural, engineering, medical, dental, and legal professionals as groups who could not have a union bargain for them. Solidarity among those workers who were allowed to unionize was largely forbidden. Both secondary picketing and job action in solidarity with striking workers in workplaces where scabs had replaced striking workers were forbidden. Finally, the legislation gave the minister the right to declare a strike-ending emergency if she or he felt that the strike potentially harmed life or property.[35] The view that the rights of property were greater than those of workers was hardly surprising given the close association of the Manning government with the large energy companies.

Documenting the problems created for workers by this legislation and lobbying for more worker-friendly legislation became a key goal of the Alberta Federation of Labour (AFL) throughout the last eleven years of the Social Credit regime and the early years of the Lougheed regime. But there were few successes.

The biggest problem for the unions remained the willingness of the government, via the Board of Industrial Relations, to sanction company unions. AFL efforts to get the government to include a definition of unions in the *Alberta Labour Act* that would exclude company-based associations failed.[36] When the AFL provided its annual brief to Premier Manning and his cabinet in 1960, they charged that the section of the act that forbade employer interference in workers' decisions to choose a bargaining unit "has become a big joke." Though the AFL had documented many cases of such interference, there had never been a penalty assessed against an offending employer.[37]

The AFL's 1960 brief portrayed a government with no interest whatsoever in defending workers' interests. The government, it noted, had failed to regulate work camps, and poor conditions dominated these workplaces. Workers often had to bring their own bedding and then slept in cramped quarters where there were few toilets, and men drank water from "unsanitary water containers, using a common drink dipper." There were some reasonable safety regulations on the books, but the Workmen's Compensation Board hired few inspectors to enforce them. "The loss of life in trenching and excavation work has been alarming in the past few years," said the brief. "In each case, this loss of life has been caused by the lack of enforcement of Safety Regulations, and the Board is not adequately staffed to provide inspectors."[38]

To keep out real unions that might try to change this state of affairs, the government gave active support to company unions, particularly in the petroleum industry. In 1968, AFL president Roy Jamha estimated that there were twenty to twenty-five thousand workers in company unions in Alberta.[39] Jack Hampson, an earlier president of the AFL, summed up the government's attitudes and actions at a Canadian Labour Congress conference on labour legislation in 1963:

> Alberta has bad Labour legislation, and it is administered by a bad government. This is so, because it is the belief of Social Credit that the Trade Union movement is an unnecessary burden on the shoulders of working people. Their view is that our economic problems would be resolved much easier by the Social Credit monetary theory — something which our Federation cannot accept.

The Board of Industrial Relations, chaired by the Deputy Minister of Labour, administers the Labour Act, and sets arbitrary rules to make life difficult for unions.

The Labour Act and the behaviour of the Board (exclusive of Labour's two representatives) are doing just what the government wants done. It has brought the growth of the labour movement to an almost complete halt. They are not allowing this to alienate the affections of the working man, however. Certifications for bargaining rights are available to company unions without membership, charter, constitutions, aims and objectives, and these ineffective organizations are growing at an alarming rate. For example, the petroleum industry, by far the largest industry in the province and the darling of Social Credit, is almost completely represented by company unions. As an example — of the eight largest oil refineries in the province, the six largest have company unions.[40]

Premier Manning's close friendships with oilmen made it particularly imperative to foreclose the option of real unions representing energy workers, and the installation of company unions seemed to offer that foreclosure. Reg Basken, a later president of the AFL, organized oil rig workers for the Oil, Chemical and Atomic Workers' Union, whose Canadian section formed the Energy and Chemical Workers Union in 1980. But when Basken had signed up a majority, the companies simply shut the rigs down for a few days to scare the workers off from a vote in favour of unionism. This form of intimidation constituted a legal labour relations practice in Alberta.[41] The companies also got away with barring unions other than the company

FIG 6-7 Oil, Chemical and Atomic workers on strike against Texaco, July 1976, Edmonton. Provincial Archives of Alberta, J2554-1.

union from talking to workers on company property, which is where most of them lived.[42]

It was not only petroleum workers, however, who suffered from the government's antipathy to unions. The Beverage Dispensers' Union, for example, was frustrated in its continuing efforts to get contracts for Edmonton hotel employees after the debacle of 1954. Organizer Doug Tomlinson turned the union's efforts to organization of the women who worked at private clubs. While they were often happy to join unions, their employers made good use of the province's labour legislation to stymie their efforts. Tomlinson's union had greater success in the northern oil sands camps:

I became an organizer when I was president too. . . . We have a section of our union in the north — in those big camps. We've got three or four thousand members up there now in Syncrude and GCOS [Great Canadian Oil Sands] and all those new camps that are opening up. The entire cooking staff and the camp attendants are members of our union. And wages are very good, they do very, very good. They get good pay. We had to fight like hell to get women to work as cooks. Making the beds up, forty units. We had an awful time getting the women in there. They finally got in and they did a good job. They were good union people. They come to union meetings.[43]

WHAT MANAGEMENT WOULD CONCEDE TO KEEP UNIONS OUT

While company unions often lacked the experience and the will to face down energy company management on issues of benefits and occupational safety, they did sometimes extract important concessions because of management's desire to avoid strikes in periods of labour shortages. The Great Canadian Oil Sands Employees Association, organized in 1967, was a standard company union. In 1973, it became the Fort McMurray Independent Oil Workers and successfully sought affiliation with the Canadian Labour Congress. It only finally joined forces with the Energy and Chemical Workers Union (ECWU) in 1987.

ECWU leader Reg Basken's description of the contracts negotiated by the Independent Oil Workers at Suncor indicates the surprising number of worker-friendly concessions that a company union in a tight labour market might sometimes win from an employer desperate to keep out real unions. His description also suggests a degree of pragmatism that some might view as conservatism on the part of certain senior union leaders: Basken clearly felt that the Independent Oil Workers went too far in getting good things for their members to the point where their contracts threatened the viability of Suncor's operations. Speaking of a discussion with a senior executive of Suncor, Basken recalls the lengths to which one company went to keep unions out:

I wasn't very polite to the McMurray Independent Oil Workers. Not at all. I said, they don't have the concept of what a settlement is. You guys have given so many things to keep the union out over the years, you've given crazy things. Do you know that you guys' insanity went to the extent that if a job becomes redundant in your mine up there, and somebody wants to stay where they were at their rate of pay, they can do that. But if they choose not to do that, they drop down to a labourer's rate. But if they choose not to drop down to a labourer's rate, they stay at their trades rate in a redundant job and play cribbage. Do you know that it's in your collective agreement? You've got the kind of stupidity that you've got to get rid of. But you offered them so many things to keep them out of the union, and they're far higher paid than any other oil worker in Canada. They've got far better conditions than any other oil worker in Canada. . . . We got the essence of an agreement worked out, which took away an awful lot of those crazy fringer ideas that were in there that were not in any other collective agreement, and wouldn't have been there if their union had been there. Because we wouldn't have been stupid enough to ask for them. No company would've given them to us. But they gave them to them to keep the union out. And they were successful for damn near twenty years. But their costs were gone through the roof. The mine at that point was in doubt as to whether it would continue.

SOURCE: Interview with Reg Basken, Edmonton, September 2003, ALHI.

Government complicity with private employers in crushing efforts to unionize had a particularly chilling effect on service workers, a rising percentage of the labour force, mainly women and mainly low-income workers. Retail workers dispersed among the small franchises at the growing number of malls and often hired only part time were difficult to organize anywhere in the country, but in Alberta, the labour legislation made their organization almost impossible. On the surface, it was easier to organize nursing homes, where relatively large numbers of workers were hired and able to find time to collectively discuss their oppression by the employer. The Parkland Nursing Home employees in Edmonton joined CUPE, and sixty of them, mainly women, went on strike in March 1977 after their employer refused to raise their wages from the provincial minimum wage to the same level that Parkland workers elsewhere in the province received. Striking picketers faced police harassment, and the company blacklisted key union activists, vowing never to reinstate them. As the strike dragged on, Warren Caragata wrote:

Early in the dispute, when picketing was making recruitment of strike-breakers difficult, the Alberta Supreme Court granted Parkland an injunction which prohibited workers on the line from singing, placed tight limits on the number of people who could be on the line and then went one step further — forcing the much-reduced picket line to form across the street from the nursing home, in front of a row of apartments. The provincial government has funnelled several thousand dollars a day in subsidies to the privately-owned home and suggested that the workers agree to a blacklist, all the while claiming neutrality.[44]

Similarly, in a story that highlights why union efforts to organize and to win better wages and working conditions for their members received negligible and usually rather negative media coverage, Caragata recounts the failed efforts of the workers at CJOC television in Lethbridge to unionize. The station was owned by Southam, the national media giant that at the time also owned the two dominant newspapers in the province, the *Edmonton Journal* and the *Calgary Herald*. Southam was determined to prevent unionization of any of its employees and, with no laws in place to prevent the hiring of scabs and no unwelcome media scrutiny of its behaviour, the station simply dismissed its striking workers.[45]

Here is a typical story of how a union's efforts were forestalled in Alberta, as explained by Laurier Payment, of Amalgamated Transit Union #569 regarding the Diamond Bus Lines workers of Jasper Place, a separate town before it amalgamated with Edmonton in 1963. In January 1961, the union hired Payment to organize the workers. In February, two workers whom he had signed were fired. But the union signed enough workers to get a board certification that month, and it put forward its proposals to the employer. The employer responded by firing two more workers and largely refusing to negotiate. In March, the union called on the board for conciliation, and the conciliators' report was received in April. While the union accepted the report, management rejected it and fired six more workers. The conciliators recommended improvements in wages and salaries in June, but by the time the supervised vote was held in August, the workers, many of whom had been hired to replace union-supporting workers, voted it down in an atmosphere of continuing management intimidation. In short, the *Alberta Labour Act*'s provisions had prevented the union from striking early on as it became clear that management was truculent, with the result that six months later, when the union might have been in a position to strike, it had lost most of its members to firings or intimidation.[46]

Even workers who belonged to unions often felt the sting of the province's anti-labour administration of labour laws. In 1962, for example, the Board of Industrial Relations exempted "inexperienced employees" from the minimum wage, which, as noted by the Alberta Federation of Labour (AFL), "in effect, means all the employees engaged in the Garment Industry."[47] Meanwhile, the Workers Compensation Board, adding to the hardships workers endured because they were injured on the job in a province that did little to prevent worker injury, was pushing injured workers "to find lighter work, which in many industries is nonexistent." The United Brotherhood of Carpenters and Joiners of America in Calgary called on the AFL in 1968 to press the government to provide workers with full benefits until they were "physically and mentally able to resume the regular work in which they were engaged at the time of injury."[48]

Though the Lougheed government made some changes to labour legislation in the province, on the whole, the anti-labour attitude persisted both in the legislation itself and in its enforcement. The *Labour Act* was revised by the new government in 1973, but the *Labour Gazette*, the AFL newspaper at the time, complained that "we have simply a new arrangement of an old composition."[49]

At the 1973 AFL convention, the United Association of Plumbers and Pipefitters Local 488 observed that construction companies were establishing spin-off companies to avoid having to abide by collective agreements. The AFL passed a resolution calling on the Board of Industrial Relations to have the authority to revoke a company's licence "when it is proved that a spin-off company is not living up to the terms of a collective agreement that is in effect with the parent company."[50] But the government rarely made changes in response to representations from the AFL, and in this case, their dismissal of union concerns had dire consequences for the construction unions, though the impacts would only become severe in the depressed 1980s. Indeed, many private sector unions, and especially the construction unions, made great gains in the 1960s and 1970s, despite the anti-labour legislation and political environment that would prove fatal to many unions when the boom finally ended in the early 1980s.

ACHIEVEMENTS AND DELUSIONS

Throughout much of the postwar period, unprecedented economic growth along with expanded social programs — though modest by European standards — plus Keynesian economic policies made it appear that the unbridled capitalism of the Great Depression was a thing of the past for Canada.[51] Following Keynes's economic prescriptions, governments, at least in theory, now increased their spending, even if it meant accumulating large short-term debts, to counter the economic cycle when private investment began to decline. Such government spending often had little impact on the poor: the large pockets of poverty in both the cities and the countryside demonstrated that the economic pie was still not shared equally. But in Alberta, in particular, many young workers, especially males, believed that they had it made. They could make big money in the energy sector even with little education and could save up to buy their own small business, a house, and a truck or two before they turned thirty. Whether or not they were unionized, labour shortages would guarantee them good wages and — provided that they did not die on the job or lose their ability to do hard, physical labour — the world was their oyster. Karl Marx might have thought that workers had nothing to lose but their chains, but these workers thought otherwise and had dreams of becoming capitalists, if only small capitalists. The end of the boom, when it arrived in the early 1980s, came as a huge shock: these workers were largely oblivious to the fact that uncontrolled capitalist booms are followed by busts and that weakly developed state apparatuses are in no position to step in to help the victims when the private economy inevitably cycles downwards.

One couldn't blame these workers — most of whom voted for right-wing parties that were in bed with their employers and who saved little of what they earned to tide them over in hard times — for being surprised since the evidence before their eyes was that Alberta had become the land of milk and honey. As this chapter's opening quotation from Jack Hubler demonstrates, the construction unions signed excellent agreements with the major commercial and residential developers in 1969 with regard to wages and even working conditions. In 1975, determined not to be sidelined by non-union contractors, the construction unions negotiated no-strike, no-lockout agreements with companies like Syncrude who were developing the tar sands of northern Alberta.[52] While these agreements

guaranteed the companies that there would be no wildcat strikes over working conditions or the treatment of individual workers, they ensured the construction workers excellent wages. The average hourly wage for a construction worker shot up from $9.35 an hour in 1975 to $13.75 in 1977, double the average industrial wage in the province.[53] The private oil companies that were part of the Syncrude consortium had negotiated "cost-plus" financing arrangements with their government partners that allowed them to pay generous wages; continuous production, for a time, became more important than keeping wages low.

Although the construction workers in Alberta negotiated provincial labour agreements, many industrial workers were members of national or international unions that bargained nationally. Alberta's workers who were involved in national contracts were sometimes more militant in their demands than their counterparts elsewhere because they compared themselves with workers in the energy and construction sectors in the province. So, for example, in 1974, Edmonton packing-house workers rejected a proposed agreement that workers in other provinces accepted. That forced a return to negotiations and resulted in a better national offer.[54]

Union activists did not take for granted the gains that they had made because of their participation in union struggles. Betty and Gerald Franklin, who moved to Hinton in 1956 and worked at the pulp mill during the 1960s and 1970s, both congratulated their unions for tangible improvements in their lives. Betty worked in the office and was a member of the Office and Professional Employees International Union. "If it hadn't been for the union, we wouldn't have had the pensions that we have. As I said, when the union got organized in the office, our wages went up substantially. If I can recall, I think mine went up about two hundred dollars a month, and thirty-five years ago, that was a lot of money."[55]

Gerald Franklin worked for the mill for thirty-five years, first as one of the construction workers who built the mill, then as a worker in the wood room and the machine room, and finally as a welder. He was active in the United Paperworkers International Union, which later became the Canadian Paperworkers Union, now part of the Communications, Energy and Paperworkers Union. "The union helped tame them down quite a bit; otherwise, they would've been hell on earth. It was bad enough as it was, at certain things. Like when I tell people now that I brought my lunch pail home lots of times the same way I took it in because I had no time to eat it, they don't want to believe me. If it hadn't have been for unions, we wouldn't have had no pensions, no overtime, quite a few benefits."[56] Franklin talked about how dangerous the jobs were and the efforts the union made to promote job safety. In the wood room, where he worked for six years ensuring that logs were level before going onto the chipper, a machine with sharp blades that chewed the logs into chips, there was a constant danger of falling logs. But in the 1960s and 1970s, the Hinton mill was a fully unionized outfit, from the International Woodworkers of America loggers who felled the trees and the truck-drivers who brought them to the mill, to the various mill workers.

Another union that gained many concessions for its members was the Brewery Workers Union. Like the paperworkers and chemical workers, the brewery workers broke from their former American-controlled union in the early 1970s and formed the Canadian Union of United Brewery, Flour, Cereal, Soft Drink and Distillery Workers. But during the 1960s and 1970s, the brewery workers were often on strike or locked out by management. In the early 1970s, Bill Flookes started working for Calgary Brewing and Malting (later bought out by Carling O'Keefe and then Molson's before being shut down in 1994) and became active in the union. Flookes recounted the militancy of his fellow workers in 1979 when the breweries in the province joined to lock out their workers in an effort to reduce the workers' demands:

At the time, the Labatts plant had a paid half-hour lunch, and we didn't have one at our plant. So you can imagine, this is seven and a half months. So we took it back to our members and our members said, we want the half-hour lunch. We got it. After seven and a half months, they were still willing to say, "We're not going back." I can remember afterwards walking around the plant talking to people and people saying, "Ha, it was worth it." Especially at lunchtime. It was an epic battle. I remember going around trying to find money so we could pay our picketers so they could eat. My first son was born during the dispute. It was hard, but for a lot of the people who went through it, it was probably one of the funny moments of their lives. . . . One fellow who celebrated his fiftieth year of working for the plant, for the old Calgary Brewing and Malting, on the picket line — I can remember having a big party for him at the strike headquarters.[57]

FROM THE BUSH TO THE TAR SANDS

Jim Cardinal, an International Brotherhood of Electrical Workers (IBEW) activist, typifies the rags to semi-riches stories of unionized skilled workers in the tar sands in the late 1970s. Like many Métis in Alberta, he grew up in a family marginalized by racism. He described his early life and his experiences as an IBEW member on strike at a relatively rare strike at Suncor in 1978:

I was born in Lac La Biche, back in 1951, and grew up in Owl River. A type of farm, but not really — almost in a homesteader-type style of living. My dad did a lot of trapping and fishing, and that's how we survived. With sometimes work here and there for farmers and stuff, that's the only type of work we had around Lac La Biche. There was twelve of us. The older ones, when I came of age they'd already moved on. By the time I grew up, there was eight left at home. . . .

[We were] very isolated. My parents went into town once a month to shop. Other than that, we ate wild meat and what we grew in the garden. . . . I didn't know how to speak a word of English when I went to school. I had to learn the yes and the no, and how to ask when I wanted to go to the washroom. Nowadays we say washroom; back then it was just the word *pee*. So, "May I go to pee?" I did speak Cree. . . .

[I worked on our] trap line. We had muskrat, beavers, and all that. It was my job, from the age of twelve and up, to maintain that area after school. It was like a job for me. But the money didn't come to me, it went to the family. It went for food and all that stuff. Many times, Dad would be gone two or three months at a time. He would leave in the fall and not come back 'til Christmas. That was part of life. He'd be gone, and I was the oldest boy. I did all the work and the trapping and looked after the animals. Not bragging or anything, but that's the way it was. That's what I had to do. Mom was a very hardworking woman. She had to do all the washing, and they had to haul all the water for that. Any hot water, you'd have a wood stove to boil it. We were busy.

Dad would work for local farmers. After I was about fifteen, then Dad and I would both go. That's where I discovered peas. I never had peas in my life until I worked for one farmer. . . .

In 1978, we had a six-week strike. They locked the gates and then the next morning when the buses came they couldn't get through. Then they wanted to cut the locks off. A bunch of us who were there wouldn't let them do that. The buses are waiting, and they're getting rocked and they're ready to be tipped over. Just to talk about a bit of '78, I was carrying a bat and walking back and forth, throwing my ball up in the air and hitting it and fetching it myself. During the strike, I got a letter from Suncor that they were going to sue me for $2 million for carrying a bat on a picket line. Some things sometimes you destroy. I ripped it up and said, "Here's what I think of your $2 million." I wish I'd have kept it; it would've been beautiful history to be able to show that.

SOURCE: Interview with Jim Cardinal, Fort McMurray, 2005, ALHI.

FIG 6-9 Jim Cardinal. Courtesy of the Alberta Federation of Labour.

The long-established United Garment Workers local at GWG in Edmonton also saw improvements. According to long-time union president Anne Ozipko, she and her associates built on the successes of her predecessor, Ann Baranyk:

> I'm not sure exactly what year the company gave us benefits, and they were benefits we didn't have to contribute to. We got long-term disability. The sick benefit didn't change, but the employees weren't contributing now, it's all paid by the company. There's a dental plan now, but the employees contribute 20 percent. The health care, when Anne Baranyk was there they were paying half. Now the employee was paying 40 percent and the company was paying the rest. Then later we got a pension, which there wasn't any [before].[58]

While unions whose members dealt with a single employer often did not manage their own pensions, construction unions, whose members worked for a variety of employers, assessed their members for pensions and managed those pensions themselves, though usually contracting with professional pension managers. Wally Shaw, a mason, noted:

> I believe our pensions and our health and welfare are probably the thing I would be most proud of. We now have a pension plan. The younger people are going to be fairly well looked after and live decently, compared to the older ones. Our older members had to retire with $300 or $400 pensions. Our younger people are going to be much better off. Our health and welfare helps families that need to be helped. Not as much as we would like maybe, but we're helping them.[59]

THE SAFETY ISSUE

Better enforcement of existing safety legislation and the right of workers to refuse unsafe work became major issues for the Alberta Federation of Labour and its member unions in the 1960s and 1970s, as it did for labour throughout North America.[60] Worker deaths were not uncommon in Canada but the deaths in March 1960 of five immigrant Italian construction workers who were building water mains under the Don River at Hoggs Hollow, now an area within Toronto, served as a catalyst to lobby for more government inspectors for workplaces. Unsafe company practices, speed-ups, and poor training of workers all played a role in the Toronto-area tragedy. As noted earlier, even before that tragedy, the Alberta Federation of Labour had called on the provincial government to increase the number of inspectors for Alberta worksites so that labour laws regarding safety would not be as regularly flouted. Despite these efforts, though, as industrial relations professor Bob Barnetson concludes, "Canadian inspectors continue to focus on persuasion, rather than coercion."[61]

Both Social Crediters and the Conservatives ignored such requests, but in 1973, the Lougheed government, following the lead of other provinces, passed the *Occupational Health and Safety Act*, which gave workers the right to know about occupational health hazards, the right to participate with management in Joint Health and Safety (JHS) committees meant to limit and correct workplace risks, and the right to refuse unsafe work. This proved mainly of benefit to unionized workers, whose representatives often demanded information from management, advertised dangers at their worksite to fellow workers, and encouraged union leaders to make workplace issues fundamental in collective bargaining. This "internal responsibility system" was implemented at a time "when the influence of labour was near its peak and the standard employment relationship was widespread." [62] Its weakness lay particularly in the lack of protection it provided for workers in non-union environments and in the "careless worker" narrative that it implied: worker injury was seen to be the result of an individual worker's ignorance and sloppiness rather than how management organized the labour process.

Studies in Ontario have demonstrated that a minority of workers know their workplace safety rights, and even when they do, few are willing to protest unsafe workplaces. Fear of losing their jobs results in very few workers invoking their right to refuse unsafe work. In any case, there are few rules governing exposure limits for chemicals, and workers are rarely in a position to be able to determine whether substances in the workplace are toxic. The establishment of JHS committees, though supported by trade unions as a means of ensuring worker input, "delegitimizes discussion that occurs elsewhere, such as in a union hall or on the shop floor." [63] Management power is only limited by a JHS when it is dealing with a powerful union. On the whole, the new occupational health framework did not prove to be an adequate substitute for what labour wanted: clear rules for all workplaces about necessary steps that must be taken to reduce workplace dangers to a minimum and tough inspection by a well-staffed inspectorate.

In unionized workplaces, however, improvements did occur. Most of the one thousand to twelve hundred workers at Celanese in the 1960s were Oil, Chemical and Atomic Workers (OCAW) members, and their leaders

were particularly committed to emphasizing labour safety in their dealings with both management and government. Willa Gorman, a union activist who began working in the plant in 1965 in the fibres area, noted:

> We worked with chemicals with absolutely no safety as we know it now. . . . The union got involved, and the safety was really brought up much more and improved over the years, through total knowledge and union involvement both. It increased the safety and the health of the workers. We talk about unions wanting money all the time; that wasn't always the case. Often it was a safety or health issue that we would discuss for a long time to get a resolution for. [64]

FIG 6-10 Working at Celanese. Provincial Archives of Alberta, PA1951-2.

MEAT-PACKING AND "ACCIDENTS"

The pace of work was a significant contributor to workplace mis-adventures for which the word "accident" seems a misnomer since it implies that an event is unavoidable. Indeed, most unfortunate events in the workplace *are* avoidable if the workplace is organized according to the principle that a worker's life and health are more important than potential profits for the employer. Meat-packing worker Vicky Beauchamp's story of her accident at Swift demonstrates that workers are forced to take unnecessary risks at work and that even when their health is compromised as a result, they often have few options but to resume the same work with little thought to the likely consequence for their long-term health:

> There was a gentleman by the name of Joe Farrell, bless his soul, he's passed on. He'd turn up the machine, and he'd really run it quickly. You had rejects coming and leakers, so you'd throw them here and there. You're trying to package this; where normally two people did it, I was doing it by myself. That day, I turn around and when this happened, I went to pile the boxes twelve to a case. So there was two boxes, which was twenty-four. I had four boxes by this time. I took two and put two in a pallet. Swung around to put two, and my table was full of wieners, and that was it. My back just jarred. I couldn't get up, I couldn't do anything.

All Joe said was, "If you can't do your job, go home." So they carried me out. . . . With their arms they made a bench and carried me out to the nurse's office. They took me to the Royal Alex, and I was off with back strain, as they said, no real injury. But eventually I was let go from the plant. This happened in April, and by the end of June I had no job. So I left, and as a result of that today I still suffer with major back problems. Somehow they didn't seem to find it at the time, but it continually plagued me. I was young, unmarried. Therefore, what does a young person do? You try to get back into the workforce as best you could. You don't want to go on welfare. . . . I tried numerous places to get employment. Although my qualifications were fairly good — I finished high school — as soon as they found out I had a back injury, oh dear. I guess we will get hold of you if need be. So you knew you were at risk, it didn't matter what employment you went into. So while Swift's packing plant was on strike, and Canada Packers and Burns, I ventured out to Gainers, because they had not been on strike. They were separate negotiations. I had applied there, thinking if these were on strike, I would go there and get back into whatever I knew to do best. Which was the meat-packing industry, which was labour intensive.

SOURCE: Interview with Vicky Beauchamp, Edmonton, 1998, ALHI.

Sometimes, on-the-job action was required to force management to accept workers' rights to refuse unsafe work. Noel Lapierre, chief shop steward for the Canadian Paperworkers Union in Hinton, gave an example that demonstrates why workers without a union rarely took advantage of their legal right to refuse unsafe work:

In 1980, twenty-six of my fellow workers lost their jobs because they refused to work in a terrible snowstorm. When I learned about it, about 2:00 p.m., I . . . called on the shop stewards from each camp for an assembly that evening. Next day, no one worked in the woods. We made it a sit-down day so that the twenty-six guys could get their jobs back. We won after the one day off work.

Lapierre was hit by a tree as he was cutting down trees in 1976 and ended up in the hospital for four and a half months with a broken back. He was off work for over thirteen months. He had also seen several fellow workers in the woods killed by falling trees.[65]

Wally Land was a coal-mine electrician in Grande Cache in the 1970s who discovered the lack of management consideration for worker safety:

There was one instance where it was a coal-mine pillar retreat method underground. They put pieces of wood in the sides of the entryways, called lagging, to protect the rib from sloughing in and blocking the road. A guy was walking into work one day and the rib sloughed in and knocked him down and killed him. It's not something you could ever foresee or plan for. More lagging in the rib probably would've saved his life. But that's not what coal mines do. They're in the business of getting the coal out, not taking the wood in.

Land described how he became politicized, beginning with an event that occurred while he was at NAIT in 1980 taking the course for the fourth year of his apprenticeship:

The six o'clock news came on after school one day. Four guys of my crew were on the news, dead. The roof caved in and killed them. . . . It really impacts you. . . . [I became] a little bit disheartened with the management of the mine, because they really didn't put a whole lot of effort into health and safety. So I became a shit disturber and a troublemaker. That ultimately ended up costing me my job at the mine. I moved to Hinton and got on with the pulp mill, and got a job with health and safety. Then it all kinda started to make sense. In some cases, underground coal mining is like a macho job. If you whine about health and safety issues, it just makes your working life a little more difficult, possibly. But guys die because other people don't stand up and say, "Hey that's wrong." I decided to stand up.[66]

LABOUR AND POLITICS

In the face of anti-labour legislation that limited the growth and effectiveness of the labour movement and placed workers' lives in danger, the traditional left wing within Alberta labour was enthusiastic about the national effort to launch the New Party, which would unite labour and liberally minded people.[67] In common with their national leadership, the Alberta wings of the Oil, Chemical and Atomic Workers (OCAW), the United Packinghouse Workers of America, and the United Steelworkers of America were active in efforts to organize the New Democratic Party (NDP),

the idea of watering down the Alberta CCF's socialist emphasis on public ownership of industry in order to attract supporters of reform of the private enterprise system. Although many of the old CCFers joined the NDP, they did not like what they viewed as its domination by trade unions and reformist, non-socialist ideology. They created the Woodsworth-Irvine Socialist Fellowship to promote socialist ideas outside the NDP framework in the hope of pressuring the NDP to readopt the socialist thrust of the Regina Manifesto. In practice, though, the national CCF had significantly modified the Regina Manifesto at its 1956 convention, making its peace with free-enterprise capitalism and calling for regulation of big corporations rather than state ownership and for an emphasis on social programs rather than public operation of the economy.[70]

When the Alberta NDP held its founding convention in Edmonton in January 1962, there were 172 labour delegates among the 379 registered delegates. Later that year, at the AFL convention, a resolution passed that urged all local unions to affiliate with the NDP and that encouraged all union members to join NDP clubs (the predecessors to formal constituency organizations for the party) and to "establish and maintain Political Action Committees to better enable local unions and Labour Councils to give full support to the New Democratic Party and the forthcoming election campaign."[71] Affiliating locals gave the NDP five cents per member per month, a figure that would increase over time. By 1967, six thousand unionists were affiliated with the NDP, but participation did not necessarily follow affiliation. During the NDP's first five years of existence in Alberta, no affiliated union sent any resolutions to provincial conventions.[72]

whose founding national convention was held in Ottawa in August 1961.[68] Locals of the first two of these unions, along with the Lethbridge District and Labour Council, called on the Alberta Federation of Labour at the provincial convention in October 1960 to support the New Party effort. But the resolution did not come to a vote because seven delegates, beginning with an International Brotherhood of Electrical Workers representative, indicated that their unions wanted to remain non-partisan.[69] While the NDP looked too left-wing to some unions, especially craft unions, it looked too right-wing to some of the staunch CCFers, who disliked

At the party's first convention, Neil Reimer, Canadian director of OCAW, was named party president. Grant Notley, a twenty-two-year-old CCF activist who had done much of the organizing of New Party clubs before the NDP's official founding, was named provincial secretary. In 1963, Reimer defeated school teacher Ivor Dent, later mayor of Edmonton, to become the first leader of the Alberta New Democrats. He had no sooner become leader when the party was propelled into its first provincial election. While it won no seats and only 8 percent of the provincial vote, that was twice what the CCF had managed in the 1959 provincial election. In 1965, Reimer came within ninety votes of winning a by-election in the heavily unionized Edson seat. The following year, NDP candidate Garth Turcott, aided by the votes of retired miners, won a by-election in Pincher Creek-Crowsnest.

Reimer and Turcott unleashed a relentless attack on the integrity of the members of the Manning Social Credit government, which Reimer regarded as a dictatorship masked as a democracy. While Reimer publicly supported all the policies proposed by the Alberta Federation of Labour, his emphasis was on the authoritarian and corrupt character of the Social Credit administration, whose veneer of religious rectitude had generally spared it from close scrutiny. Manning responded by attempting to frame the provincial election in 1967 as a clear choice between Social Credit free enterprise and NDP socialism. The voters doubled NDP support to 16 percent, but no New Democrat was elected, not even Turcott. While Manning won another large majority, the key outcome of the election was the vast increase in Progressive Conservative support. Many Albertans, it seems, accepted

the NDP message that change was needed in Alberta but preferred the conservative change offered by the Tories' new leader, Peter Lougheed, to Reimer's social-democratic alternative.[73]

The early Alberta NDP made the Saskatchewan CCF administration, which ran that province from 1944 to 1964, its model in terms of social programs and labour legislation. Reimer left the provincial NDP leadership in 1968 and was replaced by Notley, who, through intensive campaigning, was elected as MLA for Spirit River-Fairview in 1971. But the growth in Progressive Conservative support that year was at the expense of not only the Social Credit government that the Conservatives defeated but also the NDP, whose vote fell to 11 percent. A province-wide survey showed that only 8 percent of voters claimed to have voted NDP in 1971; the survey found that the figure rose only to 15 percent for trade unionists. Yet 66 percent of the unionists indicated that the party that best represented the interests of trade unionists was the NDP, causing one analyst to conclude that "labour has been seduced by high wages and the prospects of continued prosperity."[74]

Throughout the 1970s, with oil prices rising, especially after OPEC began raising oil prices dramatically in the wake of the Arab-Israeli war of 1973, the NDP was simply unable to win additional seats despite Notley's effective performance in the legislature as the voice of workers, farmers, and small-business people who lived with the consequences of the uneven distribution of the gains made from a hot energy economy. Inflation, high urban rents, and insufficient rental units left many Albertans on the outside of the great Alberta economic barbecue. But the passivity that thirty-six years of one-party government under Social Credit had

CONSERVATIVES VERSUS SOCIAL DEMOCRATS

While many of the elected leaders of the labour movement after the merger of the Alberta Federation of Labour (AFL) and the Canadian Congress of Labour (CCL) in 1956 were socialists from the old CCL, a number of the conservatives from the pre-merger AFL remained active in the 1960s. Frank Bodie, a Calgary Transit Union member, was president of the AFL in 1960 and became the union's secretary-treasurer the following year. He remained in that position until 1968, when he became a Northwest Territories government industrial relations officer. Eugene Mitchell, who succeeded him as secretary-treasurer, had cut his union teeth in the 1950s, when he was a process operator at a chemical plant in Medicine Hat called Northwest Nitro Chemicals, and he battled employer opposition in an effort to win recognition for the Oil, Chemical and Atomic Workers (OCAW) to replace the company union. He was not impressed with his predecessor's attitude to either the NDP or Social Credit:

> Bodie never took a very active role politically. Kind of dragged his feet. In fact, very close to Ernest Manning and the Social Credit. I recall one year we were making a presentation to the government. We went down there every year. Oh, cap in hand, you'd better believe it. Ernest Manning never seemed to like us. It was after we'd made our presentation to the cabinet. I know Frank Bodie stayed behind and was having a chitchat with the premier. It happened that our next executive meeting was coming up right after that. Bodie came in with a proposal to the executive board that the federation co-sponsor, along with the premier, bringing Billy Graham into the province for a tour of Alberta. I know at that time I made a motion to have him fired. The board didn't see fit to fire him at that time, but it was certainly made very clear to him that there'd be none of that stuff.

SOURCE: Interview with Eugene Mitchell, Edmonton, 29 October 2002, ALHI.

created did not abate at all as the Tories settled in to govern Alberta for an even longer period. In the circumstances, it is hardly surprising that the dissident Waffle group, which mounted a left-wing challenge within the NDP across the country in the late 1960s and early 1970s, had only modest success in Alberta. The Waffle called for nationalization of the major industries in Canada as a means both to give Canadians control over their economy, increasingly under American control, and to give workers control over their workplaces. But the unions responded with hostility to Waffle attacks on foreign control over Canadian unions, though ironically many of the Canadian sections of American unions did indeed, as mentioned earlier, form Canadian unions during the 1970s and afterwards. The Alberta Waffle called for nationalization of the energy industry, but Grant Notley and most of the NDP and labour movement called instead for higher taxation of the industry while leaving ownership in private hands.[75]

Labour used its political action committees and its various labour schools to educate its members about political issues, stressing that it was hard to win gains in negotiations if the labour laws were stacked against you, and equally hard to hold onto whatever gains you did win when management held most of the cards, thanks to close government-corporate ties. But it faced a difficult task in trying to persuade its members, much less other Albertans, to embrace a social-democratic party.

Apart from fighting for better provincial legislation, the labour movement in the province was also involved in federal politics. The Alberta Federation of Labour (AFL) and its affiliates joined the Canadian Labour Congress on 14 October 1976, in calling a one-day strike against the federal wage controls that had been

imposed a year earlier and remained in effect for three years. While almost fifty thousand Alberta workers joined the strike, the demonstrations in Alberta cities were smaller per capita than in many other areas of the country. In general, the labour leaders complained that their members seemed unwilling to join political demonstrations, regardless of the issue.[76]

Labour's protests did not win changes in provincial labour legislation or cause the national or provincial governments to end wage controls earlier than 1978. But other labour campaigns, conducted in conjunction with other groups, did have an important effect during this period. The national labour movement played the largest role among organized interest groups in winning medicare: together, they convinced the Royal Commission on Health Care appointed by Diefenbakers's Progressive Conservatives that the private insurance companies' arguments that private insurance would deliver the goods was false. The minority Liberal parliament from 1963 to 1968 proved willing to implement a variety of reforms, from medicare, to the Canada Pension Plan, to the Canada Assistance Plan. Canada's social programs, inferior overall to American social programs in the mid-1950s, had left American social provision in the dust by 1980. The Canadian labour movement's decision to finance a party left of the Liberal Party — which contrasted with the American labour movement's decision simply to back the Democrats, the American equivalent to the Liberals — was vindicated as a better means of pressuring governments in Canada to act on behalf of workers' interests.[77]

In Alberta, the labour movement, though mostly ignored by governments, could point with pride to its efforts to persuade the provincial government to pass legislative guarantees for human rights, which Saskatchewan's CCF government had pioneered in the 1940s. In 1960, the AFL, in its annual brief to the government, called for human rights legislation that would end discrimination on the basis of "race, colour or creed."[78] The federal government and six other provinces had already passed such legislation, but Alberta did not act until 1966, when it introduced the *Human Rights Act*, which, characteristically, it attempted to enforce by means of only one person. For its Canadian Centennial convention in 1967, the AFL chose the theme "Human Rights for All," and convention speakers included a representative of the Alberta Indian Association as well as academic and labour experts on human rights.[79] In 1972, the Alberta legislature passed the *Individual Rights Protection Act*, which created a Human Rights Commission and resulted in the province developing an apparatus for investigating and prosecuting cases of discrimination against individuals on the basis of sex, race, religion, or place of origin.

◆ ◆ ◆

Though Alberta suffered from the recession in the early 1960s and again in the early 1970s, on the whole, the growth of the energy sector shielded its economy from any extreme downturns while providing several major upturns. The big energy corporations were the biggest beneficiary of provincial governments that promoted private ownership of provincial resources and instituted labour policies that would ensure that workers' interests would never trump the interests of capital. But many workers managed to do quite well financially despite the labour laws, particularly if they were in sectors that experienced labour shortages, such as the construction sector, and if they had strong unions. A macho philosophy regarding worker productivity and risk-taking, promoted by government and management, was shared by many workers. Some of the union leaders recognized that the strong corporate-government link worked against the interests of workers and tried in various ways, particularly through founding and supporting the provincial NDP but also through union educational work, to change the philosophy of government in Alberta. They wanted the provincial government to take a larger role in planning the provincial economy and to make job security and on-the-job safety principal goals in that economy. During the 1960s and 1970s, they largely failed in these objectives, though they did create cadres of union militants who were prepared to fight the good fight both in the workplace and in political life. And they did manage to extract some concessions from the provincial government in the areas of occupational health and safety, and human rights.

The majority of Alberta workers, however, benefited little even as the energy boom created jobs for most of them. Keeping up with the inflationary spiral within an uncontrolled boom economy proved difficult for workers, particularly those in the service sector. As Warren Caragata commented in 1979 in his conclusion to *Alberta Labour*, "the real fight is still in the unorganized sector, where workers are denied even the basic rights won over the years by the labour movement. For unorganized workers wishing to join unions, the basic issue is still at stake — the very right to belong to a union."[80] The right of workers to join unions and to negotiate with employers would face even harsher tests in the 1980s as a major international recession stripped Alberta workers of their illusions that they lived in a place free from the economic laws of capitalism.

FIG 7-1 Mass solidarity march for Gainers workers organized by the Edmonton and District Labour Council. *Edmonton Journal*, June 1986.

7 ALBERTA LABOUR IN THE 1980s

WINSTON GERELUK

"There was total shock that we were not only fighting the company, the government and the courts, but also police from across the province," commented Ian Thorne, Energy and Chemical Workers Union staff representative, about the appearance of two hundred RCMP officers, along with dogs, on the picket line in Fort McMurray on 8 May 1986. It was an array of forces that many unions confronted in the 1980s, most spectacularly the Gainers workers in Edmonton, whose long confrontation with capitalist Peter Pocklington sparked the most visible demonstration of labour solidarity in the province's history to date.

The 1980s proved the most militant decade in Alberta labour history. An economic downturn led to employer intransigence and government introduction of neo-liberal reforms that together threatened working conditions and workers' quality of life. Legislation that was intended to destroy trade unionism in the construction sector was only the most blatant effort to make unions disappear. Workers' efforts to defend and extend earlier gains produced a decade that transformed the province's labour movement, reviving a tradition of protest politics that had characterized its earlier days. Many workers became militant because they realized that, as an Alberta Federation of Labour (AFL) convention resolution noted in 1983, neo-liberal policies "were having a devastating effect on all sectors of our community."[1] These neo-liberal policies reflected pre-war notions that business alone should direct the economy while governments and unions should support business needs as defined by large business interests.

Private sector employers, supported by government, responded to the economic crisis with efforts to make the workers, rather than those whose decisions had caused the mess, pay the price to bring back prosperity. Until the mid-1970s, the postwar compromise among business, labour, and government meant that at least some progress had been made toward "soft" human resource management at work, legal protection of worker rights, and the promise of a steady improvement in the standard of living. Now, however, workers were expected to accept increasingly precarious employment, restrictive legislation, and an ongoing campaign of cutbacks and privatization.

By 1980, the economies of the Western world had stagnated, but without the stubborn inflation of the 1970s giving way. Economists applied the term *stagflation* to this double whammy, marked by a long slowdown that turned into a recession in the last quarter of 1981. Neither Alberta workers nor their public services were spared as both the federal and provincial governments introduced restraint measures popularly associated with Margaret Thatcher in the United Kingdom and Ronald Reagan in the United States. In fact, Thatcher and Reagan simply accelerated their predecessors' policies that rejected expansion of government spending and the money supply as the means to kickstart private-market sluggishness. Instead, the focus was on restoring profits by making companies meaner and leaner, which, of course, meant accepting high unemployment. In Canada, too, monetary policy had been restrictive since 1975 and fiscal policy gradually followed.

Initially, companies claimed to offer workers long-term gain for short-term pain. For example, Lorraine Stallknecht, a Safeway clerk and president of the Fort McMurray Labour Council, recalled Safeway's complaint that it was suffering. "They were asking their workers to take cutbacks. The union really believed them, the president or CEO at the time, who was promising them [the workers] that once they got their money back, they would share the wealth. Of course, that CEO no longer exists with Safeway."[2]

THE RECESSION OF 1981

Canada's relatively brief but sharp recession in 1981–82 was deeper and more long-lived in Alberta because of the province's excessive reliance on oil. The Lougheed government's schemes for economic diversification during the boom, which had relied excessively on initiatives by the private sector, had failed. As the government itself later admitted, "many entrepreneurs in Alberta who could have further contributed to diversification committed most of their cash and efforts to expansion in the energy and real estate fields."[3] What diversification did occur was mostly in "satellite industries" serving the oil industry. Little had been done to develop a large-scale independent manufacturing base.[4]

The Lougheed government attributed the downturn to the federal National Energy Program (NEP) of November 1980. The NEP proposed oil self-sufficiency for Canada, a secure oil supply particularly for the industrial base in eastern Canada, domestic ownership of the energy industry, lower prices, development of alternative energy sources, and increased government revenues through a variety of taxes and agreements. It proposed a level of government intervention, including a greatly expanded Petro-Canada, to help "Canadianize" the entire oil industry, which the industry and the Alberta government rejected.[5]

Albertans were barraged with messages that the program was an outright attempt by the federal government to take over their resources. The Petro-Canada building in Calgary was dubbed "Red Square," and stickers on pickup trucks declared: "Let the Eastern bastards freeze in the dark!" Albertans were generally resentful when Pierre Trudeau's Liberals were returned to office in February 1980, winning only two seats west of Ontario. As political scientists Larry Pratt and Garth Stevenson note, for those who had always regarded Trudeau as opposed to the aspirations of western Canada, "the new federal initiatives, with their emphasis on the redistribution of resource wealth and a much stronger role for the national government, seemed designed to keep the West in a position of permanent subordination."[6]

Claiming that the NEP threatened the constitutional rights of ordinary Albertans, Premier Lougheed cut shipments of oil to the rest of Canada and slowed down tar sands projects.[7] The oil industry, supported by substantial elements of Canadian business and finance, "responded by cutting back new capital investment and exploration activity, and by launching a powerful lobbying campaign against the NEP."[8] Exxon's Canadian subsidiary, Imperial Oil, shelved a proposed $8 billion heavy oil project in Cold Lake, threatening five hundred jobs.[9] Customs officials at the Coutts US border crossing reported a massive exodus of oil rigs from Alberta as early as November 1980, and drilling activity dropped dramatically.[10]

On 1 September 1981, Prime Minister Trudeau and Premier Lougheed announced a compromise agreement that scaled back the initial ambitions of the NEP. But by then, the international energy industry was facing great difficulties. OPEC had lost its ability to either maintain high prices for energy or restrict oil supplies. As the Western economies slowed, demand for oil and gas fell, and prices dropped in response to a glut of available fossil fuels. Nothing that governments did seemed to persuade the oil companies that new, stable investments were possible.

As oil companies laid off thousands of employees, related services suffered, and bankruptcies, business closures, and foreclosures became commonplace. Real estate values tumbled, as imploding markets led to unprecedented migration out of Alberta. Real per capita provincial incomes dropped, only recovering in the late 1980s. Edmonton fared worse than Calgary. Though the city issued a record number of building permits during 1980 and 1981, development ground to a near halt in 1982. As the capital city, Edmonton's economy was further affected by government job cuts. When oil prices plunged from US$27 per barrel in fall 1985 to US$8 per barrel in August 1986, more jobs disappeared. By 1987, Edmonton's unemployment rate was 11.1 percent, and almost twenty-four thousand Edmontonians had turned to welfare and the Food Bank.[11]

The federal and provincial governments offered incentives to business and cutbacks to public services. Labour lawyer G. Brent Gawne later observed:

The vast wholesale migration of drilling companies out of the province, and the alarm that it caused in the streets of Calgary was seen as necessitating a fundamental change. The eighties saw a lurch to the right in Alberta, driven by a combination of factors that conspired to sacrifice the rights of workers in the misguided hope that these changes would kickstart the economy and return us all to prosperity.[12]

In a province where bumper stickers proclaimed, "Oil feeds my family and pays my taxes," the public accepted an Economic Resurgence Plan that included billion dollar royalty holidays, tax cuts, and other incentives anchored by a $5.4 billion Alberta Oil and Gas

Activity Program announced by Premier Lougheed in April 1982.[13] Other grants followed. When Shell Canada president Bill Daniel set a 30 April deadline for increased federal participation in its proposed tar sands project, Alberta and Ottawa each agreed to put up 25 percent of the $14 billion cost.[14] Even this could not stem the investment cuts, however. Perhaps the fatal blow came when Ed Czaja, president of Alsands Energy Consortium, announced that the consortium would not be proceeding with its megaproject after all, blaming a lack of confidence and poor cash flow for the decision.[15]

This was a judgment based on international energy markets, not the emaciated NEP. For the Alberta government, which could not explain its failure to diversify the economy or its subsidies of billions of dollars to energy companies to create jobs, it was expedient to blame the NEP. Why accept that international oil prices and the province's one-industry economy were the culprits when it was easier to blame Ottawa and the controversial NEP? As American prairie studies professor Frances Kaye observes, "To be sure, the drill rigs left Alberta and their departure was hastened by NEP incentives to explore on the 'Canada Lands' in the North and East — but they pulled out of Texas as well. The same bumper stickers appeared on trucks at both ends of the Great Plains: 'Please God, if You let us have another boom, I promise not to piss it away this time.'"[16]

When Brian Mulroney and his federal Conservatives came to power in 1984, one of his first acts was to dismantle the NEP but not before myths associated with the program had fueled widespread separatist sentiment in Alberta. The federal Liberals would remain "the enemy" in the minds of many, rendering Alberta a secure base for the Conservative party to the present day.

GOVERNMENT RETRENCHMENT AND LABOUR'S RESPONSE

The climate of uncertainty that attended the economic slowdown made public spending, debt, and deficits a focus for governments, setting the stage for cutbacks and hard collective bargaining in the public sector.

Cutbacks and Neo-liberalism

While it was widely assumed that these cutbacks were a response to a drop in government revenues, Alberta's politicians began to target public spending long before deficits became an issue. David Cooper and Dean Neu explain: "Political pronouncements and media coverage of the deficit/debt are reminiscent of 'Chicken Little' of children's story fame who announces that 'the sky is falling, the sky is falling' to anyone who might listen."[17] Indeed, economists Melville McMillan and Allan Warrack have shown that, despite the investment drought of 1981–82, the Alberta government's real per capita revenues grew at a healthy rate until 1986, outstripping other provinces. The same goes for government expenditures, which grew in real per capita terms until 1987.[18]

According to economist Sten Drugge, the decline in government revenues and the beginning of provincial deficits that accompanied falling oil prices in 1986 were more attributable to corporate giveaways than to spending on public services. Lougheed's 1982 plan alone doubled the tax credit on Crown royalties from 25 percent to 50 percent and the maximum annual allowable credit from $1 million to $2 million, which cost the Treasury an estimated $1.6 billion over the next three fiscal years. This amount was supplemented by further "stimulants" estimated at $5.6 billion between

1982 and 1986.[19] The annual report of the provincial Auditor General found that in the fiscal year that ended 31 March 1983, Alberta's corporate sector received $162 million more from Alberta taxpayers than it paid in taxes, royalties, and fees.[20]

An important feature of the neo-liberalism of the 1980s was the prominence of political formations and "think tanks" that consistently promoted measures to relax rules on business, downsize public services, promote the private sector, and submit wages and working conditions to market rule. The Business Council on National Issues (BCNI, now the Canadian Council of Chief Executives) emerged in the 1970s to play a leading role in influencing pro-business government policy. Chief executive officers of over one hundred of Canada's largest companies — such as Air Canada, AT&T, Bechtel, Bombardier, and Canadian Pacific — came together under the leadership of Thomas d'Aquino to define a new direction for Canada.[21]

Whereas the BCNI was simply the capitalist class without disguise, the so-called think tanks were corporate-sponsored ventures masked as independent research institutes. When a Canadian Chamber of Commerce study revealed that Canadians suspected business organizations and their research to be motivated by self-interest, a different public relations strategy became necessary.[22] The Fraser Institute, created in 1974, helped to defeat David Barrett and the first NDP government of British Columbia and was regularly solicited by media and policymakers for a "balanced business perspective." Promoting "a free and prosperous world through choice, markets and responsibility," its well-funded and aggressive program of publication and public relations attacked everything from rent controls to public education, reserving special venom for government spending, debts, and deficits.[23]

The National Citizens Coalition, another pro-business organization, formed as a lobby group in 1967 to oppose Canada's new national health care act and gained prominence during the 1980s as a leading advocate of privatization, public spending cuts, and reduced taxes. Canada's current prime minister, Stephen Harper, served as president from 1998 to 2002, during which he masterminded campaigns in support of "more freedom with less government." Favoured targets included the *Canada Health Act*, the Canadian Wheat Board, closed-shop unions, and "gold-plated" pension plans for MPs and federal government employees.[24]

Workers Serve Early Notice

Strikes by four of Alberta's largest unions took place even before the recession-related retrenchment of the early 1980s. The pattern was set in April 1980 in the United Nurses of Alberta (UNA) strike discussed in chapter 6, the first of three general nurses' strikes in the 1980s. UNA vice-president Jane Sustrik, who became a nurse shortly after that milestone strike, explained why the nurses saw the need to strike frequently. Initially employed at the University of Alberta Hospital and a member of the Staff Nurses Association of Alberta, she noted:

> I started around $7 or $8 as a nurse in 1982. Prior to that, one of my first jobs was teaching swimming as a lifeguard; I made more money teaching swimming as a lifeguard than I did at nursing. . . . So wages were a priority, to get wages in a more realistic zone compared to other health care professionals and people with equivalent education.[25]

FIG 7-2 Rallies connected with the United Nurses of Alberta strike in the 1980s were large and enthusiastic. Provincial Archives of Alberta, J5024-2.

When six thousand nurses walked out of sixty-nine hospitals in February 1982, the Alberta government enacted a Disputes Inquiry Board and demanded a vote on its findings. Instead, the UNA held its own vote, receiving a mandate for a walkout. When they finally returned to work, an arbitrator awarded a 29 percent wage increase, as well as other improvements.[26] Margaret Ethier, who served as UNA president from 1980 to 1989, attributed this and other victories to rank-and-file decision-making, backed by a fan-out system of communications that allowed the union to cope with an increasingly bureaucratized health system. Laws could not stop nurses from striking, she said. "You can fine me, but you can't make me go to work. You could get the army out and march me to work, but can you make me work? *No!*"[27]

As we saw in chapter 6, a wildcat strike in July 1980 by members of the Alberta Union of Provincial Employees was also successful in bringing the government to the bargaining table. It occurred in the midst of the Alberta Teachers' Association (ATA) walkout from Calgary School District No. 19 over the issue of class size. That labour action ended 29 September 1980, when the minister of Labour ordered the teachers back to work and created a commission to examine the relationship of class size to quality of education. The eventual report supported the teachers' position but the government dismissed the report's recommendations as too costly. However, it remains ATA policy that "maximum classroom enrolment should be 20 students."[28]

A forty-two day strike by the Canadian Union of Postal Workers (CUPW), which represents inside workers, began in 1981, just as the Government of Canada was moving to corporatize the Post Office as a Crown corporation. That year, CUPW made maternity leave a bargaining priority, and on 1 July, some twenty-three thousand postal workers began their fourth strike in seven years. After six weeks on the line, CUPW became the first national union to win maternity rights for its members.[29] Its motto —"The struggle continues!" — would describe labour relations in the Post Office for the remainder of the decade.

Turning Back the Industrial Relations Clock

The Trudeau government's wage controls of the 1970s evolved into a series of legislative controls on collective bargaining rights during the 1980s. In July 1982, the federal government limited wage increases in the federal sector to 6 percent and 5 percent over two years, later extending those limits to increases to old age security, family allowances, and federal public service pensions.[30] The Alberta government, for its part, set out to limit public sector negotiations by issuing "bargaining guidelines" established by cabinet.

At its May 1982 convention, the Alberta Federation of Labour passed several resolutions declaring wage controls an attack on democratic principles of free collective bargaining. One resolution directed that "in the event government announces it intends to impose wage controls in any form, the Executive Council immediately organize a program of industrial action to culminate in a national general strike."[31] But no such national or provincial strike materialized during the decade that followed, despite constant imposition of wage controls.

The Alberta government moved determinedly to limit unions' ability to represent their members. After being snubbed by the nurses in their 1982 strike, the government passed the *Health Care Continuation Act*, which made illegal any further strike by nurses before the end of 1983. The legislation threatened the union with severe sanctions if it failed to live up to its "peace" obligations, including huge fines, decertification, and an unprecedented prohibition on all union staff and officers, even if they had played no role in the strike, from holding office in any Alberta union.[32] In 1983, this temporary act provided the template for Bill 44, the *Labour Statutes Amendment Act*, which replaced the right to strike for all hospital workers with compulsory arbitration in which arbitrators, in turn, were limited by government policy. Penalties for disobedience included huge fines for non-compliance, the right of an employer to apply for a six-month suspension of dues, the right of cabinet to decertify a union, and relaxed service requirements for court and board orders.[33]

Claiming that too many "frivolous and vexatious" appeals were launched under Alberta's *Employment Standards Act*, the government introduced a revision in 1984 requiring workers to post a $300 bond when appealing the decisions of employment standards officers. In 1985, further amendments to the *Individual Rights Protection Act* saw the concepts of "reasonable and justifiable" introduced as a defence for employers against discrimination charges by employees. Then the government, headed by the new Premier Don Getty, amended the *Industrial Wage Securities Act* in 1985 to remove a requirement for employers in the coal industry to post security for wages. This eliminated legislation passed in the 1950s to correct long-standing practices in an industry notorious for not paying its workers.[34]

The erosion of regulatory protection during the economic downturn was particularly noticeable in the area of occupational health and safety, where unions were compelled to bargain for the most basic health and safety rights. Alberta remained the only Canadian jurisdiction that did not require Joint Health and Safety committees on worksites. Bill Flookes, president of the Brewery Distillery Soft Drink Local at the Calgary Brewing and Malting Company, recalls the conditions that moved his local to demand a committee in his plant:

> The plant differed from area to area. It's very noisy and dangerous in the packaging area. But the other areas, like the brewing areas, cellars, fermenters, not so much. Except in a lot of places you'd have to work alone, and that's one of the things we changed as well with the committee. You'd have to get in the tanks and you'd be by yourself. There were gases around, etc., and there were dangers that way.[35]

Glen Taylor, currently mayor of Hinton, recalls how empowering it was to become involved with his union's safety committee in the town's sawmill. "For the first time I was able to work with fellow employees to help an employer understand that there might be a safer or better way of working. . . . Health and safety can be a way to achieve many other things than just a safe and healthful workplace."[36]

Alberta's unions combined to challenge the Workers' Compensation system when a regulatory change in 1982 eliminated the requirement to report no-lost-time accidents, opening the door to aggressive claims management by employers. Peter Holbein, an active United Food and Commercial Workers (UFCW) Local 280P member, recalls Peter Pocklington's takeover of Swift's Edmonton meat-packing plant in 1982:

> He hired compensation specialists to cut down on his compensation bills . . . to get people to stay in the plant whether they were injured or not, and say they had light duty. But in fact a lot of it wasn't light duty. They just changed the job a little bit and said, "You can handle it now." . . . So a lot of people worked injured.[37]

One notable victory during this period of anti-labour policy and regulation was related by Mike Tamton, president of the United Mine Workers of America District 18, on behalf of miners who were denied compensation for black lung:

> The offshoot was that, in 1979, black lung was recognized as a compensable disease. We had some of the oldtimers that were able to retroactively apply for claims for black lung. They received some pensions. I'll never forget when the next time we met with some of those oldtimers, in particular an individual in Canmore, tears rolling down his eyes, when he said thank you.[38]

War Against the Construction Trades

> Yes, definitely, since '84. That was the crunch, as we called it. We got hammered, and the government did nothing about it. They locked us out and said, "This is what you're going to get." Pay went from $18 something an hour down to $12 an hour. The 24-hour lockout — you're locked out, that's it.[39]

Medicine Hat carpenter Bill McGillivray had first-hand knowledge of the shift in labour policy for the construction trades during the 1980s. As business agent for the Medicine Hat local of the United Brotherhood of Carpenters and Joiners of America (UBCJA), he could do little when contractors took advantage of an economic slowdown to turn back the clock on collective bargaining rights. Alberta's oil booms are primarily construction booms, and when construction fell precipitously in the 1980s, contractors took advantage of the huge reserve of unemployed workers to smash the construction unions.

By law, expired collective agreements usually remain "bridged" until a new one is settled and may be terminated only by strike or lockout. When construction agreements expired in 1984, the Contractors' Association implemented a twenty-four-hour lockout: they locked out their workers and declared twenty-four hours later that a collective agreement no longer existed. Workers were then offered their jobs at vastly reduced rates. To get rid of union contracts that had yet to expire, they set up "spin-off companies" to transfer work from unionized firms to non-unionized entities.[40] The Alberta government refused to take action despite repeated arguments from unions and legal scholars that these lockouts violated the legislation's intention of inducing parties to conclude an agreement and that the spin-offs were "dummy firms" established solely to escape existing agreements.

Huge wage reductions for formerly well-paid construction workers impacted local economies across Alberta. Like many others, Calgary carpenter Brad Bulloch chose not to work under the new regime, becoming a private home renovations contractor instead. He rejoined the union in 1987, in time to organize a walkout over health and safety issues. "The union is about safety, about longevity," he said. "It's about having a decent standard of living and the right to work in a safe environment so that you can grow up and cuddle your children's children. That's why I'm proud to work for this union."[41]

The Independent Contractors and Business Association chose this period to introduce the "merit shop," an industry-wide, portable benefit plan for "open-shop" (a euphemism for non-union) work. Formed in late 1985, the association grew to over thirteen hundred members, including most of Alberta's general and trade contractors, explaining its success as "a response to escalating costs of building union and excessive work disruptions and jurisdictional disputes."[42] Although a partial recovery occurred in the late 1980s, the twenty-four-hour lockout and spin-offs are still available to contractors today.

Changes in labour law reflected changing strategies in human resource management, as "soft" human resources increasingly gave way to more traditional methods of "sweating" labour. John Ventura, business agent with United Food and Commercial Workers Local 280P, found a radical change in industrial relations at

THE IMPACT OF LOSING A UNION

All of Alberta's big contractors were involved in the effort to destroy trade unionism in the construction industry during the 1980s recession. They virtually wiped out collective agreements and left workers at the mercy of contractors for their wages, benefits, and conditions. Brad Bulloch, business manager for Calgary Carpenters' Local 2103, recalled:

> One day, you were working for a union company with a full benefit package and full rate, and twenty-four hours later you were working for a non-union company at what I figured to be a 65 percent cut. It was devastating to anybody that had a mortgage, a car payment, or a family, such as me. We lost members, and some lost their lives through suicide. There were many marriage breakups, people lost their homes, lost their vehicles. In 1984, people were selling their homes for one dollar to get out of the liabilities.

Similar reports came from across the industry. In 1980, Alberta's oldest craft union, Bricklayers and Allied Craftworkers Local #1, was 806 members strong. In 1984, after the twenty-four-hour lockout reduced hourly wages from $18.00 to $12.50, members left the province or found work in other fields, and by 1986, the local's membership had declined to 254.

SOURCES: Interview with Brad Bulloch, Calgary, 16 November 2005, ALHI; "About Us," BAC Edmonton, http://www.bacedmonton.ca/about-us.

the Edmonton Gainers plant in 1984. "Prior to Pocklington, we had good management, and things got resolved — could go for years without an arbitration," he said. "In fact, when I first became a chief steward, there were only three or four grievances filed for an entire year. After Pocklington, we never had less than a hundred grievances per year." [43]

Pocklington's workers and their unions were not alone in confronting employers who refused to adapt their management strategy to accommodate a unionized regime. Bill Flookes explains:

> To a large degree, our problem was that we were the decision makers for the union, but the people we dealt with weren't. . . . A lot of times, the top of the union would be speaking to the middle of the management pyramid. As a consequence, decision makers were speaking to the people who could not make decisions, which is where a lot of frustration came in terms of relationships and communication. [44]

Workers Take On the Law

It didn't take long for Alberta's unions to challenge anti-union employers and governments. In April 1983, the day after Bill 44 with its ban on hospital strikes was introduced, Dave Werlin, the newly elected president of the Alberta Federation of Labour, declared a "War on 44." Action was overdue, he said, "to mobilize support for fundamental trade union and democratic rights and to ensure that in the future, the government would think twice before infringing even further on the freedoms and rights of the trade union movement and general public in Alberta." [45] The AFL would "solicit support from organizations outside the Federation, to organize an aggressive lobby against the government, to ultimately change the political pattern of a huge number of voters in Alberta, and to establish a 'War Chest' to come to assistance of any union which is 'persecuted or prosecuted' under the primitive provisions of Bill 44."[46] Most unions in the province, whether affiliated or not, supported a voluntary assessment of forty-four cents per member per month. When the response to public hearings on Bill 44 was so overwhelming that many requests to appear were rejected, the AFL organized its own "Real Hearings on Bill 44."[47] Although the bill passed, the campaign helped to lay the basis for the militancy that followed.

The Dandelions emerged in 1985 as a largely spontaneous response of construction workers to twenty-four-hour lockouts and spin-offs. While their unions struggled through conventional channels, unemployed workers with little prospect of decent work began to meet, vowing that just like the tough weeds, they would resist efforts to eradicate their unions. Dandelion signs appeared across Alberta, adding considerable energy to the demands of the labour movement for job creation and workers' rights. Dandelions joined other unions and organizations in Solidarity Alberta (a coalition of various justice-oriented groups that eventually merged into the Action Canada Network), even appearing at farm gates where farmers were threatened with eviction.[48]

In the same year that the Dandelions sprouted, Dave Werlin, in a policy paper for the 1985 AFL convention, charged the Conservatives with manufacturing a crisis to move against organized labour in the legislature, the courts, and worksites, and then withdraw support for public programs at a time when workers

DANDELION POLITICAL ACTION COMMITTEE

WE NEVER DIE

were experiencing depressed income levels, benefits, and social conditions.[49]

Mike Wilgus, a representative for the Bakery Workers' Union, described workers' attitudes after an extended lockout at Edmonton's McGavin's bread factory in December 1985. Restrictive labour laws and Labour Board orders prevented strikers from doing anything about strikebreakers who crossed their picket lines. "We ended up losing," he said, "but it made our people more militant. . . . More than anything else was their realization that the government had screwed them. It was the government more than the company that had taken their rights away. . . . It changed their political view."[50] Experiences of this kind contributed to major setbacks for the ruling Conservatives in the provincial elections of 1986 and 1989.

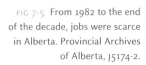

FIG 7-5 From 1982 to the end of the decade, jobs were scarce in Alberta. Provincial Archives of Alberta, J5174-2.

GROWING POVERTY AND HARD TIMES

With businesses closing, public employees losing jobs, and cutbacks in public services, signs of hard times began to appear everywhere in Alberta.[51] One of the clearest was the proliferation of food banks that paralleled the mass charity organizations of the 1930s. The Edmonton Food Bank was first opened in 1981 by the Edmonton Gleaners Association, a charity that worked with such groups as the Salvation Army, Operation Friendship, WIN House, Our House Addiction Recovery, the Unemployed Action Centre, the George Spady Centre, and church organizations to provide emergency food relief for the needy. The Calgary Inter-Faith Community Action Association followed a year later. By mid-decade, seventy such banks operated across the province, and Alberta had the highest percentage of food bank recipients in Canada, approximately 40 percent of whom were children under eighteen.[52]

Unemployed Action (or Help) Centres were another sign of the times. These were initiated by the AFL in 1983 after its convention adopted a policy paper entitled "The Bloom is Off the Rose in Wildrose Country," which directed the AFL executive to "explore ways and means of establishing Unemployment Action Centres across the Province to offer aid, assistance and organization to the unemployed and to promote dialogue on the economic and employment crisis."[53] The federal New Employment Expansion and Development program (NEED) provided a grant of $466,000 to finance staffing and operation of twelve Unemployed Help Centres across the province for a period of twelve months. In 1984, Keith Rimstead was hired as provincial coordinator and Tamara Kozlowska as assistant coordinator.[54]

Each centre was guided by a board comprising trade union, church, and community leaders. Trade unions supplied equipment and materials for the operation, and in each case, the city or town council provided free space.

While the centres were primarily committed to bread-and-butter issues facing unemployed workers, such as difficulties dealing with the Unemployment Insurance Commission, they also served as a resource for advocacy and information by organizing discussion forums and engaging in public policy advocacy around such topics as housing, human rights, and job creation. A recurring subject, Kozlowska recalls, was renters' rights, as accommodation costs were rising to record highs in many Alberta cities, and governments had done little to ease the pain for the poor and homeless.[55]

The centres attracted a diverse population. Newcomers who had come to Alberta during its boom mixed with long-time residents who had been reasonably secure before the economic downturn, but who, according to Kozlowska, "found themselves in trouble . . . . Often whole households became unemployed."[56] Kozlowska also noted differences in political outlook. "Newcomers were often aware of the Canadian reality; they had historical perspective that allowed them to recognize the nature of their hardship." Long-time Edmontonians, on the other hand, "wanted to be on the winning team. They felt hurt by what had happened; it was as if the 'family' had let them down. There was little political analysis."[57]

LABOUR'S HOUSE DIVIDED

Within the labour movement, however, political analyses *were* being offered, but not everyone viewed the dilemmas faced by the movement in the same way. The more radical trade unionists recognized that the post-war labour-relations ideal was collapsing before their very eyes. Sometimes referred to as Fordism, this model assumed a workforce doing lifelong assembly-line tasks that mechanization made ever more productive and for which the company, after negotiations with the unions, would reward workers with wage increases that took into account both inflation and productivity increases. The Fordist model viewed workers largely as toilers and consumers within a specific nation, to whom companies and governments catered because they wanted them to be productive workers with enough consumer power to buy what the nation produced. By the 1980s, in an economy that was increasingly globalized, it had become clear that corporations wanted "flexibility" to move jobs and machinery to various plants around the world in ways that maximized productivity and profits. Trade unions, with their defence of Fordism and workers' rights to lifelong work and constantly improving wages and benefits, were considered dinosaurs in this new environment, impediments to profit-making. Trade unionists who recognized the dangers of the post-Fordist world — which was crushing their former powers to negotiate with employers — saw a need for unions that could fight back politically, both in terms of electing progressive politicians and in terms of uniting a broad section of the working class plus other social groupings in coalitions that would fight the new anti-national and anti-communitarian philosophy of capital.

FIG 7-6 Button for the Alberta Federation of Labour's "War on 44" campaign, which began in 1983. Courtesy of the Alberta Labour History Institute.

It was in this context that Dave Werlin, a representative with the Canadian Union of Public Employees (CUPE), was elected president of the Alberta Federation of Labour in 1983. Werlin became the first member of the Communist Party of Canada to head a provincial labour federation. Born and raised on a farm in Saskatchewan, Werlin became involved in CUPE as a municipal worker, first in Calgary and then in Vancouver. He was appointed as a staff representative in Calgary in 1979. After serving as AFL president, he returned to CUPE in 1989 as its Alberta regional director, where he remained until his retirement in 1996. Werlin's leadership addressed a broad range of social and political issues, reviving a tradition of social unionism at a critical time in Alberta's labour history. After kicking off the "War on 44," he proceeded to take on such diverse causes as farmers facing eviction, the anti-cruise missile campaign, and the Lubicon band's battle to preserve traditional land rights against the oil and timber industries.

But others within the labour movement took much longer to accept the idea that a new trade unionism was necessary for the post-Fordist world of globalization and the return to pre–World War II attitudes toward unions on the part of employers. In 1982, the building trades unions left the AFL, in tandem with their unions' secession nationally from the Canadian Labour Congress (CLC) to form the Canadian Federation of Labour (CFL).[58] The CFL represented only American-headquartered construction unions in Canada and rejected both political partisanship and social unionism. Such ongoing issues as whether certain work "belonged" to in-house employees or to the construction trades aggravated the CFL-CLC split. There were also divisions over tripartism — that is, formal collaboration of unions with government and industry; some unions saw it as the only way to secure gains, while others believed it would lead to betrayal of workers. This disagreement became public when the CFL began dealing with the Mulroney government, while the CLC maintained a critical stance.[59]

The movement for Canadian independence also fueled the split, as national unions attracted thousands of trade union members who broke from their US-dominated internationals during the 1980s. In 1960, 72 percent of Canadian unionists belonged to US-based industrial unions, but by 1989, with expanding public sector unions and breakaways from the US-dominated unions, only 32 percent belonged to these so-called internationals. Some of these breakaways were contentious, such as the Canadian paperworkers' rupture with the International Paperworkers' Union in 1980.[60] Others were amicable. In April 1980, delegates from the Oil, Chemical and Atomic Workers (OCAW), the Canadian Chemical Workers (CCW), and an independent Quebec union of textile workers met in Montreal to form the Energy and Chemical Workers Union (ECWU), with thirty thousand members. As Wayne Roberts notes, "The new union unified the major groups of energy and chemical workers, merging the experiences of the shock troops of Canadian nationalism, partisans of Quebec nationalism, and champions of classic international-ism."[61] Neil Reimer became the national president and kept the ECWU head office in Edmonton. When the split with the Denver-based OCAW occurred in 1986, the international not only handed over all that was owed but also maintained a common strike fund and continued to work with Canadians on such issues as health and safety.[62]

DEEPENING ECONOMIC CRISIS AND THE PEOPLE'S RESPONSE

Financial problems and the collapse of some key pillars of Peter Lougheed's industrial plan for Alberta were just around the corner when he handed over the reins of government to Don Getty in 1985. By the mid-1980s, provincial revenues had shrunk so badly that the government had to borrow a record $5.5 billion to see itself through the 1986–87 fiscal year.[63]

Getty's Reforms

One of the original core of the Conservative Party that swept into power in 1971, Getty had served as Alberta's minister of Federal and Intergovernmental Affairs and then minister of Energy and Natural Resources. He left government in 1979 to serve on boards of several energy and financial companies, but came back in 1985 to be elected leader of the Progressive Conservative Party, which automatically made him premier. Getty then led his party to a reduced majority in the 1986 general election, and when he lost his Edmonton-Whitemud seat in 1989, a by-election was arranged in the electoral district of Stettler to allow him to re-enter the legislature.[64]

In 1985, the Alberta government ran its first deficit in over two decades, and when the price of West Texas crude plunged the following year, the drop in energy revenues led to a fiscal deficit of $3.4 billion. Financial woes were exacerbated by a struggling agricultural sector, a failing real estate market, and finally the collapse of several government-subsidized enterprises, including two banks, the Canadian Commercial Bank and the

Northlands Bank.[65] Calls for Thatcher-style reforms sounded anew.

The new premier's first reaction was to intervene with generous stimulus packages, giving the agricultural sector a $2 billion loan program to address high interest rates and the energy sector almost $600 million in loan guarantees, mainly to Husky Oil and Syncrude for capital projects. Pocklington received a $55 million guarantee (in addition to a $20 million loan) to upgrade his Gainers meat-packing plant. The perception grew that Getty's administration was willing to spend public money to support large businesses but was indifferent to the problems of working people.[66]

Getty then took steps to reduce and transform Alberta's public sector. While taxes were raised by $1 billion for 1986–87, program spending was cut by 6.3 percent, including decreases in grants to schools, universities, municipalities, and hospitals. Municipalities, in particular, began to feel the pinch as governments downloaded responsibility for services onto them.[67] None of this seemed to work, however, as budget deficits continued throughout Getty's term. By the time he finally retired in 1993, the debt-free government he had inherited in 1985 had accumulated a debt of $11 billion.

Even before revenues dried up, the Alberta government had begun to cut services and lay off staff. Divestment of Alberta's technical institutes, mental health hospitals, and a number of other institutions, all to separate boards, was announced in 1982.[68] In 1984, the government cancelled fourteen hundred casual jobs at the Alberta Liquor Control Board (ALCB), contracted out government temporary services, and privatized large sections of Alberta Social Services. In November 1983, thousands of government positions were cut through layoffs, contracting out, and position abolishment; this was followed by further cuts in 1984, bringing the total government jobs lost to fourteen hundred.[69]

The assault on government services began in earnest in 1985 as the government began implementing its plans to privatize ALCB liquor stores, hand over certain government services to volunteer agencies, contract out food services at universities and hospitals, and privatize provincial parks and campsites. Transportation Minister Marvin Moore advised municipal districts and counties that they would qualify for their share of regular capital roads funding only if they contracted 50 percent of the work to the private sector.[70]

The Alberta Union of Provincial Employees (AUPE) responded with a Government Watch program to document cutbacks and an advertising campaign to warn the public of their harmful effects. Social partners such as the Edmonton Social Planning Council publicized the tremendous increases in social problems created by an unemployment rate that had climbed to 10.1 percent in Alberta, problems such as alcoholism, cardiovascular disease, mental hospital admissions, and suicide.[71] Social agencies felt the bite as funding from sources like the United Way shrank and research contracts from government shrivelled. As Neil Webber, minister of Social Services and Community Health, said, "We don't fund our critics."[72]

One of the biggest issues to emerge in the 1980s was the fight to preserve the public health care system in Alberta. An alarm was sounded in 1977 when the federal government abandoned a 50/50 cost-sharing agreement with provinces in favour of a block-funding scheme that failed to tie federal funds to hospitals, medical care,

FIG 7-7 Gainers picketers stop scab buses, 1986.
Courtesy of the Alberta Labour History Institute.

or other designated services. When extra-billing and facility fees became the order of the day, the Friends of Medicare was born following an Alberta Federation of Labour convention at which delegates adopted a paper entitled "Friends of Medicare: Concerns on the Erosion of Medicare in Alberta." [73] When the Alberta government passed the *Alberta Health Care Insurance Amendment Act* in 1980, implicitly legalizing extra-billing, the Friends planted people in doctors' offices, held public hearings, surveyed and educated the public, and lobbied MLAS. Their reward was to be named "Public Enemy #1" by Alberta Conservatives at their 1983 party convention.[74]

Former Saskatchewan Chief Justice Emmett Hall, whose 1965 report had given rise to the initial *Medical Care Act*, released a second report in 1982. The subsequent *Canada Health Act* of 1984 banned extra-billing as contrary to the principle of universal accessibility.[75] The Alberta government's determination to test this ban resulted in its paying $18 million in penalties from mid-1984 to the end of 1985.[76]

At the same time, critics of public education were becoming more vocal in their calls for a more traditional pedagogy and for private and charter schools, driven by the marketplace notion that parents should choose where their children are educated. The labour movement had traditionally supported public schools as a basic precondition for democracy and argued that private schools would undermine the ability of the public system to operate. After a 1982 Supreme Court decision allowed a group of Mennonites to withdraw their children from public schools, the province commissioned *A Study of Private Schools in Alberta* by Woods Gordon Management Consultants, and then increased its funding to private schools to 50 percent of the provincial per-pupil grant. By the end of the decade, the *Alberta School Act* had been amended to provide ample legal basis for public funding of private schools.[77]

Resistance in the Mid-1980s

With deteriorating economic conditions, unions in all sectors were faced with demands for concessions, making 1985 and 1986 years of much contention. Emboldened by President Reagan's destruction of the union of American air traffic controllers in 1981, Canadian airlines began to press their employees. Pacific Western Airlines began a prolonged stand-off in 1985 with the United Auto Workers/Canadian Air Line Employees Association (UAW/CALEA), the International Association of Machinists, and the Canadian Air Line Flight Attendants Association by tabling over two hundred concessionary demands. The labour movement joined picket lines and rallies until a tentative agreement was reached with UAW/CALEA after eight weeks, but the strike continued until the other two unions could vote on a conciliator's report.[78]

In September 1985, Yellow Cab drivers struck taxi service at Edmonton's International Airport for eighteen days. AUPE was invited to certify their bargaining unit, based on an earlier organizing drive that had been thwarted at the Supreme Court on a technicality, but this attempt ended once again in failure.[79] Members of the United Nurses of Alberta employed by health units went on a ten-week strike in late 1985, agreeing to return to work in late January only when they won wage parity with nurses employed in hospitals. Their bargaining stance remained firm: "A nurse is a nurse." [80]

A ten-week strike by about nine hundred members of the Retail, Wholesale and Department Store Union against deep concession demands began late in 1985 when employers reacted to a strike against Carling O'Keefe in Calgary with a lockout at all Alberta breweries, as well as at Alberta Brewers' Agents.[81] That year also spelled the beginning of the end for the Hotel and Restaurant Employees and Bartenders Union at the Legions, when members finally abandoned their fight against a lockout at Edmonton's Montgomery Legion. The Edmonton Strathcona Branch followed suit soon after.[82]

The next summer, the Gainers meat-packing plant in Edmonton became the scene of a strike that AFL president Werlin later called "a watershed in the struggle of working people in this province." He went on to explain:

> It was a strike which, if won, would stand us in good
> stead in terms of having demonstrated our ability,
> our resilience and ability to fight back, and which, if
> lost, would have set a trend which would have spread
> throughout the whole country, a trend which Mr. Pock-
> lington and his Bay Street and St. James Street backers
> had fully intended to achieve through that strike.[83]

Peter Pocklington had started in Edmonton with several Ford dealerships; he parlayed them into a small empire that included Gainers, Palm Dairies, Canbra Foods, and the Edmonton Oilers. In 1983, he ran unsuccessfully for leadership of the federal Progressive Conservatives.[84] His attitude toward trade unions became evident in his management of Gainers. In 1984, members of United Food and Commercial Workers

Local 280P had stepped back from a strike after Pocklington's negotiators convinced them that concessions were vital to the company's survival. They settled for a two-year contract with rollbacks, graphically described by John Ewasiw, a member of the local executive:

> We took a hell of an ass-kicking in 1984 as far as wages
> and benefits were concerned. The starting rate for all
> the people in 1984 was $11.99. When he got finished,
> the starting rate was lowered to $6.99, benefits were cut
> . . . and there was no such thing as a work week from
> Monday to Friday. . . . Our sick and accident insurance
> was literally taken away. . . . Alberta Health Care
> benefits were really cut for junior people. It was just
> hacked to pieces. We thought there was no alternative.[85]

Gainers did more than roll back wages: along with the Calgary Burns plant, it broke the back of pattern bargaining, which had brought stability to Canada's meat-packing industry since the early 1940s. When profits rebounded in spring 1986, company negotiators came back to the bargaining table with further concession demands.

On 1 June 1986, workers began a six-month walkout. Local 280P president John Ventura explained, "The average worker was so ticked off by the way they had been abused by management, we couldn't have prevented a strike." Many UFCW 280P members had been on strike before, but never one like this. American meat-packing lobbyist Leo Bolanes had been hired by Pocklington on a $300,000-a-year contract to back public pronouncements that he would never settle with the union, and for the first time, members saw their employer bringing in busloads of replacement workers, precisely the reason why Bolanes was paid "the big bucks," said Ventura.[86]

The community rallied around the strikers. "Pocklington came across as being just a greedy bastard, and it was easy for people to give us their support," Ventura recalled.[87] Gainers and Pocklington became household epithets, and buttons claiming that "Gainers makes wieners with scabs" appeared in the streets. Edmontonians appeared at picket lines, at the legislature, and at Premier Getty's Edmonton home as he was hosting a breakfast for Canada's premiers. A Conservative campaign meeting for the Pembina by-election was disrupted, and Prime Minister Mulroney prevented from speaking.[88] A national boycott team travelled across Canada to spread what national representative Kip Connelly described as "probably the most successful boycott ever undertaken in Canada, maybe in North America. It really captured the imagination of consumers, and the Gainers dispute itself captured the attention of the media."[89] A poll taken at the end of 1986 showed that 75 percent of Edmontonians were avoiding products bearing Gainers' B18 federal inspection sticker.[90]

A settlement was finally reached on 11 December, after Labour Board chair Andrew Sims ordered the company, in no uncertain terms, to bargain in good faith with the union. Pocklington agreed to hire back all strikers and even guaranteed their pensions. Life began to unravel for him soon after, however, and bankruptcies, seizures, and legal prosecutions would follow him to his self-exile in California.

Two other meat-packers were struck that summer of 1986. The American meat-packing giant Tyson had turned the small Lakeside plant at Brooks into Canada's largest beef slaughter plant and was firmly resisting organizing by UFCW 473. In Red Deer, UFCW 1118 went on strike against Fletchers Fine Foods on the same day as the Gainers walkout began. Union representative Allan Johnson attributes their settlement to the fact that the company's plant in Vancouver was also out on strike. As well, said Johnson, Fletchers was owned by hog producers, who were more interested in finances than ideological warfare. The workers took the company on again in 1988, however, successfully enduring an eight-month lockout imposed to crush the union.[91]

Highly publicized strikes against the meat-packers overshadowed other industrial actions in the summer of 1986, such as the longest — and last — strike by Alberta Liquor Control Board employees, which began on 31 July 1986. Gord Christie, then president of AUPE Local 50, explained why members maintained an illegal strike for fifty-seven days:

> In the eighties, our members made $25,000 to $30,000, had a reasonable pension plan, health care benefits, dental, etc. They took those jobs and made them into wage and casual jobs without benefits, where people were on call twenty-four hours a day seven days a week, but worked two or three hours a day, if at all. That was the atmosphere we went into.[92]

In May 1986, the McMurray Independent Oil Workers (MIOW) began a strike at the Suncor Plant in Fort McMurray. Many of the members had come from unionized refineries and mines in the Maritimes, explained President Dan Comrie, and were prepared to remain firm. In 1986, MIOW had filed over four hundred grievances, and the Energy and Chemical Workers Union (ECWU) sent in staff representative Ian Thorne to assist.[93] When the company turned down a "stand

pat" union offer on 1 May 1986, and instead served lockout notice, MIOW responded with strike notice, and on the same day, affiliated with the ECWU. Suncor immediately obtained court injunctions to limit pickets and sued the union for $5 million in damages. Even though the union said it would obey another injunction on 8 May, almost two hundred RCMP officers accompanied with dogs appeared at the picket lines.[94]

Members turned out en masse to walk the lines and, when led away by police, were replaced by wives and other members. In the course of the strike, 152 arrests were made.[95] In early October, after the failure of yet another back-to-work tactic, Suncor met with ECWU director Reg Basken to negotiate a settlement offering mid-term wage increases, employee assistance programs, and a radical change in industrial-relations strategy.[96]

By the summer of 1986, members of International Woodworkers of America (IWA) 1-207 had been on strike at Zeidler plywood plants in Edmonton and Slave Lake for over a year. Founder Fred Zeidler had maintained a cool but respectful relationship with the union, but when he passed away, his son-in-law, Neil Cameron, took advantage of a depressed labour market to destroy the union. While the strike in Edmonton was relatively peaceful, aggressive tactics employed by the RCMP in Slave Lake prompted AFL president Dave Werlin to complain to the government that government involvement was strictly to serve the interests of the employer and was neither protecting citizens nor maintaining law and order. The union remained on strike until 1988, when it lost to a section in the new Labour Code that declared a strike ended once it had lasted over two years.[97]

LABOUR LEGISLATION: AMENDMENTS AND CHALLENGES
Labour Law Revised — for the Worse

Public reaction to the long hot summer of discontent in 1986 prompted the Alberta government to sponsor yet another review of labour legislation in 1987. The Alberta Federation of Labour responded by organizing Change the Law meetings across Alberta. For the first time, names and contact information of all participants were preserved on a computerized database, allowing the AFL to maintain contact with over ten thousand individuals for union-related activities. Coalitions spawned by the Change the Law campaign were put to use in worksite organizing, May Day festivals, and other activities for years after.[98]

After taking a "road show" through Alberta, across Canada, and even to other countries, Labour Minister Ian Reid drafted revisions that extended restrictions in labour law to workers in both public and private sectors. Among other changes, the Alberta Labour Relations Code demanded that a representation vote be held before the Labour Board could certify a union, even when a large majority of workers had signed cards. As well, prohibitions on employer access to employees during organizing were withdrawn, providing a green light to harass and even fire workers who had signed union cards.[99] Employers could frustrate a union drive and simply write off whatever penalty might be imposed as the "cost of doing business," said Werlin.[100] The only remedy available to the Labour Board would be to order a vote in a "poisoned" environment.

The province also began to cut worker compensation costs, just as it was pursuing fewer prosecutions for health and safety violations. When courts ruled that employer negligence was the cause of death, employers were fined an average of just over three thousand dollars per death from 1985 to 1987.[101] Workers' Compensation Board (WCB) CEO Ken Pals announced plans to further reduce the role of the WCB, causing the AFL to initiate a province-wide coalition of injured workers.[102] Demonstrators at WCB offices across Alberta demanded full public hearings and immediate action on outstanding claims and appeals.

FIG 7-9 Workers march on the Alberta legislature in 1987, demanding that the government rescind anti-labour laws. Courtesy of the Alberta Federation of Labour.

On the positive side, unions saw some progress in their long-standing demand for workers' right to know about workplace hazards to which they were exposed. In 1986, the federal government created the Workplace Hazardous Materials Information System (WHMIS), which required suppliers to provide information about materials they were shipping.[103] But Alberta did not enact WHMIS until a year later, and even then, failed to incorporate some key provisions, such as full union participation and adequate worker education. The ECWU took the impetus of WHMIS a step further, however, negotiating a deal at Edmonton's Petro-Canada refinery to deduct three cents an hour from workers' pay to finance union education and training in health and safety.[104]

There were also rumours that the government was planning to pass right-to-work laws modelled on laws in effect in parts of the US. These laws banned the "agency shop," that is, a unionized workplace in which employees must pay union dues, although they are not officially required to join the union. Opponents used the misleading term "closed shop" to imply that workers were being coerced into joining the union. No such coercion existed, but the courts had ruled in the late 1940s that because all workers benefited from the union's efforts, they should all contribute to the union's functioning. Otherwise, the union would become a "free good," a service that everyone receives whether they pay for it or not — a situation that tends to cause the service to disappear for lack of funding. A worker at a Hinton union meeting recalled assembling facts and figures about infant deaths, average wages, life spans, literacy rates, and so on that showed how the general population was suffering in right-to-work

states. "It was really lucky," he said, "that the AFL put the effort and time into organizing that battle, because I believe that the Alberta government was going to put in that legislation, and it was just stopped by a hair."[105]

Labour and the Charter

On 17 April 1982, the *Constitution Act*, which included a Charter of Rights and Freedoms, was signed by Queen Elizabeth II in a ceremony in Ottawa.[106] Alberta government officials expressed concern with a document "intended to constrain government action inconsistent with those rights and freedoms," particularly when such action is "designed to regulate the behaviour of labour or management."[107]

Canadian trade unions had done little to influence the Charter process and unsurprisingly found little immediate support in the Charter for collective bargaining rights. While a few unions sent submissions, no trade union representative appeared before the Special Joint Committee on the new constitution. The main pro-union intervention came from Svend Robinson, NDP MP for Burnaby, who proposed that section 2(d) of the Charter on "freedom of association" be amended to say "freedom of association including the freedom to organize and bargain collectively."[108] His amendment was defeated, and trade unions would wait over twenty years before they could turn to the Charter to protect these rights.

Three Charter cases in 1987 established that the freedom of association provided in section 2(d) guaranteed neither the right to strike nor the right to bargain collectively. The lead case came from Alberta, when the Alberta Court of Queen's Bench postponed a case brought by the Alberta Union of Provincial Employees to refer the issue of the right to strike directly to the Supreme Court.[109] The case dealt with the *Public Service Employee Relations Act*, the *Labour Relations Act*, and the *Police Officers Collective Bargaining Act*, all of which prohibited strikes and restricted the scope of arbitration. The outcome was damaging, as it established that the rights of trade unions could not be greater than the rights its members enjoyed as individuals. Speaking for the majority, Justice McIntyre said, "People cannot, by merely combining together, create an entity which has greater constitutional rights and freedoms than they, as individuals, possess." [110]

Justices Beetz, Le Dain, and La Forest took McIntyre's argument a step further, arguing that trade unions could not be distinguished from other forms of association when interpreting their rights.[111] But Justices Dickson and Wilson disagreed, arguing for special status for trade unions. They wrote:

> In the context of labour relations, the guarantee of freedom of association in s. 2(d) of the Charter includes not only the freedom to form and join associations but also the freedom to bargain collectively and to strike. The role of association has always been vital as a means of protecting the essential needs and interests of working people. Throughout history, workers have associated to overcome their vulnerability as individuals to the strength of their employers, and the capacity to bargain collectively has long been recognized as one of the integral and primary functions of associations of working people. . . . The right of workers to strike is an essential element in the principle of collective bargaining.[112]

Such decisions created the presumption for the next twenty years that the Charter did not protect the right to engage in collective bargaining or to strike.[113]

A separate workers' rights challenge occurred in October 1987, when Olive Dickason, a professor at the University of Alberta, complained to the Alberta Human Rights Commission that the university's compulsory retirement policy contravened section 7 of the province's *Individual's Rights Protection Act* by discriminating on the basis of age. A provincial board of inquiry agreed with her, but the university appealed the decision all the way to the Supreme Court of Canada, which decided that mandatory retirement was reasonable and justifiable within the narrow meaning of the act.[114]

A SOCIAL AGENDA FOR LABOUR

While mainstream media focused on jurisdictional battles between Edmonton and Ottawa, trade unionists were forming coalitions with social activists to lay the foundation for a robust social movement in the province. The Council of Canadians emerged in 1985 to oppose the domination of Canada's social, economic, and political fabric by American corporations. Its tours, "days of action," conferences and demonstrations were supported by the AFL and individual unions, who also began to use Council research reports and organizational capacity in their work.

Another expression of social activism in the 1980s concerned food security, as the growth in corporate control of the food industry caused increasing concern about the cost and quality of food available to Canadians. Trade unionists participated in the Peoples' Food

Commission, which held public hearings across Canada and published *Land of Milk and Money: The National Report of the People's Food Commission* in 1980.[115] Alberta coordinator Lucien Royer explained that the "Commission process naturally began to identify the linkages between international trade, food exports and imports . . . as well as issues like who controls prices."[116]

Although it had only a brief lifespan, Solidarity Alberta, founded in 1984, brought trade unions into a coalition with the unemployed, youth groups, senior citizens, Aboriginal people, farmers, the disabled, welfare recipients, the peace movement, and church organizations.[117] It merged into the Action Canada Network (ACN) in 1987, forming perhaps the largest network of national and provincial organizations and coalitions ever to appear in Canada.[118] Encouraged by the National Farmers' Union, one of the ACN member organizations, labour chose to speak out on rural issues such as the abolition of the Crow Rates. An AFL brief to a House Committee on Transportation in 1987 called on Ottawa to "nationalize the CPR, if as a private enterprise, it is unwilling to meet its public obligations."[119]

As early as 1982, the AFL joined with the Alberta Status of Women Action Committee (ASWAC) to promote equal pay for work of equal value. At the time, the average woman worker earned only 55 percent of average male earnings. By the 1980s, the National Action Committee on the Status of Women (NAC) — an activist organization dedicated to such issues as daycare, birth control, maternity leave, family law, education, and pensions — had grown into a large national coalition encompassing some seven hundred groups. ASWAC was the provincial umbrella group and was active within NAC.

The decade also saw increased attention to international solidarity, including the anti-apartheid movement and the California grape boycott launched by the United Farmworkers of America to compel California to enforce legislation won by their struggle in the 1960s and 1970s. Employers continued to spray grape fields with insecticides and herbicides, poisoning farmworkers, their families, and their communities. CUPE representative Clarence Lacombe recalls his meeting with perhaps the best-known American labour activist of the last century:

> When I was a representative in Red Deer, and also president of the Labour Council, we collected money for the California farm workers, and when César Chávez . . . came to Red Deer, I had the opportunity to talk to him. I consider him to be one of the brightest leaders in the labour movement, and somebody who's an example to other people as to what can be accomplished when you have a strong enough desire to do something.[120]

Some sections of the labour movement also played a significant role in the expanding environmental movement. AFL staffer Lucien Royer was a founding member of Save Tomorrow, Oppose Pollution (STOP) in 1980. In January 1983, STOP won a case against Panarctic Oil, which was fined $150,000, placed on probation, and ordered to draft a remedial plan after a Territorial Court in Yellowknife found it guilty of dumping waste scrap metal and chemicals into the Arctic Ocean.[121] STOP helped to found the Alberta Environmental Network (AEN), which welcomed any Alberta-based non-profit, non-governmental organization engaging in action for a healthier environment. This included the AFL, which had formed a standing environment committee in 1982. With the release of *Our Common Future* (the Brundtland Report) in 1987,[122] the focus of that committee switched to sustainable development and immediate action to stop the destruction of our global environment by unsustainable patterns of production and consumption. Roundtables on the Environment and Economy, organized both nationally and provincially, included such labour nominees as ECWU president Reg Basken.

But, as on many other issues, the labour movement was not united on environmental causes or on how to handle alliances with social movements. Many in the environmental movement regarded the labour movement's stances on the environment and on willingness to work with others for radical change as too limited by its historical ties to the dominant social model, which viewed economic growth as essential to social progress and human happiness. Ecosocialists called for a radical shift in thinking toward no-growth economies with a radical redistribution of wealth; a significant emphasis away from private property, including cars; and an end or significant rollback of polluting industries, including the petroleum, chemical, and nuclear industries. Political scientist Laurie Adkin notes that this call for the reframing of humans' relations to the ecology was met with some hostility among unions; they had, after all, fought successfully to improve the material lives of their members who had worked in industrial-era firms that were now seen as major polluters — members who had bought into the dominant paradigm of the industrially produced good life. As a result, it was hardly surprising that a union such as the Energy and Chemical Workers Union (ECWU), whose members worked in industries targeted by environmentalists as destructive, was reticent about alliances, even though it was pressuring the companies in these industries to do more to protect the health of their members and to limit environmental impacts on their communities. As Adkin observes, "The higher proportion of skilled tradespersons in the ECWU, in addition to employer campaigns, have contributed to the formation of a 'professional elite' culture among ECWU officials which is resistant to the militant, grass-roots oriented campaigns and tactics and to the formation of alliances with non-union organizations."[123]

Labour's position on peace issues in the 1950s, as we saw in chapter 5, had also resulted in divisions with some taking the pro-Western side and often red-baiting both pro-Communists and pacifists. But by the 1980s, the Alberta labour movement was more united in favour of peace initiatives. This was evident in AFL presentations in August 1985 to the Special Joint Committee on Canada's International Relations, in which the AFL objected to Canadian participation in President Reagan's Strategic Defence Initiative: this initiative would supposedly create a mythological nuclear shield around the United States while it continued to increase its own nuclear forces aimed at others. Trade unions were instrumental in a thirteen-day Anti-Cruise Easter March, which went from Cold Lake to Edmonton in May 1983, passing through towns where committees were typically formed around a CUPE local in a small-town hospital.

THE STRUGGLE CONTINUES

As the 1980s came to a close, economic conditions in Alberta deteriorated further and demonstrated the extent to which its government, locked in a close embrace with large corporations, had failed to protect the public interest. An example was the failure of the Principal Group, an Edmonton-based trust company central to Premier Lougheed's vision for Alberta. Its investment subsidiaries were shut down on 30 June 1987, by court order, and the parent company went bankrupt soon after, affecting more than sixty thousand people, including investors and employees. The government paid out $85 million to the investors but ignored the suddenly unemployed workers. A court-ordered investigation led by Calgary lawyer Bill Code revealed a decade of government failure to protect the public interest, including its duty to administer and enforce the *Investment Contracts Act*.[124]

Working people were not impressed with their governments' efforts to deal with continuing hard times. Mounting cutbacks, privatization, and layoffs led to more industrial action. The postal unions led rotating strikes in 1987 against concession demands, cutbacks, and privatization of postal services; the federal government responded with back-to-work legislation with binding arbitration. The private sector, meanwhile, saw multi-year strikes led by IWA 1-207 at Zeidler's in Slave Lake and the United Steelworkers of America at Wittke Steel in Medicine Hat, and strikes and lockouts at XL Beef and Centennial Packers in Calgary.[125]

The United Nurses of Alberta (UNA) went to the bargaining table in 1987 asking for improvements in safety, patient care, and professional responsibility, but were met with an unprecedented list of concession demands. When the Labour Relations Board issued a cease-and-desist order against a UNA strike vote, nurses at 104 UNA hospitals held a vote anyway. They began a nineteen-day strike on 25 January 1988, the seventh walkout in the union's eleven-year history. This produced severe retaliatory measures, including a board order declaring the union's actions illegal. When the UNA stayed out, it was charged with contempt of court, and seventy-five individuals were also charged, with many terminated. Moreover, Justice Sinclair found criminal contempt and imposed a fine of $250,000, followed by a second fine of $150,000, with $26,750 for civil contempt — the largest penalties in Alberta history.

The AFL formed a strike support committee with representation from all sectors of the union movement, church and women's groups, and the NDP. It also formed the Friends of Alberta Nurses Society (FANS), which collected over $425,000 in contributions to meet the stiff penalties faced by the UNA.[126] This was one of several formations organized to assist unions on the front line of attack and to change labour legislation. Other support groups were formed for the private sector strikers mentioned earlier, and the Alberta Workers' Rights Action Committee organized in 1989 to support the building trades against the introduction of merit shops in Alberta. For example, on 30 March 1989, the Action Committee held a rally at the Banff Springs Hotel to protest a meeting organized by the Merit Contractors Association and the Independent Contractors of British Columbia.[127]

The decade closed with a lengthy strike by caregivers who had been affected by privatization and closures of care facilities. On 1 May 1990, social workers, child care counsellors, and others in Alberta Union of Provincial Employees Local 006 walked out to support two key demands: downsizing case loads and implementing pay equity. Local member Guy Smith said, "We took the stand that we are for quality public services and that we cannot provide those services unless we're given the resources to do so. Part of that is having decent working conditions and decent workloads."[128]

LABOUR AND THE POLITICAL SPHERE
Electoral Politics

> When Dave [Werlin] was the president of the
> Federation of Labour, the working people in
> the province of Alberta have never had better
> leadership. I think Dave personally got more people
> to become New Democrats, to become active in
> the NDP movement, even though Dave himself has
> long admitted that he's a communist and has never
> hidden the fact.[129]

As we saw in chapter 6, Alberta labour's initial embrace of the NDP was neither universal nor effective. At the 1983 annual convention, AFL president Harry Kostiuk reported about the 1982 provincial election, "It is with some degree of despair that we must report that on November 2nd, a lot of our own members voted for the Conservatives."[130] But change was in the air in May 1986, when the Alberta New Democrats won 29 percent of the popular vote and Official Opposition status, with sixteen seats in the Legislature. The party won the same number of seats in 1989. The large number of mainly working-class constituencies that went NDP suggested that many workers believed that the party most favoured by AFL union leaders offered programs that favoured the working class. There was even a brief federal breakthrough as Ross Harvey won Edmonton-East in 1988 in a campaign focused on opposition to the Free Trade Agreement. Former NDP leader Grant Notley did not live to see any of this, however: he died on 19 October 1984, when the two-engine aircraft he was taking to his home in Dunvegan crashed into a hillside in a blinding snow storm. Ray Martin, elected as an MLA with Notley in 1982, took over as leader and was joined by Jim Gurnett, who won in the by-election to replace Notley.

While the NDP was making gains in Alberta that proved temporary, the federal Reform Party, which emerged in May 1987, quickly gained popularity in western Canada. Leader Preston Manning, son of the former Alberta premier, focused on free trade and direct democracy (with referendums, initiatives, and recall), a Triple-E Senate (equal, elected, and effective), and opposition to special status for Quebec. Underlying these were a belief in decentralization and a reduced role for government, primarily through cuts to social welfare and cultural programs.[131] Albertan Deborah Grey won a federal seat for Reform in 1989, setting the stage for the near-total collapse of federal Conservatives in 1993, when Reform became the Official Opposition in Parliament.

Labour-backed candidates enjoyed some successes on the municipal front. Ted Grimm, who served as the mayor of Medicine Hat from 1974 to 2001 (excluding one term), credits his success to his experience with the Oil, Chemical and Atomic Workers when he worked at a fertilizer plant operated in Medicine Hat.[132] As mayor, he worked hard to retain public ownership of the gas fields and utilities that had built Medicine Hat's reputation as the town with "all Hell for a basement."[133] He was under constant pressure to sell to private interests. "They knew where I stood," said Grimm. "I showed them the door. . . . I knew what would happen to the money. It would be squandered, we'd have no asset, and they would have control. I operated on the philosophy that, as far as public utilities were concerned, ownership is control."[134]

The Edmonton District Labour Council continued to play a key role in the Edmonton Voters' Association (EVA), which ran candidates for city council and school board, and championed civic issues throughout the 1980s. Brian Mason, later a leader of the provincial NDP, was elected for four terms to City Council under the EVA banner, beginning in 1989.

Jan Reimer, daughter of the provincial NDP's first leader, was first elected to City Council in 1980 as a member of the Urban Reform Group of Edmonton, and was re-elected for two more terms, becoming a spokesperson for those opposed to concessions to land developers, particularly regarding farmland. In 1989, Reimer was elected the first female mayor of Edmonton, a post she held until 1995. Highlights of her time in office include the inception of a new waste-management system (which included curbside pickup of recyclables) and her resistance to repeated efforts by Peter Pocklington to secure concessions from the city in exchange for his agreement not to move the Oilers.[135]

Labour Takes on Free Trade

The decade that began with the re-election of a Liberal government in Ottawa ended with the Mulroney Conservatives bringing in a free trade deal that would align Canada even more closely with the politics and economy of the United States. Powerful international capitalist forces had been pressing since the early 1970s for an end to national protection of local industries. A key group was the Trilateral Commission, a gathering of the elite of finance and industry that had been launched in 1972 with the goal of "checking the intrusion of national government into the international exchange of both economic and non-economic goods."[136]

Just after he was elected in 1984, Mulroney announced that Canada was "open for business." Canada Post was immediately told to operate according to a business model that would eventually result in the closing of all post offices in favour of franchised outlets and privatized service. VIA Rail had its budget slashed and was targeted for eventual shutdown, and the CBC suffered the first of its many budget cutbacks.

Mulroney's moves to cement a free trade deal with the United States began in 1985 at the Shamrock Summit at Montebello, Quebec, where he joined President Reagan in a duet of "When Irish Eyes Are Smiling." Canadian historian Jack Granatstein commented that this "public display of sucking up to Reagan may have been the single most demeaning moment in the entire political history of Canada's relations with the United States."[137] The Canada-US Free Trade Agreement, finalized in late 1987, was to eliminate barriers to trade in goods and services between Canada and the United States, facilitate conditions of fair competition within the free trade area established by the agreement, and liberalize significantly conditions for investment between the two countries. Two countries that already had more trade between them than any other two countries on earth — roughly $150 billion worth of goods a year — would be brought even closer together.

AFL president Dave Werlin and his executive council left no doubt where they stood on the issue. Participants in the 1986 AFL convention were told: "With no mandate from the Canadian voters, they are preparing to sell out our Canadian resources, our Canadian jobs, our Canadian culture, our Canadian social services, our Canadian standard of living, and Canadian sovereignty — all of it served on a platter to the U.S.-based multinational companies and their disloyal, greedy, junior partners in Canada." [138]

Before the treaty could be ratified by the Canadian Parliament, a vigorous national debate ensued, with the Pro-Canada Network, a coalition of community and labour groups, giving voice to opponents of the deal. Alberta coordinator Lucien Royer explained, "Although the outside observer would say there are so many different issues we were working on, in essence they were all facets of the same phenomenon, which is the nature of trade agreements and the nature of this particular trade agreement and what it would do to our country." [139] Anti–trade deal rallies organized in Edmonton and Calgary by the Pro-Canada Network in 1988 attracted thousands from church, community, Aboriginal, and trade union organizations. Even some leading economists and industrial leaders spoke against the Mulroney-Reagan deal. Lobbying was so intense that the Tories might have lost the "Free Trade Election" of November 1988 had it not been for the multi-million

dollar advertising blitz launched by some of Canada's largest corporations under the umbrella of the Alliance of Opportunity and Trade.

The Conservative Party was re-elected and the agreement was ratified on 4 October 1988, coming into effect on 1 January 1989. Said AFL president Werlin, "The recent Mulroney electoral victory was a major setback for working people. It means that, despite the fact that a majority of Canadians voted against free trade, implementation of the deal will be the hallmark of the Mulroney government's second term. This is the meaning of the Free Trade Deal. Freedom for the corporations: lost jobs and opportunities for Canadian workers." [140] Early signs appeared to confirm Werlin's warnings: for example, a Molsons/Carling O'Keefe merger, citing a need to compete with US brewing giants; the sale of Alberta-based Wardair because of the deregulated free trade environment; a buyout of Texaco Canada by Exxon; and the takeover of Consolidated Bathurst by American Stone, with production shifted to the parent's Michigan plant. [141]

The decade closed with a Pro-Canada Network fight against a new regressive tax, the Goods and Services Tax (GST), in which Alberta labour took the lead. Initially opposed to the GST (primarily because it represented a federal intrusion), the Alberta government of Don Getty refused to do anything about it. So, in September 1989, the Pro-Canada Network, together with the Calgary and District Labour Council, launched a postcard campaign, which over the next few months delivered over a million postcards to federal MPs representing Alberta ridings. This was combined with a lobby campaign of Alberta MLAs and MPs, creating division among the Conservatives that forced Prime Minister Mulroney to use a heavy hand on his backbenchers, even throwing two out of the caucus.

◆ ◆ ◆

As the 1980s ended, the labour movement in Alberta could look back upon a decade of militancy and achievement. They had taken advantage of a deep recession and blatant anti-union action in Alberta to educate workers about the dangers of allowing only corporations and corporate-minded governments to make the decisions affecting workers' lives. The Alberta Federation of Labour and individual unions had demonstrated to governments and corporations alike that they would not allow workers' rights to be trampled upon without fighting back. The trade union movement had created alliances with other opposition-minded civil society groups on issues of common concern, and the NDP, the party that labour had created, reached the peak of its strength in the province. Unfortunately, all of these hard-fought gains could be quickly eroded, as events in the following decades would prove.

FIG 8-1 The Alberta Union of Provincial Employees and the Canadian Union of
Public Employees celebrate the signing of an agreement with the Calgary Regional
Health Authority, the culmination of a strike of hospital and home care workers
in 1995 that began with a walkout by laundry workers. Courtesy of Gord Christie.

8 REVOLUTION, RETRENCHMENT, AND THE NEW NORMAL THE 1990s AND BEYOND

JASON FOSTER

[When we heard the plant was going to close] a lot of them came to the realization, it's an old plant, it's gonna shut down. . . . They all thought they could walk out and get jobs. In the first couple of rounds of layoffs . . . it was mostly the younger guys that went, with least seniority. They all did walk into reasonably high-paying jobs in the oil industry, because they needed the people. But as we came to the end and the guys were getting from their twenties and thirties into their forties, they were finding it a little more difficult to find work. A lot of the guys in their middle to late forties wanted to stay in the Edmonton area. Well these jobs didn't exist in the Edmonton area, or were tougher to get. The last hundred that went in June are like me, they're fifty and over. . . . You're looking at four thousand people who lost their jobs and a significant income. If you start turning that into terms of families, you're talking maybe twelve thousand people that have been affected by this. Now they're not taking as big a role in their communities. They're not able to, they don't have the income anymore. . . . But the politicians didn't want to . . . pay any attention.[1]

They tried to say it's violent. The first three days were probably the best and the worst. My first experience of actually being on strike. The first day the buses were stopped. It was like, wow, this is cool. . . . Then the second day when they came across the cornfields on the buses . . . that tells you how much they really care about their team members' safety, when they're willing to bounce them across the cornfield to bring them into the plant. Then that night comes. I'm home and I can hear sirens. I'm like, oh god what's going on out there. Next thing I hear a bunch of supervisors get off a bus and start beating picketers. . . . Then the next day comes, the buses are stopped, production don't go. Then that night, they were trying to give Doug papers . . . they run him off the road. I don't know about you, but to me that's attempted murder. When you're running somebody off the road, going a hundred kilometres an hour down the highway, it's bad enough to hit an animal at that speed, let alone you got cars trying to box you in and run you off the road. It was like, oh my god . . . will they stop at nothing to make sure this union is out?[2]

Two stories. The first, from former Celanese worker Bill Climie, is about the closure of a petrochemical plant that served as a mainstay for Fort Saskatchewan for fifty years. The second is Ashley Grandy's tale of the ugly Lakeside Packers strike in Brooks, a unionization drive pitting a diverse workforce against a fiercely anti-union employer. Each story provides glimpses of an Alberta in transformation in the last decade of the twentieth century and the first of the twenty-first. The new Alberta was more diverse but more hostile to workers than ever, which in turn incited new groups of workers to fight for justice. Other workers, however, like many during the boom of the 1970s, shared the government's vision of new prosperity as a supercharged tar sands boom took hold in the early 2000s (though like that earlier boom, it was followed by a bust). Like Alberta's workers, the labour movement's responses to a neo-liberal government enmeshed with corporate forces committed to leaving the province's fate to global markets also varied — from resistance to capitulation.

Alberta's era of full-blown neo-liberalism began 5 December 1992, at the Northlands Agricom in Edmonton, when Ralph Klein won the leadership of the Progressive Conservative (PC) Party and the premiership. He defeated his opponents by essentially running against the Getty government in which he had served as a cabinet minister, promising to make massive budget cuts to end deficit financing and eventually provincial debt altogether.

An account of the 1990s and 2000s must start, then, with Ralph Klein and his election. But despite his central and flamboyant role, the real story is that of Albertans and how they responded to the forces of globalization and the rise of neo-liberalism.

CONTEXTUALIZING A REVOLUTIONARY ERA

The cracks in the postwar Fordist compromise accelerated in the 1990s. The global shift of power to transnational corporations continued as trade rules were weakened and the international flow of capital was liberalized. The strength of international bodies such as the International Monetary Fund and the World Bank intensified, culminating in the focused power of the World Trade Organization, formed in 1995. Labour politics and social democracy entered a phase of deep crisis, unsure how to respond to the new world order of free capital and constrained states.

The Canada-US Free Trade Agreement was expanded in 1993 to include Mexico, becoming the North American Free Trade Agreement (NAFTA), without the debate and acrimony that accompanied its predecessor. Canada also experienced a serious recession in the early 1990s, placing great pressure on government budgets and throwing thousands of workers into unemployment. In 1992, unemployment reached 11 percent.[3] Canada's constitutional issues also contributed to an atmosphere of malaise and unease, as both the Meech Lake Accord and the Charlottetown Accord were defeated, discrediting mainstream political actors, reinvigorating the Quebec sovereignty movement, and promoting the rise of the right-wing Reform Party.

The retreat from Keynesian economics, evident in the 1980s recession, was even more marked in that of the 1990s. Trudeau had accepted the continuation of the Bank of Canada's tight-money policies when the recession occurred in 1982, but, while he had avoided Keynesian counter-cyclical spending, he had not cut government programs much. By contrast, the Mulroney government cut social spending, especially grants to provinces. It also reduced workers' protections with a series of restrictive reforms to Unemployment Insurance.[4] The Chrétien government in the mid-1990s further restricted access to unemployment benefits. Instead of drawing attention to high unemployment rates, politicians raised the alarm about "unsustainable deficits" and "big government."

The last decade of the 1900s and the first of the 2000s witnessed a transformation in Alberta's economy, politics, and society. The period began with Albertans highly dependent upon oil and gas for their economic prosperity and trying to escape an extended recession. Governments were attempting to diversify into secondary processing and manufacturing. Oil prices then rebounded and Alberta's economic fortunes bounced up with them, leading to an unprecedented boom in the middle part of the era, only to end up once again on the rough end of an economic downturn. Alberta ended the period more deeply tied to energy, and in particular tar sands, less diversified than twenty years earlier and with a dying manufacturing base.[5] Alberta, the home of Prime Minister Stephen Harper, had become Canada's energy superpower and was playing a more central role in the politics of the nation.

Alberta was not immune to global economic changes, which accompanied continued deindustrialization in advanced capitalist countries and growth in service industries. This so-called post-industrialism has brought an increased polarization of society. In Alberta, alongside the growing number of Hummers and mansion-sized houses was a burgeoning group of increasingly vulnerable workers, on whose sweat much of the province's prosperity rested. Many of these workers were part of the changing face of Alberta as migration from other provinces and international immigration brought scores of new workers into the province, and with them, different traditions, perspectives, and cultures. This transformation would challenge the labour movement and its ability to adapt to new realities.

Electorally, the overall picture remained unchanged, but with swirling eddies underneath. The 1993 provincial election found the PCs experiencing their first real threat in twenty years and saw the wipeout of the Official Opposition New Democrats, supplanted by an invigorated Liberal Party. But the Liberals proved a paper tiger in the next four elections as the Tory grip on power strengthened. The Liberals remained an anemic second party, while the NDP struggled to maintain a toehold in a handful of Edmonton ridings. The security of the PCs' electoral fortunes played heavily in the political dynamics of the era, though the province's oil barons reigned supreme, as demonstrated in part by the emergence of the Wildrose Alliance, discussed below.

On the surface, little changed regarding unionization levels in Alberta, with about 27 percent union density in 1990 compared to 25 percent in 2010, a remarkably small drop given the seismic changes of the era.[6] However, the face of labour changed significantly. Demographic changes and stagnation in private sector unionization led to an increase in women and people of colour within Alberta unions. The former union world of the white male goods-producing worker evaporated. By the early 2000s, a majority of union members were women. Growing numbers were workers of colour. Most unionized jobs were in the public sector, and four out of five were in service occupations.[7] And neither new unionists nor old had a friend in Premier Klein.

BIRTH OF A REVOLUTION

Ralph Klein became premier at a time when the range of political debate was significantly constricted and public perception was that "something" had to be done to fix the crisis. Klein — a former mayor of Calgary, where he was regarded as a moderate Liberal and a straight-talking, hard-drinking populist[8] — recast himself as the tough leader capable of making hard decisions to turn things around.

The 1992 PC leadership vote was spawned by the resignation of Don Getty, premier since 1985, whose government was plagued by scandals, spiraling deficits, and plummeting popularity in opinion polls. A series of ventures aimed at economic diversification — including NovAtel (cellular telephones), Millar Western (pulp mill), MagCan (magnesium processing), and the Lloydminister heavy oil upgrader — had become financial disasters. The budget deficit hit $1.5 billion in 1991/92. Klein handily defeated Edmonton-based cabinet minister Nancy Betkowski to win the party leadership on the second round of balloting, becoming premier nine days later on 14 December 1992. Many observers argue that the leadership race result represented an ideological shift that changed the course of the party. Betkowski represented the moderate, urban tradition of Lougheed, while Klein appealed to rural Tories and hard-line, neo-liberal elements.[9]

But while Klein represented a change in style, it is questionable how much his leadership affected the direction of the Progressive Conservative Party. The moderate Lougheed image was exaggerated and reflected the political context of the time. The PCs had already begun to swing rightward under Getty in the early 1990s, as the influence of the upstart Reform Party affected the activist base of the provincial Tories.[10] Klein's personal ambition to pursue a radical neo-liberal course merely accelerated trends already occurring within the PC Party and within Canadian politics in general.

After becoming premier, Klein quickly delivered a message that his government would be markedly different than that of his predecessor. He reduced the size of cabinet and eliminated the Department of Occupational Health and Safety, which had existed since the early 1980s. To assuage angry voters, he eliminated the MLA pension plan. As a clear harbinger of things to come, the Klein government's first key social policy decision was to drastically reduce welfare rolls and introduce "workfare" (where social assistance recipients must work for their benefits). As longtime Calgary activist Gord Christie pointed out, "Their very first piece of business was to attack the people on social assistance. At the time, we had nearly the lowest social assistance rates in Canada. . . . We cut those, not just cut those, we trashed those rates. The very first thing they attacked were the most disadvantaged people in our society."[11] The May budget on the eve of the provincial election provided a sneak peek into the government's plans following re-election.

The June 1993 election was unlike any other in Alberta history, in particular for the convergence of Liberal and PC platforms. Liberal leader Laurence Decore called for "brutal cuts" to government budgets and restriction of government's role. Klein countered with a call for "massive cuts."[12] Both parties accepted neo-liberal assumptions about fiscal challenges and proposed nearly identical solutions. A blindsided NDP defended the status quo but found no audience thanks to a successful corporate and media campaign of "deficit hysteria" that made even the former Tory status quo appear too radical. After the election, with a majority secured, Klein moved swiftly on his promised agenda of massive cuts that would rock public services and public sector workers to their foundation. "Ralph [was] off and running," observed Christie, adding:

> You had a government who was elected on slash and burn, you had an opposition who ran on slash and burn, and you truly had no opposition. All of a sudden, it was full speed ahead on health care, education, civil servants, environment, you name it. . . . The first opposition I saw to this, we participated in, is when they passed the budget in the spring of '93. . . . Jim Dinning and Ralph Klein had a news conference down at McDougall Centre where they're announcing the agenda, all the massive cuts. Myself and a few other activists were down [there too] to raise some hell about it.[13]

DIMENSIONS OF A REVOLUTION

The two years that followed marked what may be the most tumultuous period in modern Alberta history. As in any revolution, some groups were more affected than others: women, seniors, people with disabilities, and the poor paid a disproportionate price. Public sector unions were also in for the fight of their life. The government took action on multiple fronts at once, moving with unusual speed, determination, and focus. Key minister Steve West articulated the strategy clearly: "Taking more time never makes that job easier. It just allows your opponents time to mount their campaigns. . . . You need

to move as quickly as possible."[14] The following section examines the dimensions of these swift assaults, who was affected, and how Alberta workers and their unions responded.

Budget Cutbacks

The 1993–94 budget announced an aggressive plan to reduce government spending by 20 percent over three years. The impact of the reductions was widespread. In health care, cuts quickly led to bed reductions, longer wait times in emergency rooms, and hospital closures. Simultaneously, the government regionalized health care delivery, adding further confusion into the system. In education, funding for kindergarten was slashed by 50 percent and class sizes for all grades were increased.

FIG 8-2 United Nurses of Alberta President Heather Smith addresses a rally against cutbacks at the Alberta legislature, 1994. Courtesy of the United Nurses of Alberta.

FIG 8-3 Calgary General Hospital
was blown up in 1998 on orders
from the Klein government.
Courtesy of Frank Reaume.

The government also permitted semi-private "charter schools" to open. In advanced education, funding grants were cut by 21 percent and tuition began to rise significantly. Services for people with disabilities were cut back, and Assured Income for the Severely Handicapped (AISH) rates were frozen. Seniors were particularly hard hit, with the amalgamation of five programs into a single, new, income-tested Alberta Seniors Benefit, which proved deleterious to middle-income seniors and of only marginal benefit to the poorest retired Albertans.[15] Probably the biggest target of the deficit hawks were recipients of welfare. In addition to the announced workfare program, the government reduced benefits for clients deemed capable of work and systematically reduced the total caseload. Between March 1993 and August 1994, recipients fell from about 122,000 to 68,000 — a drop of 44 percent — while fewer than one in ten had moved into gainful employment.[16] Meanwhile 6,600 core government jobs were eliminated in three years, along with 3,000 nursing positions and thousands of jobs in education and advanced education.[17]

The short-term impact of all this was cuts to services, longer waiting lists, and higher costs to individuals. But more significant, and by design, were the long-term effects: a weakened public sector less able to effectively deliver public services. Coupled with the other vigorously pursued side of the government agenda, tax reduction, the Conservative goal was to shrink permanently the capacity of the state to play a role in public life.

Wage Rollbacks

A central component of the expenditure reduction strategy took dead aim at public sector workers both in the core public service and in health care, school boards, universities and colleges. In fall 1993, Klein asked all public sector workers to voluntarily accept a 5 percent wage reduction followed by a two-year wage freeze, and he entrenched his "request" by ordering that payroll funding envelopes be reduced by 5 percent, effectively forcing the hands of the unions and their employers.

Initial union responses promised a fight. "You are headed for one of the biggest labour battles that you've ever seen in this province," thundered Alberta Union of Provincial Employees (AUPE) president Carol Anne Dean.[18] She called for a general strike in February 1994.[19] Other labour leaders also promised to mobilize their members to take "drastic action." Health care unions and education unions formed coalitions to fight the plan. Some unions, including the Alberta Teachers' Association (ATA), ran extensive ad campaigns to support their position. The government responded by meeting with health care unions to discuss overall health care restructuring, but discussions went nowhere.

THE CONSEQUENCES OF CUTBACKS: HEALTH CARE

I remember a large portion of my time was spent in layoff meetings during those mid-nineties. . . . In '92 was the first wave. At the time it was devastating; it was a smaller chunk though than what we were to see. At that meeting, I remember them calling the nurses together from what was termed the nursing float pool, which was this group of nurses that floated wherever the need was. They called in the managers to the same meeting. . . . They told everybody there at the same time in the room that the nursing office was going to be eliminated. The IV team was another one . . . they were going to be eliminated. It struck me that you're telling your staff, your managers and staff nurses, together: it was a bizarre occurrence. That was the first wave that had happened. But as we got into the mid-nineties they started to do those kinds of layoffs by units. They would call in the nurses that were going to be laid off into a room. They would have the manager there, they would have some HR people there. My heart knows that it was the right place for the union to be there, but it was some of the hardest days I'd ever experienced as a union leader, to see the young nurses coming in. They were our future, so I knew we were about to get rid of an entire generation. . . . It hit you very hard in the face to be sitting in those meetings and realize that some of those young people who had young children and were maybe not married for long, and probably had a mortgage and all kinds of goals and visions and dreams, and were having that totally brought to a halt immediately. . . .

But my sense is that the morale of the staff nurses or the frontline bedside nurses has never recovered from that. . . . It's been crisis after crisis since then. . . . We've never had the time to recover.

— Jane Sustrik, University of Alberta Registered Nurse; Staff Nurses of Alberta, and United Nurses of Alberta Executive Member

SOURCE: Interview with Jane Sustrik, Edmonton, 19 April 2007, ALHI.

The willingness to take on the Klein government began to crumble. In December 1993, Canadian Union of Public Employees (CUPE) health care locals agreed to the rollbacks in return for guarantees against contracting out. "These people got job security," said CUPE representative John Malthouse. "There is a ban on subcontracting until March 31, 1995. That's historic. We couldn't have paid for that agreement earlier in the year."[20] The ATA settled local by local in early 1994. ATA president Bauni MacKay justified the settlements as "'an essential move' designed to keep the focus on the bigger picture where it belonged, that the very essence of public education was under attack."[21]

AUPE held out longest, after members rejected a tentative agreement in June 1994. But Klein threatened that the reductions would be achieved through layoffs: a few months later, members accepted a barely changed offer. Eventually, most unions negotiated settlements that entrenched the reductions and subsequent wage freeze through combinations of wage reductions, unpaid time off, and other concessions. A few small locals, refusing to accept the agreement, eventually had the rollbacks imposed by arbitration.

Several factors produced this outcome. First, the government's determination to achieve its fiscal goals gave unions a stark choice of wage reductions or layoffs. Second, political mobilization of public sector workers was underdeveloped at the time. Many members, such as nurses and teachers, perceived themselves as professionals but not union activists. Also, many members, as Albertans, accepted the government's framing of the deficit problem and saw pay reductions as a reasonable way to "do their part." Unions struggled financially since layoffs translated into loss of members, and thus revenue, and the simultaneous need to spend additional resources to defend members. It is estimated, for example, that public sector unions lost 20 percent of their membership in this period; AUPE lost almost 30 percent of its core government members in three years.[22] Finally, union leadership adept at collective bargaining processes but less confident at political mobilization opted for strategies with which they were most comfortable. Nevertheless, anger over the 5 percent reduction simmered for years and would eventually create difficulties for the government after the heat of the revolution had cooled.

Privatization

At the core of the neo-liberal project is the goal to transform the functions of the state to benefit the interests of capital, including moving state services onto the market. Privatization was a key component of the so-called Klein Revolution.

Privatization as such was not new to conservative Alberta. Lougheed had reprivatized Pacific Western Airlines in 1983. The Getty regime had privatized Alberta Government Telephones in 1991. However, the Klein government was the first to embark on a wide-scale effort to privatize public services and to adopt privatization as an ideological given rather than a pragmatic policy option. Minister Steve West claimed, without supporting evidence, "There isn't a government operation, a government business, a Crown corporation that is as efficient as the private sector, and indeed they're 20 to 40 per cent less efficient."[23] West announced the first two privatizations in fall 1993. The government closed public registry offices and contracted to private registry providers on a fee-for-service basis. Similarly,

FIG 8-4 Vance Rodewalt, a *Calgary Herald* cartoonist, shows
the Klein government cutting the dummy named "Alberta"
in half, January 1995. Glenbow Archives M-9457-50.

government-owned distribution and retail of alcohol through Alberta Liquor Control Board (ALCB) stores was replaced with private liquor stores serviced by a private monopoly distributor, transforming thirteen hundred jobs into private retail jobs that averaged half the ALCB wages.[24] Ray Gorse, AUPE activist and chair of the ALCB local, expressed the fears of ALCB workers in an *Edmonton Journal* article: "I joined the liquor board seven years ago because it was a nice, secure job with a fairly good pension plan." With the government's announcement, he was left wondering what the private stores would pay: "What's minimum wage? . . . Ralph Klein and Steve West are destroying a lot of lives."[25] The union howled, but both moves were politically popular.[26]

Other privatizations quickly followed: highway maintenance, provincial park operation, Alberta Tourism, and the publicly owned radio and TV networks, CKUA and ACCESS. In all cases, privatization led to financial scandal and turmoil, as in the bankrupted CKUA and Alberta Tourism, or to higher costs and lower service quality.[27] And in a different form of privatization, the government passed legislation changing the status of the Workers' Compensation Board to an autonomous corporation, no longer accountable to the minister of Labour. This launched an extended period of reductions in worker benefits and increased claim denials meant to lower employer premiums.

The privatization push stalled in the mid-1990s. Several planned selloffs — including contracting out enforcement functions in employment standards and environmental protection, and selling the Alberta Treasury Branches — were eventually rejected due to political pressure. However, privatization takes many forms. In the late 1990s and early 2000s, the government turned to public-private partnerships (P3s) as a model for construction and operation of new facilities. Under P3, rather than have the state pay for the costs of constructing a new facility, a private sector partner pays costs up front and then receives an annual payment from the government for an extended period. Many large construction projects in the mid-2000s, including Anthony Henday Drive in Edmonton and eighteen schools around the province, were constructed as P3s, a model that has been shown to defraud the public in the long term.[28]

A Communications Revolution

Perhaps the most enduring component of the Klein Revolution was the reshaping of the nature of political debate in Alberta and of public perception about the province. Klein, as a former reporter, demonstrated particular skill at communication, using it to frame issues and debate in a fashion designed to make the neo-liberal agenda appear inevitable. He quickly centralized government communications by heading up the Public Affairs Bureau (PAB) and giving it significantly increased resources: the number of "spin doctors" under the PAB expanded from 47 in 1993 to 133 in 2001.[29] This revamped department provided Klein with unprecedented ability to manage communications, aided by an acquiescent press gallery.

Three strategies were employed to control political debate, all central to the neo-liberal project. First, the government personalized criticism, attacking opponents in ad hominem fashion. Former bureaucrat (and future Liberal leader) Kevin Taft was branded a "communist" for his book *Shredding the Public Interest*, which exposed Klein's fiscal policy as fraudulent.[30] Albertans mobilizing against plans to privatize health care were labeled "left-wing nuts."

Second, advocates critical of the government were denigrated as "special interest groups." Klein dismissed women, people with disabilities, labour unions, gays and lesbians, and anti-poverty organizations as special interests. The implied ideological message was that the government represented the so-called public interest and was preventing narrow interests from hijacking the political agenda. This dichotomy was personalized in Klein's creation of "Martha and Henry," who represented the "severely normal" Albertan. Klein filled the vessel of Martha and Henry with values, political positions, and attitudes that reflected the neo-liberal project.

The third strategy may have been the most effective: defining what makes Alberta great. The PAB concocted a slogan, nominally to promote Alberta business externally, but, in effect, to "brand" Alberta. The chosen phrase was "The Alberta Advantage," and it embodied the neo-liberal Klein agenda: low taxes, competitive business environment, low unionization, trained and flexible workforce, business-friendly government. When delivered as a boast to Albertans, as it often was, it served the function of telling Albertans what values defined them. The framing was so successful that even Albertans adversely affected by the cuts repeated the phrase when contesting who received the advantage, thus accepting the bulk of its implied political assumptions.

By the end of the 1990s, neo-liberal framing loomed large over Alberta politics. While much of the Klein Revolution dissipated after 1997, the communications revolution continued to leave its mark on Alberta well into the twenty-first century.

LABOUR'S RESPONSE

The government's sweeping agenda sparked furious debate and reaction among Albertans. The atmosphere in the province during 1994 and 1995 crackled with tension, anger, and disagreement. Some commentators suggested that labour "missed an opportunity" by not more aggressively challenging the Klein agenda.[31] Labour certainly grasped the direness of the attack. "Every gain and every benefit that our predecessors have made is under attack," AFL president Linda Karpowich told delegates to the 1994 convention. "Make no mistake. We're in the fight of our lives. It will take the strength of the entire labour movement to win this struggle."[32]

In 1994, led by the AFL, a popular front was assembled. The Common Front aimed to draw together Albertans from many sectors — labour, church, non-profit, students, and so on — to develop a common response to the political challenges. The Common Front organized some coordinated actions, including a few rallies and public meetings, but for the most part, it fizzled. A November 1994 rally at the legislature garnered only three hundred attendees.[33] The AFL's desire to keep a firm control over the direction of the Front frustrated many non-labour participants, and the Front was never adequately resourced.

But pockets of resistance remained. Small advocacy groups of people affected by cuts formed and offered sporadic actions, including Albertans for Social Justice, the Alberta Disability Forum, and Poverty in Action. Solitary protesters, such as two hunger strikers who camped in front of the WCB in the summer of 1999, also tried to draw attention to their situation. Occasionally, larger mobilizations would arise over single issues, including the fifteen hundred Mill Woods residents who rallied to save Edmonton's Grey Nuns Hospital.

An important research advocacy group was born during the tumultuous 1990s. The Parkland Institute was formed as a provincial version of the Canadian Centre for Policy Alternatives, a left-wing think tank supported by labour. Its launch in 1996 marked an effort by labour to match the efforts of right-wing think tanks like the C.D. Howe Institute, the Fraser Institute, and others. Since its inception, Parkland, housed at the University of Alberta, has provided credible research to

support political advocacy. Its roles in opposing health care privatization and in pushing the oil royalty issue to the forefront were particularly noteworthy.

Government workers themselves could have provided the media — to the extent that it was willing to publicize more than the official Klein government's perspective on the revolution — with details of the cutbacks' impacts on their clients and themselves. But ministers made it clear that "their" employees were not free to tell their stories to the public, to whom both they and the government were responsible, and Mike

FIG 8-5 *AFL Labour News* reports on the walkout of the Calgary hospital laundry workers in 1995. Courtesy of the Alberta Labour History Institute.

Alberta Federation of Labour 1912

Labour News

Vol. 2, No. 9   Alberta's Alternate News Voice   December 1995

Calgary hospital workers stage dramatic wildcat strike

by Gil McGowan, AFL Staff

Photo Credit: Roxanne Smart

The mouse that roared. That's how some people are describing the 120 hospital laundry workers who led a massive wildcat strike in Calgary between November 14th and 24th. At the peak of the strike, more than 2,700 workers from six hospitals and nine nursing homes walked off the job to protest the Calgary Regional Health Authority's decision to privatize

awarded to the lowest bidder.

Researchers from the two unions representing laundry workers — AUPE and CUPE — discovered that K-Bro submitted the highest bid. The company would have charged $36 million over five years to handle laundry from Calgary hospitals. That's $8 million more than it would cost to keep the service "in-house."

tracting-out.

The ranks of striking workers swelled even further on November 23, when several hundred lab technologists — members of the Health Sciences Association — joined the strike. Additional support came from the United Nurses of Alberta and the Staff Nurses Association who both launched "work-to-rule campaigns".

Cardinal, minister of Family and Social Services, threatened publicly to fire ministry employees who spoke out. Youth counsellor and Alberta Union of Provincial Employees activist Guy Smith defied this order in 1996 and was suspended for three weeks, with a threat of dismissal if there was a recurrence.[34]

Initially, no efforts either profoundly affected the government's direction or propelled Albertans en masse to speak up against the cuts. Public opinion polls reported that while a majority felt negatively affected by the cuts, similar numbers supported the government's agenda.[35] Why? First, the government assault occurred on many fronts simultaneously, creating significant challenges to mobilization. Second, union response proved fractious: private sector unions failed to defend their public sector comrades. Communications, Energy and Paperworkers Union (Western) vice-president Rolf Nielsen offered a simple explanation for the passivity of private sector workers: "The private sector hasn't been hit with rollbacks like the public sector."[36] In addition, Alberta unions had no significant experience with co-operative political organizing and lacked sufficient trust to wholeheartedly engage in collective activism. One local president lamented afterwards, "If we were more unified we could have done something about our circumstances, but certainly that is not the case today. We're fragmented and driven apart, . . . we turn our guns inward and fight against each other, which I think is really sad."[37]

Third, most of the unions involved had done little before Klein's cuts to educate and mobilize their members to engage in political battle. Thus, when the Klein agenda confronted public sector unions so aggressively, unions proved flat-footed in their response.

LAUNDRY WORKERS VERSUS THE REVOLUTION

On 14 November 1994, about sixty laundry workers at the Calgary General Hospital, members of the Canadian Union of Public Employees (CUPE), called in sick, effectively launching an illegal, wildcat strike. The next day they were joined by an identical group of workers at Foothills Hospital, members of the Alberta Union of Provincial Employees. Why? After taking a 28 percent pay cut in the previous round of bargaining, both sets of workers had just been informed that their jobs were being privatized to K-Bro Linens.

Over the next ten days, the strike escalated to an estimated twenty-five hundred workers across six hospitals and nine nursing homes, while hundreds more workers in other health facilities engaged in work-to-rule and other actions. The atmosphere was highly charged. The strikers had caught the public imagination. CUPE activist Jimmy Arthurs remembered:

> We had great support from the people driving to work. Lots of tooting on horns and waves — it was just unreal the support we got from the community. . . . They had seen the devastation to the health care industry that the Klein government had created with their cutbacks, their slash-and-burn tactics. So there was a great understanding of what we were going through and what the laundry workers were suffering. Here they are, some of the lowest paid workers within the health care industry, and their jobs are going to be contracted out to the private sector with no rights or benefits granted to them, and no retraining.[38]

THE BIRTH OF A WILDCAT STRIKE

They have a cafeteria upstairs and they had all the laundry workers there. At that spot they announced to the laundry workers that the laundry was closing. . . . The emotion and the anger, to say the least, was very high. . . . The turning point for everything was when we asked them if anybody was feeling sick. Okay, what do you mean, what's that about? I said, "Well, you must be feeling sick over the news you've just received. . . . So how many people think that they should be going home sick?" All but two people put up their hand. So we sent them all home sick. We told the fellow that was waiting outside — at that time he was in charge of the laundry . . . that the laundry workers were all going home sick, they're feeling ill, they don't have the ability to work today. He asked me, "Will they be back?" I said, "Well, not if I can help it." Then we set a meeting that evening for seven o'clock. . . . It was at that point that a motion was made to actually set up the picket lines the next day at five in the morning. . . . We went up the next day, the signs went up at five o'clock. Everybody did show up. What the idea was is that the trucks moved early in the morning from the laundry, so the intent was to stop the trucks from moving out. That took place from about five o'clock to eight o'clock. Everybody said, okay, well, they actually needed a break at that time. . . . So everybody left and we came back at two o'clock, then the whole process escalated at a high pace from there. The Thursday night we actually went to a meeting that AUPE was having with their laundry workers. . . . So first it was the General Hospital laundry that went out, the next day the Foothills group set up their picket signs, and from that point, the Thursday and Friday, different departments started to come out of the hospital. It just kept growing.

— Len Fagnan, CUPE Local 8 President

SOURCE: Interview with Len Fagnan, Calgary, 24 April 2009, ALHI.

Within the Alberta Federation of Labour, senior labour leaders discussed how to use the strike to build political momentum. There was discussion of escalating to a general strike, an option ultimately rejected. After ten days, the government "blinked": it provided a financial package to the Regional Health Authority so that it could delay contracting out for eighteen months. (It occurred as planned eighteen months later.) Both bargaining units, in separate simultaneous ratification meetings, accepted the deal. Reaction to the settlement was divided. Some saw the strike as an overdue first victory against Klein — it was the first time he had backed down from an announced decision. Others lamented the lost opportunity to escalate labour's response to the political attacks of the previous two years.

THE REVOLUTION PETERS OUT, THE NEW NORMAL MOVES IN

The laundry workers' strike signalled a shift in Alberta's political climate. While the victory was small and temporary, it seemed to take the wind out of the government's sails. Klein had reduced government spending by 28 percent in real per capita terms, but now cuts began to ebb, and the remainder of the decade witnessed spending increases. By the early 2000s, with Alberta in a new boom, public sector workers, remembering the painful 5 percent rollback, successfully achieved sizeable wage increases. While the Alberta government retained its neo-liberal credentials, the frenetic crisis of the first two years was not repeated.

It is important not to overstate the impact of the laundry workers' strike on the provincial government. The government's loss of zeal coincided with rising energy revenues. It balanced its books in 1995, posting a $900 million surplus. Without the rhetorical drive of deficits, the justification for additional cuts withered. But the effects of the cuts to services would be felt for years. Klein had won the battle, and by stepping away from a full-scale counterattack and instead negotiating resolution on the government's terms, labour may have signalled that the core of the government's neo-liberal agenda was not at risk, thereby entrenching it. The laundry workers' strike may serve as a symbol of the beginning of a "new normal" of weakened unions, emboldened employers, and a slow creep of gains by neo-liberalism.

Taking Medicare to Market

Efforts to expand private, for-profit elements of health care delivery were key to Klein's neo-liberal agenda. However, privatizing medicare proved far more difficult than selling off liquor stores. The spectre of reduced public health care sparked a quick response from Albertans, and labour demonstrated a willingness to forcefully mobilize and to engage the government's health agenda.

Klein built on the efforts of his predecessors to impose marketization on medicare. The government used the crisis created by earlier cuts to raise doubts about medicare's financial sustainability. In spring 1994, Premier Klein made the government's ideological goal explicit: "Private hospitals and clinics should be allowed to expand in Alberta."[39] With that clear signal from government, health entrepreneurs began circling, hoping to buy closed hospitals or use closed wings to establish for-profit surgery centres. Lifeshare Healthcare

Systems West lobbied to buy the Holy Cross Hospital in Calgary. A shadowy group under the moniker Hotel de Health proposed to take over a floor of the Leduc hospital. A third group wanted to open a facility in Banff for well-heeled Americans. Such proposals were actively encouraged by the government. Cathy Jones, a union activist and board member of the Headwaters Regional Health Authority, remembered the determination of the government to forge ahead regardless of the research results:

> Headwaters was targeted as a favoured community because of Banff and Canmore, and the wealthy [who] would come here to recuperate if we had a private hospital. So we had to look into the American, British, and Australian systems. It is my personal opinion that after going through that research . . . that we cannot go for private care systems the way those three countries have, for one practical reason. . . . The numbers of doctors and nurses and physiotherapists and pharmacists aren't enough to cover two systems.[40]

For many reasons, including public outcry and financial difficulties, most of these proposals dissipated. In 1996, the most serious bid to establish a private hospital was launched by Health Resources Group (later renamed Health Resource Centre), which wanted to lease part of the closed Grace Hospital in Calgary to operate an orthopaedic surgery centre. After initial defeats, the group received a licence to operate, and during the latter part of the 1990s, it survived in large part due to patients sent by the Canadian military and the Workers' Compensation Board, which fast-tracked injured workers so they could return to work. In 2010, however, the Health Resource Centre filed for bankruptcy, forcing the government to take over its operation. By that time, the government was allowing the centre to bill medicare for patients and had reduced capacity in the public system accordingly.

Since the 1980s, Alberta has hosted a series of private clinics, mostly eye surgery centres that billed medicare for the procedure and charged patients a "facility fee" for other costs. But the facility fees flouted the *Canada Health Act*, and Alberta was fined $3.5 million between 1995 and 1997 before finally ending the fees by increasing the medicare payment to these clinics.

The combination of cutbacks and attempts to expand private health care sparked a uniquely strong response from Albertans. The reduced quality of service and proposed bed closures led to large protests and angry letters to newspapers and MLAs. Particularly vocal outcries came from seniors, health care workers, consumers' advocates, and activists in communities directly affected by closures. But two factors galvanized citizen anger around health care while other issues failed to unite Albertans.

First, a pre-existing vehicle served as a public face for opposition to health care privatization and cutbacks. While Friends of Medicare (FOM) had fallen into dormancy following the 1980s extra-billing fight, it had retained enough structure, name recognition, and credibility to quickly rejuvenate in the early 1990s. This was in stark contrast to most other issues, where players during a period of great stress needed to learn to work together and build trust before their fledgling coalitions could prove effective. FOM had the advantage of incorporating a broad spectrum of Albertans into its actions. The second key factor was the willingness of unions, particularly health care unions, to put their institutional weight behind this ready-to-go organization. Union leadership, especially from the United Nurses of Alberta and the Health Sciences Association of Alberta, as well as from the Alberta Federation of Labour, offered financial resources and institutional support for FOM's activities.

FOM mobilized quickly, putting out press releases on all health-related matters, and organized the largest petition drive in Alberta history, presenting more than eighty thousand signatures to the legislature. In its campaigns, FOM tapped into fears about "American-style health care," evoking a strong emotional reaction that the government never had an answer for. But FOM's strength was tested in 1999 with the introduction of Bill 37, designed to legalize for-profit "non-hospital surgical facilities" and allow them to bill medicare for services. The new facilities were functionally the same as hospitals without emergency departments. FOM fanned fears about the bill, forcing the government to quickly back away and announce a blue ribbon panel to "review" the bill's risks to medicare.

In 2000, following the panel's report, the government introduced Bill 11, which mimicked Bill 37; the primary changes were some restrictions on the facilities' operations and some patient protection. FOM organized the largest campaign against the Klein government to that time, including television ads, two massive rallies in Edmonton and Calgary, and community mobilization. Nightly protests, attended by thousands, as the bill was being debated in the house, capped the campaign. "It became an organic thing when in May of

2001 people rallied at the steps of the legislature. They just kept coming night after night after night," recalled Elisabeth Ballermann, president of the Health Sciences Association of Alberta.[41]

The bill passed, but changed little. Due to the intense public response, the government was reluctant to move too aggressively, and it even introduced regulations that diluted its impact. Furthermore, it remained uneconomical to operate a private, for-profit hospital, and few entrepreneurs were willing to risk the investment.

In 2006, the Klein government made one last attempt to further a private health agenda, announcing plans to develop a "Third Way" for health care that would expand the role of private insurance companies in health care, increase user fees, and examine possible services to be delisted. Using the term "Third Way" was a conscious effort to side-step thorny comparisons to US-style health care. Once again, the FOM launched a campaign to oppose the strategy, rolling out ads and establishing Constituency Action Teams in every provincial riding in the province to mobilize community-level opposition. The campaign was less effective in building popular activism than the Bill 11 campaign had been, but it solidified public opinion against private health care options.

At the 2006 Conservative leadership review, Ralph Klein received an embarrassing 55 percent support from PC Party members, which led immediately to his resignation as premier. The backlash to the Third Way plan was widely considered a contributing factor in Klein's downfall. Following his resignation, incoming Premier Ed Stelmach put the Third Way to rest publicly.

FIG 8-6 Thousands gather in Edmonton's Agricom in 2000 to protest Bill 11, provincial legislation that expanded the private delivery of health services. Courtesy of the Alberta Labour History Institute.

While FOM's role in Ralph Klein's downfall is unclear, it is clear that the organization played a leading role in preventing the privatization of Alberta health care. The campaigns — a mixture of grassroots organization, research, and media savvy — were effective in winning battles that had been unsuccessful with other issues. How FOM was able to "punch above its weight" is best encapsulated by Elisabeth Ballermann: "One of my fondest memories is of course when Ralph Klein at some point said the Friends of Medicare have run this million-dollar campaign. I knew at the time what kind of resources we had marshalled. . . . We hadn't even spent a tenth of that."[42]

Remaking Labour

At the dawn of the Klein era, labour feared anti-union labour law reforms on the model of New Zealand, Australia, and many US states. An early salvo in 1994 saw the government dissolve the Public Service Employee Relations Board and merge its functions into the Labour Relations Board. In 1995, the following motion narrowly passed in the legislature: "Be it resolved that the Legislative Assembly urge the Government to initiate a study to examine the implementation of Right to Work legislation in the province of Alberta." [43] Right-to-work, a concept that originated in the southern United States, gives every worker the right to opt out of union membership, effectively overturning the Rand formula and thus weakening unionization. [44] The AFL quickly built a campaign against the initiative, adopting the phrase "The Right to Work . . . For Less." The Building Trades Council also mobilized, accusing supporters of "an irrational hatred of unions and the benefits that unions provide to workers." [45] Fortunately for labour, many large unionized employers also opposed the initiative, fearing destabilization of labour relations. The committee set up to examine right-to-work legislation received 225 submissions, the vast majority of which opposed a right-to-work provision. [46] The committee's final report recommended against the initiative.

Following the defeat of right-to-work, the government changed its approach. Rather than full-scale changes to legislation, it settled into supporting the status quo while quietly reshaping key elements of the system. A particular target was the Labour Relations Board. In 1999 the government, in an unprecedented move, fired the chair of the board, Bob Blair, over accusations that he was not sufficiently employer friendly. Then they overruled a selection committee and appointed a member of the anti-union construction employers' group Merit Contractors to the board, the first time a non-union employer had joined the board. In the decade that followed, union activists believed it became more difficult for unions to receive a fair hearing at the Labour Relations Board. The president of United Food and Commercial Workers Local 401, Doug O'Halloran, then in the middle of a difficult round of negotiations, expressed a common frustration regarding time delays:

> [Last] March we filed this bargaining-in-bad-faith charge. They had it scheduled for December 21 of this year. . . . That is how terrible this labour board is. The company snap their fingers, they get a hearing the next moment. At this stage, we're fighting the company, we're fighting the Labour Board, and we're fighting the people in the plant that don't want the union. [47]

The only significant Labour Code changes came in 2008, when, after years of lobbying by Merit Contractors and other anti-union groups, the government passed a bill banning two practices common in the construction sector: "salting," involving a union organizer soliciting employment with a non-union employer to start an organizing drive; and "merfing" (an acronym for Market Enhancement Recovery Fund), in which employers invest in a fund to subsidize wages or benefits, making their bids more competitive. The bill also stripped ambulance workers of the right to strike.

Building-trades unions barely mobilized against the changes, despite the problems they posed for their members. Other unions, not affected by the amendments, remained on the sidelines. The change was widely seen as payback for the ill-fated anti-Tory campaign waged by labour during the 2008 provincial election.

THE QUIET WITHERING OF WORKER RIGHTS

Throughout the 1990s and 2000s, the government launched numerous reviews of employment standards, but few substantive changes resulted. In 2010, the Employment Standards Code stood mostly as it had in 1989, with a few minor changes to maternity leave and other provisions.

In contrast, the *Occupational Health and Safety Act* and its regulations underwent significant overhaul. Extensive amendments in 2002 increased penalties, afforded new powers to the minister, and enshrined key safety principles. However, many initiatives beneficial to workers were promised but never implemented, such as publishing the names of the worst offenders and mandating Joint Health and Safety committees.[48]

The most significant change to the government's occupational health and safety regime was the formation of the Partnerships Program in 1990. Partnerships established a "collaborative" relationship between employers and the government and de-emphasized active regulatory enforcement, which led to a hollowing out of state enforcement capacity. The enforcement arms of the Occupational Health and Safety and Employment Standards departments received disproportionately large cuts in the 1990s: Alberta Federation of Labour

research conducted in 2000 found that Occupational Health and Safety suffered a 42 percent budget reduction in that decade.[49] In 2010, the Auditor General released a scathing report indicting Occupational Health and Safety enforcement as ineffective and disorganized. The evisceration of that department is aptly illustrated by the reduction in workplace health and safety prosecutions: an average of 39 a year between 1985 and 1988; 10 between 1989 and 1994; and 2 between 1995 and 1999. After some modest re-investment, the average number of prosecutions between 2004 and 2009 rose to 12.[50]

Alberta's minimum wage also underwent a slow withering of spending power, languishing as the lowest in Canada for most of the 1990s — it rose from $4.50 in 1990 to only $5.90 in 2000.[51] After 2000, periodic rounds of agitation from the AFL, the Parkland Institute, and anti-poverty groups resulted in one-time increases, such as in 2005 to $7.00. Labour earned a short-lived victory in 2007, when the government tied the minimum wage to average weekly earnings. But the economic downturn scuttled the policy in 2010.

Division 8 and the De-unionization of Construction

Alberta's Labour Relations Code contained an unused, largely forgotten section (Division 8) permitting an employer to bypass the normal construction bargaining regime and negotiate a single master ("wall-to-wall") agreement for a project. In 2004, the government invoked the provision on behalf of Canadian Natural Resources Limited (CNRL) for its massive Horizon tar sands project. The effect was to permit CNRL to cut a deal with the Christian Labour Association of Canada

(CLAC), a union that espoused close collaboration of unions and management, and was widely disparaged in labour circles. For CNRL, it meant restricting wage gains during a time of tight labour supply. The building-trade unions howled but could do little. In an analysis, the AFL stated, "[The AFL] believes that what's happening with the Horizon Project is yet another example of the Alberta government using its legislative power to tip the playing field in favour of a large employer — in this case, one of Canada's wealthiest energy corporations. CNRL has been handed a big stick that will almost certainly be used in an attempt to beat building trades workers into submission."[52]

The move gave CLAC a leg up in the booming tar sands construction. It also sparked a divisive fight between building-trades unions and the Communications, Energy and Paperworkers Union (CEP), which also negotiated an agreement with CNRL, raising the ire of traditional building-trades unions. The feud lasted until CEP abandoned its construction experiment in 2009.

Labour Relations Board Credibility, Bill 27, and Using the Courts to Fight Back

The era's other major piece of labour legislation was Bill 27 in 2003. The amendment was requested by health care employers responding to the amalgamation of Regional Health Authorities. The bill defined the parameters of health care bargaining, creating four functional groups — direct nursing care, paramedical and technical, auxiliary nursing care, and general support services — and region-wide bargaining units, thus forcing a series of runoff votes. It also removed the right to strike from community health care workers.

Health care unions, led by the United Nurses of Alberta (UNA) and CEP, launched a legal challenge against the legislation, while the AFL submitted a series of freedom-of-information inquiries to find out the extent of employer involvement in the bill's creation. The inquiries unexpectedly revealed that the Labour Relations Board was actively engaged in drafting Bill 27, an egregious breach of its mandate. For many unionists, this confirmed long-held suspicions of the board, and a large scandal erupted. The AFL commissioned reputed administrative law scholar Dr. Lorne Sossin to evaluate the breach and propose a set of protocols. In spring 2007, the Labour Relations Board agreed to implement protocols loosely based upon the Sossin recommendations in return for withdrawal of the legal challenge.

The unions' legalistic response to Bill 27 was an example of a growing trend across Canada. Unions were more often turning to the courts to address perceived legislative injustices. This strategy was at times successful. Some key Charter of Rights and Freedoms decisions struck down restrictions on secondary picketing, guaranteed the right to unionize for farm workers, and enshrined collective bargaining as a Charter right. However, this approach had limitations. Many legal scholars suggested that the courts are not well disposed to union rights and the Charter is not constructed to recognize collective rights.[53] In addition, unions' growing hesitancy to resort to collective action and their increased reliance on lawyers to defend worker rights reflect the slow decline of union activism in Canada.

THE CHANGING FACE OF THE LABOUR MOVEMENT

Alberta's labour movement in 2010 looked different from the movement constructed after World War II. Unionization rose at less than half the rate of employment growth in the province, which was dominated by industries with low union density such as oil and gas, high technology, and the service sector. Private sector organizing almost ceased: application success rates were below 50 percent, with new certifications generally small and precarious. The Christian Labour Association of Canada possessed the highest certification rate.[54] Public sector unions therefore rose in prominence, profoundly affecting the direction of the labour movement. The period from 1990 to 2010 also witnessed the rise of female labour leadership and, more tentatively, space for workers of colour. Internal fights and financial difficulties hobbled the AFL for much of the period, limiting its role to that of a support player and ending a short-lived period of a more activist AFL sparked by departure of the building-trades unions in the 1980s.

The vociferousness of the government's attack during these two decades, rather than galvanizing public sector unions, divided them, creating tension and competition, particularly in health care. Animosity was strongest between the Canadian Union of Public Employees (CUPE) and the Alberta Union of Provincial Employees (AUPE), a feud fueled by CUPE's early settlement during the 1993 negotiations. Through the 1990s and 2000s, the two unions waged a series of raids and counter-raids. The unions presented their attacks as attempts to ensure stronger representation for health care workers, but in reality, their battle amounted to a resource-draining turf war that distracted both unions and opened a long-lasting rift in the labour movement. While AUPE was more victorious in runoff votes, CUPE was able to cast its opponent as a "black sheep" in the labour movement. The conflict climaxed in 2001 when AUPE, still Alberta's largest union, was suspended from its national affiliate for raiding and thus became ineligible for AFL membership. AUPE blamed CUPE and the AFL for the expulsion and continued a campaign of raiding in retaliation, further entrenching tension and division. AUPE remained outside of the house of labour for the rest of the decade.

AUPE's departure sparked a financial crisis at the AFL, forcing layoffs and restricting its political capacity. The AFL had also not benefited from the collapse of the Canadian Federation of Labour in the late 1990s. Most building-trades unions remained outside the federation, opting to remain with the Building Trades Council. The financial struggles only eased with the affiliation of the United Nurses of Alberta and the Health Sciences Association of Alberta a few years later. Both unions were constitutionally non-partisan and most of their members considered themselves professionals rather than unionists. Their arrival shifted the AFL's political strategies: ties with the NDP weakened and rallies and public meetings gave way to more focus on advertising, lobbying, and communication strategies.[55]

Strikes

Strikes were infrequent in Alberta between 1990 and 2010. Work days lost to work stoppages were consistently a fraction of rates in the other large provinces.[56] Strike failures at Zeidler and in construction during the 1980s had set the stage for subsequent union reluctance to use the strike weapon.

Private sector employers imitated the government and implemented more sophisticated union-busting tactics. The use of private security firms to patrol picket lines and intimidate strikers became commonplace. American-style consultants filtered into Alberta to advise employers how to remain union-free, break existing unions, and survive long strikes. These trends, combined with restrictive picketing rules and use of replacement workers, made striking a challenging proposition.

Some important disputes did arise, however, drawing mixed levels of broader labour and/or public support.

FIG 8-7 Striking Lynnwood home care workers join the picket line in Edmonton in 2000. Courtesy of the Alberta Union of Provincial Employees.

The location and nature of the disputes reflected the changing nature of Alberta labour. The engagement in these strikes of new kinds of workers — immigrants, women, younger workers, and professionals — posed challenges to traditional union methods of mobilizing but also opened opportunities for new models of collective action, only partly realized by the end of the era.

The Public Sector Fights Back

The 1995 laundry workers' strike turned the tide in public sector labour relations, emboldening public sector unions. In 1997, the United Nurses of Alberta (UNA) pushed the government to the brink of a province-wide strike just weeks before a general election, gaining sizeable wage increases. Soon after, three health care unions (CUPE, AUPE, and the Canadian Health Care Guild) representing hospital support staff and auxiliary nursing staff jointly staged an illegal walkout that earned the workers their first wage increase in five years.

Then, on 24 May 2000, ten thousand AUPE health care workers, largely LPNs and nursing assistants, staged a dramatic illegal walkout. Their main issue was wage equity with other health professionals, as expressed by striker Myrna Wright:

> I believed in what we were doing. It was the team we were on . . . and the fact that we'd been so underpaid and [for] so many years had been promised the other half of the loaf of bread, and we never got it. . . . When you saw what the RNs got . . . you can't go back and tell your people to take it, because it's not worth it. It wasn't worth it and we were being discriminated against.[57]

Less than forty-eight hours later, a tentative agreement, hammered out personally between AUPE president Dan MacLennan and Premier Klein, ended the strike. The deal provided wage increases of between 8 percent and 16 percent, and a further guarantee of no contracting out.

The aftermath of the 2000 strike was significant. AUPE was fined $400,000 (reduced to $200,000 on appeal) for contempt of court and the Labour Relations Board imposed a two-month dues suspension, costing the union hundreds of thousands more. More legal challenges ensued, but in 2009, the courts affirmed the legality of the double penalty.

In 2002, it was the teachers' turn. A battle had been brewing between the Alberta Teachers' Association (ATA) and the province since the 1994 cuts. In 2001, the good settlements won by the UNA and AUPE signalled to teachers the opportunity to regain lost ground. With school board contracts expiring, representing over half the province's teachers, the ATA abandoned its decentralized and moderate approach, and developed a province-wide coordinated bargaining strategy, an overtly political act intended to send a signal to the government. ATA president Larry Booi emphasized that the strategy was not primarily about increasing wages: "I believe the emotional driver for the strike was the classroom conditions issue. I'm not saying that wages weren't important. But classroom conditions have been a burning issue for at least a decade." [58]

On 4 February, teachers in nineteen locals struck; they were soon joined by three more. The strike affected 21,000 teachers and more than 350,000 students (two-thirds of all students in the province). [59] After thirteen days, the government declared an "emergency" and

ordered the teachers back to work. However, the courts overturned the order, ruling that the government had not demonstrated that an emergency existed. This led to failed one-on-one negotiations between Klein and Booi. The government instead passed legislation imposing restrictive arbitration, angering teachers even further, but by that point, classes had resumed and strike energy had dissipated. Arbitration tribunals eventually settled agreements with sizeable wage increases, but most classroom condition issues remained untouched.

FIG 8-8 Alberta Teachers' Association president Larry Booi addresses a teachers' rally at the legislature in 2002. Courtesy of the Alberta Labour History Institute.

The Changing Face of Private Sector Strikes

The 1990s and 2000s witnessed workers in traditionally low unionization sectors beginning to stand up for their rights by leading a series of strikes, many to gain a first contract. Strikes and lockouts in traditional industrial areas continued, mainly as battles for survival rather than to acquire gains for workers. Workers at the Gainers plant (now called Maple Leaf Foods) walked out again in 1997, but for the last time, as the plant was shuttered during the strike. Through the next ten years, more strikes occurred to forestall rollbacks, layoffs, and plant closures: Finning International workers struck unsuccessfully to prevent rollbacks in 1997; workers at the Georgia Pacific gypsum plant prevented plant closure through striking in 1998; Altasteel workers struck in 1999 to stop layoffs and wage rollbacks; in 2007, the Molson Brewing Plant in Edmonton was closed following a short strike; and in 2009, workers at Old Dutch waged a strike for a union shop.

The bulk of strikes were in newer sectors. In 1997, ten thousand Safeway workers struck province-wide to oppose employer demands for a two-tier wage structure and to protest broken promises from a 1993 agreement when the union took concessions to prevent the company's collapse. But the strike, while regionally effective, could not overcome the sheer size of Safeway's operations, said United Food and Commercial Workers president Doug O'Halloran:

> We have a strike vote of 93 percent across the province. We end up with eighty-five picket lines across the province. The strike is seventy-five days long. The one thing that we underestimated was Alberta's only 7 percent of the company's market. Their business, except for Calgary, was shut down to about 15 percent. Stores that were doing $400,000 were doing $15,000 or $20,000. Safeway were running trucks up to Fort McMurray with nothing on them.[60]

The resulting deal disappointed the workers. "The people were pissed off at Safeway, they were pissed off at us, because that's all they were getting and they were paying high dues," says O'Halloran, blaming the changing industry. "In hindsight now, if we had known what was going to happen with Canada Safeway, we may as well put them out of business back then."[61]

The Safeway strike can be seen as a transitional strike. While grocery has a long history of unionization, changes in the industry toward discount bulk stores, globalized product chains, and downward wage pressure undermined the status of workers in the sector, causing them to share more in common with other retail workers than with oil refinery workers.

In the years that followed, a series of strikes erupted

across the province in the areas of media, casinos, and hotel/catering staff. In 1999, the Communications, Energy and Paperworkers Union (CEP) surprised many by successfully certifying a bargaining unit of journalists at the *Calgary Herald.* However, their opponent, outspoken conservative media baron Conrad Black, installed a management team intent on busting the union. The dispute escalated to a lockout in November 1999, which lasted eight months. Intimidation from Herald security and even the Calgary Police was formidable. Strike leader Andy Marshall experienced much of it first hand:

> We held our first rally a month into the strike. . . .
> We had a couple of thousand people at least, in northeast Calgary one evening. . . . We intended to make it difficult for them to get the trucks out. This involved a big sacrifice, because the trucks don't come out until two o'clock in the morning. . . . But when everyone showed up in the evening, there were Mounted Police on another street, which was very intimidating. During the evening we had a rally and speeches, then we lined up on the road at the entrance to the Herald. The police came, walked down the street in a line, tapping their shields, slow step by slow step toward these very innocent, gentle people, who just wanted a first contract. . . . On subsequent nights, it was even nastier, where the police manhandled people, were very rough. . . . When I was sitting on the ground and a policeman came up, the first thing he did was knock my glasses off so I can't see. He went for my eye, that's right, and started putting his finger in my eye. . . . It was quite staggering to see the role of the police in a strike. . . . In my view, the police are co-opted by companies and by the authorities to act against people who are legally striking.[62]

LORD BLACK VERSUS HIS WORKERS

We were in the strike headquarters planning our day. Gordon Christie from the Labour Council phoned up. He said, "Conrad Black's in town. . . . He's come to a Canadian Imperial Bank of Commerce shareholders meeting being held in Calgary." A handful of us went down to the inn on Fourth Avenue and sure enough, we heard Conrad was in the meeting room there with the shareholders, maybe 150 people. So we began picketing on the street. There were some media there. . . . I thought, "I've gotta talk to Black, I've gotta catch him." So I waited at the doors, and he's the first out at lunchtime, him and his great big bodyguard. I said, "Mr. Black (he wasn't a lord then), I'm Andy Marshall and I want to talk to you." He said, "I've heard all about you." He strode off, so I went along behind him. He stopped at the steps, so we talked some more. I said, "I think we could solve this strike quite easily." He went into a tirade. . . . That's when he said, "You're a gangrenous limb that we've got to chop off." . . . He sort of wagged his fingers in my face. He said, "You've got two choices. You come back to work tomorrow or we're going to wait you out, we're going to decertify you." . . . So what he proposed was, we have absolutely no intention of bargaining with you. So come back tomorrow, no contract. Or we just wait you out, no big deal. So what he said on camera with absolute impunity was illegal. . . . It was totally against even Alberta's labour laws. You have to bargain in good faith. There he was saying, "I have no interest or no intention of bargaining in good faith with you." That interview knocked the stuffing out of people.

— Andy Marshall, former *Calgary Herald* reporter

SOURCE: Interview with Andy Marshall, Cochrane, 18 November 2005, ALHI.

FIG 8-10 Members of the United Food and Commercial Workers strike the Shaw Convention Centre, Edmonton, 2002. Courtesy of the Alberta Labour History Institute.

The workers could not inflict economic hardship on the *Herald,* and as the strike wore on, morale sagged. "I know there have been longer strikes and tougher strikes, but I could see the suffering," said Marshall. "People were coming unglued. . . . By May, the vice-president said to me, 'We've got to finish this, because it'll just peter out to nothing.'"[63] Eventually a buyout package was negotiated and the union was decertified.

Other media workers also struck in the early 2000s. Reporters and technicians at A-Channel Edmonton (later City TV) struck in 2004 for a first agreement. A four-and-a-half-month strike produced an agreement. The union has since been decertified. CBC workers went on strike in 1999, 2001, and 2005. Globalization was behind rising conflict in the sector. With content increasingly produced centrally and advertising dollars scattered among myriad new media forms, layoffs in local newsrooms and the downgrading of local production became inevitable.

A second group of newly unionized workers during the Klein era were workers in casinos and hospitality, who were among the lowest paid in the labour market. Consequently, disproportionate numbers of newcomers, young workers, and visible minorities worked in this sector. Unions struggled to organize these workers, making some inroads, only to face anti-union employers. Several disputes ensued. In 2002, catering staff at the Edmonton Convention Centre, recently and precariously unionized by the United Food and Commercial Workers, walked out for a first contract. The strike was plagued by picket line crossing and apathy from the public and the broader labour movement. The employer, the city-funded Economic Development Edmonton, stonewalled until City Council, concerned about the strike's effect on the upcoming Grey Cup game, forced a resolution.

Four years later, the same union took a group of dealers and serving staff at Palace Casino on a strike that lasted ten months. Doug O'Halloran summarized Palace wages:

> An average dealer makes $8.80 an hour, a server makes $7.01 an hour, a woman who's been dealing for five years makes $9 an hour. . . . No sick days, full time or part time. The full time can pay for half their benefits, and the benefits aren't that great. We've got these oil workers coming in and saying, "Well, go get a job. Why are you out here on the picket line? If you only make $7 or $8 an hour, why don't you go work somewhere else?" They don't understand that the people love the place of work.[64]

The challenge in the hospitality sector compared to traditional industries, as CUPE discovered in their 2005 strike at Casino Calgary, was to create economic hardship for the employer. First, it was easier for managers to fill striking workers' functions. Second, especially in first-contract strikes, there was insufficient solidarity to prevent large-scale line crossing. Third, the picket line had to also achieve the more difficult task of preventing customers from entering.

Unique challenges forced the unions involved to develop new tactics, such as producing radio ads and billboards, attempting to influence community leaders, and launching consumer boycotts. Increased international ownership of these companies forced unions to engage in actions around the globe (for example, in Australia to settle the Palace Casino strike). Also, unions framed the strikes differently — adding public health issues, safety, community standards, and other concerns to draw public sympathy. Not all of these strikes were successful, but they demonstrated the need of unions to respond to unique needs of workers in particular industries.

NEW WORKERS AND NEW MOVEMENTS

Labour took some time to respond to new voices in new struggles. For example, unions were bystanders in the battle between a gay Christian college instructor fired for his sexual orientation and the weight of the government's bigotry. In the 1990s, Delwin Vriend

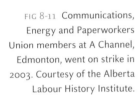

FIG 8-11 Communications, Energy and Paperworkers Union members at A Channel, Edmonton, went on strike in 2003. Courtesy of the Alberta Labour History Institute.

became a symbol for the new face of justice and equity in Alberta. His victory through the courts took seven years and resulted in sexual orientation being enshrined in the Charter of Rights.

Labour's difficulty in embracing new political activists continued when Prime Minister Jean Chrétien announced in 2002 that the G8 Summit would be held in Kananaskis. Issues of global power and globalization had exploded onto the public consciousness in 1999 with the so-called "Battle in Seattle," where sixty thousand protesters disrupted a meeting of the World Trade Organization.[65] That confrontation marked the maturation of a new movement of youthful political activists questioning the validity of global capitalism. The 1999 protests spawned large-scale activism at all key global political meetings.

As the Kananaskis meetings approached, the Alberta Federation of Labour and the Communications, Energy and Paperworkers Union attempted to form a working coalition with local activists to organize protests. Two challenges emerged. First, the summit took place in a mountain resort ninety minutes west of Calgary, complicating both access and logistics. Second, the coalition struggled to mesh labour's traditional, institutional approach to organizing with the brash, impatient energy of the anti-globalization activists, which bogged down organizing efforts. The eventual protests, held in Calgary, were smaller and less confrontational than those elsewhere, drawing attention to the relative weakness of both labour and the anti-globalization movement in Alberta.

However, some union activists took on the G8. Canadian Union of Postal Workers member Cindy McCallum-Miller recalled:

The postal workers had collected a whole bunch of letters from citizens of Calgary to the leaders of the G8 to say why we didn't want the kinds of programs that they were going to try and put in place. . . . Postal workers were going to break through the barricades and we were going to go and deliver those letters to the G8 leaders. My proudest moment was the fact that [Jean-Claude Parrot] and I were the first two that were to cross the police lines.[66]

As the 2000s rolled along, the polarity of oil prosperity and deplorable working conditions became glaring. Three groups of vulnerable workers drew the attention of the labour movement: farm workers, adolescent workers, and temporary foreign workers.

Farm Workers

Agricultural work has long been exploitative. Hard physical labour, small economic margins, and a "family first" mindset combine to create low pay, excessive hours, and little attention to safety. The plight of farm workers received renewed attention in the early 2000s, sparked by two factors. First, in the 1990s, the United Food and Commercial Workers in Ontario and British Columbia launched an ambitious drive, modelled on the United Farm Workers in California, to organize farm workers and overturn laws prohibiting farm worker unionization. Their legal battles drew national headlines as the Supreme Court overturned the prohibition in 2001.[67] Second, the murder of Terry Rash, a farm worker near Taber, on 20 August 1999, sparked public outrage in the province.

There were about twelve thousand farm workers in Alberta earning less than ten dollars per hour on average and working highly sporadic, demanding work schedules.[68] Unlike Ontario and British Columbia, where most farm workers were migrant workers, most Alberta farm workers were resident Albertans. Farm workers were exempt from most employment protections, including Workers' Compensation Board coverage, Occupational Health and Safety regulations, and working-hour limits.

A small advocacy group for farm workers, Farm Workers Union of Alberta, formed in the early 2000s to raise awareness of farm worker issues. However, the group's decision to not actively organize limited its potential gains and it faded away. In 2005, the Alberta Federation of Labour launched "End the Drought," a short-lived campaign to pressure the Alberta government to extend basic employment standards to farm workers. This initiative also soon fizzled.

The momentum against farm worker protection was significant. As labour relations professor Bob Barnetson explains, "Agricultural workers have historically had no meaningful access to provincial policy making and also lack powerful allies who might assist them in seeking statutory inclusion."[69] Labour's half-hearted adoption of the issue was insufficient to overcome historical barriers.

Temporary Foreign Workers

In the mid-2000s, the tar sands boom led to significant shifts in the labour-market balance. Employers in many industries complained of difficulty attracting and retaining workers. The government agreed, decrying a "labour shortage" and calling for immediate action. The labour movement was skeptical. "Apparently we are to believe," responded the Alberta Federation of Labour (AFL), "that when minimum wage employers can't find people who want to work at unpleasant jobs for miserable wages, it's a crisis."[70]

In 2002, the Liberal federal government changed the rules to its niche-oriented temporary foreign worker (TFW) program. The program had existed for decades as a small program facilitating the temporary employment of scientists, university professors, engineers, and other high-skilled occupations. When the Liberals expanded its scope to include building trades, retail clerks, cooks, labourers, and gas station attendants, few additional safeguards were added to protect the more vulnerable low-skilled workers. In 2007, the Harper government increased the number of workers and eligible occupations further, which profoundly shifted Canada's immigration policy to resemble entrenched European migrant worker programs. Alberta employers were quick to take advantage of the expanded program. In 1998, only a few hundred TFWs lived in Alberta. By 2004, the number had grown to 13,236, and by 2009, to 65,748.[71] Alberta had the highest proportion of TFWs in the country — 1.8 percent of its population. Most were low-skilled workers from developing nations.

Reports of exploitation soon emerged. Employers took advantage of TFWs' vulnerable legal status and the shortcomings in government enforcement. The AFL hired Edmonton lawyer Yessy Byl in 2007 to act as a TFW advocate providing case assistance to TFWs in need and offering education and policy advocacy. Within the first six months, Byl received more than 1,400 inquiries, handled 123 individual cases, and made dozens of representations on behalf of TFWs. She found widespread abuse and exploitation by employers and employment brokers and neglect by both levels of government. Brokers illegally charged fees to TFWs, and employers failed to pay overtime, paid lower than promised wages, and often charged exorbitant rents for employer-supplied accommodation. Sixty percent of those employers with TFWs who were inspected had breached either the Employment Standards Code or the *Occupational Health and Safety Act*, yet few penalties were ever assessed.[72] Few TFWs were granted permanent residency.

Employers unwilling to share the boom's prosperity used the TFW program to construct a new vulnerable labour pool as an end-run around the higher wages demanded by Canadian workers. Though TFWs were trumpeted as a short-term solution to labour shortages, their influx continued even after the 2008 economic crisis arrived since employers still wanted expendable workers.[73]

Adolescent Workers

The search for new workers during the tar sands boom also targeted adolescents. Employment of twelve- to fourteen-year-olds had been restricted to a few occupations, such as newspaper delivery. An employer wanting young workers outside those occupations needed special approval from the director of Employment Standards. During the 1990s, applications grew more common, and in 2004, more than 550 permits were granted to restaurant owners.[74]

In June 2005, without public notification and at the request of the restaurant industry, the government allowed restaurant employers to hire twelve- and thirteen-year olds without informing the government. The

AFL raised the alarm about potential impacts. Although political pressure forced the government to amend the new policy slightly, requiring employers to submit a checklist for each adolescent they hired, research conducted by the AFL the following year found that most employers were failing to submit the forms. In 2007, the government relaxed the rules even further, permitting adolescents to work in kitchens of bars, but this time, public backlash forced a reversal. By 2008, however, as many as eleven thousand nine- to eleven-year-olds and forty thousand twelve- to fourteen-year-olds were employed in Alberta.[75] Much like TFWs, the loosening of rules around adolescent workers allowed low-wage industries to tap a labour pool of more vulnerable workers and thereby keep wages low.

NEW CANADIANS WIN AT LAKESIDE

The remaking of Alberta workplaces is best symbolized by the 2005 strike at the Lakeside Packing plant in Brooks, a town of thirteen thousand on the Trans-Canada Highway that had for generations represented the rural cowboy spirit. Its largest employer, Lakeside Packers, was a leader in the transformation of the meat-packing industry, driving down wages and shedding its union in 1984. Union-organizing efforts through the 1990s met with failure due to aggressive and at times illegal tactics by the employer.

By the early 2000s, an influx of new workers — at first from Newfoundland and other provinces, and later from Sudan, Somalia, Cambodia, the Philippines, and other developing nations — changed the face of Lakeside and Brooks by creating a diverse, divided workforce. Working conditions were deplorable. "They

FIG 8-12 United Food and Commercial Workers members strike Lakeside Packers in Brooks in 2005. Courtesy Alberta Labour History Institute.

value the cows, not the workers," said Peter Jany, a Sudanese worker. "When you get injured, cut yourself or whatever, they fire you."[76]

In 2004, a wildcat protest by mostly Sudanese workers sparked a renewed interest in the union. United Food and Commercial Workers organizer Archie Duckworth remembers being invited.

> In May of 2004, the Sudanese community had been negotiating with the company to create better working conditions. The company had apparently promised them this. When that failed, approximately a hundred people walked off the floor and insisted that they wanted to talk to the management to solve some of the issues . . . pay, injuries, and being treated with respect and dignity. . . . The employer at that time decided to turn around and fire the hundred people. Then the Sudanese community came and asked us to come back in and try to organize the plant. So that's when I came back on the scene and we started our campaign.[77]

With a new alliance of African newcomers and former union supporters, the union shifted tactics. It produced campaign literature in eight languages, and made a concerted attempt to include all cultural groups. The certification succeeded with a razor-thin 51.4 percent, largely divided along newcomer–long-time Albertan lines.[78] Lakeside, owned at the time by Arkansas-based giant Tyson Foods (sold in 2009 and renamed XL Foods), refused to negotiate, and the two sides marched towards a dispute. The strike began on 17 October 2005. The picket line was tense and violent. Nearly half the workers crossed the line, but in the early days of the strike, the union successfully halted production. Newfoundland ex-pat Ashley Grandy felt that such an ugly strike could only happen in Alberta. "Any other province in Canada, this would not happen. I believe B.C. and Quebec have anti-scab laws. If this was Newfoundland . . . nobody would get into that plant, absolutely nobody."[79]

The strike's turning point was a high-speed car chase involving four plant managers and union local president Doug O'Halloran. O'Halloran was permanently disabled after being run off the road. Two weeks later, a first agreement was settled. O'Halloran remembered the immediate aftermath of the chase:

> After the accident, we had to be very careful, because the workers were so annoyed they were going to go burn the plant, literally. . . . The workers couldn't believe that they would run their president off the road. . . . [But] believe it or not, there was a positiveness to it all. I think that the company had such a backlash of public opinion because of me being run off the road, it actually brought the strike to an end.[80]

PETER JANY'S JOURNEY TO BROOKS

I was born in southern Sudan. We have been [at] war in Sudan for long time, approximately forty-two years before I was born. . . . There is a lot of problems, people die for hunger. Some people die of water, some people die [of] disease, some people die by fire, some people die thirsty. . . . I came with my family — my wife and two kids. . . . If you read international policy, Canada is number one country for human rights. Then I decided, why don't I go to Canada? Maybe, God willing, I would be in better life, letting my children go to school, a peaceful country. . . .

So when I was looking for a job in Edmonton, it was really very hard. Some people even when I call they said, "No, your English is not good, you're not qualified to work." Then I go to school, I looking for part time [work]. . . . I worked as a housekeeper. Very good job, I liked that. So I worked there part time for $7 an hour. . . .

Then I went to Bow Valley College. They give me a grant, seventeen hundred dollars for a month for all my family; we are five people. . . . After one year, they find out that I was in Alberta for only three months when I went to school. They say to be approved for student funding, you [must] have one year in Alberta. They said . . . you violated the law. We need this money back,

around twelve thousand dollars. . . . I have no job at that time, my wife has no job. . . . I got depressed. . . . What should I do? My wife is not going to school, I'm not going to school. We come here for better life, we come for the future of our kids. . . . The next day, I decide to come to Brooks. . . . When I come in 2001 [to] Lakeside I work in processing. What we do in there is process the meat. I was [what] they call [a] stripper. I have a scar, you see this one? That's [from] a hook. When I pull it, it caught my finger here. Very hard job.

One day I slipped because the floor is wet. I get my ankle twisted. . . . I want to see the doctor. My supervisor told me, "No, you cannot see the doctor." I said, "Look, my ankle now is this way." He says no. I say, "What is the reason?" . . . He says, "I don't allow you to go, because if you go to see the doctor, that will be a bad report, and then we are not going to get a bonus." I say, "[What] bonus?" He says, "We get a jacket, green jacket." That is a policy for them as a supervisor, if you keep [your workers] from seeing the doctor, they get a bonus.

SOURCE: Interview with Peter Jany, Brooks, 1 November 2005, ALHI.

In the years that followed, Lakeside remained divided and the union continued to meet with resistance. Duckworth, who serviced the local after the strike, said it took time for management to accept the union's legitimacy. "When we first started out . . . they weren't willing to give one inch in a collective agreement. They didn't care about the workers; they cared about getting rid of us." [81]

Lakeside is one of the few organizing and strike victories for Alberta labour in the two decades beginning in 1990. It is noteworthy that African and Asian workers took a leadership role in standing up for their rights.

THE FALL OF MANUFACTURING

During the 1990s, the government ended attempts to diversify the Alberta economy. Experiments with loan guarantees and investment in burgeoning industries ended ingloriously in a heap of scandals and millions of dollars lost in the early 1990s. The Klein neo-liberals used the failures to discredit notions of active government. The political influence of the oil industry increased, leading to a shift in economic policy from encouragement of secondary processing of energy resources to more aggressive exploitation and exportation.

This shift stimulated rapid expansion of tar sands development, creating massive construction projects north of Fort McMurray. Tar sands production increased from 350,000 barrels daily in 1990[82] to 1.3 million barrels daily in 2008, with expectations of up to 5 million by 2030.[83] The migration of capital and workers to the tar sands created a crisis in other sectors. Calls for a slowdown, a moratorium, and greater regulation of tar sands development went unheeded by the government.

For labour, the tar sands represented a dilemma. For construction unions, the boom meant thousands of well-paid industrial construction jobs, albeit tempered by employers' increased use of temporary foreign workers, Christian Labour Association of Canada members, and non-union workers. However, unions in other sectors could not ignore the political, economic, social, and ecological consequences of the boom. The labour movement's ambivalence is reflected in two AFL reports released in 2009. "Down the Pipeline" supported secondary processing of crude oil and gas while accepting ongoing tar sands development.

"Green Jobs," by contrast, supported a move away from carbon-intensive industry. At the end of the 2000s, the labour movement remained ambivalent, wanting to align itself with the concerns of environmentalists but unwilling to question underlying assumptions about the industry's growth.

Preoccupation with tar sands development and neo-liberalism also led to the decline of manufacturing in Alberta. The 1997 closure of the Gainers plant symbolized Alberta's shifting economy. Northeast Edmonton, historically the hub of the meat-packing industry, had a single, small independent packing plant left in 2010. Strip malls, casinos, and tracts of empty land replaced former plants. The 2007 closure of Edmonton's Molson plant, where beer had been brewed uninterrupted since 1913, also marked the end of an era.[84]

The fifty-year-old Celanese petrochemical plant in Edmonton was shut down in 2007, while the Edmonton GWG jeans factory (GWG was then owned by Levi Strauss & Co.) closed in 2004, each representing the collapse of their industries. Workers' lives were altered forever — in the first industry, mostly older male workers; in the second, female newcomers. The GWG announcement shocked Kim Ngo and her co-workers: "When we heard the announcement that they were going to close, everybody cried. I cried. At night time I said, 'Is it a dream? I hope it is a dream.' We did not want to lose it. Some of us even think, 'Could we reduce the wage so that we all can stay?'"[85] The productive, profitable plant fell victim to Levi Strauss's decision to move all production off-shore. Edmonton Mayor Bill Smith called the closure "almost inevitable in the global economy," an analysis that ignored forty years of corporate decisions.[86]

Most laid-off workers struggled to find comparable employment, even with the assistance of job centres and training funds. Bill Climie, a lab technician at Celanese, is an example:

The majority of resumes nowadays go through one or two companies; they get fed through a computer, scanned in, and key words are flipped out, and you get spit out. Because my resume has no dates on it anymore, because my university degree is thirty years old . . . my resume never makes it to a person, I'm guessing. Even these small and medium companies that could use my training and my expertise, they can't afford to hire HR people to review a thousand resumes, so they go through these companies. So my resume still doesn't make it onto their desk.[87]

Alberta entered the new century with a dramatically changed economy and workforce. Gone were the blue overalls of factory workers, replaced by the white shirts of nurses, teachers, and oil executives. As laid-off worker Sam Cholak noted: "We can't all be in the service industry. You have to make something here to be viable. Services only go so far and that's it. . . . You have to have manufacturing; you have to take your raw resources and make something with it, right here."[88] The Alberta government disagreed, repealing requirements for energy upgrading and forging ahead with an export-oriented economy.

THE END OF KLEIN AND BEYOND

The Klein era ended on 31 March 2006, when PC Party members handed Ralph Klein his first political defeat in a leadership review. While Ed Stelmach's surprise leadership victory in December 2006 changed the personality of the premiership, the immediate post-Klein period was one of continuity. Stelmach continued most Klein policies, including rapid tar sands development. Little changed for Alberta workers. The March 2008 election gave a large majority to the PCs. Its aftermath signalled that the "new normal" of the Klein era would continue.

In earlier elections, Alberta's unions had adopted traditional campaign strategies: providing money and campaign workers to specific parties — in general the AFL-affiliated unions to the NDP and the building trades predominantly to the Liberals — and encouraging members to vote for the desired party. But labour approached the 2008 election differently. Attempting to replicate successful campaigns in Ontario and Saskatchewan in which labour ran its own issue campaigns parallel to the party campaigns, the Building Trades Council, the United Nurses of Alberta, the Health Sciences Association of Alberta, the Alberta Union of Provincial Employees, and the Alberta Federation of Labour partnered to create Albertans for Change, a $2.3 million advertising campaign designed to encourage anti-Conservative voting.[89] Seven television ads attacked Stelmach, claiming he had "no plan." Public reaction to the Albertans for Change campaign was, however, negative.

The strategic change by the AFL highlighted the shifting power base within labour toward the non-partisan health care unions and away from the traditional NDP-supporting private sector unions, a shift that continued in the election's aftermath when the AFL Executive Council debated a proposal to lead an effort to persuade the Liberals, Greens, and NDP to co-operate in the next election. The AFL proposal paralleled efforts of a cluster of groups, fueled by discouraging election results, to push the two main opposition parties to co-operate in some fashion. The AFL's dalliance with cross-partisan support raised significant tensions with the Alberta NDP and the Canadian Labour Congress.

A New Round of Cuts, or Not

Alberta was shaken harder by the 2008 country-wide economic crisis than any other province. Eighty thousand jobs were lost in ten months,[90] and labour shortages turned into surpluses with cascading consequences. The province's budget faced the spectre of renewed deficits. This led to rhetoric of budget cuts and the need for public sector workers to "share the pain" once again. Through 2009 and 2010, however, overall spending increased but at a slower rate. Still, financial challenges emerged in advanced education, health care, and education. The economic crisis hit Albertans unevenly: some barely noticed the shift in economic fortunes, and the wealth gap widened.

Unions responded by forming Join Together Alberta, a coalition of labour and community groups. But in a pattern similar to that of 1994, concessionary collective agreements were signed without disruption as unions accepted the belt-tightening rhetoric. While union fears of a new round of Kleinesque cuts had not materialized in 2010, patterns established during the 1990s replayed themselves. Efforts to mobilize activism against cuts were sporadic, and unions accepted the assumptions of financial difficulty presented by employers.

Health Care Reform Redux

The economic crisis was used to shake up the health care system once again and promote private health care experiments. In 2009, the Regional Health Authorities were eliminated and a province-wide "superboard" was created, leading to chaos in the system. The health minister used the crisis to place health care privatization back on the table. Long waiting lists, emergency room queues, and staffing shortages returned. The government acted on many fronts at once, moving to close Alberta Hospital, the province's largest mental health hospital; reduce seniors' health benefits; and close long-term care beds. Public outcry, however, focused by Friends of Medicare, led to a retreat from most of the announced cutbacks, though rhetoric of adding more "market" conditions to health care continued.

The Rise of a New Political Force

By 2010, a new political party was posing a potentially serious challenge to the Tories. The Wildrose Alliance Party (WAP) was formed out of an amalgamation of small, right-wing fringe parties in early 2008.[91] A protest party of ideological conservatives, it had little impact on the 2008 election. However, marginally increased royalty rates angered the oilpatch, leading to an influx of donations from angry oil executives to the WAP, if only to pressure the governing Conservatives to rescind energy royalty increases. The election as leader in fall 2009 of former *Calgary Herald* lockout journalist Danielle Smith sparked a quick rise for the party, which had already won a Calgary by-election that fall. The party's popularity forced the government to backtrack on the new royalty regime.[92]

For labour, the rise of WAP was a matter of concern. At its 2010 policy convention, the party passed resolutions restricting the right of teachers to strike and loosely advocating right-to-work legislation. The party also supported unbridled tar sands development and more aggressive health care privatization.

While most observers argued that the rise of WAP marked a long-awaited shift in Alberta politics, another view is possible. The preliminary success of WAP can be seen as another marker of the new normal. By selling his revolution on neo-liberal rhetoric and principles, Ralph Klein lifted the expectations of those Albertans who wholeheartedly accepted that ideology. His government, through its words as much as its actions, also legitimized a perspective of radical free-market politics. When the realities of governing dampened the Conservatives' ideological fervour, emboldened true believers felt the confidence to strike up their own political movement. The rise of WAP is significant not because of the party itself, but because it may represent the culmination of forces unleashed by Klein.

◆ ◆ ◆

The most recent era in Alberta labour history began with a revolution and ended with the entrenchment of a new normal. Labour was unprepared for the onslaught that came at them in the 1990s, unable to muster sufficient response to the series of cuts and rollbacks. Internal divisions and insecurity handcuffed working Albertans and allowed neo-liberalism to advance further than in other provinces. By acquiescing to key assumptions about the nature of the problem, unions unintentionally signed a deal re-establishing the boundaries of political debate and labour relations in the province. That new normal is characterized by a defensive, divided labour movement hesitant to use its potential strength of solidarity and, in contrast, confident employers and conservative politicians advancing their agenda unscathed.

But during this era, workers still rose to protect justice, jobs, and their values. Although these struggles often ended in defeat, the growth of new voices and new faces among Alberta workers was heartening. Those most likely to raise their fists in the 1990s and 2000s were new to the labour movement and often new to Canada. Whether at Lakeside Packers, at Palace Casino, or in union halls, workers challenged parts of the new normal, rising up to say that justice should not be denied. Furthermore, unions learned from these workers and tried to understand their lived experience. The labour movement responded to the evolving working class. The new voices will become established voices in the next era of Alberta labour history and may find ways to shred the new normal.

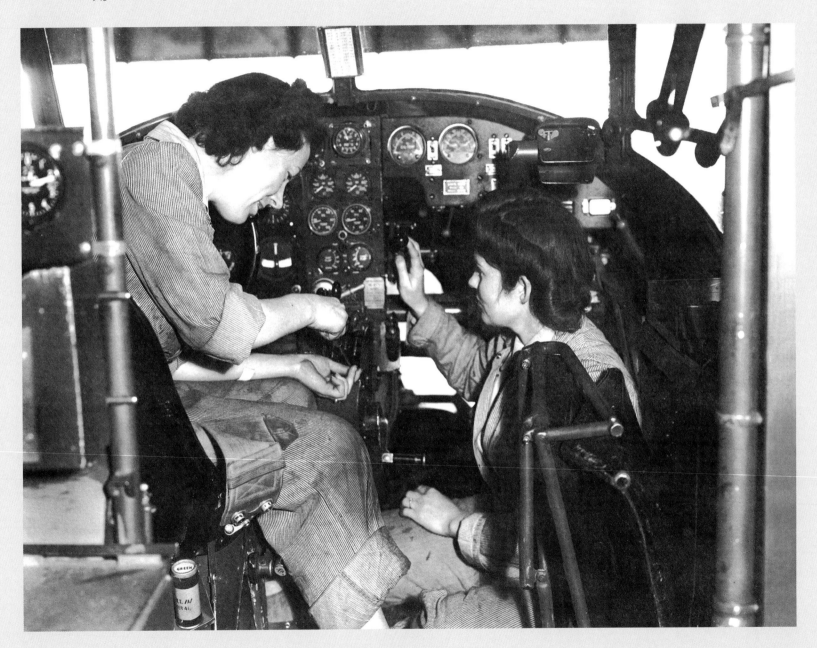

9 WOMEN, LABOUR, AND THE LABOUR MOVEMENT

JOAN SCHIEBELBEIN

Victoria Belcourt Callihoo, a Métis woman from northern Alberta born in 1861, was only thirteen years old when she first joined the buffalo hunt. Her mother "was a medicine woman who set broken bones and knew how to use medicinal herbs." After the men killed the buffalo, she recalled, "the women would go out to help bring in the meat, and then the slicing of the meat began. We girls would then keep a little smoke going all day to keep flies away from the meat. The meat would be hung on rails that rested on two tripods at each end." [1]

Callihoo's story demonstrates the varied work roles that women have played throughout Alberta's history. As we saw in chapter 1, for most of the province's history — that is, before Europeans arrived — women played crucial roles both in the home and as providers of food. The Native women who married European fur traders continued to play their traditional roles, as chapter 2 explains. But the arrival of European women in what is now Alberta introduced a gendered division of labour in which women were gradually mainly confined to domestic roles without pay while men were involved in paid labour. This chapter traces women's gradual incorporation into the paid labour force and the ways in which that entry into paid labour was fraught with gendered identities that limited women's pay and possibilities of advancement. The chapter also follows women's involvement with the trade union movement in their efforts to improve their position within the labour force, and the positive and negative experiences that such involvement entailed.

WOMEN'S WORK, PAID AND UNPAID

As colonialism descended upon Alberta, the extended-family units of production that had characterized the millennia of pre-contact Native hunting and gathering history in the province gave way to European nuclear-family farming units of production. The division of labour was based on gender, but women's roles on farms were varied. Women tended to and provided education for their children. They were responsible for

MRS. OSBORNE BROWN

Using colourful pamphlets to promote settlement on the Prairies to British women, the CPR minimized the harshness of the land and the modest commercial incomes of its farmers. But these early-twentieth-century pamphlets included testimonies from prairie farm women that nonetheless provide some indication of the commercial pursuits of farm women. Mrs. Osborne Brown of Wales (it was an indication of women's subordination that they generally referred to themselves publicly using their husband's first name rather than their own) described her experiences as follows:

> We had a garden and I bought a pair of chickens and a young pig. This was our "stock." The garden behaved well; my vegetables from the first proved very remunerative, and eggs and chickens were in great demand. We set out the wild fruit trees, and in a few seasons we had lots of fruit to add to our market sales. By this time we had purchased several cows and my butter-making proved the biggest returns in a cash way. In winter, when you'd suppose a farm couldn't yield any cash returns, the long evenings gave my embroidery needle a chance to assist, and I sold a great deal of this kind of work.

SOURCE: Canadian Pacific Railway, *Women's Work in Western Canada: A Sequel to "Words from the Women of Western Canada,"* 56.

the household and for the health care of their family. Many were also involved in the production of goods — including vegetables, eggs, meat, butter, bread, cloth, yarn, soap, and candles — that were not only used by their family but also sold to provide needed household income. Off-farm paid work in the late 1800s was limited mainly to domestic work, with teaching and nursing offering more intereresting opportunities, though at the time they were poorly paid occupations that did not enjoy the status of recognized professions.

The first nurses in Alberta were Grey Nuns, who did missionary as well as nursing work among Aboriginal populations. They built a hospital-school-orphanage in St. Albert in 1870. Alberta's first lay nurse was probably Mary Newton, who arrived in Hermitage, near Edmonton, from London, England, in 1886. She worked in a "small log hospital" there and advertised "that she would do nursing and midwifery in private homes for ten dollars a week."[2] The first regularly equipped hospital in what was to become Alberta opened in January 1890 in Medicine Hat, which also became the site of Alberta's School of Nursing in 1894. Medicine Hat had the only hospital between Winnipeg and Vancouver at the time. It employed two nurses: Grace Reynolds, who had received her nurse training in Leeds, England, and held the position of matron until she married the hospital's superintendent, and Mary Ellen Birtles, a nursing graduate from Winnipeg General Hospital. Apart from the doctor, they were the only staff in the twenty-four-bed hospital, and the only time off that either woman received was to allow them to attend church on Sunday. In her memoirs, written in 1939, Birtles described the two nurses' responsibilities, which were in no way limited to nursing:

> Miss Reynolds and I managed the work between us. She prepared the meals and looked after the downstairs work; I attended to the furnace and did the upstairs work, dusting etc. besides attending to the patients. When any surgical work had to be done we had to arrange the work accordingly. Miss Reynolds gave

the anesthetic and I looked after the instruments and waited on the doctor. There was no sterilizer so we had to resort to boiling the instruments in a large saucepan with a steamer on it for towels and dressings.[3]

The Alberta District Nursing Service (ADNS, renamed the Municipal Nursing Service in 1950) was created in 1919 in response to a need for midwifery and emergency medical services in the province's remote areas. Until 1924, maternal and infant mortality rates in Canada were highest in the Prairies, with maternity being second only to tuberculosis as the leading cause of death among women.[4] It was women's groups, most notably the United Farm Women of Alberta, who pressured the Liberal provincial government into creating the ADNS, which grew steadily from three nurses in 1919 to thirty-seven in 1951, and then declined until it was phased out in 1976. Throughout, municipal nurses provided "emergency treatment, obstetrical supervision, home nursing, immunization, and environmental sanitation in sparsely populated areas distant from medical and hospital services."[5]

FIG 9-2 Women saw lumber for a homestead. Provincial Archives of Alberta A6914.

FIG 9-3 A woman works the loom at the Golden Fleece Woolen Mill in Magrath, 1940. Provincial Archives of Alberta, BL 301-3.

Domestic and personal service jobs in Alberta accounted for a large percentage of jobs for women and girls: 46 percent of all employed females in 1911, 33.4 percent in 1921, and 37.8 percent in 1931.[6] While most domestic servants were young unmarried women, married working-class women also worked as domestics in order to earn money for their families to survive. Emma Mohr tells the story of her mother, Catherine Henning, who worked as a maid in the early 1900s while her grandmother helped care for her and her siblings. The family lived in Josephsburg, a village northeast of Edmonton.

Mother decided to earn a bit of extra money to help buy the many necessary household items which were still needed. She got a part-time job as a maid for the Johnstone Walkers, owners of the first Johnstone Walker store in Edmonton. Her usual mode of transportation was on foot, and in order to save her shoes she walked barefoot and carried her shoes. She stayed in Edmonton three or four days a week, then walked home to see how things were. . . . Wages were very low, and were taken out in merchandise in some cases. She often talked about the time she worked for days to earn a fairly large tin box with a tight-fitting lid in which to store flour or any perishable food, as the house had no screen doors to keep out flies or insects. The Johnstone Walker store got its supplies packed in these tin boxes. This particular one had contained tea.[7]

Wages for domestic servants were poverty wages, and the women were often isolated, particularly those who lived with the family for whom they worked. Employers generally expected them to be highly deferential. For these and other reasons — such as long hours, lack of privacy, and lack of prestige — factory work tended to be preferred over domestic work by many working-class women when they could get it, and Great Western Garment Company (GWG) would provide almost a century of women who had few other career prospects, and especially immigrant women, with factory employment. As Emma Gilbertson explained:

Before I was married and before I ever went to Edmonton [and worked at GWG], I kept the house for the school inspector in Camrose. His wife . . . passed away so I looked after three children for him for fifteen months, kept house. . . . He married his second wife's sister and when he was going to marry her, they wanted me to stay on and work and I didn't want to 'cause . . . I was boss of, you know, in charge . . . of the kitchen and everything on my own. I didn't want somebody to be over me.[8]

From an initial workforce of eight seamstresses, GWG quickly increased its staff to a hundred employees in the first year of operation. Sewing men's work clothing for piecework rates rather than wages, "thousands of immigrants found their first jobs at the 97th street factory, learning English as they manufactured farmers' overalls, soldiers' uniforms and denim jeans."[9]

Assunta Dotto, an Italian immigrant and sewing machine operator, was one of them. Initially, she had cleaned houses "for a dollar a day." She preferred GWG, where she made lasting friendships:

There were two girls, Irma and Irene, that were born here. Our friendship lasted for sixty years. Irene especially was helping me with English. The girls in my line, they were really, really good . . . they never laughed if my pronunciation was bad. They helped me. A lot of times, we called on Irene to be the interpreter and if I misunderstood what they were saying, they all had a good laugh. I had a good circle of friends and I was really happy.[10]

While many women preferred factory work to domestic service, piecework made for hectic and generally poorly remunerated employment. Helen Allen, who started working at GWG in 1939 at the age of eighteen, said, "You didn't get much for piecework. I mean, I think the average wage that I got would be between twelve and fifteen dollars a week, and that's for a forty-eight-hour week." In addition, sewing machine operators were not paid for time spent fixing mistakes: "If you made a mistake, you'd get the bundle back and you could rip, you might rip for a few hours a day. . . . You wouldn't get paid for the ripping."[11]

GWG also employed men, and, in common with other garment manufacturers throughout Canada, organized work based on gender. Men were generally employed as cutters and pressers while women worked as sewing machine operators. Women's wages were lower than men's: "In general," notes historian Linda Kealey, "women's work in the clothing trades was labeled unskilled or less skilled then men's, and the sexual division of labour was reinforced by low wages."[12]

Office work, once exclusively the domain of men, gradually opened to women in step with the concept of scientific management and new technologies in the office, such as the typewriter. Calgary's eight stenographers and typists in 1902 had increased to 750 by 1914.[13] While the office work environment was cleaner and safer than that of a factory, the jobs available to women in offices were also classified as low skilled and were therefore low paid, offering no opportunity for advancement. According to scholars Ruth Frager and Carmela Patrias, women "did not generally displace men, who continued to be hired as accountants and bookkeepers and for other jobs with prospects for advancement. Women took the new, routinized jobs. The monotonous, dead-end character of the work meant that they could be paid poorly."[14]

In the early years of European settlement, women, particularly in urban centres, were limited to teaching

FIG 9-4 Teacher and pupils in a one-room school in Nisbet, 1908.
Glenbow Archives, NA-3976-35.

elementary school; secondary teaching, which was viewed as the instrument for moulding young men for the workforce, remained the domain of men.[15] Unsurprisingly, elementary school teachers were paid far less than secondary school teachers, the early years of education being peculiarly viewed as requiring less skill to teach.[16]

Women's inferior economic status, particularly in Alberta's growing urban centres, encouraged many women to become prostitutes. Prostitution expanded in Alberta with the construction of the CPR and an all-male labour force unable to bring their families with them.[17] Similar imbalances between the sexes promoted prostitution in the early mining towns. In the late 1880s and early 1900s, the authorities had little incentive to curb prostitution since it helped make possible the retention of transient male workers.[18] That changed, however, as the province's population grew. Many early Alberta settlers were of Anglo-Saxon background and brought with them strict views concerning acceptable roles for women — namely, wife and mother. They demanded that the police crack down on prostitution and other "moral offences" such as drinking and gambling. In her examination of prostitution in Calgary between 1905 and 1914, Judy Bedford documents an increase in police arrests of prostitutes and keepers of common bawdy houses "to placate the angry moralists."[19]

Rather than recognize that most women who turned to prostitution did so for economic reasons, moralists and reformers blamed the "foreign element." In fact, most prostitutes and johns were Anglo-Canadians, and a majority of prostitutes convicted in Calgary in 1914 were married women.[20] That did not stop the newspapers from blaming Chinese employers of young women for prostitution, as the following excerpt from an editorial in the *Lethbridge Herald* in 1909 reveals:

One of the most regrettable things noticed in the towns and cities of Western Canada is the presence of young girls working in semi-respectable restaurants and boardinghouses. These places, very often, are breeding places of crime of the worst kind. It is noticed particularly that in the Chinese places of the lower order young girls, fourteen, fifteen and sixteen years of age are employed and it is known their position there is anything but what it ought to be. These girls, and society, should be protected, even if against their own wills. . . . No girl under eighteen years of age should be allowed to work in these places, which are fatal to their moral well-being and therefore create and maintain a menace against society."[21]

FIG 9-5 "Houses of ill repute" in Calgary in the early twentieth century. Glenbow Archives, NA-673-9.

Employment prospects for women remained precarious in the interwar period. In 1929, the *Edmonton Journal* reported a series of arrests of teenage girls who took up prostitution either because they couldn't find work or could only find unremunerative jobs. For example, one young woman found work in the cafeteria of Ramsey's Department Store, but the $7.50 per week that she earned did not even pay her room and board. "She took to wandering the streets as the only form of recreation available to a poor and lonely girl and shortly fell in with a taxi-driver. She began to share lodgings with him and he asked her to 'hustle for him.' . . . In the course of several months, Miss X moved from pimp to pimp."[22]

The movement of women into the paid workforce, whether as prostitutes or in legal occupations, did not occur without resistance before World War II. The reform movement, led by organizations such as the Imperial Order Daughters of the Empire and the National Council of Women of Canada, whose members were primarily middle- and upper-middle-class married women, objected to women working in the paid labour force because of the perceived negative impact on women's health, femininity, and high moral standards. They felt it would lessen women's desire to become wives and mothers, which were seen as their natural roles in a patriarchal society.[23] Some of their objection to women having new opportunities for work, however, seems to have been based on self-interest: they wanted women to be available to work as domestics in their homes, and they therefore exempted paid domestic labour from their critique of women's work.

But it was not only bourgeois reformers who objected to women working. So too did organized labour.

In 1898, the Trades and Labour Congress (TLC) "called for the exclusion of women from the labour force as part of its platform of principles," a position they held until 1914.[24] The primary concern for the TLC was the impact of women workers on men's jobs and wages. In their view, employers took advantage of the large number of women seeking work to push wages down, which then affected wages of male workers, whom the labour movement, along with the rest of society, regarded as the legitimate family "breadwinners."[25]

There was particular hostility to married women working. Women often stopped working for pay when they married, not only because of prevailing social attitudes but also because many employers would not employ married women.[26] Even the federal government restricted the employment of married women until 1955. But most married women who took paid work did so either because their husbands earned wages too low to manage the household or because their husbands had died or deserted the family.[27] The mothers' allowance introduced by the provincial government in 1919 provided some assistance but was set well below the poverty level. John Lloyd recounts the story of his grandmother, who took a job working in a coal mine to support her family after her husband was killed:

> It fell upon my grandmother's shoulders to make a living for her young family, and this she did by taking a job at the pit head. The job: shoveling coal out of the mine cars that came up from underground. Because she was only a woman she got about half the wages of the men who did the same work alongside. . . . Money was scarce, and so she also took the job of caretaker at the local school.[28]

Objections to women working grew during periods of high unemployment, such as the Great Depression of the 1930s. But despite pressures on women to free up jobs for unemployed men, the gendering of jobs meant that employers were usually hiring women and men for different jobs. There were relatively fewer job losses during the 1930s in the service and clerical jobs for which women were hired than in the jobs reserved mainly for men.[29] Those "women's jobs" paid poorly and were often fraught with dangers. Clare Botsford, working as a waitress in the 1930s from the age of twelve or thirteen, made a dollar a day for a twelve-hour shift and then walked home at two in the morning. "Your employer had no responsibility to see that you got home safely," she said. "If you got hurt on the job, just don't bother coming back. There was no workers' compensation."[30]

Labour shortages inevitably drowned out the voices opposing paid work for women. During both world wars, with many Canadian men joining the armed forces, demand for women workers increased, and some were even hired to do jobs typically done by men, although for less pay. In World War II, women were hired to work in the munitions industry. Aircraft Repair in Edmonton opened shortly after the outbreak of the war to overhaul, repair, and assemble military aircraft. In 1943, it employed a thousand women in its workforce of twenty-four hundred.[31] Some Alberta women also agreed to move to Ontario, sometimes on a temporary basis, to work in that province's more substantial munitions industry.[32] Norah Plumley Hook stayed in Alberta and later recalled her work experiences at Aircraft Repair:

I was hired on July 12, 1941, expecting that with sewing experience, I would be working in the fabric department. This was not meant to be. . . . Another girl and I were escorted to the Sheet Metal Department. As the first girls in that department, we were being tested, "to see if girls *could* do Sheet Metal work." Our first job was filing — not fingernails or documents! . . . In due time, we went on to many different aspects of sheet metal work. We took out dents and straightened ailerons, cowlings, flaps and undercarriages and all metal parts with equally strange names.[33]

The wartime economy also stimulated some expansion of traditional women's employment. Government contracts went to GWG during both wars to manufacture soldiers' uniforms. During World War II, "GWG workers, almost all women, were considered essential workers. The plant ran three shifts, 24 hours a day, seven days a week and produced 25,000 articles of military clothing a week."[34] Meanwhile, a shortage of teachers during the war caused school boards such as Edmonton Public Schools to remove their ban on the employment of married women as teachers.[35]

But expanded opportunities for women's work proved temporary. By 1951, only one-quarter of Canadian women of working age were in the labour force, and most were single women in traditional women's labour ghettoes.[36] Clerical work was on the increase for women. While it supplied just over 16 percent of jobs for females in 1931 in Alberta, that figure jumped to 28 percent in 1961 and almost 38 percent in 1981.[37]

A dramatic increase in women's employment started in the 1960s in Alberta. The labour force participation of females over ten had doubled between 1931 and 1961 to 26 percent. By 1991, when figures were kept for females over fifteen, the comparable figure was 59.5 percent, and in 2009, 64 percent.[38] Since the mid-1970s, Alberta has had the highest percentage of employed women in Canada, although women's employment in the province still remained 10 percent lower than men's in 2009.[39]

The increase in women's employment occurred partly because of economic need, but such need was hardly new in the 1960s. A bigger factor may have been the gradual change in social attitudes regarding gender roles, as the second wave of feminism and the report in 1970 of the Royal Commission on the Status of Women attested. Anne Ozipko, a machine operator at GWG, told an often-heard story.

> I started there in May '44. . . . I got a week off to get married in 1945. Then I went back to work. I worked until 1947. Then my son was born so I stayed home for a number of years. I didn't go back to work until . . . 1963. I had three kids and stayed at home with them. So when I came back, I went to work nightshift because my husband wasn't in favour of my working. But I insisted I was going, so I worked from 4:30 to 11:30 every night, because we needed the money. Our son was very good in school and . . . he was almost ready for university and we couldn't afford the tuition. The girls wanted a piano and I couldn't afford a piano. So I went to work so I could make some money.[40]

Like Anne Ozipko, postwar women tended not to leave the labour force when they married, waiting instead until they had their first child and then returning to work when their children were older. Gradually, it became common for women to leave paid work only for a brief period after giving birth. In 1976, the percentage of Canadian women who were both employed and had children under sixteen years of age living at home was 39.1 percent; in 2009, it was 72.9 percent.[41] This has led to more women experiencing what is referred to as the "double burden" — a double workload of paid and unpaid labour, as women are still primarily responsible for household work and child care.

What has changed only slowly are the types of occupations in which most women are employed. While increasing numbers of women have entered professional and managerial jobs over time, most women workers, particularly in the public sector, continue to work in a narrow range of traditionally female occupational areas, including clerical and administration, sales and service, health care, and education.[42] Furthermore, the jobs women hold in these areas tend to be at the lower level. While over time, more women were promoted to management positions, most have not risen above junior levels of management.[43]

Not only has occupational segregation of women and men persisted over time; so too has pay inequality. In 1921, women's annual wages as a proportion of men's were 59 percent for Calgary and Edmonton, and in 2007, the median income for women employed full time was 66 percent of men's full-time incomes, the worst figure for gender disparity of any Canadian province.[44] That figure understates the real gender gap in wages because women made up 70 percent of the part-time workforce in Alberta in 2007.[45]

WOMEN AND THE LABOUR MOVEMENT

One of the ways in which women workers have addressed their inferior economic status is through unionization. Though Alberta's early unions were almost exclusively male, a notable exception was the United Garment Workers of America, which unionized the mostly female workforce at Edmonton's GWG plant only three months after it opened in January 1911.[46] Few other women were unionized because women's work was viewed by employers as unskilled, meaning that they could be easily replaced if they agitated to improve their pay and working conditions. Many worked in isolation (e.g., as domestic servants) or in small workplaces that were difficult for unions to organize.

Another problem was the mainstream labour movement's lack of interest in organizing women workers. Their primary goal was to secure a "family wage" for their members — "a wage big enough for a male breadwinner to support his wife and children. . . . As workers, women were seen as temporary, needing protection only while they laboured before marriage."[47] Organized labour sought this protection by advocating protective labour legislation, such as factory acts that reduced working hours and improved working conditions and minimum wage legislation. Alberta's *Factory Act* was passed in 1917. It included "provision of a minimum wage of $1.50 per shift for all adults and $1.00 per shift for all apprentices in any factory, shop or office building," making Alberta the first province to enact minimum wage legislation.[48] But few women worked in factories. When the province did establish a minimum wage for women workers in 1920, it carefully excluded domestic workers and farm workers, thus

leaving a substantial group of women without a minimum wage guarantee.

In 1922, the United Farmers of Alberta (UFA) government established a minimum wage board to set minimum wage rates for women in various industries. As in other provinces, its purpose was "to set wage rates for female wage-earners on an industry-by-industry basis after consultation with representative employers and employees."[49] That often produced limited protection for the workers. In retail, for example, companies were exempted from paying women minimum wage during the first year of their employment, which served as an incentive to fire women after their year's "apprenticeship" was finished.[50]

FIG 9-6 The United Garment Workers of America label used by GWG workers. Courtesy of the Alberta Labour History Institute.

FIG 9-7 A waitress serves customers in a Calgary café, 1954. Glenbow Archives, NA-5600-6480a.

Even at that, the board's rulings were poorly enforced. For example, in May 1935, 150 waitresses and kitchen staff at twenty-five Edmonton restaurants went on strike at the height of the Depression because they were being paid on average $4.50 per week and working up to twelve hours a day, despite the minimum wage board having set their pay at $9.50 for a forty-hour week. Hundreds of unemployed men on relief, who were also on strike at the time, supported the women by joining their picket lines. The strikers formed the Restaurant Workers' Union, and — with the help of the secretary-treasurer of the Edmonton Trades and Labour Council, Alf Farmilo — they were successful in getting the majority of restaurant owners to sign an agreement to pay the minimum wage.[51]

Much of women's participation in the labour movement in the early history of the province was through women's auxiliaries and union label campaigns. Most women's auxiliaries were associated with crafts unions; one exception was the Western Federation of Miners auxiliary. Historian Linda Kealey suggests that the tasks women's auxiliaries performed were mainly "stereotypically female" and "accentuated men's roles in the workplace and women's roles as supporters of trade unionism through their social and educational activities as wives, mothers, and consumers."[52] But in addition to organizing social events, women attended joint meetings with the union members. Auxiliaries also sometimes "featured access to insurance schemes that provided sickness and death benefits in an age in which no government or employment-related benefits were required."[53] The International Typographical Union women's auxiliary was prominent in promoting the use of the union label. One of the organization's vice-presidents, Mrs. B.W. Bellamy of Medicine Hat, was a major figure in the Western women's auxiliary movement and, in 1918, became the first woman to participate officially in an Alberta Federation of Labour convention.

Alberta women were also active in the labour movement through the Women's Labour Leagues (WLL). WLLs were socialist organizations that first appeared in Canada prior to World War I but became more widespread and active after the war, when they were reinvigorated by the Communist Party of Canada (CPC). The Canadian Federation of Women's Labour Leagues was formed in 1924, but the Trades and Labour Congress rejected the federation's request for affiliation on the grounds that "a separate organization of women would ultimately weaken the working class movement; and that women had ample opportunity to join unions, and hence gain representation at conventions."[54] More likely, they rejected the WLLs because of their ties to the CPC.

By 1927, there were thirty-seven WLL locals across Canada, including affiliates in Calgary, Edmonton, Lethbridge, and communities in the Crowsnest Pass. Unlike women's auxiliaries, WLL locals were unaffiliated with specific (male-dominated) crafts unions, and, while they undertook some of the same activities as women's auxiliaries, their main focus was the rights of women workers. They advocated for the unionization of women workers and supported their use of the strike as a way to fight for better pay and working conditions. They also pressured governments to pass protective labour legislation — at the same time, "keeping an eye on the limits of legislative initiatives and, whenever they could, exposing violations."[55] For example, the Calgary WLL had pressed for the creation of the Minimum Wage Board and for a working-class woman to be appointed to it to represent her class. Subsequently, Edmontonian Harriet J. Ingam, president of the Garment Workers' Union, was indeed named to the board.[56] They were unsuccessful, however, in getting the government to include domestic workers within the minimum wage legislation.

The Calgary WLL was founded in 1919 by Mary Corse and Jean McWilliam. Corse was a trustee on the Calgary Board of Education, a voting delegate on the Calgary Trades and Labour Council, a member of the International Typographical Union women's auxiliary, and an activist in the Dominion Labour Party. McWilliam was president of the Calgary Defence Committee for jailed strikers and founded the Women of Unemployed Committee. She also ran a boarding house "where radicals were welcome and able to enlist her support."[57] Both women testified before the federal government's Royal Commission on Industrial Relations in 1919 (the Mathers Commission). They argued that the low pay and poor working and living conditions that most women workers experienced were a source of resentment and radicalism. Jean McWilliam testified:

> I was put on a committee to investigate conditions in the hotels and restaurants around the city here. Girls were living with sleeping accommodation down in the basement. . . . One little girl got into trouble and her baby was born three months after she was married. The baby was only four pounds in weight because the girl almost starved to death. That little girl's baby died on the 14th of this month of malnutrition and starvation. . . . Death has entered her family, who is responsible?[58]

However, even though they fought to improve the lives and working conditions of women, the WLLs did not challenge prevailing social attitudes about women's roles. They opposed the right of married women with employed husbands to work and petitioned the Calgary School Board in 1923 "to reduce married women on staff, supporting instead the concept of a family wage and married women's duty to raise a family."[59] This was also the position of the Federation of Women's Labour Leagues: its national newspaper, *The Woman Worker*, argued in favour of the male breadwinner model.[60]

It wasn't until the 1960s and 1970s that the rate of unionization of women workers began to increase significantly, paralleling the sharp increase in women's labour market participation, particularly in the public sector. As outlined in chapters 6 to 8, unionization in the public sector proceeded rapidly in the 1960s and 1970s, and after 1960 women became increasingly prominent in strikes and union leadership in Alberta. Today, over two-thirds of all women in Canada who are covered by a union work in the public sector.[61] In 2008,

women's unionization rate in the public sector was 71.9 percent, compared to 68.5 percent for men, while in the private sector only 12.2 percent of women were covered by a union, compared to 19.8 percent of men.[62]

What has been the impact of unionization on women? First, unions have had a positive impact on women's wages. Nationally, in 2003, women aged fifteen and over who were covered by a union contract earned an average of $19.94 an hour, compared with $14.55 an hour for women not covered by a union, thus making the union wage premium 37 percent.[63] The union wage premium for men was 17.7 percent. Of course, other factors also influence wages, such as public versus private sector employment. When these are factored out, according to the Equal Pay Coalition, "women in unionized jobs earn, on average, $2 more than non-unionized women in similar jobs."[64]

Some activists became involved in their union because they recognized its role in improving their wages and wanted to keep it strong. Cindy McCallum Miller, a postal worker and Canadian Union of Postal Workers activist in Banff, Alberta, recalled how she became an instant activist:

> I was only hired for the summer, but it so happened that two of the part timers had moved on, so there were two vacancies and I got one of them. On September 30, my probation ended and I became a part timer, and the next day I became local secretary-treasurer. I did that . . . because it was a small local and the people had held positions so long that they were really looking for someone else to start taking on the responsibility. I was approached by one of the long-time activists and I said, "Yeah, whatever you need." She was quite

FIG 9-8 Jean McWilliam emigrated from Scotland in 1907 and ran a boarding house in Calgary. She was a founder of the Women's Labour League. Glenbow Archives, NA-2173-2.

shocked that I would volunteer so quickly. I said, "I owe you something and this is my way of paying back." She said, "You don't owe me anything." I said, "No, not you particularly, but I owe this local something. I owe this union something." . . . At that time we were making $11.86 an hour. That was double what anybody else in Banff was making. If you were working in a gift store, you were making $4.50 to $5.00 an hour. If you were working at the local banks, you might be making a little bit more. If you were in a position of responsibility in one of the hotels, you might be making $7 an hour. I made $11.86 the day I walked into that job. That wasn't because all of a sudden somebody out there had recognized all these great skills that I'd always had. It was because of that collective agreement and because of those struggles. So I knew that I owed somebody something.[65]

The female-male wage gap within the unionized workforce is also significantly lower than in the non-unionized workforce. In 2010, women covered by a union earned 93.7 percent of what men covered by a union earned, whereas women not covered by a union earned only 79.4 percent of what their male counterparts earned.[66] One of the ways in which organized labour has attempted to address the disparity between women's and men's incomes in the last few decades is by advocating for pay equity. Pay equity goes beyond the notion that women and men doing the same job should receive the same pay; it also includes efforts to compare the value of jobs that are dissimilar. This involves establishing criteria for comparing different jobs: educational requirements, complexity of tasks, degree of responsibility, degree of danger, and the like. Thus,

FIG 9-9 Faye Broeksma, pictured in 1971, was Edmonton's first female letter carrier. Provincial Archives of Alberta, J693.

pay equity is summed up in the phrase "equal pay for work of equal value." In other words, as the Alberta Federation of Labour Women's Committee noted, "a woman doesn't have to do the same job as a man to qualify for the same pay. Instead, if her lower paid job is equal in *value* to a higher paying one done by a man, then she gets paid the same wages." This involves recognizing that women historically have been ghettoized in certain low-paying occupations and attempting "to correct the undervaluing of work traditionally done by women" by examining and comparing the skill, effort, responsibility, and working conditions of typically female and male jobs through a job evaluation process.[67]

Susan Keeley, a former daycare worker for the City of Calgary, explained how daycare workers for the city used the concept of pay equity to get their wages raised in the 1980s and onwards. First, she and her unionized co-workers "went to the city and talked to them about our wages and how low we were paid. We got a 15 percent wage increase in between contracts because of that." In turn, that proved to be "basically the real impetus to get the job evaluation program off the ground. Through that job evaluation program, the daycare workers received another 47 percent wage increase." For Keeley, the progress that the local made galvanized her to become a committed activist.[68]

While many unions have sought wage parity during collective bargaining, they have also advocated for pay equity legislation, with an emphasis on employer responsibility rather than complaint-driven action. Union women view this legislative focus as especially advantageous because it would make pay equity a universal right rather than simply a collective-bargaining goal for the minority of working women who enjoy union protection.[69] Currently, Alberta is the only province without either pay equity legislation or a pay equity negotiation framework.[70] The only recourse for women who feel they are suffering pay discrimination because of their gender is through the Alberta Human Rights Commission, which can be costly and exhausting; furthermore, Alberta human rights law only guarantees equal pay for equal work.

In addition to higher wages, unionized workers have higher non-wage benefits (e.g., pensions, health plans, paid time off work) than their non-unionized counterparts. A unionized worker is three times more likely to have an employer-sponsored pension plan and twice as likely to have a medical plan than is a non-union worker.[71] A benefit of particular concern to working women is maternity leave, which includes two important elements: job-protected leave, which is the right of women to take time off work during pregnancy and after the birth of their child while retaining entitlement to the job they held at the same pay and benefits they enjoyed before the leave; and the provision of pay and benefits during the period of leave. Both of these are reinforced by Article 10.2 of the United Nations Declaration on the Elimination of Discrimination Against Women, which was ratified by Canada in 1967. The article, in an effort to protect the right to work for all women, calls for "measures . . . to prevent their dismissal in the event of marriage or maternity," "paid maternity leave with the guarantee of returning to former employment," and "the necessary social services, including child-care facilities."[72]

MATERNITY LEAVE

Legislation guaranteeing security of employment while on maternity leave is a provincial responsibility except for federal employees, who are covered by federal labour standards. Alberta was one of the last provinces to enact such legislation. In 1975, the government introduced Bill 71, an amendment to the *Alberta Labour Act*. In moving the second reading, Minister of Labour Neil Crawford acknowledged that some unions had negotiated maternity leave in their collective agreements and that "the benefits of this progressive type of thinking" should be extended to other workers not covered by these agreements.[73] For example, Civic Service Union 52, which represents many City of Edmonton employees, won limited job-protected maternity leave in 1967. Female employees who resigned for maternity reasons were to be considered as having been on leave without pay if they accepted re-employment with the city within six months of the date of their resignation.

However, Bill 71 did not guarantee job-protected maternity leave for all women: the amendment stated only that the Labour Board *may* make an order requiring an employer to grant a pregnant employee maternity leave without pay for up to twelve weeks before the estimated date of delivery of the child and six weeks after the birth of the child. It wasn't until 1980 that the Alberta government enacted maternity leave legislation with which all employers were required to comply. The amount of leave was basically the same as that contained in Bill 71, but to be eligible, a worker had to have been employed by her employer for at least twelve months.

Upon recommendation of the Royal Commission on the Status of Women, the federal government began providing income support for expectant and new mothers in 1971 through the unemployment insurance (UI) system. Mothers with twenty or more insurable weeks could claim up to fifteen weeks of benefits after a two-week waiting period, but since Alberta did not have maternity leave legislation at that time, Albertans who took maternity leave to claim UI benefits risked losing their job. In 1990, the *Unemployment Insurance Act* was amended to include ten weeks of parental leave, which could be used by either parent, in addition to maternity leave. In 2000, parental leave was increased to thirty-five weeks, thereby increasing maternity and paternity leave from six months to a year.

GETTING MATERNITY LEAVE

When an Edmonton dental hygienist asked for maternity leave from the four-person dental office where she worked in late July 1990, she was unaware of her rights under provincial labour law. She told her employer of two years that she would come back 22 weeks later, that is, the beginning of January. He agreed verbally and she thought everything was set. But that November, the 25-year-old hygienist got a call from the dentist who told her he decided to keep her replacement instead. "At that time (November) he was sort of indicating that he might not want me back because I wouldn't be reliable," she said. "Even before I left he was asking me what I would do if the baby was sick. . . . That's some way to treat an employee after two years of service. That's the hardest part — being treated like that."

SOURCE: Bob Boehm, "Baby-making vs. Profit-making," *Edmonton Journal*, 28 April 1991.

Only after the changes to the *Unemployment Insurance Act* in 2000 did Alberta feel compelled to extend its maternity provisions and introduce paternity provisions to match the federal Employment Insurance (EI) regulations. Before the changes were implemented in 2001, Alberta had the shortest maternity leave provision in Canada — just eighteen weeks (Quebec provided a full year). Audrey Cormack, Alberta Federation of Labour president at the time, welcomed the changes, commenting that "mirroring the changes made to federal EI creates a level of jurisdictional equity that we rarely see in Alberta."[74]

Many unionized workers on maternity leave have the benefit of additional income support through their collective agreement. The first national union to win paid maternity leave for its members was the Canadian Union of Postal Workers (CUPW). It was one of their key demands in their 1981 strike. Before the strike, CUPW's collective agreement with the Treasury Board provided six months unpaid maternity leave with no accumulation of annual leave credits and no superannuation contributions. Men were entitled to only one day of paid leave for the birth of a child, and all members to one day of paid leave for adoption of a child. CUPW's program of demands going into the 1981 negotiations included twenty weeks paid maternity leave and five days each of paid paternity leave and adoption leave. The Treasury Board offered twenty-six weeks unpaid maternity leave, which could be taken by either parent. The board also offered to pay the equivalent of unemployment insurance (UI) benefits for the two-week waiting period during which claimants received no UI benefits but was unwilling to increase paid paternity and adoption leave beyond one day.[75]

Frustrated with the progress of negotiations, CUPW requested a conciliation board. In the meantime, they prepared educational materials on the key issues under dispute, which they distributed both to their members and externally. The backgrounder on parental rights was distributed to hundreds of women's groups. As sociologist Julie White notes, it

> stated the union's position that child bearing was a social as well as an individual responsibility, that women workers were penalized financially for their role in child bearing and fathers deprived of the opportunity to fully participate. . . . [It] also pointed out how little cost was involved, given that only one percent of the total number of employees took maternity leave each year.[76]

The cost to the employer was estimated at 0.25 percent of payroll or two cents per hour per employee. In June, the Conciliation Board report recommended seventeen weeks paid and nine weeks unpaid maternity leave, as well as two days each of paid paternity and adoption leave. CUPW accepted the recommendation as the basis for further negotiation; the Treasury Board did not.

The strike began on 29 June and ended on 12 August. In the last days of the strike, the union won seventeen weeks paid maternity leave, though paid paternity and adoption leave remained at one day each. In her analysis of the strike, Julie White argues that feminists in CUPW faced quite a challenge in persuading members as a whole that paid maternity leave was not only a just demand but worth striking for. Women were a minority in the union at only 43 percent of the membership. However, resistance came not only from male members but also from older women who had gotten by without it and thought that younger women were being too demanding in expecting this benefit. The union, however, kept the issue alive. As Pat Miller, CUPW national director for the Western Region, put it:

There was a lot of shouting and yelling from inside the union, "What the hell am I on strike for — maternity leave?" We overcame that. . . . And as we went along we convinced those that weren't convinced, and the momentum swayed. . . . That was just another segment for the education process on the rights of women and the problems of women. It woke up a lot of people.[77]

Ten years after CUPW's historic strike, another step forward with respect to maternity leave was made when an Alberta human rights board of inquiry ruled in favour of Alberta nurse Susan Parcels that women are eligible for the same benefits as employees on sick leave during the health-related portion of their maternity leave, that period when their doctor says they are unable to work. The Alberta Health Care Association appealed the ruling to the Court of Queen's Bench, but it was upheld in April 1992. The first time Parcels had taken maternity leave, she was in a management position and the employer — Red Deer Auxiliary Hospital — had covered her benefits. So in 1989, when she informed them she was taking a second maternity leave, she was surprised to be told she had to prepay all of her benefits:

When I went down to human resources and said I need to make arrangements for my coverage to continue while I'm off for the next six months they said, "Okay, you'll need to prepay eight hundred and some odd dollars." I said, "Why? . . . I didn't do this before." . . . I said I had to have coverage because I am the sole provider for our benefits for our family.[78]

Parcels's husband had just learned about a recent Supreme Court decision (Brooks v. Safeway) in which the court ruled that pregnancy is a valid health-related reason to be absent from work and therefore must be treated like other health-related absences. So Parcel filed a complaint with the Alberta Human Rights Commission. Even though the United Nurses of Alberta (UNA) was named in her complaint, they supported her from the beginning: "There were so many good people that were just right behind me. I have to say, UNA was one of them. They were named in the claim . . . because the collective agreement was gender biased, was sexually discriminatory, so they were named. But they never acted like they were on the opposite side of my case — ever."[79]

Apart from better wages and benefits, women have benefited from unionization in terms of human rights. Collective agreement provisions related to pay structures, promotions, and layoffs "tend to minimize the most overt forms of discrimination on the basis of gender and race," as one labour advocate has noted.[80] Many unions have also negotiated clauses to mitigate sexual harassment in the workplace. For example, as the result of a sexual harassment case won by the union, Canada Post was ordered by an arbitrator to provide an anti-sexual harassment course

FIG 9-10 International Women's Day march, 1980.
Provincial Archives of Alberta, J4957-2.

for its supervisors and employees.[81] Sociologist Julie White examined data collected in 1992 from 1,235 collective agreements covering close to 2.5 million workers in Canada and found that 63.1 percent of these workers were covered by an agreement with an anti-discrimination provision and 42.7 percent with a sexual harassment provision.[82]

Of course, women who have no union at all are only covered by the limited benefits and protections that employers are required to provide by law. Some "pink ghettoes" in which women have been able to unionize in other provinces, such as child care, remain largely non-unionized in Alberta. While Quebec's public day-care system is heavily unionized, only a small group of civic-run daycares are unionized in Alberta. The result is that child care workers are better remunerated overall in Quebec than in Alberta, though wages overall in Alberta are far higher than Quebec. Sociologist Tom Langford argues in a recent book on daycare in Alberta that the low level of unionization in daycare reflects a "power deficit" for Alberta women: "As a consequence, with very few exceptions, workers lack the institutional means to directly bargain for a distribution of resources that better reflects their valuable contributions to child care."[83]

WOMEN'S STRUGGLES WITHIN UNIONS

While women have clearly benefited from unionization, they have had to fight and organize *within* their unions in order to get the labour movement to pay attention to and take action on issues of concern to them. In the course of doing so, they have come up against sexism and discrimination. Canadian Union of Public Employees (CUPE) activist Clancy Teslenko recalled:

SUSAN PARCELS, NURSE

I didn't want to be front row centre. I wanted the process to continue without me being some sort of figurehead for it. It feels awkward when something is about you and it's that controversial. I come from rural central Alberta and I was raised in a very traditional community setting. I had a great upbringing. . . . But it didn't prepare me for the world of working women outside of that community; . . . you're either going to get married to a farmer or you're going to go and be a teacher or a nurse. That's the traditional way that women in the rural community looked for the next step in their life. Am I going to be a wife and a mother or am I going to be a nurse or a teacher? You didn't often get both. So at seventeen, I was . . . like okay, I've been a candy striper for three years, I guess this means I go to nursing. . . . So when I came back to this community and I had made this noise with the Human Rights Commission, my family . . . couldn't believe it. . . . No, that's not our granddaughter, or niece. That's not our cousin. Because it really did play with their traditional beliefs. . . . They're Social Credits from way back. . . . You don't do this. You don't take your government to court and change things like this.

SOURCE: Interview with Susan Parcels, Edmonton, n.d., ALHI.

I remember going to a CUPE convention in Lethbridge . . . . By that time, I was married and I had a child. . . . There was a resolution that I had written and put forward . . . about providing subsidies for child care. I not only did that. I had resolutions on health and safety. I had resolutions on government issues, political issues, everything. I wasn't focused on women's rights. When this resolution came up, I had gone up to the mike and spoke on it. As I was leaving the mike, . . . one of the brothers turned to me and said, "Why don't you stay home with your kids?" I was absolutely floored that he would say that to me. At that point it was 1990. The unions had been talking about equal rights. There'd been acceptance at the national [level] . . . . So I went back in and I went to the mike and I said that I couldn't believe what had just happened on this floor. From there, the rally started. After I got off the mike, I don't know how many brothers and how many sisters got up and condemned what was done. . . . The president of his local came and talked to me and I told him what happened. He went and dealt with that member, and that member came and apologized. For that to happen was a big thing. We actually ended up being quite good friends after that. It was more of an "okay, I've done wrong. I'm here to learn."[84]

One of the ways in which women have raised issues and pressed for change is by forming women's committees. These committees' activities have ranged from advocating changes within the unions of benefit to women to discussing model clauses to be obtained through collective bargaining and to struggles for broader social change.[85] The Alberta Federation of Labour (AFL) Women's Committee was established in

1983. In 1985, its members brought forward resolution #85/401 at the AFL's twenty-ninth annual convention to establish four new positions specifically for women on the AFL Executive Council. The purpose of this affirmative action resolution was to address underrepresentation of women in leadership positions within the AFL. In 1987, in celebration of the AFL's seventy-fifth anniversary, the Women's Committee published a collection of essays on topics ranging from the effects of technology and free trade on women to the need for publicly funded daycare. In 1989, they called for a woman labour activist to be honoured annually at an AFL event in recognition of International Women's Day (8 March). The first award went to Jean Ross of the Canadian Union of Public Employees in 1990. The committee has also organized forums on equality, raised funds for organizations such as the Alberta Council of Women's Shelters, written policy papers on topics such as child labour and violence against women, and held women's caucuses at the AFL/CLC schools.[86]

In recent decades, unions and the AFL have made efforts to address issues of concern to women and improve their economic and social position in the workplace and society. However, there is still much work to be done. The persistent gender wage gap is a reminder of larger gender inequalities throughout Alberta. Gender inequality also continues within the labour movement itself: for example, men are overrepresented in senior elected and staff positions within unions while women are concentrated at lower levels. Organized labour has undertaken measures to increase the participation of women in unions — for example, by providing child care for women to attend conventions and schools — but more can be done. The workload often expected of union activists and leaders is a barrier to women, particularly those who have family responsibilities.[87]

The 1987 AFL Women's Committee's collection of essays includes one by a male unionist — Bill Berezowski — who was a member and staffer for the International Union of Mine, Mill and Smelter Workers, who served on a number of AFL committees, and whom the Women's Committee called their "honorary feminist." His challenge to the labour movement to fight for gender equality still rings true today:

> The fact that, after a millennium of generations, women still get the "dirtiest" and least rewarding jobs, are still the last hired, first fired and last promoted and are still paid less for the work they perform than their male counterparts is not only a blot on our civilization but a blot on the labour movement as a whole. Unless such issues as that of equal pay for work of equal value are raised to the level of importance we grant to changing unfair labour laws, solving unemployment and winning strikes, never will the extra burden be lifted from the shoulders of our sister workers. Nor will we win the other battles bosses and governments place before us. Simple arithmetic proves the point. More than half of the actual or potential work force is women. Unless this half comes forward in full equality, the labour movement battles with one arm.[88]

MARILYN WARREN, PUBLIC SERVICE ALLIANCE OF CANADA (PSAC)

In 1976, I was chosen as the Alberta and NWT Co-ordinator for our union's Equal Opportunities for Women program. . . . I would also be a member of a small group of women who would try to get funding. . . . The time came for the resolution to hit the floor. We were sure we would have a fight on our hands but we had right on our side, so we couldn't lose, right? . . . To make a long, sordid story short, those speakers who were to speak for us didn't and to make matters worse they spoke against us. . . . We lost the funding and I lost my illusion as to how much our "brothers" wanted to help us. Brotherhood was only for brothers, not sisters. . . . I was elected to attend the next convention and made sure a proposal for funding was in the resolutions. I found things had changed somewhat. . . . Many of the old power brokers [were gone]. . . . There were also more women at this convention. . . . When we called a women's caucus, one hundred and fifteen women attended . . . a change from three years ago, when twenty-four of us showed up. . . . When the resolution came to the floor I was first at the mike. . . . When my five minutes were up, members of our Alberta Caucus took up the cause. We stacked the mikes four deep and before we were all through, the last member called for the question. It was wonderful! We had our 1¢. . . . It was a start.

SOURCE: AFL Women's Committee, *Claiming Our Past . . . Shaping Our Future: A Collection of Essays in Celebration of the Alberta Federation of Labour's 75th Anniversary*, 17–19.

10 RACIALIZATION AND WORK

JENNIFER KELLY AND DAN CUI

The other day I received a communication from a party at Aurora, Nebr. who said he was colored and wanted to go to Canada. He is a laboring man, and while he says he is a good worker, etc. I was under the impression from your circular, that you did not wish Negroes going into Canada and for that matter wrote him. To-day he comes back with a letter stating he is in communication with officials in Canada, of whom he mentions J. Bruce Walker at Winnipeg and says that they urge him to come. The man may be a good worker and may make a good settler, but from our experience in the states, I judged the Canadian Officials were not desirous of having Colored people enter Canada and as such interpreted your circular of above date.[1]

This letter — written in 1910 by W.V. Bennett, a Canadian immigration agent working in the United States, to the Canadian superintendent of immigration — illustrates well the intertwining of race and labour in Canadian immigration policies and the so-called settlement of Alberta. Throughout its history, the Canadian state has decided, often using the category of race, which groups of people it wanted to bring to Canada and for what purposes. While equating "whiteness" with intelligence, honesty, and civilization, the government subscribed to stereotypes of "non-white" groups, characterizing all members of a group as the same rather than considering them as individuals. Like other categories based only on what the eye perceives, however, ideas of "whiteness" evolved over time, with some groups being considered more white than others. For example, until the late 1800s, the Canadian government viewed certain Europeans, particularly Slavs and southern Europeans, as genetically inferior people. Efforts to recruit families and individuals with these backgrounds began only in the 1890s because there were too few "preferred" immigrants available from Britain, France, and Germany. Although the state always regarded them as more white than non-Europeans, it took several generations for Slavs and southern Europeans to be accepted fully as white.

FIG 10-2 These railway workers from the early 1900s had their family roots in Italy and central Europe. Library and Archives Canada, C-46161.

Non-Europeans, who were usually darker than people of European descent, continued to be viewed by the state as the least desirable immigrants. After World War II, in particular, the view of the Canadian Immigration Department was that the world was divided between Europeans and non-Europeans, the latter being inferior to the former and only acceptable for Canadian residence and citizenship under special circumstances. Prime Minister Mackenzie King made the government's position clear in the House of Commons in 1947: "Large-scale immigration from the orient would change the fundamental composition of the Canadian population," he warned, and he assured the House that government policy would prevent such immigration.[2] The notion that people's skin colour or other physical attributes set them apart from other existing or potential citizens is part of the process of racialization, which uses the concept of race to make judgments about people's intrinsic worth on the basis of their outward appearance.

Hence, during the early twentieth century, when there was a need for immigrant workers — especially farmers — in western Canada, the Canadian government racialized certain people as non-white and therefore unfit for Canadian citizenship. Those few non-white workers who were allowed into Alberta and Canada before the 1960s were often officially regarded as temporary migrants, expendable and returnable to elsewhere once the economic need for their labour ended. This issue of expendability has been an aspect of immigration policy since at least the nineteenth century and underlies today's temporary foreign workers scheme (discussed below). Further, non-white workers, including Aboriginal groups, were often marginalized and corralled into specific segments of the Alberta labour market; they were regarded as only able to work effectively under supervision and in certain types of jobs. The overall effect of this marginalization and the racialized response to particular groups of workers has been that they are then vulnerable to being deported or sacked and are thus likely to be more acquiescent to the demands of employers and the state.

This systemic racialization of workers, immigration policies, and, ultimately citizenship, persisted until the 1967 Immigration Regulation introduced the "point system" — a change agreed to mainly because of the decline of preferred traditional immigrants from northern Europe. This chapter uses archival records and oral history interviews undertaken by the Alberta Labour History Institute and other organizations to trace the various discourses that have been used to racialize working people in Alberta from 1900 to the present.[3]

COLONIAL RELATIONS, WORK, AND ABORIGINAL GROUPS, 1900–45

As chapter 1 suggests, Canada's Aboriginal peoples were the first group of Albertans to face racialization by the Canadian state. The pre-Confederation relationship of Europeans with Aboriginal peoples based on the fur trade gave way after 1867 to "national" policies in which the Canadian state viewed the Aboriginal peoples' control of the land, acceptable during the fur trade period, as contrary to the interests of capital. A nation was to be developed through the promotion of a national railway system and the opening up of the West to a stable agricultural class, who would produce wheat and other agricultural products for exchange on world markets. Such measures were intended to maintain and stabilize industrial capitalism in central Canada. As sociologists Harley Dickinson and Terry Wotherspoon note, "Indians were commonly regarded as impediments to economic development and nation-building processes, at least insofar as they occupied territories regarded as vital to national expansion."[4]

So the state sought to train and resocialize Aboriginal youth in residential and industrial schools with a view to changing traditional work habits and ways of engaging with the land. It used education in its attempt to replace the Aboriginal kin-based economies with capitalist economic structures in which Aboriginals would provide a source of cheap labour. Education professor Brian Titley describes the Red Deer Industrial School of late-nineteenth-century Alberta, for instance, as a place where work took precedence over the academic program: "The boys were kept busy working on the farm putting in crops of oats, potatoes, turnips, carrots, and other vegetables. . . . Eight boys were receiving instruction in carpentry. . . . The girls were learning to cook and make clothes and other tasks of a domestic nature."[5] Education thus played a critical role in the reproduction of entrenched class, power, and gendered meanings of specific types of work. Canadian social structures and "common sense" understandings of nation, citizenship, and labour were consequently stabilized.

As well, title to and use of most traditional Aboriginal land as private property was ensured through treaty arrangements that resulted in the separation of First Peoples onto reserves. Despite First Nations being separated from mainstream society and given a marginalized status, their contribution to the Canadian economy was noteworthy. In 1911, a Department of Indian Affairs report stated "that Indians had begun to make a significant contribution to economic activity in the form of wage labour, agricultural work, and other industrial pursuits." Further, "Indian participation in various economic activities generated substantial revenues: more than $1.54 million in wages, $1.0 million in agriculture and beef production, $0.82 million in hunting and trapping, $0.69 million in fishing and $0.85 in other industries."[6] Aboriginals' wages varied considerably, with the average annual wages in Alberta, the Northwest Territories, and Prince Edward Island being less than $5.00 per capita compared to $22.00 in Nova Scotia, New Brunswick, and Ontario. Recast as cheap, largely unskilled labour, Aboriginal peoples became an underclass within Alberta for whom racial stereotyping made social advancement rare. Linked to their poverty were the social effects of poor health and low educational achievement, which also worked against economic independence.

Aboriginals' residential school experiences and dislocation from their lands severely limited traditional ways of engaging with the land, and other work opportunities became increasingly scarce as time passed. While they did find work in the early period of capitalism (trapping, cutting wood, casual work in construction, and work on railroads and forestry), later changes in how production was organized decreased work opportunities. For example, although Aboriginal groups initially engaged in paid work and ran small enterprises in the North, white private entrepreneurs from elsewhere in the country, assisted directly or indirectly by state policy, eventually replaced them, leaving them few alternative forms of work. As a result, Aboriginal groups, who generally had fewer years of education than most Canadians, often faced high unemployment rates. Historian Joan Sangster notes that during the interwar years, "white trappers continued to expand their catchment areas, infringing on traditional Native trapping grounds; moreover, as seasonal/casual work in the North was decasualized, with whites filling jobs previously done by Native men in construction, rail, and forestry, Native families became more dependent on trapping in a time of declining fur prices."[7]

Linking Race, Labour, and Immigration

Into this mixture of colonial relations with Aboriginal groups came immigrants — not just those from the preferred groups of northern Europeans but also non-whites.[8] Attempts by African-Canadians from the United States to settle in Alberta as farmers became the catalyst for discussions as to who was an ideal Canadian and what the results of "race mixing" might mean for a future workforce and society. The Canadian parliamentary discussions concerning immigration to the western provinces made it clear that immigrants from China and the Indian subcontinent were as unwelcome as African immigrants.[9] Chinese workers who arrived in Alberta in the 1880s were greeted with hostility by the local media. The *Calgary Herald* stated in 1884, "We do not want Chinamen in Canada. It is desirable that this country shall not be peopled by any servile race."[10] Chinese immigrants were wanted only when there was a shortage of cheap and willing labour. For example, in the early 1880s, Chinese were hired to build the most dangerous mountain passes of the Canadian Pacific Railway. Subsequently, the government imposed head taxes to discourage the workers who hadn't died in these dangerous jobs from bringing their families to Canada. With limited educational opportunities and in the face of employer unwillingness to hire non-whites for white-collar jobs, Chinese Canadians were concentrated in a small number of occupations. Sociologist Peter S. Li notes that records of Chinese immigrants entering "Canada between 1885 and 1903 indicate that male labourers made up 73 percent; merchants and storekeepers, 5.7 percent; and cooks, farmers, laundrymen, miners and others for the remaining."[11]

Such informal immigration restrictions gradually gave way to laws formally restricting the entry of unwanted racialized groups. Race was incorporated as a restrictive legal category in Section 38 (c) of the *Immigration Act* in 1910. Responding to perceived radicalism by particular European-origin groups during the war, this section of the act was amended in 1917 to include reference to nationality as well, thus excluding "any nationality or race of immigrants of any specified class or occupation, by reason of any economic industrial or other condition temporarily existing in Canada or because such immigrants are deemed unsuitable." [12]

Changes to the act in 1910 were supplemented by a memorandum that indicated how understandings of race were linked to employment and which groups were preferred:

> The policy of the Department at the present time [1910] is to encourage immigration of farmers, farm labourers, and female domestic servants from the United States, the British Isles, and certain Northern European countries, namely, France, Belgium, Holland, Switzerland, Germany, Denmark, Norway, Sweden and Iceland. . . . It is the policy of the Department to do all in its power to keep out of the country . . . those belonging to nationalities unlikely to assimilate and who consequently prevent the building up of a united nation of people of similar customs and ideals. [13]

The following year, a Government of Canada Order-in-Council explicitly pronounced the "Negro race" unsuitable "to the climate and requirements." [14] Prominent Alberta-based local groups such as the Edmonton Board of Trade and the Imperial Order Daughters of the Empire also argued against the immigration of peoples of African descent. Despite such resistance from the authorities and some of the general population, black Americans did manage to come to northern Alberta early in the twentieth century. The descendant of one of these early pioneers was Willie Toles:

FIG 10-3 Chinese-Canadian rail workers, ca. 1900. Courtesy of the Alberta Labour History Institute.

My father homesteaded. My granddad picked those homesteads for himself and his boys in 1909. In 1910 he came back and he built his house and worked on the Athabasca railroad before the bridge was here. He worked on the train before it got to Athabasca. Went back [to the US] and then came back in 1911 before the big immigration. One of his sons came in the cattle car. [15]

Formation of Communities: Racialized, Segmented Labour Practices

Government policies and institutionalized racism more generally placed huge constraints on workers racialized as non-white. Those workers responded with a variety of strategies, sometimes aimed at mere survival but sometimes with the goal of broadening their work opportunities. Some Chinese workers became

FIG 10-4 John Ware, photographed with his family in 1895, was an African-Canadian homesteader and rancher in the Millarville area. Glenbow Archives, NA-263-1.

self-employed and opened their own businesses such as laundries, restaurants, grocery stores, and garden markets. Others were hired by ranchers on a seasonal basis while still others worked as cooks, houseboys, and hotel workers. Most of these jobs were grueling and involved low wages and long workdays without any days off. An examination of laundry work, the most common job for early Chinese labourers in Alberta, provides us with important insights into the work practices and health issues faced by a racialized and exploited group, sometimes by employers of the same nationality. A Chinese laundryman who worked at William's Laundry in Calgary for twenty years recalled his experiences and unfulfilled dream of a better life:

> Since there was no hot water, I had to boil water in order to clean clothes. I scrubbed all the clothes with my bare hands. As a result, my hands had far too much contact with soap and washing soda. They always had blisters and bled. . . . Although I came to Canada in order to earn more money than I could have in China, I never made much money here.[16]

An *Edmonton Journal* article noted that in 1918, it was not uncommon for a Chinese laundryman to work sixteen hours per day seven days a week for about fifteen dollars a month — fifty cents per day.[17]

While workers of African descent, like Chinese workers, opened small businesses to gain employment and to provide service to the wider community during the early twentieth century, both groups became associated with and confined to specific types of work. For African-Canadian women in the cities, domestic work was at one time the most prevalent job, although there were exceptions: in the early 1920s, Edmonton newspapers carried reports such as that of black entrepreneurs like Mesdames Bell and Proctor opening a dressmaking and fancywork store in downtown Edmonton. Men of African descent from the United States, and later the Caribbean, became associated with work as sleeping-car porters on railways such as the Edmonton District and British Columbia (EDBC) railway and the Northern Alberta Railway. As part of a small community, men like Edwin Clifton Anderson, who came to Edmonton in 1919 from Mississippi and worked on the EDBC railway, became important members of local black churches such as the Emmanuel African Methodist Episcopal. He and others were keen to engage in what they viewed as racial uplift through forms of adult education.[18] The experiences of these workers of African descent in Alberta were similar to those in other provinces. In reference to Winnipeg sleeping-car porters, Sarah Jane Mathieu points out that "though often migrant workers, they affirmed their right to a livelihood as well."[19] Dan, a porter during the late 1940s and early 1950s, outlines what learning the job entailed (J. and L.L. represent the interviewers):

> D. [We learned] what we had to do, how to do it, how to keep out of trouble and that sort of thing, how to make beds, because at that time the porters made the beds, sometimes we had to make twenty-four, counts upwards and downwards, trained how to make the beds and how to make them the same way, and how to greet people. . . .

> L.L. Before you started as a porter, did you know anything about the work, about the conditions of a porter, what the job conditions were all about?

> D. Not really, not really, but you learned when you start working.

> L.L. So there were never any negative connotations about being a porter as far as you remember or anything like that?

> D. Not at all, basically I was trained [that] if you do anything, you do it right. I guess that's how I still do things.

> J. You talked of greetings. You had to greet people, could you give an example of how you were supposed to greet people?

> D. Everything was "Ma'am" and "Sir" and you had to help the ladies if they wished to, you didn't take it all, but you offered to do it, you take their arm, that sort of thing.[20]

While traditional historians regard the railroad as a defining moment of building Canadian geographic nationalism and capitalism from "sea to sea to sea," the railway can also be viewed as an early embodiment of the contribution of racialized minorities to the building of Canada. Chinese labour laid the tracks and African-Canadian labour provided the porter service needed to enable the construction of leisure and profitability for the railway owners. Some early South Asian pioneers were also linked to the railway: while there would be no large South Asian communities in Alberta before the 1950s, some of those few (mainly Sikhs) who did make it to Alberta during the early twentieth century were employed on railroads in roadbed clearing and track-laying.[21]

A split-labour market in which they were confined to the low-paying section of work tasks thus affected most racialized workers. Unions during this period tended to acquiesce to the dominant racist ideas about non-white workers and often saw them as a threat to working conditions and pay, as well as to moral authority. A motion recorded in the Proceedings of the Ninth Annual Convention of District 18, United Mine Workers of Alberta, February 1912, argues that "Orientals should be debarred from employment in restaurants; and that it be a criminal offense for an Oriental to employ white girls in any capacity."[22]

The experiences of non-white workers, who were not regarded as full Canadians, were influenced by stereotypes based on simplistic understandings of race as linked to biology, personality, and work habits. While African-Canadian men were pigeon-holed into service jobs such as sleeping-car porters or "shoeshine boys," Chinese-Canadian men became associated with stereotypically feminine labour such as laundry work and cooking. According to cultural studies professor Lily Cho, 50 percent of Chinese immigrants worked in restaurants in 1921, and this increased to an astonishing high of 70 percent by 1931.[23] Reinforcing these racial stereotypes was some of the popular literature that appeared during this period of heightened social exclusion, an example being a book by popular author and women's activist Emily Murphy.[24] Murphy's *The Black Candle* blamed and demonized Chinese immigrants for creating opium dens and blacks for luring white women away from home and hearth, reinforcing arguments for social exclusion and segregation of non-white workers.

At least in part as a result of the dissemination of these notions, many Chinese, blacks, and Indigenous people faced exclusion from public social areas such as restaurants and hotels. In the 1920s, in both Calgary and Edmonton, local community members brought forward petitions urging Edmonton City Council to ban blacks from swimming in local pools. In the *Edmonton Bulletin,* a letter and article appeared discussing segregated bathing and an appeal to the City Council. Commissioner Yorath, the city manager at that time, stated that he personally thought that a white man and a black man shouldn't enter a pool at the same time.[25] This idea of social exclusion was extended to attempts at maintaining social distance through preventing those racialized as non-white from working in public service jobs such as shop workers and bus drivers.

Racism, supported by institutions, had direct consequences for workers in terms of their ability both to locate remunerative work and to receive state support when that was not possible. A laundry worker recalled that during the Depression, many desperate Chinese labourers in Alberta committed suicide due to unemployment and starvation: "I only survived because of money sent to me by my brother in China."[26] Furthermore, during the Great Depression, unemployed Chinese labourers in Calgary received relief payments of only $1.12 per week compared to $2.50 for non-Chinese. The city justified this promotion of racism on the basis that the Chinese "had a low living standard to begin with" and that it was not a civic responsibility for Calgary's City Council to support Chinese people.[27] Reinforcing this negativity toward Chinese workers was the racist *Chinese Immigration Act* of 1923, not rescinded until 1947, which restricted entry to members of the diplomatic corps, children born in Canada, merchants, and university students. The act stipulated that every person of Chinese origin living in Canada was

required to register with federal officials within twelve months after the act came into effect; those leaving for more than two years would lose Canadian domicile. While the act was in force, only a handful of Chinese were allowed to enter the country.

World War II brought changes for Japanese workers, who were declared enemy aliens and were relocated from many of the coastal areas of British Columbia to become cheap labour for white farmers in the beet fields of Alberta. One evacuee remembered the process:

FIG 10-5 Chinese-Canadian restaurant workers in the 1930s. Glenbow Archives, ND-2-109.

We had to go to Vancouver and then register in Hastings Park. We were called enemy agents, which I could never understand. We were all registered there, and waited for the time to be evacuated out from the coastal area.

We had an option there. If we knew somebody in the agricultural area of Alberta or anywhere outside of BC, we had an option to put our name in and go there. So we went to Raymond, because I had a sister who was married in Raymond and living there for a number of years. In that way we were lucky to go somewhere that we knew someone, and a little support there too.

It was all sugar beets. We were all designated for beet labour. The wife and I, we went to one farm there that the quota was twenty-five acres that we had to handle. If you had a big family you'd probably get a hundred acres, and you'd get a percentage of that from the farmer, whatever they get.[28]

The beet fields of southern Alberta were also a worksite for many Aboriginal workers. From the 1950s, the Federal-Provincial Farm Labour Committee and Indian Affairs encouraged Aboriginal groups to work on Alberta's beet farms. This was seasonal, casual labour. Joan Sangster notes: "Aboriginal workers were pushed into seasonal sugar-beet labour in the 1950s because the state saw them as particularly suited for migrant, seasonal, physical, low paid work; moreover bureaucrats knew the practices of kin-based labour — associated with fur and fish — could be incorporated into the regime of agricultural work."[29] These forms of seasonal employment continued to grow in the postwar period.

A SHIFT TOWARD HUMAN RIGHTS AND ORGANIZED LABOUR AFTER 1946

With the removal of the *Continuous Passages Act* in 1947 — an act that had prevented anyone from immigrating to Canada from countries that did not have direct passage to Canada (which excluded Asians and Africans from eligibility) — and the changing dynamics of independence for South Asian countries, immigration quotas for Asians and Africans were slightly increased. Still, 96 percent of immigrants from 1946 to 1962 came from Europe and the United States, and most of those who came from Asia and Africa were white.

In the postwar period, the attitudes of organized labour with regard to non-white workers gradually changed. Historian Ross Lambertson notes that "before the war, organized labour was usually governed by the same racist values as the majority of Canadians."[30] After the war, organized labour retained its traditional wariness of a large influx of immigrants: it feared the creation of a glut of workers, which would undermine wages and conditions. We can see this perspective clearly in the following "Immigration" resolution that was presented at the Alberta Federation of Labour convention on 17 November 1947, by the Electrical Workers Local B-1007, Edmonton:

WHEREAS The Dominion Government and some Provincial Governments have indicated that a policy of large scale immigration will be undertaken and many Displaced Persons will be accepted into this country, and

WHEREAS periodic periods of prosperity and full employment, and periods of depression and reduced employment have recurred time and time again in the past, and

WHEREAS in periods of reduced employment a surplus or glut of Labor may swamp the Labor market, and a situation of this nature will be further aggravated by additional immigrants and Displaced Persons, in the future; therefore be it

RESOLVED That the Dominion and Provincial Governments be charged with the responsibility of keeping these immigrants employed and a period of relative prosperity maintained.[31]

But despite its reservations about immigration, organized labour, responding to the Nazis' racism and attempted genocide, developed a split in its once-united insistence that some races should be preferred over others as immigrants. Joan Sangster suggests that "the more conservative Trades and Labour Congress (TLC) favoured economically selective immigration as well as the 'exclusion of races that cannot be assimilated into Canadian life.'" In contrast, "the more liberal Canadian Congress of Labour (CCL), whose ties to the CCF (Co-operative Commonwealth Federation) and campaigns against anti-Semitism had likely led to more enlightened views, spoke of the need for a deracialized policy."[32]

Brotherhood of Sleeping Car Porters

While union responses to racism varied, it was not uncommon for unions to join with management to exclude workers deemed non-white. In 1943, the legendary African-American leader of the International Brotherhood of Sleeping Car Porters (BSCP), A. Philip Randolph, visited Canada to assist with organizing a Canadian section of the US-based Brotherhood. Present at the

final signing of the agreement was P.T. Clay, who became president of the Calgary branch of the BSCP. The catalyst for this separate organization of workers was the racism that workers of African descent faced on the railway, not just from their employer, the Canadian Pacific Railway, but also from the Canadian Brotherhood of Railway Employees and Other Transport Workers, who negotiated a two-tiered union agreement with the railway company. Two groups were established for seniority purposes: Group I contained a variety of employees such as dining-car employees and sleeping-car conductors; Group II was exclusively for sleeping-car porters. Since an employee could advance only within his designated group, blacks were slotted forever as porters and could not be promoted to conductor. Despite this lack of mobility, however, the pay was regular and allowed for a degree of self-organization that was not always available through other avenues in the 1940s and 1950s. Unionization with the BSCP meant, as one sleeping-car porter remembered, that "in 1945 our standard of living was raised because we were getting more money; our children were able to at least finish high school and the odd one had a chance to attend one of the leading universities."[33] In general, though, in both the Canadian National Railway and the Canadian Pacific Railway, black men were isolated in the lowest paid and most physically strenuous service positions.[34]

The concentration of sleeping-car porters in a racialized enclave and their resistance to racism in their workplace through organized labour provided the base for developing a political consciousness around broader human rights issues. In recognition of unions as being about more than just wage bargaining, A. Philip Randolph visited Calgary in the 1950s and encouraged the development of a branch of the Alberta Association for the Advancement of Coloured People (AAACP). Hazel Proctor, whose father was a porter in Calgary, remembered the event:

> I recall meeting the president of the porter's union, Randolph I believe was his name, because my father was a porter. In fact, that was the first time I sang to someone other than with my dad. My dad said, "Okay, this man is here from the States, we're going to do this song." So dad played for me and I sang this song for Mr. Randolph. Yes. So that was quite something that he came to our city and met with us. It wasn't AAACP at the time, but he met with the community, and all the porters were there.[35]

One of the main issues for the AAACP was discrimination in both employment and housing. Dick Bellamy, a former sleeping-car porter who was active in the formation of the AAACP in the early 1950s, suggested, "The object of this organization shall be the betterment of colored people, to seek equality as Canadian citizens and the promotion of participation in all social and civic activities."[36]

The 1950s and 1960s saw an increasing push from organizations such as the Jewish Labour League (Sid Blum) and the Brotherhood of Sleeping Car Porters (Arthur Blanchette) to promote fair employment practices, fair accommodation practices, and human rights across Canadian society and within organized labour.[37] The Alberta Federation of Labour (AFL) correspondence and convention minutes show that while some labour councils urged member unions to actively pressure Premier Manning's government to adopt fair employment practices legislation, the government was slow to take anti-discrimination initiatives. In the 1950s and 1960s, resolutions (such as the one reproduced below) were consistently put forward, by the Calgary Labour Council, in particular, urging the executive of the AFL to press the Alberta government to adopt the *Fair Employment Practices Act* as the federal government and other provincial governments had done.

RESOLUTION NO. 61
Submitted by the Calgary Labour Council.

WHEREAS the Government of Canada and the Provincial Governments of Nova Scotia, New Brunswick, Ontario, Saskatchewan, British Columbia and Manitoba have enacted legislation covering Fair Employment Practices, and

WHEREAS the Province of Alberta is increasing in population and wealth, and is fast becoming industrialized quite prominently, and

WHEREAS employment problems of a discriminatory nature will arise more sharply than ever before as a result of this growth,

THEREFORE BE IT RESOLVED that the Alberta Federation of Labour, more strongly than ever before, urge the Alberta Government to implement an Act covering Fair Employment Practices, similar to those put into effect by the Federal Government and other Provincial Governments, and

BE IT FURTHER RESOLVED that the Executive of the Federation petition or lobby each member of the Legislature at the next session, so that we may accomplish our aims in this direction.[38]

Organized Labour Begins to Challenge Racism and Discrimination

From the early 1950s, some groups who were the target of racial or religious discrimination recognized the need to work with more mainstream local groups such as the Council of Christian and Jews. The council, active in the 1960s, had a Brotherhood Week across the country. Local notables such as Grant MacEwan and Francis Winspear supported the Calgary section. Others such as Premier Manning sent messages of support for Brotherhood Week, and Alan White was a national executive member. Yet despite some of the elite members of Alberta society being associated with Brotherhood Week and the Council of Christians and Jews, Premier Manning's Social Credit government was slow to pass legislation banning discrimination in the province. Manning, for religious and ideological reasons, opposed interference with the rights of owners, employers, and landlords, but the individual rights championed by human rights campaigners often conflicted with the rights of owners of capital.[39] In the mid- to late 1950s and early 1960s, non-white workers and their supporters were able to use emerging human rights discourse to challenge barriers that maintained all-white occupations in public service and professional jobs. For example, in 1954, Violet King of Calgary became the first black woman in Canada to qualify as a lawyer. Subsequently, jobs such as bus driver and firefighter became possible for marginalized workers living in Edmonton and Calgary.

The provincial government began to respond to pressure for human rights legislation in 1966 by passing the *Human Rights Act*, which forbade anyone, directly or indirectly, to "deny to any person or class of persons the accommodation, services, or facilities available in any place to which the public is customarily admitted," specifying the prohibited reasons for exclusion as "race, religious beliefs, colour, ancestry or place of origin."[40] The Alberta Human Rights Branch, established to enforce the legislation, began to receive a variety of complaints, with the dominant ones being discrimination against First Nations and Métis groups in the areas of housing and employment. Overall, the branch reported that the leading group with complaints from its inception in 1966 to spring, 1969, was "Canadian Native" with thirty-one, followed by "Negro" with eleven.[41] The mood among Alberta politicians can be assessed by a document entitled "Minister's Message," which was put out by the Human Rights Branch, Department of Labour, in 1969. The tone of the document was slightly ambivalent:

> In Western Canada we like to pride ourselves on the fact that people are readily accepted without prejudice or class distinction. By and large, this is true; but unfortunately, we have had situations from time to time in which people were denied employment, turned away from hotels or refused service in shops or eating places because of their skin colour, racial origin, or religious beliefs. So even though discrimination in these fields is not rampant, it was our belief that, in the interest of human dignity, it was necessary to have recourse in law for this type of abuse.[42]

By 1967, Calgary and Edmonton were experiencing huge growth and were drawing far more immigrants than Manitoba and Saskatchewan combined. Active

during this period was the Alberta Human Rights Association (AHRA), a lobby group that had links to the AFL and the Canadian Labour Congress (CLC) through the activism of trade unionists such as Frank Bodie. These contacts eventually produced a more formal association between the AHRA, on the one hand, and the AFL and CLC, on the other: in 1968, for example, the AFL donated secretarial services for free to the AHRA.[43] Even though much had already been achieved by labour in the area of human rights, a CLC memo sent to all affiliates in 1967 warned that "while its Standing Committee on Human Rights worked indefatigably in marshalling the strength of the labour movement and other elements in society to secure appropriate legislation, there was much left to be done."[44]

Education was regarded as a strong antidote to racism, and several high-profile leaders in the national human rights field were invited to Edmonton and Calgary to make educational presentations on how to further the cause. The AFL invited both Alan Burovoy, secretary of the Jewish Labour League, and George McCurdy of the federal Fair Employment Practices Branch, Department of Labour, to Edmonton during the 1960s. McCurdy, who had strong union ties, had been a member and former education and research director of the United Brotherhood of Carpenters and Joiners of America for twelve years.

PROFESSIONAL IMMIGRANTS AND CREDENTIALS

Immigration and labour policies affected the size and formation of non-white communities — for example, the descendants of the few African-Canadians allowed to migrate in the early 1900s remained the main group of such workers in Alberta until 1956, when the federal cabinet relaxed Section 61 of the 1952 *Immigration Act* and enabled female labour from the Caribbean to serve in Canadian homes. Many of these domestic workers were educated and skilled women who seized the opportunity to come to Canada even if it meant a few years in low-economic-status work:

> In those days, it was difficult to get into Canada. The only way you could get into Canada is what they used to call a domestic servant, and later on they called it the homecare givers and home keepers. So they had that program open. And what they were doing in those days, even though it sounded like a low type of activity in Canada, but they were taking all of the best-educated people from [the island] and sending them on that scheme. I tried to come on my own. I was not able to, so I decided, "Okay, if this is the only way I can enter Canada, I will." And I did come up on that scheme.[45]

The immigration law restrictions against non-whites were relaxed first in 1962 and then more fully in 1967, and the government implemented a new system of evaluation based on "points," which assessed all immigrants on the same skills and training-related criteria. Many workers from countries in Asia, the Caribbean, and Latin America, previously deemed unsuitable, began to emigrate to Canada.

Traditionally, it has been assumed that early 1960s immigrants from the Caribbean, and other non-traditional sources of labour, were destitute. In fact, because of the strict entry rules for non-white workers, many had trade skills and others were professionals. For example, workers were allowed into Alberta if they could contribute to decreasing the teacher shortage in northern Alberta or if they had skills and knowledge garnered in the Trinidadian oil industry.[46] One skilled recruit from Trinidad recalls his early days in Fort McMurray:

> That was the first plant they had built extracting the oil from the oil sand. It was one of the first plants. I'd never worked in a plant like that before, so this was something new. They used big bucket wheels to dig the sand. They put it in a big drum and hot water to help dilute or extract the first set of oil, then it goes into other stages before they can get it to refine. . . . In Trinidad, we have refineries and I'd worked there before. But the weather, this was a big problem. The weather, I didn't know what it was like.[47]

Many new immigrants, while able to get jobs in their field of work, were nonetheless encouraged or required to undertake additional upgrading at colleges or universities. In the case of teachers from the Caribbean who came to rural areas of Alberta to work, many found that their low salaries on the pay grid meant that upgrading was necessary to increase earnings and opportunities. One professional worker who emigrated from a Caribbean island in the early 1960s recalls her first experiences with immigration authorities on arrival in Canada and their assumptions about inferior educational systems in the Global South. They told her that she would need to retake a grade 12 English course. "I told them, 'English Grade 12? . . . But I've spoken English my whole life.' I may have had a West Indian accent at that time, 'but my English is better than your English.'"[48]

As the shortage of teachers disappeared in the 1970s and teaching became a better-paid occupation requiring specialized university training, new immigrants faced a tougher process relative to that experienced by Jamaican immigrants in the mid-1960s. Many had to return to university, but earning a living while one acquired the necessary credentials was a struggle. Teacher Norma Ellis explained why she finally decided to take that route:

> They said that I had to go into university. Previous years it was different. I wasn't able to teach. I started university in September 1970 for a two-year graduate diploma, and I graduated and then started teaching in 1973.

> They were scared of blacks. I remember calling one lady about babysitting. She didn't know about how her daughter would feel about a black person babysitting. After a while, I gave up on finding a job outside of teaching.[49]

ECONOMIC BOOM AND BUST: AN INCREASE IN NON-WHITE WORKERS IN THE 1970S AND 1980S

From the OPEC increases in oil prices in 1973 to the precipitous drop in international oil prices in 1982, Alberta enjoyed a period of stunning economic growth. Immigrants who came to Alberta between 1975 and 1980 benefited from this boom, whereas those who came after 1981 were faced with an economic recession.[50] In 1976, Calgary and Edmonton each took in almost 50 percent more immigrants than Winnipeg. Many of these new immigrants, unlike the early-twentieth-century groups, were non-white workers from the Global South. The census in 1971 recorded the presence of only 7,900 Asians in Calgary, a modest number compared to 225,000 British people, 110,000 western Europeans, and 32,000 eastern Europeans.

The growing non-white cultural communities formed ethnically and regionally based organizations that attempted to create better working conditions and expand employment opportunities for their members. Many immigrant workers at the time were young and had skills and training in either a profession or a trade. Of the 5,900 immigrants who came to Calgary in 1976, almost 30 percent were in their twenties, and another 18 percent were in their thirties. Because many of these workers were highly educated and skilled, their expectations were high, and it was a shock for many that they were only able to get work that underutilized their skills and education. Many found no work at all since employers wrote off their work experiences in their home countries and demanded Canadian experience before hiring.

During 1979 and 1980, about seventy-five hundred Southeast Asian refugees entered Alberta. The total number of Southeast Asian immigrants subsequently rose owing to the sponsoring of family and relatives both by these new arrivals and by those who had come earlier. By mid-1984, Alberta was home to an estimated fifteen thousand Southeast Asian immigrants, 92 percent from Vietnam. One study found that during the 1970s and 1980s immigrants from the Global South experienced the highest unemployment rates and the slowest economic integration of all immigrants to Canada. So, for example, three years after their arrival, at least one-third of Vietnamese newcomers were not employed in their intended occupations. Interestingly, the obstacles cited by workers were language and non-recognition of credentials. While some experienced occupational mobility, many underwent downward mobility reinforced by the post-oil-boom recession.[51]

Throughout the 1970s and 1980s, black and Asian employees consistently earned lower average wages than their white counterparts, even when figures were adjusted for education, gender, age, region, and industrial sector. Also, although these decades saw no rigid occupational segregation, there was a tendency toward ethnic concentration in certain sectors in Canada that often disadvantaged some non-white groups. For example, figures from the 1980s showed that blacks were overrepresented in the service sector by about 40 percent and in manual labour by about 30 percent, and underrepresented in management by more than 60 percent. In 1981, groups previously categorized as non-white were transformed yet again under another label: visible minority.[52]

THE 1990S TO TODAY: FROM KLEIN CUTBACKS TO STELMACH STAGNATION

This term, visible minority, came into prominence through its use in the federal *Employment Equity Act* and in census data.[53] All the same, the old stereotypes about newcomer workers persisted within worksites in the 1990s and into the early twenty-first century. Many mainstream workers regarded those racialized as non-white as lacking in trade union acumen and as uncommitted to trade union principles. However, during that period, workers whose heritage lay in Asia, the Caribbean, and Africa began to prove that they were just as concerned about trade unionism and workers' rights as their so-called white colleagues. Two significant examples marked the involvement of racialized groups: the 1995 Calgary laundry workers strike and the 2005 Lakeside meat-packers strike in Brooks, both of which are discussed in detail in chapter 7.

The laundry workers included a number of women from Asia and the Caribbean who were instrumental in calling for a strike to protest their working conditions at a Calgary Hospital and the contracting out of their work to K-Bro Linens, a private company.[54] The 2005 meat-packers strike involved workers — many of whom were recent immigrants of Sudanese heritage — whose poor working conditions led to support for unionization and an eventual strike. The plant had tried to unionize on previous occasions but to no avail. One woman working at Lakeside Packers explained her decision to support the union:

> Yeah, people would ask me, why are you with the union? I'm like, they're going to help us change this

plant, because that plant needed change desperately. The people of the community didn't understand that. Like I said before, they weren't in the working conditions we were in, people getting things said to them that shouldn't be getting said to them, and just the whole way the plant was run and the way we were getting treated. The people of the community didn't understand it and they didn't see it, so it didn't mean nothing to them.[55]

Another worker at Lakeside Packers described the health and safety issues in the plant:

> I call my community. . . . This is killing us. Some people their hand claw like this from the hook. Some people get damage in their backs, shoulder, leg, everything. But the company wouldn't accept. We told them, you have to slow the speed down, because the big problem is the speed. They say business is business, and I say okay. So job condition is bad. They treat us like garbage. While we are the production, they don't keep us happy.[56]

For other workers, both racialization and discontent with general working conditions were at play at Lakeside Packers. One of the male workers noted:

> At that time . . . one black guy, Sudanese from Africa, has a problem with that white guy. This white guy sprayed hot water 180 degrees in this guy's chest. They didn't fire the white guy who sprayed the hot water; they fired the black guy. So the following morning . . . we were telling our friends, "Today we're not going to work until the company find a solution

to it, or they also fire the white guy." The news go around. . . . [When they arrived] they hung around outside. When we were coming from home, we join them. At that time we were over two hundred people outside. Only a few in kill floor, they only had about four black guys working on the kill floor that day.[57]

Work conditions have also been an issue for Aboriginal workers. The comments of one long-time worker in Fort McMurray illustrate how racism can come to shape worksites and how unionization has, at times, helped with countering this racism: "We [used to] get the dirtiest job. That's the management part. That [situation] the union has fixed over at Suncor. That's changed now."[58] But while workers at that site experienced positive change, work experiences for Aboriginal employees continue to be problematic. In 2009, the unemployment rate among Aboriginal people aged fifteen and over rose to 13.9 percent from 10.4 percent the previous year. At the same time, the unemployment rate for non-Aboriginals rose to just over 8 percent in 2009 from 6 percent in 2008. Employment rates among Aboriginals dropped 3.2 percentage points from 2008 to 2009 to 57 percent. For non-Aboriginals, they dropped less than 2 percentage points to about 62 percent. In particular, there was a 30 percent employment decline for Natives in manufacturing, compared to just 8 percent among non-Native manufacturing workers. A similar decline was noted in construction, with a 16 percent drop for Native workers compared to 5 percent for non-Natives. Myron Sparklingeyes, acting executive director of the Oteenow Employment and Training Society, suggests that the reason for the growing unemployment may well be the fact that "Aboriginal people are the last hired and first fired. It's an unfortunate reality."[59] Sparklingeyes' comments bring to light the continuing vulnerability of Aboriginals in Alberta's economy, which has been consistently subject to a boom-and-bust cycle.

In more recent times, one of the most significant initiatives undertaken by non-white workers was the formation of the Workers of Colour caucus at national and provincial levels. Both the Canadian Labour Congress and the Alberta Federation of Labour have been instrumental in encouraging this initiative although not all union officers recognize the importance of providing a space for the caucus to meet on their own. There is still resistance to groups caucusing outside of main union meetings. Having joined with Aboriginal workers, the group is known formally as Workers of Colour and Aboriginal Workers Committee (WCAWC). According to a committee report, these two traditionally marginalized groups have joined together because "of expediency and the need for support on the issues that are common to both groups. . . . This has helped . . . address some of the problems that would otherwise be fragmented."[60] Some caucus members chafe at the restrictions that the union movement places on their activities, in particular discouraging them from involving workers who are not yet represented by a union. One member suggested that if the committee could recruit workers of colour and Aboriginal workers directly, union activity among marginalized workers might increase.[61] Despite these restrictions, however, the WCAWC in Edmonton has begun to broaden its base by recognizing common issues of concern with gay workers.[62]

The difficulty, common in the 1960s, of getting Canadian employers to recognize foreign credentials has continued to be a significant issue for immigrant workers in Alberta. Visible-minority professional immigrants face persistent devaluation and rejection of their credentials.[63] For some, that leads to lower incomes than earned by those doing similar work but who gained their credentials in North America or western Europe. For others, particularly those whose credentials are rejected altogether, it often means a shift from prior professional and managerial jobs to "occupations in sales, services, processing, and manufacturing."[64] Even the right-wing C.D. Howe Institute's *Backgrounder Report on Immigrants' Declining Earnings–Reasons and Remedies* suggests that the incomes of recent immigrants are declining when compared to immigrants who came in the 1970s.[65]

When the oil, mineral, and construction industries were booming during the early years of the twentieth century, these industries pushed the government to import migrant workers from abroad to temporarily fill the economic needs in Alberta. Recognition of credentials was not a problem because of the need for workers. An article published in the *Edmonton Journal* in 2006 notes, by contrast:

> It is ironic that right now, the booming West is once again relying on Asian workers to build its core infrastructure and fill its service jobs. Alberta is bringing in hundreds of temporary workers from countries such as China, the Philippines and Sri Lanka, not just to build oil sands processing plants but to work in restaurants or take care of children and seniors. In the circumstances, there's never been

a better time to remember the injustices of the past and avoid any need for future contrition.

From 2002 to 2008, the number of temporary foreign workers (TFWs) present in Canada, most of them in clerical or manual work, increased from 100,000 to 250,000. This increase happened in tandem with new policies that restricted the time those workers could stay in Canada. Workers were limited to a stay of only four years, after which they would be banned from re-entering Canada for the next six years. These restrictions certainly made it harder for temporary workers to gain residency or skilled employment through experience, thus creating a disposable workforce.[66]

In 2009, when the recession struck and jobs were no longer plentiful, the Alberta government refused to renew contracts for TFWs who had not yet hit the four-year wall. In July 2010, Alberta Labour Minister Thomas Lukaszuk commented regarding the TFW scheme, "In my opinion, it was a program that had fulfilled its mandate, [by] suddenly providing a large number of workers."[67] Lukaszuk has since broken ranks with Conservative colleagues to argue for more immigration rather than continuing with the TFW program.[68] Among all provinces and territories, Alberta experienced the biggest boost in TFWs — from 13,236 in 2004 to 65,748 in 2009.[69] Gil McGowan, president of the Alberta Federation of Labour, is critical of the TFW program: "This is a program that is so dysfunctional it probably has to be scrapped entirely. . . . What essentially we have done is create a European style guest-worker program. . . . We think both the federal and provincial government ought to go back to the drawing board."[70] These comments are a far cry from those of many early-twentieth-century trade union leaders who sided with employers in order to maintain pay and working conditions that privileged so-called white workers. However, the basic issue of the role of migrant labour in Canada has not been resolved: if someone is good enough to work in Canada, why are they not good enough to become citizens of the country if they so choose?

◆ ◆ ◆

Both Canada's policies toward Aboriginal peoples and its immigration policy have been, from the country's early years, based on the economic needs of elites and on their perceptions of who is an ideal citizen. These preferred citizens and workers, favoured through policy, were ideally not only white, but of British origin and Protestant. At times, the early- to mid-twentieth-century policies revealed a tension between the economic needs of the state and capital, as identified during times of labour shortage, and the social desire of individuals to maintain an all-white policy. Alberta's dominant social classes — including commercial factions such as the Board of Trade and farm and labour organizations, and even its cultural feminist elite — were at the forefront of racist incitements contrived to discourage those deemed unsuitable from settling on the Canadian Prairies. While such views on immigration and work were pervasive and complex, they occurred through an active process. As historian Sarah Carter points out, "the mainly British-Canadian elite that dominated business, politics, education, women's organizations and other realms worked to ensure that a sense of British-ness, combined with whiteness, became equated with Canadianness."[71] The legacy of this production of a racialized ideology is the understanding that the history of non-white labour is tied to encouraging the immigration of a specific type of worker. While there have been changes in the attitudes of workers and organized labour in relation to non-whites, today's scenario is also strangely familiar.

CONCLUSION
A HISTORY TO BUILD UPON

ALVIN FINKEL

Yvon Poulin was only seventeen in January 2004 when he died after falling head first into a bailer while at work near Peace River. Labour studies scholar Bob Barnetson elaborates on this preventable death on the job:

> During his three months on the job, Poulin complained about a lack of training. He was also looking for less dangerous work elsewhere. After his death, inspectors found Poulin's employer had failed to ensure an alarm system was installed to warn workers when the machine was in operation. Poulin's employer used a legal loophole to have charges under the *Occupational Health and Safety Act* dismissed.[1]

In 2008, as the Alberta economy reached the peak of one of its many booms, 166 workers died in industrial accidents: a death on the job every 2.2 days.[2] They died from exposure to dangerous substances, harmful environments, transportation accidents, contact with equipment and utilities, falls, fatigue, fires, and explosions. Many more workers lost worktime due to complications from overexertion in an economy where many hours of overtime and working for weeks without a break became common in many sectors, especially construction. Assaults became more common, particularly on overburdened health care workers.

Alberta's rate of work fatalities in 2008 made it one of the most dangerous places to work in the Western world, despite the fact that deaths on the job are preventable. The province's worker fatality rate of 5.9 per 100,000 was far greater than that of Canada as a whole at 4.2 deaths per 100,000 workers.[3] Still, Canada had the fifth-highest rate of workplace deaths in the OECD, with only relatively poor countries — South Korea, Turkey, Mexico, and Portugal — posting worse records.[4]

The maiming and murder of workers continued unabated because the Alberta government, with its pro-employer bias, had the worst record among Canadian provinces of prosecuting employers who failed to meet safety standards. No one in Alberta has been jailed for causing a worker's death, and in the rare case where there is both a prosecution and a conviction, the fines that are paid are modest. Promises for over a decade by labour ministers in Alberta to step up prosecutions have proved to be no more than hot air. Alberta was also the only province that exempted farm workers from labour standards, and thirteen farm workers died on the job in the province in 2009. The Government of Alberta spent five times as much in 2009 on insurance rebates to Alberta companies with government-endorsed safety certificates than it spent on inspecting job sites and enforcing occupational safety laws. The safety rebates are available to companies with worker fatalities, even those with multiple deaths.[5]

Meanwhile, the province's Workers' Compensation Board is accused by the Alberta Federation of Labour of focusing not on ways to help injured workers but on ways to deny their claims and reduce benefits for injured workers. Alone among Canadian provinces, the board pays bonuses to employees who get workers off compensation and back to work.[6]

This carnage on the job and the government's cavalier response give the lie to notions that Alberta, with its fossil fuel economy and high average incomes, is a workers' paradise. It also comes as no surprise that Alberta has the lowest union density in the country. While the national average of workers in Canadian provinces who are members of unions or who are covered by collective agreements was 31.4 percent for 2009, only 25 percent of workers in Alberta were in those categories. Not surprisingly, most of the provinces with above-average union density have recent experience of social democratic governments: Quebec at 39.8 percent and Manitoba at 37 percent, and Saskatchewan and British Columbia close behind. The outlier is Newfoundland and Labrador, which has a 39 percent union rate, though it has never had an openly pro-labour government.[7] Clearly, there is a relationship between the inability of unions in Alberta to represent more than a quarter of the paid labour force and their inability to affect government policy in such areas as occupational health and safety.

But Alberta's unions consistently attempt to represent the province's workers despite the disappointingly low density of unionization and the challenges of cooperation among a number of separate organizations that sometimes work together well but often go their own merry ways. Of 418,000 workers covered by a collective agreement in 2009, about 125,000 were members of the 31 unions that belonged to the Alberta Federation of Labour. Another 75,000 were members of the Alberta Union of Provincial Employees, while the Building Trades Council claimed 60,000 members and the Alberta Teachers' Association counted about 43,500 members. The Christian Labour Association of Canada, whose claim to being a union the above-named groups rejected because of its pro-employer bias, had 15,000 members.[8]

As the statistics in table c.1 demonstrate, there is now a huge gap in unionization rates between public service jobs and private sector jobs. Only one worker in eight in the private sector is covered by a collective agreement, while seven in ten workers employed by governments enjoy such coverage. But only one worker in five is in the public sector, and if the public sector cutbacks that have characterized the neo-liberal era continue, that percentage will decline with time. So the trade union movement faces the double challenge of trying to reinvigorate its private sector presence while defending public sector workers who are mostly unionized but who are under constant ideological attack from employer-friendly governments and their powerful media.

TABLE C.1 **ESTIMATED UNION COVERAGE, 2010 ANNUAL AVERAGES**

	Total Employees (000s)	Unionized Employees (000s)	Union Members (%)
Agriculture	10.2	0	0.00
Forestry, fishing, mining, oil and gas	129.2	14.9	11.5
Utilities	18.3	8.5	46.4
Construction	147.6	39.9	27.0
Manufacturing	116.8	21.7	18.6
Trade	274.8	30.3	11.0
Transportation and warehousing	83.8	26.6	31.7
Finance, insurance, real estate and leasing	84.6	6.8	8.0
Professional, scientific and technical services	95.8	5.0	5.2
Business, building and other support services	51.7	4.1	7.9
Educational services	123.5	83.8	67.9
Health care and social assistance	195.6	104.1	53.2
Information, culture and recreation	69.4	14.4	20.7
Accommodation and food services	115.3	5.8	5.0
Other services	70.0	4.8	6.9
Public administration	86.9	57.4	66.1
Public Sector Rate	**367.9**	**259.5**	**70.5**
Private Sector Rate	**1305.6**	**158.8**	**12.2**
All Industries	**1673.5**	**418.3**	**25.0**

NOTE: Figures exclude self-employed Albertans.
SOURCE: Statistics Canada.

As we have seen throughout this book, it is, for the most part, not the unions that are at fault for the low rates of unionism in Alberta. Rather, it is anti-labour legislation promulgated from the Manning Social Credit period to the present that has limited the ability of workers to have representation on the job. The current global context is dominated by post-Fordism: that is, an increasing emphasis on "flexible" workers to whom employers promise neither long-term employment nor much in the way of benefits while governments cut away the social programs that at one time would have helped these workers as they move from employer to employer with periods of unemployment in between. In such an environment, unions will face quite a challenge trying to increase the extent of their coverage of the workforce. It is challenging in any context to organize transient workers, workers in small work units, workers who work mainly from their homes, and workers under constant threat of dismissal and/or deportation, all of which are growing segments of the international labour force. It is doubly difficult to organize such workers in Alberta, where governments are so friendly to employers that the two often seem enmeshed.

It is easy to be cynical about anything changing in Alberta. Its corporate elite is firmly entrenched and controls the governing Progressive Conservative Party, the rising opposition Wildrose Party, and most of the media, giving it an unchallenged means of inundating workers with its message that unfettered free enterprise works best for Albertans. Many of the province's workers are transients who hope to return to their home provinces after they have collected a nest egg. They don't want to upset the apple cart in between.

But as this book reveals, each generation has produced workers who have been willing to take chances to fight for social justice, whether via their unions or in the political arena. Though unknown to most Albertans, the most egalitarian forms of government were established in the province during the millennia of First Nations settlement, as chapter 1 revealed. The fur-trade period, with its partnership between Natives and Europeans, probably deserves second place. It was followed by the brutal dispossession of Native lands and the imposition of a colonial society, as we saw in chapter 2.

Chapter 3, dealing with the creation of a proletariat or working class during the early settlement years, indicated that conservatism and radicalism existed side by side in the workforce, with similar splits within the fledgling trade union movement. The early Alberta Federation of Labour united the unions that tried to effect change largely by legal means despite the extent to which the laws made defending the rights of workers very difficult. Most of its members were organized on the basis of a particular skill, not on an industry-wide basis. By contrast, the radical miners and the Industrial Workers of the World reflected a revolutionary perspective that rejected notions that workers could achieve gains while the capitalist system persisted. The IWW proposed that workers organize on an industrial basis without making distinctions among each other on the basis of crafts, a form of organization that it claimed left most labourers without an organization.

As chapter 4 suggested, that debate continued during World War I and the interwar period. The conscription debate and the huge increase in the cost of living during the war kept the pot boiling that gave the One Big Union widespread support among Alberta workers. But a combination of the state, employers, and craft unions ensured that the OBU's life was short-lived. One wing of the 1920s labour movement believed that an electoral alliance with the United Farmers of Alberta would gradually deliver changes of benefit to working people, and during that decade, some gains were made. But as such gains were undone during the Depression, the Communist Party, while weak electorally, gained an important following as a leader of both the unemployed and unionists.

Chapter 5, outlining events between 1940 and 1960, told a story both of improved wages for many workers, at least those connected with the rising fossil fuel industry, and the evolution of a reactionary industrial relations regime meant to make the province attractive to the oil and gas industry. Debates within the trade union movement continued, but few revolutionaries were left in this period of economic growth and a vicious Cold War that limited robust social debate in Canada. Unions were viewed as conspiratorial organizations by Premier Ernest Manning, not much better than the rats that Alberta government policy was trying to keep out of the province. Ironically, the Alberta Federation of Labour, before it merged with the Industrial Federation of Labour of Alberta in 1956, had lost its fighting spirit and tended to kowtow to both employers and the government. Only the presence of the industrial unions, which operated within the constraints of Manning's anti-union legislation, kept the spark of resistance alive in the province.

In chapter 6, we saw the gradual rise of a new militancy in the period from 1960 to 1980, with the public sector leading the way. This brought many women into the membership, and eventually the leadership, of a trade union movement that had been disproportionately male. But it left many women and men working in small enterprises in the private sector still beyond the reach of trade unionism and any measure of social justice.

Chapter 7 analyzed the 1980s, when a major Alberta recession called into question the popular view after World War II that capitalism had solved its internal contradictions and could offer economic growth and near-full employment forever. Having been spared the high unemployment that other provinces had experienced in the 1970s, Alberta workers were not amused at their suddenly precarious economic position. Nor were they willing to stand idly by while their government poured billions into private corporations facing bankruptcy, at the same time recognizing the existence of a working class mostly by passing anti-labour legislation. A series of major strikes in both the public and private sectors demonstrated the greatest militancy that workers in the province had evinced since the Great Depression. Even their voting patterns in some areas of the province shifted leftwards to the New Democratic Party, which had been fighting for workers' rights since its formation in 1961 but did not enjoy clear electoral success until the 1980s. Used to working on its own to effect social change, the labour movement increasingly linked up with progressive social movements, sometimes playing a leading role, at other times a supportive role.

Chapter 8 described the intensification of the neoliberal government and employer counter-offensive to this growth in labour militancy. Attempting to divide public and private sector workers and exacerbate divisions within society as a whole, the government of

Ralph Klein tore up the social contract of the postwar period in which health, education, and social services were seen as entitlements of the population and public servants the loyal deliverers of these services. The government complained that the province was broke, its publicly delivered services bloated, and public servants pampered. Cuts, privatizations, and attacks on the destitute became the order of the day. The labour movement, after its militancy and occasional victories in the 1980s, seemed somewhat exhausted by the time Klein came to power. Its opposition to the neo-liberal regime appeared anemic until 1995, when Calgary hospital laundry workers, taking the lead on their own, caused their union to mount a popular resistance to job cuts. It wasn't followed up with a truly massive campaign by labour to defend its rights, but the Klein government was unnerved and the Klein Revolution slowed down. Efforts to counter neo-liberal ideology seemed to founder overall, even though a large section of the working-class population of the province seemed skeptical about the government's directions.

Women, both as workers and as home caregivers, were disproportionately victimized by policies that had as their underlying philosophy the notion that the state owed no one — except big corporations, whom conservatives believed were the engines of economic growth — a measure of help. The gradual reduction in health care, education, and social services jobs not only took away the unionized jobs of some women but forced many others to serve as unpaid caregivers to a larger extent than they might have if social and health programs had been properly funded. As chapter 9 suggested, while Alberta women were increasingly in the labour force, their pay was lower proportionately to men than that of women in other provinces, and services such as daycare and homecare, which recognized that women still bore the major responsibility for family care and housework, were always underfunded and, in the Klein period, often disappeared altogether.

Chapter 10 traced the gradual removal of whites-only policies in Canadian immigration and both the opportunities and challenges faced by visible minorities in Alberta. Again, the province was slower than other provinces to pass and enforce human rights legislation. Visible minorities often found that their professional experience acquired in their homelands was not recognized in Canada. Meanwhile, the view of governments and corporations that certain groups of migrants, in which visible minorities loomed large, would work particularly cheaply and uncomplainingly led to the hiring of tens of thousands of temporary foreign workers during the economic boom that began in 2002. Despite efforts of trade unions to speak for the interests of these workers, many employers tended to ignore labour laws as they dealt with this vulnerable population who were too afraid of being deported to complain when their human rights were violated.

◆ ◆ ◆

Clearly, the Alberta labour movement has its hands full in trying to deal with the many problems associated with an increasingly "marketized" and "globalized" economy in which a relatively small group of international corporations and financiers play with people's lives and make it seem useless, even sinful, for governments to intervene on behalf of the public interest. Labour has at times also supported a global economy, but its vision has been completely different: it has called for production for use, not for profit, and a sharing of international resources and wealth. In the future, it will have to revive such notions and create the international alliances that can make them a reality if it wishes to provide a counter-model to the one that global capitalism has developed.

Alberta's unions correctly attacked the provincial Progressive Conservative government during the 2008 provincial election for having "no plan" about how to ensure that the province's energy-fuelled prosperity create long-term economic stability, responsible environmental stewardship, and a better distribution of the province's wealth so that homelessness and want, the flip side of the coin of the conspicuous consumption of corporate executives, disappears. But the unions have struggled with creating a detailed vision of their own. Objectively, most of labour's campaigns for several decades now have been efforts to preserve previous victories from the Fordist era rather than to gain new victories. Labour lacks a unified vision to guarantee better lives for workers and more worker participation in society's decision making. The union movement and its allies have had some successes, such as preventing the privatization of medicare and limiting the extent of privatization of education and other programs. But on the whole, workers are losing ground.

Particularly as a result of the Klein Revolution and its aftermath, capital's share of provincial wealth relative to that of labour has increased, and the public sector has been weakened. Economist Greg Flanagan notes that Alberta spent only 13 percent of its provincial GDP on government services in 2003, compared to 22 percent in 1993, at the beginning of the Klein era. While spending across all provinces also fell during that period, the national average dropped only from 27 to 22, making Alberta easily the stingiest province. Flanagan notes that "the role of government as stabilizer was abandoned, as regulator was considerably reduced, and as provider of public goods was diminished."[9] The poor suffered most from cutbacks while the wealthy received most of the benefits from tax changes that created an artificial sense of a "debt wall" in Alberta.[10] The flat tax instituted by Ralph Klein deprived the Treasury of $5.5 billion in annual income in 2006 alone. Meanwhile, the government's corporate tax receipts remained static while corporate profits before taxes quadrupled from 1989 to 2008. In 1989, corporate profits per person in Alberta amounted to $3,600. By 2008, that figure, adjusted for inflation, had risen to $15,000. Little wonder then that while provincial GDP rose 76 percent in the two decades after 1989, personal income rose only 39 percent. Between 1989 and 2008, spending per person on health care rose 37 percent and on schools a mere 6 percent, while social service spending *fell* a full 15 percent. Corporate profits, on the other hand, rose 314 percent.[11]

Norway, a country of just under five million people, offers an alternative that the labour movement in Alberta studied closely in the early 2000s. Its history is quite different from Alberta's. A country with a long history of social-democratic governments before it struck North Sea oil riches in the late 1970s, Norway has managed to create one of the world's most prosperous economies and one of its most socially just societies in terms of wealth distribution and protection of labour rights. Both Alberta and Norway adopted the notion to establish public trust funds that would invest some of the oil royalties received by the state to ensure that funds be available to create new industries and protect social programs in the period after the fossil fuels are tapped out. Alberta established the Alberta Heritage Savings Trust Fund in 1976 and initially placed 30 percent of oil royalties in the fund. Beginning with the 1982 recession however, the government began using the royalties that it collected from the energy companies for current expenditures and retirement of debt so as to maintain a low-tax regime.[12] On 31 March 2011, the government reported that the Trust Fund was worth $15.2 billion. By contrast, in 1991, Norway established the Statens Pensjonsfond, its sovereign wealth fund, which took ownership of two-thirds of Statoil, the largely state-owned energy firm that dominates the country's fossil fuel industry, and subsequently placed virtually all of its energy earnings in the fund. In May 2011, the fund's value was reported as $525 billion, or thirty-five times the value of the Alberta Heritage Savings Trust Fund.[13] Norway's social programs left Alberta's and Canada's in the dust, but they were paid for by steep, progressive taxes, not from the earnings of the Statens Pensjonsfond, which were seen as savings for a post-oil period. Norway's sovereign fund invested heavily in alternative energy sources and in environmental projects more broadly, accepting a role of social responsibility that Alberta's private-enterprise energy industry lacks.[14]

Norway's labour movement — facing a growing neo-liberal movement that resulted in relatively right-wing governments being elected in 1997 and 2001, as well as a Labour Party that included a neo-liberal faction — created the Campaign for the Welfare State (CWS) in 1999. Although this organization initially grouped only six unions, it gradually came to embrace almost the entirety of Norwegian labour. It demanded an end to privatization and cutbacks, and called for the expansion of social programs. The CWS was powerful enough to persuade three political parties — the Labour Party, the Socialist Left Party, and the Centre Party — to promise in writing before the 2005 election that they would implement the CWS program if elected; it also forced them to commit to a pre-electoral coalition so that they could not weasel out of their promises by failing to work together after the election. That coalition was elected with 60 percent of the votes in 2005 and re-elected in 2009.[15]

The higher taxes in Norway have not created the unhappy society that conservatives suggest it should. Quite the contrary. Norway, as one of the most egalitarian countries among the advanced capitalist nations, can boast of some of the most impressive social statistics in the world. It reports low rates of poverty, crime, obesity, mental health problems, and infant mortality. An important international study found that the poorest 20 percent of Norwegians had better social statistics than the wealthiest 20 percent of Americans.[16] This finding was one of the pieces of evidence used by the authors of this study to determine that countries that achieve the most equal distribution of wealth end up with the happiest populations overall. While the richest 20 percent of Americans were obviously very much happier and healthier than the poorest 20 percent in their own country, just living in a rat-race society where a change in their economic circumstances could put them out on the streets appears to be enough to imperil their health so that they are worse off than the relative poor in Norway, where state social security assures that almost everyone feels that he or she has a stake in society. In

2010, as it had been for many years, Norway sat atop the United Nations' Human Development Office's list of the best places to live in the world, a ranking based on such factors as average incomes, degree of poverty, equality among the sexes, and educational attainments. Canada ranked eighth.[17]

Whether a "Norwegian vision" is sellable in conservative Alberta is questionable. Two non-government organizations in which the trade union movement is influential, Public Interest Alberta and Join Together Alberta, have been making tentative steps toward raising issues about the "next Alberta" by focusing on the shackles placed on meeting public need by the conservative commitment to low taxes regardless of ability to pay. But they place a much greater emphasis on preserving existing jobs than on campaigning for a radical extension of the welfare state or greater socialization of industries such as the energy industry. However, the Alberta labour movement, along with the Canadian Labour Congress and the NDP, is currently campaigning for a doubling of Canada Pension Plan benefits, a national daycare program, and the expansion of the medicare program to include homecare, pharmaceuticals, denticare, and holistic alternative medical treatments. Through its involvement with Public Interest Alberta, it is also involved in national campaigns to end poverty.[18]

As we approach the future, the lessons of our forefathers and foremothers in the labour force and the labour movement will hopefully guide us to seek a more just society as they did. When the Alberta Federation of Labour formed in 1912, it regarded itself as speaking for all working people. Through the years, the AFL, along with other labour organizations, has tried in different ways to improve the lives of workers. As the federation approaches its second century, it behooves all trade unionists, whether they are members of the AFL or not, and indeed all working people, to think about how the AFL and the broader labour movement can build upon past achievements of working people in Alberta to shape an agenda for this century. The key goals will be, as they have always been, to create for and by working people a stable economy with safe, clean jobs over which workers exercise some control and with first-class health, education, housing, and public transport, as well as liveable communities with breathable air and a variety of affordable recreational and arts activities within reach. As it has been in the past, the fighting spirit of the trade union movement will be crucial to achieving such goals.

This book has relied a great deal on the words of workers themselves about Alberta's past and future. And so it ends with the words of a coal miner, Enoch Williams, who served as mayor of Blairmore from 1936 to 1951. Interviewed in 1969 at the age of eighty-five, Williams said:

> All of this here comes from the resources of the country, the resources of the world, and God, if there is a God, he never put it there for the benefit of a few. He put it there for the use of all of his people. At least, I'm simple enough to think that. And the only way we're ever going to get to the bottom is say "NO, there's no more oil, fellow, and there's no more gold, there's no more copper, there's no nothing anymore — all things that's in the ground belongs to the people. And it's going to be — not for profit, but for use for and by people." And I'm simple enough to believe that that's it.[19]

NOTES

Introduction: Those Who Built Alberta

1   Harry H. Hiller, *Second Promised Land: Migration to Alberta and the Transformation of Canadian Society*.

2   Doreen Barrie, *The Other Alberta: Decoding a Political Enigma*.

3   Aritha Van Herk, *Mavericks: An Incorrigible History of Alberta*.

4   Warren Caragata, *Alberta Labour: A Heritage Untold*.

1 *Millennia of Native Work*

1   Treaty 7 Elders and Tribal Council, with Walter Hildebrandt, Sarah Carter, and Dorothy First Rider, *The True Spirit and Original Intent of Treaty 7*, 85.

2   Harold Cardinal and Walter Hildebrandt, *Treaty Elders of Saskatchewan: Our Dream Is That Our Peoples Will One Day Be Clearly Recognized as Nations*, 12.

3   Ibid., 14–16.

4   Terence N. D'Altroy, *The Incas (People of America)*.

5   Jack Brink, *Imagining Head-Smashed-In: Aboriginal Buffalo Hunting on the Northern Plains*, 81.

6   Trevor R. Peck, *Light from Ancient Campfires: Archaeological Evidence for Native Lifeways on the Northern Plains*, 25.

7   Ibid., 444.

8   Ibid., 191, 431, 445.

9   Ibid., 452.

10 Arthur J. Ray, *I Have Lived Here Since the World Began: An Illustrated History of Canada's Native People*, 32–33.

11 Treaty 7 Elders, *The True Spirit*, 83–104.

12 Kerry Abel, *Drum Songs: Glimpses of Dene History*, 20–23. On the Dene, see also Keith J. Crowe, *A History of the Original Peoples of Northern Canada*.

13 David G. Mandelbaum, *The Plains Cree: An Ethnographic, Historical and Comparative Study*; Jennifer Brown and Robert Brightman, eds., *The Orders of the Dreamed*.

14 Canada, *Report of the Royal Commission on Aboriginal Peoples*, vol. 1, *Looking Forward, Looking Back*, 66–72. On the Blackfoot, see also Treaty 7 Elders and Tribal Council, *The True Spirit and Original Intent of Treaty 7*; Betty Bastien, *Blackfoot Ways of Knowing: The World of the Siksikaitsitapi*; and Adolf Hungry-Wolf, *The Blackfoot Papers*.

15 Frances W. Kaye, *Goodlands: A Meditation and History on the Great Plains*, 26.

16 David Thompson, *Explorations in Western America, 1784–1812*, 81.

17 Bastien, *Blackfoot Ways of Knowing*, 24.

18 Indian Brotherhood of the Northwest Territories and Métis Association of the Northwest Territories, "Past and Present Land-Use by Slavey Indians of the Mackenzie District"; Arthur J. Ray and Donald Freeman, *Give Us Good Measure: An Economic Analysis of Relations between the Indians and the Hudson's Bay Company before 1763*, 17.

19 Crowe, *A History of the Original Peoples*, 24.

20 Elder Danny Musqua, quoted in Cardinal and Hildebrandt, *Treaty Elders of Saskatchewan*, 39.

21 Canada, *Report of the Royal Commission on Aboriginal Peoples*, 71.

2 *The Fur Trade and Early European Settlement*

1   "The Royal Charter for Incorporating the Hudson's Bay Company, A.D. 1670."

2   Two powerful histories of the conquest of Native territories in the Americas are Ronald Wright, *Stolen Continents: Conquest and Resistance in the Americas*, and Eduardo Galeano, *Open Veins of Latin America: Five Centuries of the Pillage of a Continent*.

3   Fernand Braudel, *The Mediterranean and the Mediterranean World in the Age of Philip II*, vol. 1, 227; G.V. Scammell, *The World Encompassed: The First European Maritime Empires, c. 800–1650*, 236–57.

4   Galeano, *Open Veins*, 32, 41.

5   Scammell, *The World Encompassed*, 349.

6 Ibid., 350.

7 Olive Patricia Dickason, with David T. McNab, *Canada's First Nations: A History of Founding Peoples from Earliest Times,* 90–91; Wright, *Stolen Continents,* 106–13; Roger L. Nichols, *Indians in the United States and Canada: A Comparative History,* 39–88.

8 Alfred W. Crosby, *Ecological Imperialism: The Biological Expansion of Europe, 900–1900.*

9 Maureen K. Lux, *Medicine That Walks: Disease, Medicine, and Canadian Plains Native People, 1880–1940.*

10 Nichols, *Indians,* 13.

11 Arthur J. Ray and Donald Freeman, *Give Us Good Measure: An Economic Analysis of Relations Between the Indians and the Hudson's Bay Company Before 1763,* 162.

12 James P. Ronda, "'We Are Well as We Are': An Indian Critique of Seventeenth-Century Christian Missions"; Denys Delâge and Helen Hornbeck Tanner, "The Ojibwa-Jesuit Debate at Walpole Island, 1844."

13 Arthur J. Ray, *Indians in the Fur Trade: Their Role as Trappers, Hunters and Middlemen in the Lands Southwest of Hudson Bay, 1660–1870.*

14 Trevor R. Peck, *Light from Ancient Campfires: Archaeological Evidence for Native Lifeways on the Northern Plains,* 435.

15 Ibid., 433.

16 Betty Bastien, *Blackfoot Ways of Knowing: The World of the Siksikaitsitapi,* 17.

17 Clifford Wilson, "Anthony Henday," *Dictionary of Canadian Biography Online, v*ol. 3, *1771–1770,* 2000, http://www.biographi.ca/009004-119.01-e.php?id_nbr=1400.

18 Lux, *Medicine That Walks,* 18. In "Constructed and Contested Truths: Aboriginal Suicide, Law, and Colonialism in the Canadian West, 1823–1927." Lesley Erickson notes that this faith in traditional healing practices persisted in the treaty period that followed the end of the fur trade.

19 Bastien, *Blackfoot Ways of Knowing,* 18.

20 Arthur J. Ray, *I Have Lived Here Since the World Began: An Illustrated History of Canada's Native People,* 168–70.

21 Carolyn Podruchny, *Making the Voyageur World: Travelers and Traders in the North American Fur Trade,* 26.

22 Ibid., 133, 151–59.

23 On the militancy of the Orkneymen, see Edith Burley, *Servants of the Honourable Company: Work, Discipline, and Conflict in the Hudson's Bay Company, 1770–1879.*

24 Carol M. Judd, "Native Labour and Social Stratification in the Hudson's Bay Company's Northern Department, 1770–1870," 307.

25 Ibid., 310.

26 Sylvia Van Kirk, *Many Tender Ties: Women in Fur-Trade Society in Western Canada, 1670–1870,* 121. Covering similar ground to Van Kirk is Jennifer S.H. Brown, *Strangers in Blood: Fur Trade Company Families in Indian Country.*

27 Van Kirk, *Many Tender Ties,* 171–72, 201.

28 Ray, *I Have Lived Here,* 172.

29 Glyndwr Williams, "Highlights of the First 200 Years of the Hudson's Bay Company," 13; Lyle Dick, "The Seven Oaks Incident and the Construction of a Historical Tradition, 1816 to 1970."

30 Dick, "The Seven Oaks Incident."

31 W.L. Morton, "Pierre-Guillaume Sayer," *Dictionary of Canadian Biography Online,* vol. 7, *1836–1850,* http://www.biographi.ca/009004-119.01-e.php?BioId=37771.

32 Frits Pannekoek, *A Snug Little Flock: The Social Origins of the Riel Resistance of 1869–70;* John Foster, "The Country Born in the Red River Settlement."

33 Judd, "Native Labour," 311.

34 The federal government's acquisition of most of the Hudson's Bay Company lands and its subsequent approach to these lands are detailed in Kirk N. Lambrecht, *The Administration of Dominion Lands, 1870–1930.*

35 Vernon Fowke, *The National Policy and the Wheat Economy,* Part 1; Jeffery Taylor, "Capitalist Development, Forms of Labour, and Class Formation in Prairie Canada," 169.

36 The estimate of the value of the HBC lands is based on CPR records from 1916. The CPR also received 5 percent of the land of western Canada and reported in 1916 that land sales added to the value of lands yet to be sold totalled $188 million: Robert Chodos, *The CPR: A Century of Corporate Welfare,* 22.

37 D.N. Sprague, *Canada and the Métis, 1869–1885,* 67–74.

38 See Bob Beal and Rod Macleod, *Prairie Fire: The 1885 Northwest Rebellion.*

39 The classic statement of federal aims is John L. Tobias, "Protection, Civilization, Assimilation: An Outline History of Canada's Indian Policy."

40 Sheldon Krasowski, "Mediating Treaties: Eyewitness Accounts of Treaties Between the Crown and Indigenous Peoples, 1871–1876."

41 Ibid., 2.

42 Two books that attempt to retrace the Elders' perceptions of how Native peoples viewed the treaty process are Treaty 7 Elders and Tribal Council, with Walter Hildebrandt,

Sarah Carter, and Dorothy First Rider, *The True Spirit and Original Intent of Treaty 7*, and Harold Cardinal and Walter Hildebrandt, *Treaty Elders of Saskatchewan: Our Dream Is That Our Peoples Will One Day Be Clearly Recognized as Nations.*

43 Ray, *I Have Lived Here*, 215–17; Brian Titley, *The Frontier World of Edgar Dewdney*, 47; John L. Tobias, "Canada's Subjugation of the Plains Cree, 1879–1885."

44 Brian Titley, *A Narrow Vision: Duncan Campbell Scott and the Administration of Indian Affairs in Canada.*

45 Helen Burke, *The People and the Poor Law in Nineteenth Century Ireland*, 111–16. The similar reluctance of the British to provide relief in India, leading to millions of deaths, is discussed in Ravi Ahaja, "State Formation and 'Famine Policy' in Early Colonial South India."

46 Hugh Shewell, *"Enough to Keep Them Alive": Indian Welfare in Canada, 1873–1965*, 70.

47 Sarah Carter, *Lost Harvests: Prairie Indian Reserve Farmers and Government Policy*, 79–129.

48 Walter Hildebrandt, *Views from Fort Battleford: Constructed Visions of an Anglo-Canadian West*, 36.

49 Ray, *I Have Lived Here*, 230–33.

50 Sarah Carter, *The Importance of Being Monogamous: Marriage and Nation Building in Western Canada to 1915.*

51 J.R. Miller, *Shingwauk's Vision: A History of Native Residential Schools*; John Milloy, *A National Crime: The Canadian Government and the Residential School System — 1879 to 1986*; Sharon Venne, "Understanding Treaty 6, An Indigenous Perspective," 195.

52 Carter, *Lost Harvests.*

3 *One Step Forward: Alberta Workers, 1885–1914*

1 A.A. den Otter, *Civilizing the West: The Galts and the Development of Western Canada*, 76.

2 Ibid., 99, 105.

3 Edmund W. Bradwin, *The Bunkhouse Man: A Study of the Work and Pay in the Camps of Canada*, 270.

4 Donald Avery, *"Dangerous Foreigners": European Immigrant Workers and Labour Radicalism in Canada 1896–1932*, 27.

5 The *Victoria Colonist* claimed fifteen hundred deaths, but Chinese merchants in Victoria argued that there had been twenty-two hundred. Andrew Onderdonk, the contractor for the western section of the the CPR, admitted only six hundred.

6 Warren Caragata, *Alberta Labour: A Heritage Untold*, 6.

7 Bradwin, *The Bunkhouse Man.*

8 Greg Hall, *Harvest Wobblies: The Industrial Workers of the World and Agricultural Laborers in the American West, 1905–1930*, 8.

9 Bettina Bradbury , *Working Families: Age, Gender and Daily Survival in Industrializing Montreal*, 250; Peter Baskerville and Eric W. Sager, *Unwilling Idlers: The Urban Unemployed and Their Families in Late Victorian Canada*, 112–17; Jane Humphries, "Enclosures, Common Rights, and Women: The Proletarianization of Families in the Late Eighteenth and Early Nineteenth Centuries."

10 Caragata, *Alberta Labour*, 16.

11 Charles Allen Seager, "A Proletariat in Wild Rose Country: The Alberta Coal Miners, 1905–1945," 24–25, 63.

12 Ibid., 25–26, 34, 35.

13 On the general climate of employer-labour relations, see the account of the Homestead strike of 1892 in David Montgomery, *The Fall of the House of Labor: The Workplace, the State, and American Labor Activism, 1865–1925.*

14 Ibid., 121.

15 Ibid., 123.

16 Ibid., 276.

17 Ibid., 278.

18 Seager, "A Proletariat in Wild Rose Country," 202.

19 Ibid., 203.

20 Caragata, *Alberta Labour*, 19.

21 Seager, "A Proletariat in Wild Rose Country," 203.

22 Ibid., 204–5.

23 Ibid., 207–8.

24 William M. Baker, "The Miners and the Mounties: The Royal North West Mounted Police and the 1906 Lethbridge Strike."

25 Ibid., 75.

26 Den Otter, *Civilizing the West*, 290.

27 Ibid., 296.

28 Seager, "A Proletariat in Wild Rose Country," 212–13.

29 Den Otter, *Civilizing the West*, 297.

30 Ibid., 217.

31 Caragata, *Alberta Labour*, 21. The major work on Mackenzie King's philosophy regarding labour relations is Paul Craven, *An Impartial Umpire: Industrial Relations and the Canadian State, 1900–1921.*

32 Seager, "A Proletariat in Wild Rose Country," 218.

33 Ibid., 220.

34 Ibid., 237–42.

35 Ibid., 245–52.

36 Allen Seager, "Socialists and Workers: Western Canadian Coal Miners, 1900–21."

37 Seager, "A Proletariat in Wild Rose Country," 232.

38 Ibid., 255–56. Electoral cooperation between organized labour and local Liberal parties was not uncommon in the late nineteenth and early twentieth centuries. It involved a Liberal constituency association agreeing to nominate a candidate supported financially by trade unions as the local Liberal candidate. Such candidates were generally known as Liberal-Labour, or even "Lib-Labs."

39 Ibid., 61.

40 Den Otter, *Civilizing the West*, 180, 273–74.

41 *Census of Canada, 1911*, vol. 1, *Areas and Population by Provinces Districts and Subdistricts*, Table 2.

42 Seager, "A Proletariat in Wild Rose Country," 98–99.

43 Ibid., 103.

44 Excerpt from M.B. Venini-Bryne, *The Buffalo and the Cross*, cited in ibid., 104.

45 Karen Buckley, *Danger, Death and Disaster in the Crowsnest Pass Mines, 1902–1928*, 9.

46 Calculations based on data from the *Census of Canada, 1911*.

47 Den Otter, *Civilizing the West*.

48 For non-wage survival tactics, see Bettina Bradbury, "Pigs, Cows and Boarders: Non-Wage Forms of Survival Among Montreal Families, 1861–91"; Baskerville and Sager, *Unwilling Idlers*, chap. 6, 112–28; for specific accounts of livestock raising and children's and women's contributions, see Krystyna Lukasiewicz, "Polish Community in the Crowsnest Pass," 1–10; the critical value of women's and children's work for family survival is detailed in Humphries, "Enclosures, Common Rights and Women," 17–42.

49 David Jay Bercuson, "Labour Radicalism and the Western Industrial Frontier: 1897–1919," 169.

50 Caragata, *Alberta Labour*, 32; Buckley, *Danger, Death and Disaster*, 1–7.

51 David Bright, *The Limits of Labour: Class Formation and the Labour Movement in Calgary, 1883–1929*, 18–21.

52 R.C. Macleod, *The North-West Mounted Police and Law Enforcement, 1873–1905*, 157.

53 Caragata, *Alberta Labour*, 9.

54 Seager, "A Proletariat in Wild Rose Country," 202; and Bright, *Limits of Labour*, 78.

55 *Census of Canada, 1911*; *Census of Canada, 1901*, vol. 3, *Manufactures*; and *Census of Population and Agriculture of the Northwest Provinces: Manitoba, Saskatchewan, Alberta, 1906*.

56 Bright, *Limits of Labour*, 79–83; and Caragata, *Alberta Labour*, 43–51, 21–28.

57 Bright, *Limits of Labour*, 41–46.

58 Montgomery, *The Fall of the House of Labor*, 214–23.

59 James R. Conley, "Frontier Labourers, Crafts in Crisis and the Western Labour Revolt: The Case of Vancouver, 1900–1919," 15, 16, 34–37.

60 Robert H. Babcock, *Gompers in Canada: A Study in American Continentalism Before the First World War*, 76–77.

61 A. Ross McCormack, *Reformers, Rebels and Revolutionaries: The Western Canadian Radical Movement, 1899–1919*, 44–48; Caragata, *Alberta Labour*, 13, 14.

62 Bright, *Limits of Labour*, 84–87; Caragata, *Alberta Labour*, 23–25.

63 Caragata, *Alberta Labour*, 43–46.

64 Michael J. Piva, *The Condition of the Working Class in Toronto, 1900–1921*, 56–58.

65 Bright, *Limits of Labour*, 33–35.

66 Calculations based on data from the *Census of Canada, 1911*, vols. 1 and 6.

67 Bettina Bradbury, "Gender at Work at Home: Family Decisions, the Labour Market, and Girls' Contributions to the Family Economy," 179.

68 John Bullen, "Hidden Workers: Child Labour and the Family Economy in Late Nineteenth-Century Urban Ontario."

69 Bright, *Limits of Labour*, 35–36.

70 Alvin Finkel, "The Rise and Fall of the Labour Party in Alberta, 1917–42," especially 64–65.

71 R.T. Naylor, "The Canadian State, the Accumulation of Capital, and the Great War," 61–64.

72 David Schultze, "The Industrial Workers of the World and the Unemployed in Edmonton and Calgary in the Depression of 1913–1915."

73 Donald Avery, *Reluctant Host: Canada's Response to Immigrant Workers, 1896–1994*, 21; Cecilia Danysk, *Hired Hands: Labour and the Development of Prairie Agriculture, 1880–1930*, 17.

74 Avery, *Reluctant Host*, 25, 26.

75 Danysk, *Hired Hands*, 58, 59.

76 Ibid., 46–62.

77 Ibid., 85–88.

78 Ibid., 67–70.

79 Ibid., 115–18, 145–48.

80 John Herd Thompson, "Bringing in the Sheaves: The Harvest Excursionists, 1890–1929."

81 Ibid., 470, 471.

82 Ibid., 480, 481.

83 Ibid., 478, 479.

84 Ibid., 471, 482.

85 Ibid., 486; Danysk, *Hired Hands*, 126–30.

86 Danysk, *Hired Hands*, 116.

4 War, Repression, and Depression, 1914–39

1 Peter Campbell, "Understanding the Dictatorship of the Proletariat: The Canadian Left and the Moment of Socialist Possibility in 1919," 62.

2 H.A. Logan, "Rise and Decline of the One Big Union in Canada," 249.

3 David Bright, *The Limits of Labour: Class Formation and the Labour Movement in Calgary, 1883–1929*, 109.

4 Gerald Friesen, *The Canadian Prairies: A History*, 329.

5 *Edmonton Morning Bulletin*, 6 August 1914.

6 *Calgary Daily Herald*, 12 August 1914.

7 *Calgary Daily Herald*, 13 August 1914.

8 David Bright, *The Limits of Labour*, 110.

9 David Bright, "'We Are All Kin': Reconsidering Labour and Class in Calgary, 1919," 70.

10 A. Ross McCormack, *Reformers, Rebels, and Revolutionaries: The Western Canadian Radical Movement, 1899–1919*, 118–36.

11 Tim Cook, *At the Sharp End: Canadians Fighting the Great War, 1914–1916*, 28–29; Desmond Morton, *When Your Number's Up: The Canadian Soldier in the First World War*, 9; and Ronald Haycock, *Sam Hughes: The Public Career of a Controversial Canadian, 1885–1916*, 202. Haycock claims that 70 percent of the first sixty thousand enlistments were British-born.

12 Howard Palmer and Tamara Palmer, *Alberta: A New History*, 169.

13 *Edmonton Bulletin*, 6 August 1914.

14 Frances Swyripa, "The Ukrainian Image: Loyal Citizen or Disloyal Alien," 58.

15 Ibid., 59.

16 Gregory S. Kealey, "State Repression of Labour and the Left in Canada, 1914–1920:

The Impact of the First World War," 291; Morton, *When Your Number's Up*, 9.

17 Bright, *The Limits of Labour*, 99–100; R.T. Naylor, "The Canadian State, the Accumulation of Capital, and the Great War," 27.

18 Quoted in David Schulze, "The Industrial Workers of the World and the Unemployed in Edmonton and Calgary in the Depression of 1913–1915," 52.

19 John C. Weaver, "Edmonton's Perilous Course, 1904–1929," 31.

20 Schulze, "The Industrial Workers of the World," 54–55.

21 Bright, "'We Are All Kin,'" 68.

22 *Lethbridge Daily Herald*, 19 February 1917.

23 McCormack, *Reformers, Rebels, and Revolutionaries*, 121.

24 *Lethbridge Daily Herald*, 19 February 1917.

25 *Red Deer News*, 20 August 1915.

26 *Crag and Canyon*, August 1916.

27 Canada, Census and Statistics Office, *Canada Year Book*, 1922–23, 279. Figures do not include board.

28 *Calgary Daily Herald*, 14 August 1916.

29 *Canada Year Book*, 1922–23, 416.

30 Paul Michael Boothe and Heather Edwards, eds., *Eric J. Hanson's Financial History of Alberta, 1905–1950*, 63.

31 *Canada Year Book*, 1922–23, 752–53.

32 *Calgary Daily Herald*, 10 November 1916.

33 *Calgary Daily Herald*, 13 November 1916.

34 *Calgary Daily Herald*, 27 November 1916.

35 Allen Seager and David Roth, "British Columbia and the Mining West: A Ghost of a Chance," 246, and Judy Fudge and Eric Tucker, *Labour Before the Law: The Regulation of Workers' Collective Action in Canada, 1900–1948*, 93.

36 *Canada Year Book*, 1916–17, 493.

37 Friesen, *The Canadian Prairies*, 296–98.

38 See the table "Industrial Disputes by Province, 1901 to June 30, 1919," in Royal Commission on Industrial Relations, *National Industrial Conference of Dominion and Provincial Governments with Representative Employers and Labour Men, on the Subjects of Industrial Relations and Labour Laws, and for the Consideration of Labour Features of the Treaty of Peace, Ottawa, September 15–20, 1919* (Ottawa: King's Printer, 1919), xxx.

39 Haycock, *Sam Hughes*, 225–57.

40 Anthony Mardiros, *The Life of a Prairie Radical: William Irvine*, 46.

41 Fudge and Tucker, *Labour Before the Law*, 92.

42 Bill Waiser, *Park Prisoners: The Untold History of Western Canada's National Parks, 1915–1946*, 5–6.

43 *Edmonton Morning Bulletin*, 16 February 1916.

44 Waiser, *Park Prisoners*, 6.

45 Krystyna Lukasiewicz, "Polish Community in the Crowsnest Pass."

46 Udo Sautter, "The Origins of the Employment Service of Canada, 1900–1920," 106.

47 David Bright, "'We Are All Kin,'" 74.

48 Canada, Royal Commission on Industrial Relations, *Official Report of Proceedings*, xlii.

49 Warren Caragata, *Alberta Labour: A Heritage Untold*, 82–83.

50 Ibid., 83.

51 *Edmonton Morning Bulletin*, 6 May 1919.

52 Canada, Royal Commission on Industrial Relations, *Official Report of Proceedings*, 4, Appendix.

53 *Calgary Daily Herald*, 14 March 1919.

54 Though mostly unsympathetic to his subjects, David J. Bercuson has provided the

major book-length history of the OBU to date in *Fools and Wise Men: The Rise and Fall of the One Big Union.* A recent assessment of the OBU in the context of radical debates of the period more generally is Ian McKay, *Reasoning Otherwise: Leftists and the People's Enlightenment in Canada, 1880–1920.*

55 Logan, "Rise and Decline of the One Big Union in Canada," 252.

56 Copies of all issues of the *Alberta Labour News* can be found in the Alfred Farmilo Papers at the Provincial Archives of Alberta.

57 Tom Mitchell and James Naylor, "The Prairies: In the Eye of the Storm," 178.

58 The events of the Winnipeg General Strike are traced in David Jay Bercuson, *Confrontation at Winnipeg: Labour, Industrial Relations, and the General Strike*; J.M. Bumsted, *The Winnipeg General Strike of 1919: An Illustrated Guide*; and Mitchell and Naylor, "The Prairies," 176–84.

59 Palmer and Palmer, *Alberta*, 203.

60 The end of the Winnipeg Strike and the strike's aftermath are explored in Reinhold Kramer and Tom Mitchell, *When the State Trembled: How A.J. Andrews and the Citizens' Committee Broke the Winnipeg General Strike.*

61 Mitchell and Naylor, "The Prairies," 199.

62 Ibid.

63 Alvin Finkel, "The Rise and Fall of the Labour Party in Alberta, 1917–1942."

64 *Edmonton Morning Bulletin*, 23 May 1919.

65 *Canada Year Book*, 1922–23, 280.

66 Ibid., 435.

67 Canada, Department of Labour, *Labour Gazette*, January 1933, 69–73.

68 See *Edmonton Journal*, 20 July 1921. See also Canada, Department of Labour, "Action Towards the Alleviation of the Unemployment Situation," *Labour Gazette*, August 1921, 996–98.

69 C.T. Hall, *Redcliff's Fifty Golden Years: The Early History of Redcliff*, 32.

70 Allan Chambers, *Spirit of the Crowsnest: The Story of Unions in the Coal Towns of the Crowsnest Pass.*

71 Caragata, *Alberta Labour*, 89–93.

72 Carl F. Betke, "The United Farmers of Alberta, 1921–1935," 14–31.

73 Finkel, "The Rise and Fall of the Labour Party in Alberta, 1917–1942," 66.

74 Ibid., 72.

75 Ibid., 73.

76 Ibid., 75.

77 Palmer and Palmer, *Alberta*, 226.

78 Finkel, "The Rise and Fall of the Labour Party in Alberta, 1917–1942," 78.

79 Ibid.

80 Ibid., 82–83.

81 Bill Waiser, *All Hell Can't Stop Us: The On-to-Ottawa Trek and Regina Riot*, 9–40; Alvin Finkel, *The Social Credit Phenomenon in Alberta*, 14–18.

82 Waiser, *All Hell Can't Stop Us*, 171–212, 261–75.

83 See David Bright, "The State, the Unemployed, and the Communist Party in Calgary, 1930–5."

84 See, for example, Eric Strikwerda, "The City and the Depression on the Canadian Prairies: Edmonton, Saskatoon, Winnipeg, 1929–1939," PhD dissertation, York University, 2000, 156–57. For additional discussion, see Strikwerda, *The Wages of Relief: The City and the Depression on the Canadian Prairies, 1929–1939*. Edmonton: AU Press, 2012 forthcoming.

85 Farmers across the Canadian prairies faced trouble from numerous quarters. Environmental disasters aside, many farmers had overextended themselves through the latter part of the 1920s, both in terms of buying more acreage as well as obtaining credit for agricultural products and new technologies. Added to this were the Wheat Pools' overly ambitious expectations of export market needs, which caused them to boldly hold prairie cereal grains off the world market, anticipating that so doing would raise the world wheat price and benefit prairie farmers. See Friesen, *The Canadian Prairies*, 384–85; Palmer and Palmer, *Alberta*, 252–54, and Bill Waiser, *Saskatchewan: A New History*, 292–302, 312–13.

86 *Edmonton Bulletin*, 19 December 1932.

87 City of Edmonton Archives, RG 11, Class 149, File 17, 6 December 1932, Shute to Knott. The RCMP had only recently taken over provincial policing in Alberta, though it might be noted that most members of the force were drawn from the ranks of the disbanded Alberta Provincial Police.

88 *Edmonton Bulletin*, 21 December 1932.

89 Ibid.

90 On the history of the Progressive Party, see W.L. Morton, *The Progressive Party in Canada*, and Robert A. Wardhaugh, *Mackenzie King and the Prairie West*. On the UFA, see Bradford James Rennie, *The United Farmers and Farm Women of Alberta, 1909–1921.*

91 "The Regina Manifesto, Adopted at First National Convention Held at Regina, Saskatchewan, July, 1933," http://economics.uwaterloo.ca/needhdata/Regina_Manifesto.html. On the early history of the CCF, see William Brennan, ed., *Building the Cooperative Commonwealth: Essays on the Democratic Socialist Tradition in Canada*, and Walter Stewart, *The Life and Political Times of Tommy Douglas.*

92 Alvin Finkel, "Obscure Origins: The Confused Early History of the CCF."

93 Finkel, *The Social Credit Phenomenon in Alberta*, 14–40.

94 Ibid., 38, 68–69.

95 Ibid., 41–72.

96 Ibid., 43–44.

97 Ibid., 51–58.

98 Ibid., 58; Alvin Finkel, "The Cold War, Alberta Labour, and the Social Credit Regime."

99 Caragata, *Alberta Labour*, 112.

100 Ibid., 110–19.

101 Caragata, *Alberta Labour*, 128–32.

5 *Alberta Labour and Working-Class Life, 1940–59*

1 C.P. Stacey, *Arms, Men and Governments: The War Policies of Canada, 1939–1945*, 66. Library and Archives Canada's official numbers suggest that 4 percent of all who served were killed: "Second World War Service Files: Canadian Armed Forces War Dead," Library and Archives Canada, http://www.collectionscanada.gc.ca/databases/war-dead/index-e.html. On psychological injury, see Terry Copp and Bill McAndrew, *Battle Exhaustion: Soldiers and Psychiatrists in the Canadian Army, 1939–1945*.

2 Donald E. Graves, *South Albertans: A Canadian Regiment at War*, 33–34.

3 Farley Mowat, *And No Birds Sang*, 218–19.

4 Graves, *South Albertans*, 130–31.

5 Stacey, *Arms, Men and Governments*, 589. Nationally, 89 percent of requests for postponement were granted.

6 Interview with Norah Hook by Catherine Cole, Edmonton, 12 May 2004, GWG Project. Interview with Assunta Dotto by Catherine Cole and Joan Schiebelbein, Edmonton, 20 April 2004, GWG Project.

7 Interview with Tets Kitaguchi, Hinton, 28 October 2005, Alberta Labour History Institute (hereafter ALHI).

8 Ron Laliberte and Vic Satzewich, "Native Migrant Labour in the Southern Alberta Sugar-Beet Industry: Coercion and Paternalism in the Recruitment of Labour," 73.

9 Patrick Lenihan, *Patrick Lenihan: From Irish Rebel to Founder of Canadian Public Sector Unionism*, 138–47.

10 Ibid., 150–51.

11 Interview with Nelly Engley, Edmonton, 21 April 2004, GWG Project; interview with Anne Ozipko, Edmonton, 4 April 2003, ALHI.

12 See Stuart Marshall Jamieson, *Times of Trouble: Labour Unrest and Industrial Conflict in Canada, 1900–66*, 288–91. The national dimensions of the strike wave are discussed in Gregory S. Kealey and Douglas Cruikshank, "Strikes in Canada, 1891–1950," 376–78, and in tables 11.10 and 11.11 (362–63).

13 Aaron McCrorie, "PC 1003: Labour, Capital, and the State."

14 Elaine Geddes, "Alberta Labour Legislation under the Social Credit Government: 1935–1947," 69–70.

15 Ibid., 83–86.

16 Bryan Palmer, *Working-Class Experience: Rethinking the History of Canadian Labour, 1800–1991*, 285–86.

17 Howard Palmer and Tamara Jeppson Palmer, *Alberta: A New History*, 298–99; Gerald Friesen, *The Canadian Prairies: A History*, 429–33.

18 David Monod, "The End of Agrarianism: The Fight for Farm Parity in Alberta and Saskatchewan, 1935–48."

19 Interview with Walter Makowecki, Edmonton, n.d., ALHI.

20 Monod, "The End of Agrarianism," 133–41.

21 Laliberte and Satzewich, "Native Migrant Labour," 74–76, 80.

22 Alvin Finkel, "The Cold War, Alberta Labour, and the Social Credit Regime," 137–38.

23 Tom Langford and Chris Frazer, "The Cold War and Working-Class Politics in the Coal Mining Communities of the Crowsnest Pass, 1945–1958," 54.

24 Comment from Bill Skura, in interview with Al Fontana, Emma Fontana, Veronica Fontana, Pauline Grigel, John Kinnear, Clara Marconi, Albin Panek, Glen Poulton (Blondie), Emily Root, Ray Root, Bill Skura, Gary Taje, and John Yeliga, Coleman, Alberta, 10 November 2005, ALHI (hereafter "group interview").

25 Comment from Clara Marconi, in group interview.

26 Interview with Joyce Avramenko, Edson, Alberta, August 2003, ALHI.

27 Comment from Bill Skura, in group interview.

28 Avramenko interview.

29 Comment from Pauline Grigel, in group interview.

30 Comment from Bill Skura, in group interview.

31 Ibid.

32 Tom Langford, "An Alternate Vision of Community: Crowsnest Miners and their Local Unions during the 1940s and 1950s," 149.

33 Bruce Ramsey, *The Noble Cause: The Story of the United Mine Workers of America in Western Canada*, 184.

34 Langford, "An Alternate Vision of Community," 150.

35 Ramsey, *The Noble Cause*, 184–85.

36 Langford, "An Alternate Vision of Comunity," 150, 152–56.

37 Interview with Canmore nurses, n.d., ALHI.

38 David Finch and Gordon Jaremko, *Fields of Fire: An Illustrated History of Canadian Petroleum*, 47–49.

39 Peter McKenzie-Brown, Gordon Jaremko, and David Finch, *The Great Oil Age: The Petroleum Industry in Canada*, 45.

40 Warren Caragata, *Alberta Labour: A Heritage Untold*, 133–34.

41 "An Alberta Schoolboy's History of Oil," in *The Roughneck*, November 1947. Reprinted in Alister Thomas, ed., *The Super Roughneck: 50 Years of Canadian Oilpatch History as Reported in* The Roughneck, 14.

42 Interview with Neil Reimer, Edmonton, December 2004, ALHI.

43 Interview with Neil Reimer for Celanese Project, Edmonton, November 2007, ALHI; Wayne Roberts, *Cracking the Canadian Formula: The Making of the Energy and Chemical Workers Union*, 36.

44 David Breen, "1947: The Making of Modern Alberta," 241–42.

45 Alvin Finkel, *The Social Credit Phenomenon in Alberta*, 111.

46 Ian Maclachlan, *Kill and Chill: Restructuring Canada's Beef Commodity Chain*, 228–31.

47 Finkel, *The Social Credit Phenomenon in Alberta*, 109–10.

48 Maclachlan, *Kill and Chill*, 231–32.

49 Interview with Elizabeth Kosma, Edmonton, 12 May 2004, GWG Project.

50 Interview with Mary Romanuk, Edmonton, 2 April 2004, GWG Project.

51 Romanuk interview.

52 Ozipko interview.

53 Doug Owram, "1951: Oil's Magic Wand," 575.

54 Owram, "1951," 576–77.

55 Interview with Lorne and Agnes Wiley, Medicine Hat, n.d., ALHI.

56 Alvin Finkel, *Social Policy and Practice in Canada: A History*, 104–6, 153–56; and Finkel, *The Social Credit Phenomenon in Alberta*, 122.

57 Finkel, *The Social Credit Phenomenon in Alberta*, 123.

58 Finkel, *Social Policy and Practice in Canada*, 115–17.

59 Ibid., 131–33.

60 Finkel, *The Social Credit Phenomenon in Alberta*, 123.

61 Ibid., 144, 149–50.

62 Geddes, "Alberta Labour Legislation," 96–97.

63 Statutes of Alberta, 1947, chap. 8 (certification at s. 59); Geddes, "Alberta Labour Legislation," 98–101.

64 Statutes of Alberta, 1948, chap. 76.

65 Caragata, *Alberta Labour*, 140–41; *The Back Row: Labour's Cold War in Alberta*, at 15:40.

66 Finkel, *The Social Credit Phenomenon in Alberta*, 112.

67 Interview with Norman Bezanson, Edmonton, May 2001, ALHI.

68 Kitaguchi interview.

69 Interviews with Neil Reimer, Edmonton, December 2004 and 25 October 2002, ALHI.

70 Interview with Neil Reimer for the Celanese Project, Edmonton, November 2007, and ALHI interview, 25 October 2002.

71 Interview with Doug and Eva Tomlinson, Edmonton, n.d., ALHI; Caragata, *Alberta Labour*, 141.

72 Tomlinsons interview.

73 Caragata, *Alberta Labour*, 139–40.

74 Reimer, Celanese Project interview.

75 Reimer, Celanese Project interview.

76 Neil Reimer, in *The Back Row*, at 22:36.

77 Ibid., 140; Finkel, *The Social Credit Phenomenon in Alberta*, 112–13.

78 Finkel, *The Social Credit Phenomenon in Alberta*, 108–9.

79 Ernest C. Manning, in *The Back Row* at 11:54.

80 On anti-communism in Canada in general, see Reg Whitaker and Gary Marcuse, *Cold War Canada: The Making of a National Insecurity State, 1945 to 1957*. On the specific implications of the anti-communist campaign for gays and lesbians, see Gary Kinsman and Patrizia Gentile, *The Canadian War on Queers*, especially 53–114.

81 Interview with Ben Swankey, Burnaby, BC, July 2003, ALHI.

82 Ibid.

83 Lenihan, *Patrick Lenihan*, 153–54.

84 Makowecki interview.

85 Ibid.

86 Swankey interview.

87 Interview with Jack Phillips, Vancouver, 2003, ALHI.

88 Tomlinsons interview.

89 Reimer interview, Edmonton, 7 November 2002.

90 Reimer interview, Edmonton, 25 October 2002. Reimer brought in several OWIU members from CIL to create the impression for Celanese workers, who were working in a plant too large for everyone to know everyone else, that the OWIU-supporting contingent was large.

91 Finkel, *The Social Credit Phenomenon in Alberta*, 113.

92 Interview (no. 3) with Dave Werlin, n.p., n.d., ALHI.

6 *The Boomers Become the Workers: Alberta, 1960–80*

1 Interview with Jack Hubler, Edmonton, n.d., Alberta Labour History Institute (hereafter ALHI).

2 "Calgary and Southern Alberta — Women," University of Calgary Applied History, 1997, http://www.ucalgary.ca/applied_history/tutor/calgary/FRAMEwomen.html.

3 Interview with Susan Keeley, Calgary, 11 September 2007, ALHI.

4 Alberta, Municipal Affairs, "Alberta's Official Population from 1960 to 2002," http://www.assembly.ab.ca/lao/library/egovdocs/alma/2002/136927.pdf.

5 Alberta Chambers of Commerce and Certified General Accountants Association of Alberta, *Vision 2020: Phase 1 Report: Demographic Impacts on Alberta's Provincial Budget — Fiscal Projections Through 2020.*

6 Statistics Canada, "Ethnic Diversity and Immigration."

7 R. Ogmundson and M. Doyle, "The Rise and Decline of Canadian Labour, 1960 to 2000: Elites, Power, Ethnicity and Gender," 417.

8 Ernest B. Akyeampong, "The Union Movement in Transition."

9 Gil Levine, "The Waffle and the Labour Movement."

10 John Richards and Larry Pratt, *Prairie Capitalism: Power and Influence in the New West*, chap. 7.

11 Alvin Finkel, *The Social Credit Phenomenon in Alberta*, 131.

12 Provincial Archives of Alberta, Alberta Federation of Labour fonds (hereafter AFL fonds), 77.54, item 455, "Press Release," 9 October 1968.

13 *Statutes of the Province of Alberta*, 1968, chap. 298, s. 26–43.

14 Interview with Bill Broad, *AUPE News*, 3 October 2006.

15 Jeffery Taylor, "Compulsory Arbitration and the Right to Strike: The Experience of Alberta's University Faculty."

16 Interview with Walter Watt, Edmonton, n.d., ALHI.

17 Interview with David William Potter, Edmonton, n.d., ALHI.

18 On the changing position of nurses in Canada in the postwar period and the roles that nurses played in achieving changes, see Kathryn McPherson, *Bedside Matters: The Transformation of Canadian Nursing 1900–1990.*

19 Interview with Barb Charles, Medicine Hat, 31 November 2008, ALHI.

20 The number of nurses on strike is reported in Human Resources and Skills Development Canada, "Orders Suspending the Right to Strike or to Lock Out."

21 Rebecca Priegert Coulter, "Alberta Nurses and the 'Illegal Strike of 1988,'" 408–10.

22 Human Resources and Skills Development Canada, "Orders Suspending the Right to Strike or to Lock Out."

23 Interview with Marg Ethier, Edmonton, September 2003, ALHI.

24 The number of teachers on strike when back-to-work orders were issued is reported in Human Resources and Skills Development Canada, "Orders Suspending the Right to Strike or to Lock Out." On the patterns of teachers' strikes in Alberta more generally, see Alberta Teachers' Association, Local 10, "Strikes by Alberta Teachers Since 1942,

" http://local10.teachers.ab.ca/SiteCollectionDocuments/Local10.teachers.ab.ca/PDF%20files/STRIKES.pdf.

25 Interview with Bernie Keeler, Edmonton, 6 May 2005, ALHI.

26 Interview with Gil Levine, Edmonton, n.d., ALHI; Patrick Lenihan, *Patrick Lenihan: From Irish Rebel to Founder of Canadian Public Sector Unionism.*

27 "Important Dates in CUPE's History," *CUPE*, 6 May 2003, http://cupe.ca/history/timelines.

28 Interview with Fred Pyke, Edmonton, n.d., ALHI.

29 Interview with "L.D.," n.d., ALHI.

30 "About CSU 52," Civic Service Union 52, http://www.csu52.org/about.htm.

31 "About Us," Non-Academic Staff Association, University of Alberta, 2004, http://www.nasa.ualberta.ca/aboutus.cfm.

32 Bryan D. Palmer, *Working-Class Experience: Rethinking the History of Canadian Labour, 1800–1991*, 321–22.

33 Interview with Andre Van Schaik, Edmonton, n.d., ALHI.

34 Richards and Pratt, *Prairie Capitalism*, 236, 242.

35 Finkel, *The Social Credit Phenomenon in Alberta*, 114–15; *Statutes of the Province of Alberta*, 1960, chap. 54.

36 The definition favoured by the AFL was "an International, National, or Provincial organization of employees, or a local branch chartered by and in good standing with such an organization." AFL fonds, 77.54, item 3, Alberta Federation of Labour, CLC, Fifth Convention, *Report of Proceedings*, Calgary, Alberta, 26–29 October, 1960.

37 AFL fonds, 77.54, item 3, "Memorandum from Alberta Federation of Labour," to Premier Manning and cabinet members, 25 January

1960.

38 Ibid.

39 AFL fonds, 77.54, item 455, "Press Release," 9 October 1968.

40 AFL fonds, 77.54, box 3, D. CCL 4 — Departments — (i) Political Education, "Report of Canadian Congress of Labour Legislative Conference," Saskatchewan Hotel, Regina, 5 August 1963.

41 Interview with Reg Basken, Edmonton, September 2003, ALHI.

42 Warren Caragata, *Alberta Labour: A Heritage Untold*, 144–45.

43 Interview with Doug and Eva Tomlinson, Edmonton, n.d., ALHI.

44 Caragata, *Alberta Labour*, 146.

45 Ibid.

46 AFL fonds, 77.54, item 13, Alberta Federation of Labour, "Report of Proceedings, 6th Convention," 18–20 October 1961.

47 AFL fonds, 77.54, item 15, Alberta Federation of Labour, "A Brief Regarding Board of Industrial Relations Garment Industry Order No. 17 (1962)," 14 January 1963.

48 AFL fonds, 77.54, item 455, "AFL Convention Resolutions 1968," Lethbridge.

49 AFL fonds, 83.29/314, *Labour Gazette*, June 1973.

50 AFL fonds, 83.29/314, "Alberta Federation of Labour Convention Proceedings, 1973."

51 John Maynard Keynes proposed that governments abandon notions of pro-cyclical spending, that is, expanding money supply and government programs during good times in the private sector and contracting them in bad times. Instead, he argued that by increasing spending and the money supply in times of recession, governments could

limit their impact. They could then balance their books by spending prudently once the economy revived.

52 Richards and Pratt, *Prairie Capitalism*, 236.

53 Jack F. Masson and Peter Blaikie, "Labour Politics in Alberta," 282.

54 Allan Chambers, *On the Line: The Struggles of Alberta's Packing Plant Workers*.

55 Interview with Betty Franklin, Hinton, 23 April 2005, ALHI.

56 Interview with Gerald Franklin, Hinton, 23 April 2005, ALHI.

57 Interview with Bill Flookes, Calgary, 2005, ALHI.

58 Interview with Anne Ozipko, Edmonton, n.d., ALHI.

59 Interview with Wally Shaw, Edmonton, August 2003, ALHI.

60 Bob Barnetson, *The Political Economy of Workplace Injury in Canada*, 38.

61 Ibid., 44.

62 Ibid., 61.

63 Ibid., 62.

64 Interview with Willa Gorman, Edmonton, October 2007, ALHI.

65 Interview with Noel Lapierre, Hinton, 2005, ALHI. Translated from the French by Alvin Finkel.

66 Interview with Wally Land, Hinton, 2005, ALHI.

67 The CLC convention in 1958 passed a resolution supporting the creation of a new political party, which it described as a "broadly based people's political movement which embraces the CCF, the labor movement, farm organizations, professional people and other liberally-minded persons interested in basic social reform and reconstruction through our parliamentary system of government"

(quoted in *The Western Socialist* 28, no. 223 [1961]: 12).

68 Robin Hunter, "Social Democracy in Alberta: From the CCF to the NDP," 74–75.

69 AFL fonds, 77.54, item 3, Alberta Federation of Labour, "Report of Proceedings, 5th Convention," 26–29 October 1960.

70 Olenka Melnyk, "Dreaming a New Jerusalem in the Land of Social Credit: The Struggles of the CCF in Alberta," 53–55.

71 AFL fonds, 77.54, item 14, Alberta Federation of Labour, "Report of Proceedings, 7th Convention," 31 October–2 November 1962.

72 Hunter, "Social Democracy," 81–82.

73 Tom Langford, "'So Dauntless in War': The Impact of Garth Turcott on Political Change in Alberta, 1966–71."

74 Masson and Blaikie, "Labour Politics," 278, 282 (quotation is from 282).

75 Larry Pratt, "Grant Notley: Politics as a Calling," 35.

76 For example, when the AFL sponsored a demonstration at the legislature in 1970 to protest the government's inaction on unemployment, the leadership were disappointed both by the lack of participation by locals and by the unemployed themselves. AFL fonds, 83.29/62, "Executive Board Report to the Fifteenth Convention, the Alberta Federation of Labour."

77 Alvin Finkel, "Trade Unions and the Welfare State in Canada, 1945–1990," 59–77.

78 AFL fonds, 77.54, item 3, "Memorandum from Alberta Federation of Labour," to Premier Manning and cabinet members, 25 January 1960.

79 AFL fonds, 77.54, item 461, "Alberta Federation of Labour Twelfth Convention," 1967.

80 Caragata, *Alberta Labour*, 145.

7 Alberta Labour in the 1980s

1 Alberta Federation of Labour (1983), President's Report to the 27th Annual Convention.

2 Interview with Lorraine Stallknecht, Fort McMurray, 20 October 2005, Alberta Labour History Institute (hereafter ALHI).

3 Alberta, *White Paper: Proposals for an Industrial and Science Strategy for Albertans, 1985 to 1990,* 30.

4 Ed Shaffer, "Oil, Class and Development in Alberta," 120.

5 Larry Pratt, "Energy: The Roots of National Policy."

6 Larry Pratt and Garth Stevenson, *Western Separatism: The Myths, Realities and Dangers,* 10.

7 Paul Stanway, "When Alberta Got Too Rich, Ottawa Unleashed the NEP," 228.

8 Pratt, "Energy," 26.

9 *Calgary Herald,* 19 November 1980.

10 *Calgary Herald,* 20 November 1980.

11 Kenneth Cox, "The Bust," 35–44.

12 G. Brent Gawne, Labour History Day Address, Alberta Labour History Institute, 2 August 2004.

13 Shaffer, "Oil, Class and Development," 121.

14 *Edmonton Sun,* 29 April 1982. Shell Canada President Bill Daniel set a 30 April deadline for federal participation in the project.

15 *Edmonton Journal,* 1 May 1982.

16 Frances W. Kaye, *Goodlands: A Meditation and History on the Great Plains,* 286.

17 David Cooper and Dean Neu, "The Politics of Debt and Deficit in Alberta," 165.

18 Melville L. McMillan and Allan A. Warrack, "One Track (Thinking) Toward Deficit Reduction," 136–37.

19 Sten Drugge, "The Alberta Tax Advantage: Myth and Reality," 183. See also Larry Pratt, "Energy, Regionalism and Canadian Nationalism, 1982–86," 188.

20 Auditor General of Alberta, *Report of the Auditor General for the Year Ended March 31, 1983,* 74.

21 David Langille, "The Business Council on National Issues and the Canadian State."

22 See Alvin Finkel, *Our Lives: Canada After 1945,* 134.

23 See the Fraser Institute website at http://www.fraserinstitute.org. See also Cliff Stainsby and John Malcolmson, "The Fraser Institute and the Government: Corporate Free Lunch."

24 Nick Fillmore, "The Right Stuff: Inside the National Citizens' Coalition," *This Magazine,* June/July 1986, 4–11.

25 Interview with Jane Sustrik, Edmonton, 19 April 2007, ALHI. The SNAA merged with the UNA in 1985.

26 Interview with Marg Ethier, Edmonton, September 2003, ALHI.

27 UFCW, *Collective Bargaining in Canada: A Human Right or Canadian Illusion,* 2.

28 David Flower, "Public Education as the Trojan Horse: The Alberta Case."

29 Bryan Palmer, *Working-Class Experience: Rethinking the History of Canadian Labour, 1800–1991,* 321.

30 Government of Alberta, Bill C-124, "Public Sector Compensation Restraint Act," 4 August 1982.

31 Alberta Federation of Labour, *Resolutions, 26th Annual Convention,* 1982, Resolution 57.

32 Government of Alberta, *Health Care Continuation Act,* a temporary emergency Act, S.A. 1982, c. 21.

33 Government of Alberta, Bill 44, *Labour Statutes Amendment Act,* 30 November 1983.

34 G. Brent Gawne, Labour History Day address, Alberta Labour History Institute, August 2004.

35 Interview with Bill Flookes, Calgary, 2005, ALHI.

36 Interview with Glen Taylor, Hinton, 2 May 2003, ALHI.

37 Interview with Peter Holbein, Edmonton, 11 November 1996, ALHI.

38 Interview with Mike Tamton, Calgary, 16 October 2007, ALHI.

39 Interview with Bill McGillivray, Medicine Hat, 3 June 2005, ALHI.

40 Interview with Sam Lee, Edmonton, 5 June 2004, ALHI.

41 Bulloch interview.

42 "Association History," Merit Contractors Association, http://www.meritalberta.com/dnn1/About/History.aspx.

43 Interview with John Ventura, Edmonton, 20 November 1998, ALHI.

44 Flookes interview.

45 Alberta Federation of Labour, "President's Report to the 28th Annual Convention," 1984.

46 Ibid.

47 Ibid.

48 Interview with Ken Mackenzie, 16 October 2010, ALHI. See also Winston Gereluk, "Hostile Terrain: Organizing the Energy Industry Has Been a Battle from the Beginning," 22 April 2011, Alberta Federation of Labour, http://www.afl.org/index.php/May-2011/hostile-terrain-organizing-the-energy-industry-has-been-a-battle-from-the-beginning.html.

49 Alberta Federation of Labour, "For Jobs and Recovery: Reduced Work Time — No Loss

49 in Pay," position paper for the 29th Annual Convention, 1985.

50 Interview with Mike Wilgus, Edmonton, 16 November 2005, ALHI.

51 Edmonton Social Planning Council, *Annual Report,* 1982.

52 Retrieved 10 April 2010 from http://www.afbna.ca/, but the information no longer appears on the page.

53 Alberta Federation of Labour, 27th Annual Convention, 1983, Resolution no. 5.

54 Alberta Federation of Labour, Executive Council Report to the 28th Annual Convention, 1984.

55 Interview with Tamara Kozlowska, Edmonton, 13 July 2010, ALHI.

56 Ibid.

57 Ibid.

58 Alberta Federation of Labour, Executive Council Report, 26th Annual Convention, 1982.

59 Palmer, *Working-Class Experience,* 400.

60 Wayne Roberts, *Cracking The Canadian Formula: The Making of the Energy and Chemical Workers Union,* 143.

61 Ibid., 201.

62 Ibid., 163.

63 Paul Bunner, "Crash, Layoff, Exodus, Repeat: Welcome to the Lost Decade," 6.

64 Andrew Nikiforuk, "The New Quarterback," 114–27.

65 Sheila Pratt, "The Grip Slips," 102–13.

66 Nikiforuk, "The New Quarterback," 120.

67 Edmonton Social Planning Council, *Annual Report,* 1985.

68 Alberta Union of Provincial Employees, Report of President, Sixth Annual Convention, 1981.

69 Alberta Union of Provincial Employees, Report of President, Tenth Annual Convention, 1985.

70 Alberta Union of Provincial Employees, Report of President, Eleventh Annual Convention, 1987.

71 Harry Dembicki, *Unemployment — Reaping the Costs.*

72 Reported in Marsha Mildon, *A Wealth of Voices: A History of the Edmonton Social Planning Council, 1940–90,* 184.

73 Winston Gereluk, *We Are the Friends of Medicare.*

74 Interview with Karen Olson, Edmonton, 22 March 2010, ALHI.

75 *Canada Health Act* (1984), c. 6, s. 1.

76 Interview with Dr. Richard Plain, Edmonton, 27 March 2010, ALHI.

77 Alberta Teachers' Association (ATA), Teaching in Alberta: History of Public Education, "The Controversial Eighties," 2010, http://www.teachers.ab.ca.

78 Alberta Federation of Labour, Executive Council Report, 30th Annual Convention, 1986.

79 Alberta Union of Provincial Employees, Report to the AUPE Provincial Executive Meeting, 8 February 1986.

80 UNA, *The First Twenty-five Years,* 11–12.

81 Alberta Federation of Labour, Executive Council Report, 30th Annual Convention, 1986.

82 Ibid.

83 B. Johnstone, "Interview: Alberta Labour at the Crossroads," *Athabasca University Magazine* Special Labour Supplement 10, no. 5 (May 1987): 19–20.

84 Terry McConnell and J'lyn Nye with Peter Pocklington, *I'd Trade Him Again: On Gretzky, Politics and the Pursuit of the Perfect Ideal,* 101–15.

85 Interview with John Ewasiw and Mary Ewasiw, Edmonton, 20 September 1998, ALHI.

86 Ventura interview.

87 Ibid.

88 David May, *The Battle of 66 Street: Pocklington vs. UFCW Local 280P,* 71–72.

89 Interview with Kip Connelly, Edmonton, 14 July 1999, ALHI.

90 May, *The Battle of 66 Street,* 73–83.

91 Allan Chambers, *On the Line: The Struggles of Alberta's Packing Plant Workers*; interview with Albert Johnson, Red Deer, 24 October 2010, ALHI.

92 Interview with Gord Christie, Calgary, 21 May 2008, ALHI.

93 Roberts, *Cracking the Canadian Formula,* 142.

94 Ibid., 143–44.

95 Ibid., 144.

96 Interview with Reg Basken, Edmonton, 20 May 2005, ALHI.

97 Alberta Labour Relations Code (hereafter ALRC), R.S.A. 2000, c. L-1. s. 90.

98 Interview with Lucien Royer, 1 August 2009, ALHI.

99 ALRC, s. 148(2)

100 Alberta Federation of Labour, Executive Council Report to the 33rd Annual Convention, 1989.

101 Alberta Federation of Labour, Report of the Occupational Health and Safety Committee to the 33rd Annual Convention, 1989.

102 Alberta Federation of Labour, Executive Council Report to the 31st Annual Convention, 1987.

103 WHMIS was implemented through coordinated federal, provincial, and territorial legislation, led by changes in 1986 to the

federal *Hazardous Products Act* and the related *Controlled Products Regulations*.

104 Roberts, *Cracking the Canadian Formula*, 219.

105 Comment recorded at meeting in Hinton, Alberta, organized by the Alberta Labour History Institute, 27 October 2005.

106 *Constitution Act*, 1982, enacted as Schedule B to the *Canada Act, 1982* (UK) 1982, c. 11, which came into force on 17 April 1982.

107 Hunter v. Southam Inc [1984] 2 SCR 145. Reconfirmed in Delisle v. Canada (Deputy Attorney General) [1999] 2 S.C.R. 989.

108 Canada, Special Joint Committee of the Senate and the House of Commons on the Constitution of Canada, No. 33 (9 January 1981), 69.

109 [1987] 1 S.C.R. 313 [Alberta Reference]. The other two cases were Public Service Alliance of Canada v. Canada [1987] 1 S.C.R. 424 [PSAC], and Retail, Wholesale and Department Store Union v. Saskatchewan [1987] 1 S.C.R. 460 [Saskatchewan Dairy Workers].

110 [1987] 1 S.C.R. 313 [Alberta Reference].

111 Ibid.

112 Ibid.

113 This jurisprudence would be radically reversed in 2007 in Health Services and Support, Facilities Subsector Bargaining Assn. v. British Columbia, 2007 SCC 27, [2007] 2 S.C.R. 391.

114 Dickason v. University of Alberta [1992] 2 S.C.R. 1103.

115 People's Food Commission, *The Land of Milk and Money: The National Report of the People's Food Commission*. See http://food securecanada.org/sites/foodsecurecanada. org/files/The%20Land%20of%20Milk%20 and%20Money.pdf.

116 Royer interview.

117 Alberta Federation of Labour, Executive Council Report to the 29th Annual Convention, 1985.

118 Royer interview.

119 Alberta Federation of Labour, President's Report, 28th Annual Convention, 1984.

120 Interview with Clarence Lacombe, Red Deer, 2 May 2003, ALHI.

121 Royer interview.

122 United Nations World Commission on Environment and Development, *Our Common Future*.

123 Laurie Adkin, "Ecology and Labour: Towards a New Socialist Paradigm," 214.

124 Brian Brennan, *Boondoggles, Bonanzas, and Other Alberta Stories*, 170–78.

125 Alberta Federation of Labour, Executive Council Report, 33rd Annual Convention, 1989.

126 United Nurses of Alberta, *The First Twenty-five Years*, 14–15.

127 Alberta Federation of Labour, "Report of the Alberta Workers' Rights Action Committee," 34th Annual Convention.

128 Interview with Guy Smith, Edmonton, 4 March 2009, ALHI. Guy Smith was elected president of AUPE later in 2009.

129 Lacombe interview.

130 Alberta Federation of Labour, Report of the Committee on Political Education, 27th Annual Convention, 1983.

131 George Melnyk, *Beyond Alienation: Political Essays on the West*, 54–57.

132 Alberta Labour History Institute community meeting, Medicine Hat, 20 January 2005.

133 Brennan, *Boondoggles*, 41–43.

134 Interview with Ted Grimm, Medicine Hat, 8 November 2005, ALHI.

135 McConnell, *I'd Trade Him Again*, 241–57.

136 See the official website of the Trilateral Commission at http://www.trilateral.org/.

137 Will Ferguson, *Why I Hate Canadians*, 112–13.

138 Alberta Federation of Labour, Executive Council Report, 30th Annual Convention, 1986.

139 Royer interview.

140 Alberta Federation of Labour, Executive Council Report, 30th Annual Convention, 1986.

141 Alberta Federation of Labour, Executive Council Report, 33rd Annual Convention, 1989.

8 *Revolution, Retrenchment, and the New Normal: The 1990s and Beyond*

1 Interview with Bill Climie, Edmonton, 4 September 2007, Alberta Labour History Institute (hereafter ALHI).

2 Interview with Ashley Grandy, Brooks, 1 November 2005, ALHI.

3 Dave Gower, "A Note on Canadian Unemployment Since 1921."

4 Patricia Evans, "Eroding Canadian Social Welfare: The Mulroney Legacy, 1984–1993."

5 The original term for bituminous oil production in northern Alberta was *tar sands*. In the 1990s, the energy industry, trying to polish its image, switched to the term *oil sands*.

6 Statistics Canada, *Labour Force Survey*, 1990 and 2010.

7 Statistics Canada, "Unionization," *Perspectives on Labour and Income* 18, no. 3 (Autumn 2006): 18–42.

8 Don Martin, *King Ralph: The Political Life and Success of Ralph Klein*.

9 Mark Lisac, *The Klein Revolution*.

10 Trevor Harrison, "The Reform-Ation of Alberta Politics."

11 Interview with Gord Christie, Calgary, 21 May 2008, ALHI.

12 *Edmonton Journal,* 19 May 1993.

13 Christie interview.

14 *Calgary Herald,* 14 June 1997.

15 Fred Engelmann, "Seniors: The End of a Dream."

16 Jonathan Murphy, "Workfare Will Make You Free: Ideology and Social Policy in Klein's Alberta."

17 For elimination of core government jobs, see Yonaton Reshef and Sandra Rastin, *Unions in the Time of Revolution: Government Restructuring in Alberta and Ontario,* 21. For nursing job cuts, see UNA, *United Nurses of Alberta: Twenty-Five Years of History,* http://www.una.ab.ca/about/historypages/UNA%20History%20-%201994.

18 *Edmonton Journal,* 25 November 1993.

19 *Edmonton Journal,* 25 February 1994.

20 *Edmonton Journal,* 17 November 1993.

21 Raymond Gariépy, "Journey Through a Turbulent Time," *ATA News,* 17 August 1999.

22 Reshef and Rastin, *Unions in the Time of Revolution,* 21, 69.

23 *Alberta Hansard,* 15 March 1994.

24 Greg Flanagan, *Sobering Result: The Alberta Liquor Retailing Industry Ten Years After Privatization.*

25 *Edmonton Journal,* 13 September 1993.

26 The case for privatization of these services is now seen as dubious. In 2009, Alberta had the highest alcohol prices in the country, and selection in most stores was reduced compared to the pre-privatization era. Government promises for greater convenience never materialized. This is evidence that once privatization occurs, it becomes almost impossible to reverse.

27 For example, see the Parkland Institute's studies on highway maintenance (Lisa Prescott, *Un-accountable: The Case of Highway Maintenance Privatization in Alberta*) and liquor retail (Flanagan, *Sobering Result*).

28 For example, the costs of building and operating hospitals via P3s versus building them as public works was demonstrated in Allyson M. Pollock, Jean Shaoul, and Neil Vickers, "Private Finance and 'Value for Money' in NHS Hospitals: a Policy in Search of a Rationale?"

29 Shannon Sampert, "King Ralph, the Ministry of Truth, and the Media in Alberta," 43. See also Simon Kiss, "Selling Government: The Evolution of Government Public Relations in Alberta."

30 Kevin Taft, in *Shredding the Public Interest: Ralph Klein and Twenty-Five Years of One-Party Government,* demolishes the arguments that the Klein government used to make the province appear to have no alternative but to make massive cuts in services in order to deal with its deficits and debts.

31 See Reshef and Rastin, *Unions in the Time of Revolution.* A similar thesis is presented by Jeff Taylor in "Labour in the Klein Revolution."

32 *Edmonton Journal,* 28 April 1994.

33 *Edmonton Journal,* 9 November 1994.

34 Natasha Mekhail, "Free Radicals: Edmontonians Who've Mobilized, Motivated and Raised A Little Hell," *See Magazine,* Edmonton, 1 May 2003; Rich Vivone, *Ralph Could Have Been a Superstar: Tales of the Klein Era,* 110–11.

35 Karen Hughes, Graham Lowe, and Allison McKinnon, "Public Attitudes Toward Budget Cuts in Alberta: Biting the Bullet or Feeling the Pain?"

36 *Edmonton Journal,* 30 April 1994.

37 Reshef and Rastin, *Unions in the Time of Revolution,* 73.

38 Interview with Jimmy Arthurs, Calgary, 30 April 2009, ALHI.

39 *Edmonton Journal,* 13 April 1994.

40 Interview with Cathy Jones, Canmore, 18 November 2005, ALHI.

41 Interview with Elisabeth Ballermann, Edmonton, 23 March 2010, ALHI.

42 Ibid.

43 *Alberta Hansard,* 7 March 1995.

44 See William Moore, "The Determinants and Effects of Right-to-Work Laws: A Review of Recent Literature." The Rand formula, developed by Supreme Court Justice Ivan Rand in a 1946 dispute between Ford Motor Company of Canada and the United Auto Workers, ordered an automatic check-off of union dues by employers in unionized workplaces. Rand argued that since all of the workers would benefit from the union's successes in achieving better wages and working conditions, none of them should be allowed to treat the union as a "free good." They all had to pay dues. While this was a benefit to unions, Rand also ruled that unions had to enforce collective agreements and prevent wildcat strikes, as well as pay steep fines when they failed to do so.

45 *Edmonton Journal,* 1 December 1995.

46 *Alberta Hansard,* 3 May 1995.

47 Interview with Doug O'Halloran, Calgary, November 2005, ALHI.

48 The government experimented with a new, collaborative consultation model that

theoretically gave more influence to labour but in practice entrenched standard power imbalances. See Jason Foster, "Talking Ourselves to Death."

49 Alberta Federation of Labour, "Double the Workplace Deaths, Half the Government Funding," press release, 26 April 2000, http://www.afl.org/index.php/Press-Release/doubletheworkplacedeathsh.html.

50 Eric Tucker, "Diverging Trends in Worker Health and Safety Protection and Participation in Canada, 1985–2000."

51 AFL, *Running to Stand Still.*

52 AFL, *The Horizon Project: Showdown over Labour Rights.*

53 See Judy Fudge, "Labour Is Not a Commodity: The Supreme Court of Canada and the Freedom of Association," and Eric Tucker, "The Constitutional Right to Bargain Collectively: The Ironies of Labour History in the Supreme Court of Canada."

54 Jason Foster, "State of the Unions: Trends in Unionization in Alberta."

55 The materials in this section are based on the author's observations as a participant and observer.

56 Statistics Canada, *Perspectives on Labour and Income,* various issues.

57 Interview with Myrna Wright, Pincher Creek, 4 March 2009, ALHI.

58 *Edmonton Journal,* 22 April 2002.

59 Reshef and Rastin, *Unions in the Time of Revolution.*

60 Interview with Doug O'Halloran, 13 March 2007, ALHI.

61 Ibid.

62 Interview with Andy Marshall, Cochrane, 18 November 2005, ALHI.

63 Ibid.

64 O'Halloran interview.

65 The 1997 Asia-Pacific Economic Cooperation summit in Vancouver offered an initial glimpse into the movement amassing in resistance to globalization. However, the scale and global media coverage of Seattle marked it as a key turning point.

66 Interview with Cindy McCallum Miller, Edmonton, 11 November 2008, ALHI.

67 See Dunmore v. Ontario (Attorney General), 2001 S.C.C. 94, (2001).

68 Alberta, Economic Development, *Alberta Wage and Salary Survey,* 2003.

69 Bob Barnetson, "The Regulatory Exclusion of Agricultural Workers in Alberta."

70 Alberta Federation of Labour, *Labour Economic Monitor,* Summer 2006.

71 Canada, Citizenship and Immigration Canada, "Facts and Figures 2009 — Immigration overview: Permanent and Temporary Residents."

72 Eric Reitsma, Alberta Director of Enforcement, speech to 7th Annual Alberta Health and Safety Conference, 21 October 2008.

73 See Jason Foster, "Making Temporary Permanent: The Silent Transformation of the Temporary Foreign Worker Program" (available from the author).

74 *Edmonton Journal,* 24 June 2005.

75 Bob Barnetson, "Regulation of Child and Adolescent Employment in Alberta."

76 Interview with Peter Jany by author, Brooks, 30 November 2005.

77 Interview with Archie Duckworth, Brooks, 10 October 2007, ALHI.

78 Jason Foster, "Conflict and Solidarity: How the Lakeside Workers Won Their Union."

79 Grandy interview.

80 O'Halloran interview.

81 Duckworth interview.

82 Joe Pok, "Oil Sands Development in Alberta and the Implications on Sulphur Supply," presentation to 2002 International Fertilizer Industry Association Annual Conference, Quebec City, 16 October 2002.

83 Andrew Nikiforuk, *Tar Sands: Dirty Oil and the Future of a Continent.*

84 Calgary's Molson plant was closed in 1994. By 2010, only one major brewery, the Edmonton Labatt plant, was operating in the province.

85 Catherine C. Cole, "The Levi's Era."

86 Ibid.

87 Climie interview.

88 Interview with Sam Cholak and Tom Enright, Edmonton, 24 November 2007, ALHI.

89 *Edmonton Journal,* 23 April 2008.

90 Statistics Canada, *Labour Force Survey,* 4 September 2009 and 5 December 2008.

91 The Alberta Alliance had, surprisingly, won a seat in the 2004 election and captured 8.7 percent of the vote, but had stalled, prompting the merger on the eve of the provincial election in 2008.

92 Anthony M. Sayers and David K. Stewart, "Is This the End of the Tory Dynasty? The Wildrose Alliance in Alberta Politics."

9 *Women, Labour, and the Labour Movement*

1 Linda Goyette and Carolina Jakeway Roemmich, *Edmonton: In Our Own Words,* 81.

2 Saskatchewan Union of Nurses and United Nurses of Alberta, *100 Years of Nursing on the Prairies.*

3 Brian Gale, "Challenging Times for Early Hospital Staff."

4 Sharon Richardson, "Frontier Health Care: Alberta's District and Municipal Nursing Services, 1919 to 1976," 2.

5 Ibid., 7.

6 Michael Palamarek, *A History of Women and Politics in Alberta, 1900–1988: A Report for Senator Martha P. Bielish*, 10.

7 Goyette and Roemmich, *Edmonton*, 187.

8 Interview with Emma Gilbertson, Edmonton, 22 June 2004, Alberta Labour History Institute (hereafter ALHI).

9 Goyette and Roemmich, *Edmonton*, 179. For a history of GWG, see Royal Alberta Museum, "Piece by Piece: The GWG Story."

10 Interview with Assunta Dotto, Edmonton, 20 April 2004, GWG Project interviews.

11 Interview with Helen Allen, Edmonton, 25 May 2004, ALHI.

12 Linda Kealey, *Enlisting Women for the Cause: Women, Labour and the Left in Canada, 1890–1920*, 63.

13 Hugh A. Dempsey, "Confessions of a Calgary Stenographer," 2.

14 Ruth A. Frager and Carmela Patrias, *Discounted Labour: Women Workers in Canada, 1870–1939*, 66.

15 Paul Phillips and Erin Phillips, *Women and Work: Inequality in the Canadian Labour Market*, 25.

16 Julie White, *Sisters and Solidarity: Women and Unions in Canada*, 18.

17 James H. Gray, *Red Lights on the Prairies*, x.

18 Judy Bedford, "Prostitution in Calgary, 1905–1914," 1.

19 Ibid., 2.

20 Ibid., 8.

21 Belinda Crowson, "Ethnic Diversity in Lethbridge's Red Light District, 1880s to 1944," 6.

22 Rebecca Coulter, "The Working Youth of Edmonton, 1921–1931," 143.

23 Elise Schneider, "Addressing the Issues: Two Women's Groups in Edmonton," 16.

24 White, *Sisters and Solidarity*, 34.

25 Phillips and Phillips, *Women and Work*, 28.

26 Ibid., 34.

27 Frager and Patrias, *Discounted Labour*, 24.

28 Paul Stanway, *The Albertans: From Settlement To Super Province, 1905–2005*, 66.

29 Frager and Patrias, *Discounted Labour*, 84.

30 Interview with Clare Botsford, Edmonton, 1 August 2001, ALHI.

31 Goyette and Roemmich, *Edmonton*, 250.

32 Ruth Pierson, "Women's Emancipation and the Recruitment of Women into the Canadian Labour Force in World War II," 150.

33 Linda Goyette and Carolina Jakeway Roemmich, *Edmonton: In Our Own Words*, 34.

34 Goyette and Roemmich, *Edmonton*, 250.

35 Alberta Teachers' Association, *Teaching in Alberta: History of Public Education*, "World War II," 2010, http://www.teachers.ab.ca.

36 Phillips and Phillips, *Women and Work*, 36.

37 Palamarek, *A History of Women*, 10, 87.

38 Ibid., 87; Vincent Ferrao, "Paid Work," 6.

39 Ferrao, "Paid Work," 6.

40 Interview with Anne Ozipko, Edmonton, 4 April 2003, ALHI.

41 Ferrao, "Paid Work," 9.

42 Andrew Jackson, "Gender Inequality and Precarious Work: Exploring the Impact of Unions Through the Gender and Work Database."

43 Ferrao, "Paid Work," 23.

44 Veronica Strong-Boag, "The Girl of the New Day: Canadian Working Women in the 1920s," *Labour/Le Travailleur* 4 (1979): 147; Parkland Institute, "Alberta's Wage Gap Highest in Canada," press release, 8 March 2010, http://parklandinstitute.ca/media/comments/albertas_wage_gap_highest_in_canada.

45 Parkland Institute, "Alberta's Wage Gap Highest in Canada."

46 Catherine C. Cole, "Union Activities at GWG."

47 Margaret Hobbs and Joan Sangster, eds., *The Woman Worker, 1926–1929*, 36.

48 Margaret E. McCallum, "Keeping Women in Their Place: The Minimum Wage in Canada, 1910–25," 31.

49 Kealey, *Enlisting Women*, 162.

50 Coulter, "The Working Youth," 89–90, outlines the Hudson's Bay Company's attempt to avoid paying the minimum wage by claiming that women workers required a three-year apprenticeship period.

51 Jim Selby, "Women Win 'Illegal' Restaurant Strike in Edmonton in 1935."

52 Kealey, *Enlisting Women*, 87.

53 Ibid., 80.

54 Ann Ball, "Organizing Working Women: The Women's Labor Leagues," 20.

55 Hobbs and Sangster, *The Woman Worker*, 72.

56 Patricia Roome, "Amelia Turner and Calgary Labour Women, 1919–1935," 432.

57 Ibid., 435.

58 Excerpt from testimony at the Mathers Commission meeting in Calgary, May 1919, quoted in Warren Caragata, *Alberta Labour: A Heritage Untold*, 84.

59 Roome, "Amelia Turner," 433.

60 Hobbs and Sangster, *The Woman Worker*, 39.

61 Jackson, "Gender Inequality," 15.

62 *Perspectives on Labour and Income,* July 2009, http://www.statcan.gc.ca/pub/75-001-x/topics-sujets/unionization-syndicalisation/unionization-syndicalisation-2009-eng.htm.

63 Jackson, "Gender Inequality," 13. The union wage premium is the union wage minus the non-union wage as a percentage of non-union wage.

64 Equal Pay Coalition, "Pay Equity and Unions."

65 McCallum Miller interview.

66 Julie Cool, *Wage Gap Between Women and Men,* Parliamentary Information and Research Service, Library of Parliament, 29 July 2010, http://www.parl.gc.ca/Content/LOP/Research Publications/2010-30-e.htm.

67 AFL Women's Committee, *Claiming Our Past . . . Shaping Our Future: A Collection of Essays in Celebration of the Alberta Federation of Labour's 75th Anniversary,* 54.

68 Interview with Susan Keeley, Calgary, 11 September 2007, ALHI.

69 White, *Sisters and Solidarity,* 66.

70 Equal Pay Coalition, "Other Provinces."

71 Jackson, "Gender Inequality," 6.

72 Edmonton Social Planning Council, *Maternity Leave in Alberta,* 1.

73 *Alberta Hansard,* 3 December 1973, 1359.

74 "Alberta Changes Parental Leave Rules," CBC News, 7 February 2001, http://www.cbc.ca/news/story/2001/02/07/clint070201.html.

75 Julie White, *Mail and Female: Women and the Canadian Union of Postal Workers,* 150–51.

76 Ibid., 152.

77 Ibid., 162.

78 Interview with Susan Parcels, Edmonton, n.d., ALHI.

79 Ibid.

80 Jackson, "Gender Inequality," 9.

81 AFL Women's Committee, *Claiming Our Past,* 13.

82 White, *Sisters and Solidarity,* 93.

83 Tom Langford, *Alberta's Day Care Controversy From 1908 to 2009 — and Beyond,* 314.

84 Interview with Clancy Teslenko, Calgary, 16 November 2005, ALHI.

85 White, *Sisters and Solidarity,* 122. Also see Debbie Field, "The Dilemma Facing Women's Committees," 293.

86 "AFL Women's Committee," Alberta Federation of Labour, 6 November 2009, http://www.afl.org/index.php/About-AFL/afl-womens-committee.html.

87 Adriane Paavo, "Union Workload: A Barrier to Women Surviving Labour-Movement Leadership."

88 AFL Women's Committee, *Claiming Our Past,* 122.

10 *Racialization and Work*

1 Immigration Branch Records, "Immigration to Western Canada," PR1977.0054/12, AFL files; NAC 7346 , W.V. Bennett, Agent at Omaha, Nebraska to W.D. Scott, Superintendent of Immigration, Ottawa, 17 January 1910, Library and Archives Canada.

2 Canada, House of Commons, *Debates,* 1 May 1947, 2646.

3 Immigration interviews are from Immigration Branch Records, PR1977.0054/12; NAC 7346.

4 Harley Dickinson and Terry Wotherspoon, "From Assimilation to Self-government: Towards a Political Economy of Canada's Aboriginal Policies," 411.

5 Brian Titley, "Red Deer Indian Industrial School: A Case Study in the History of Native Education," 57.

6 Dickinson and Wotherspoon, "From Assimilation to Self-government," 413.

7 Joan Sangster, *Transforming Labour: Women and Work in Postwar Canada,* 207.

8 The African-Canadian immigrants who came during the early twentieth century (1908–12) formed predominantly black communities such as Amber Valley, Junkins (Wildwood), and Keystone (Breton). Several family and community memoirs have been written about this period. Examples include Velma Carter and Wanda Leffler Akili, *The Windows of Our Memories,* 2 vols., and Gwen Hooks, *The Keystone Legacy: Reflections of a Black Pioneer.*

9 Canada, House of Commons, *Debates,* 22 March and 3 April 1911.

10 J. Brian Dawson, *Moon Cakes in Gold Mountain: From China to the Canadian Plains,* 44. Chinese workers came to British Columbia following the end of the Gold Rush in California. From British Columbia, many made their way to Alberta looking for employment during the building of the railroad.

11 Peter S. Li, "Chinese: Arrival and Settlement," *The Encyclopedia of Canada's Peoples,* http://www.multiculturalcanada.ca/Encyclopedia/A-Z/c10/3.

12 Lisa M. Jakobowski, *Immigration and the Legalization of Racism,* 16.

13 Ibid.

14 Library and Archives Canada, Cabinet Documents, 1911 Order-in-Council, 12 August 1911, paper C-117932.

15 Charles Irby Collection, Charles Irby interviews, interview with Willie Toles, Amber Valley, 1970, University of California, Santa Barbara Archives.

16 Excerpt from J. Brian Dawson and Nicholas Ting, *The Chinese Experience in Canada: Life Stories from the Late 1800s to Today,* http://www.abheritage.ca/pasttopresent/en/settlement/chinese_laundry_worker.html. See also John Jung, *Chinese Laundries: Tickets to Survival on Gold Mountain.*

17 "Dan Mah's Odyssey," *Edmonton Journal,* 12 March 1989.

18 For more on early African-Canadian communities in the Edmonton area, see Dan Cui and Jennifer R. Kelly, "'Our Negro Citizens': An Example of Everyday Citizenship Practices."

19 "Unable to gain the respect of their white co-workers, they [the Winnipeg railway porters] formed a union of their own in 1917, the Order of Sleeping Car Porters — the first black railway union in North America." Thus, ironically, western Canada, rather than the United States, was the site of the first North American segregated union. Sarah-Jane Mathieu, "North of the Colour Line: Sleeping Car Porters and the Battle Against Jim Crow on Canadian Rails, 1880–1920," 5. Also of interest is Agnes Calliste's "Sleeping Car Porters: An Ethnically Submerged Split Labour Market."

20 Interview with Daniel Lafierre conducted by Leander Lane, 2009 Racialization, Immigration, Citizenship (henceforth RIC). RIC is a SSHRC-funded research project to develop an understanding of the formation of African-Canadian communities in Alberta from 1900 to the 1960s. Leander Lane is a descendant of the early black settlers in Alberta and Saskatchewan.

21 Jaswinder Gudwara, *Splintered Dreams: Sikhs in Southern Alberta.* After World War I,

a small number of Sikhs began to farm in southern Alberta (near Lethbridge) and to begin to create a viable community that would include the few students who attended the University of Alberta. These South Asians remained few in number throughout the 1920s, when the only legal new arrivals were the wives and children of those already here.

22 Proceeding of the Ninth Annual Convention of District 18, United Mineworkers of Alberta, February 1912. "Conventions, 1910–73," M-2239-151, Glenbow Archives.

23 Lily Cho, *Eating Chinese: Culture on the Menu in Small Town Canada.*

24 Emily Murphy, *The Black Candle.*

25 *Edmonton Bulletin,* 12 July 1924.

26 Dawson and Ting, *Chinese Experience.*

27 See "Calgary's Chinese Community," a website developed by the Applied History Research Group at the University of Calgary, at http://www.ucalgary.ca/applied_history/tutor/calgary/chinese.html. Comments taken from Brian Dawson and Nicholas Ting's research.

28 Interview with Tets Kitaguchi, Alberta Labour History Institute (hereafter ALHI) "Road Show," 2005, 4.

29 Joan Sangster, *Transforming Labour,* 213.

30 Ross Lambertson, "'The Dresden Story': Racism, Human Rights, and the Jewish Labour Committee of Canada," 8. On labour's attitudes to immigration before World War II, see David Goutor, *Guarding the Gates: The Canadian Labour Movement and Immigration, 1872–1934,* and David Goutor, "'Standing by Our Principles': The Trades and Labor Congress of Canada and Immigration, 1933–1939."

31 Provincial Archives of Alberta, Alberta Federation of Labour fonds (hereafter AFL fonds), 77.54, item 3, AFL, CLC, Fifth Convention, Report of Proceedings, Calgary, Alberta, 26–29 October 1960.

32 Sangster, *Transforming Labour,* 58.

33 Notes from a speech given by Dick Bellamy to the Unitarian Fellowship in the 1950s, R12294-0-2-E, Library and Archives Canada.

34 James S. Walker, "African Canadians: Economic Life," *Encyclopedia of Canada's Peoples,* http://multiculturalcanada.ca/Encyclopedia/A-Z/a16/4.

35 Interview with Hazel Proctor, Calgary 2001, ALHI.

36 Notes from a speech given by Dick Bellamy.

37 Ross Lambertson, "The Dresden Story."

38 AFL fonds, 77.54, AFL, CLC, Fifth Convention, Report of Proceedings, Calgary, Alberta, 26–29 October, 1960: "Resolutions to Be Presented to the Convention of the AFL, Calgary, October 26, 1960."

39 On Manning, see Alvin Finkel, *The Social Credit Phenomenon in Alberta,* 106, 136–38.

40 Province of Alberta, *Human Rights Act,* 1966, Part 1, Code of Conduct, Discrimination and Prohibition, 214.

41 PAA, AFL fonds, 77.54, 12/380, Department of Labour, Human Rights Branch, *Human Concern* 1, no. 1 (1969): 3.

42 "Minister's Message," in *Human Concern* 1, no. 1 (1969), published by the Human Rights Branch, Department of Labour, 1.

43 PAA, AFL fonds, 77.54/10/307, E.A Mitchell, Assistant Executive Secretary, AFL, to Dr. Seth Fisher, president, AHRA, 28 October 1968. The association had a membership base that included academics, trade unionists, and

other concerned citizens. For more information on the origins of the organization, see "Canada's Human Rights History — Alberta," http://www.historyofrights.com/ngo/alberta.html.

44 PAA, AFL fonds, 77.54, 10/307, Donald MacDonald, secretary-treasurer, CLC, to all Canadian Labour Congress Chartered and Affiliated Unions, Labour Councils, and Federations, 28 July 1967.

45 Interview with female participant, Edmonton, 2009, RIC.

46 See Dan Cui and Jennifer Kelly, "A Historical Exploration of Internationally Educated Teachers: Jamaica Teachers in 1960s Alberta."

47 Interview with oil worker from Trinidad, Edmonton, 2007, RIC.

48 Interview with female participant, Edmonton, 2008, RIC.

49 Ethnic Survey, interview with Norma Ellis, RCT B75-32, Glenbow Archives.

50 Ironically, those who entered Alberta during its boom period and found work were also those most likely to overlook language and vocational training. They were affected most harshly by the recession in the 1980s.

51 A.H. Richmond, *Comparative Studies in the Economic Adaptation of Immigrants in Canada.*

52 According to the Statistics Canada website: "Counts of the visible minority population in Canada were first produced using 1981 Census data. Data on the visible minority population in 1981, 1986, and 1991 were derived primarily from responses to the ethnic origin question, in conjunction with responses from the place of birth and mother tongue questions." Statistics Canada, "Visible Minority Population and Population Group Reference Guide — Historical Comparability," last modified 5 April 2011, http://www12.statcan.ca/census-recensement/2006/ref/rp-guides/visible_minority-minorities_visibles-eng.cfm.

53 The *Employment Equity Act* (S.C. 1995 c. 44) defines visible minorities as "persons, other than Aboriginal peoples, who are non-Caucasian in race or non-white in colour." Categories in the visible minority population variable include Chinese, South Asian, Black, Filipino, Latin American, Southeast Asian, Arab, West Asian, Korean, and Japanese.

54 As part of its Project 2012 joint research project with the AFL, the Alberta Labour History Institute has produced an excellent booklet, *Fighting Back: The 1995 Calgary Laundry Workers Strike,* by Allan Chambers.

55 Various interviews with Lakeside Packers workers, Brooks, ALHI.

56 Interview with Peter Jany, ALHI "Road Show," 2005.

57 Interviews with Lakeside Packers workers.

58 Ibid.

59 *Edmonton Journal*, 21 July 2010. See also "Natives Bore Brunt of Job Losses," Aspect: BC's Community-Based Trainers, 14 May 2010, http://www.aspect.bc.ca/resources/natives-bore-brunt-job-losses-canada-statscan-study-shows.

60 Report of the AFL Workers of Colour and Aboriginal Workers Committee, AFL Convention, 2009.

61 Interviews with members of Workers of Colour and Aboriginal Workers Committee, Edmonton, 2010, RIC.

62 Ibid.

63 G.S. Basran and L. Zong, "Devaluation of Foreign Credentials as Perceived by Visible Minority Professional Immigrants."

64 Shibao Guo and Per Andersson, *Non/Recognition of Foreign Credentials for Immigrant Professionals in Canada and Sweden: A Comparative Analysis.*

65 Christopher Worswick, "C.D. Howe Insitute Backgrounder No. 81: Immigrants' Declining Earnings: Reasons and Remedies," 5.

66 Paula Simons, "Harper's Head Tax Apology Rights Canada's Racist Past," *Edmonton Journal*, 24 June 2006.

67 Trish Audette, "Foreign Worker Program Reassessed," *Edmonton Journal*, 21 July 2010.

68 *Edmonton Journal*, 18 July 2011.

69 Citizenship and Immigration Canada, "Facts and Figures 2009 — Immigration Overview: Permanent and Temporary Residents," http://www.cic.gc.ca/english/resources/statistics/facts2009/temporary/03.asp.

70 Ibid.

71 Sarah Carter, "Britishness, 'Foreignness,' Women and Land in Western Canada, 1890s–1920s," 43.

Conclusion: A History to Build Upon

1 Bob Barnetson, *The Political Economy of Workplace Injury in Canada*, 11.

2 Alberta Employment and Immigration, "Occupational Fatalities and Fatality Rates, Alberta 1999 to 2008," http://employment.alberta.ca/documents/WHS/WHS-Pub_memorandum_WHS_analysis_2008_statistics.

3 Information from Alberta Federation of Labour, 23 July 2010, posted on Injured Workers All Across Canada, in response to "WCB Provides Generous Bonuses to Its

Employees by Reducing Benefits to Injured Workers," 21 July 2010, http://iwocac.ning.com/group/albertaabusedinjuredworkers/forum/topics/wcb-provides-generous-bonuses?xg_source=activity.

4 Andrew Sharpe and Jill Hardt, "Five Deaths a Day: Workplace Fatalities in Canada, 1993–2005" (Ottawa: Centre for the Study of Living Standards, 2006), http://www.csls.ca/reports/csls2006-04.pdf.

5 Alberta Federation of Labour, *AFL in the News*, "Alberta Vows to End Abuse of WCB Rebates: Lukaszuk Sets Out New Guidelines," 3 June 2011, http://www.afl.org/index.php/AFL-in-the-News/alberta-vows-to-end-abuse-of-wcb-rebates-lukaszuk-sets-out-new-guidelines.html.

6 Information from Alberta Federation of Labour, 23 July 2010, posted on Injured Workers All Across Canada, in response to "WCB Provides Generous Bonuses to Its Employees by Reducing Benefits to Injured Workers," 21 July 2010. Material on the carnage against workers in Alberta has also been compiled by Mike Hruska of Edmonton for the Alberta Democratic Renewal Project. This material, which draws on government reports, ILO documents, and newspaper reports, is unpublished but is available from the Democratic Renewal Project, http://

drproject.ca/contact.php. For a national perspective, see Bob Barnetson, *The Political Economy of Workplace Injury.*

7 Human Resources and Skills Development Canada, calculations based on Statistics Canada, *Labour Force Historical Review 2009* (Table 078), Ottawa: Statistics Canada, 2010 (Cat. No. 71F0004XVB).

8 These are the figures claimed by these organizations on their websites rather than independently verified figures.

9 Greg Flanagan, "Not Just About Money: Provincial Budgets and Political Ideology," 122.

10 The effects of the cutbacks on the poor are demonstrated in the essays in Gordon Laxer and Trevor Harrison, ed., *The Trojan Horse: Alberta and the Future of Canada,* and in Trevor Harrison, ed., *The Return of the Trojan Horse: Alberta and the New World (Dis)Order.*

11 Kevin Taft, presentation to Join Together Alberta gathering, Edmonton, 23 June 2011. Figures available at "Public Spending Stayed Flat as Economy Grew," on Taft's MLA website, 12 July 2011, http://www.edmontonriverview.com/er/.

12 Alberta, Financial Investment and Planning Advisory Commission, *Report and Recommendations* (2008), 22.

13 Brendan Ross, "Norway's $525 Billion Sovereign Wealth Fund Essentially an Index Fund," *Seeking Alpha,* 26 May 2011, http://seeking alpha.com/article/271957-norway-s-525-billion-sovereign-wealth-fund-essentially-an-index-fund.

14 G.L. Clark and A.H.B. Monk, "The Legitimacy and Governance of Norway's Sovereign Wealth Fund: The Ethics of Global Investments."

15 Asbjørn Wahl, "Building Progressive Alliances."

16 Richard Wilkinson and Kate Pickett, *The Spirit Level: Why More Equal Societies Almost Always Do Better.*

17 A. Lee, "Best Places to Live in the World — 2010," ZoomHealth, 4 November 2010, http://www.zoomhealth.net/BestPlacestoLiveIntheWorld-2010.html.

18 The Alberta Federation of Labour's most recent commentary on its political objectives and the strategy that it hopes to follow to pursue them is found in Alberta Federation of Labour, 2011 Convention, Political Action Paper, 1 May 2011.

19 Interview with Enoch Williams conducted by David Millar, 1969. MG 31, vol. 2, file: Enoch Williams, Library and Archives Canada, pp. 10–11, as reproduced on the website of sociology professor Tom Langford, University of Calgary, http://people.ucalgary.ca/~langford/.

BIBLIOGRAPHY

Archival Sources

Alberta Federation of Labour, Convention Reports
Alberta Hansard
Alberta Union of Provincial Employees, Presidential Reports
Canada, House of Commons, *Debates*
City of Edmonton Archives
    Correspondence of Chief of Police A.J. Shute and Mayor
        Dan Knott, 1932
    Glenbow Archives
    District 18, United Mineworkers Workers of Alberta,
        "Conventions, 1910–73"
    Library and Archives Canada
    Immigration Branch Records
    Notes from a speech given by Dick Bellamy to the Unitarian
        Fellowship in the 1950s, R12294-0-2-E
    "Second World War Service Files: Canadian Armed Forces
        War Dead," http://www.collectionscanada.gc.ca/
        databases/war-dead/index-e.html
    Provincial Archives of Alberta
    Alberta Federation of Labour fonds
    Alfred Farmilo Papers

Government Publications

Akyeampong, Ernest B. "The Union Movement in Transition."
    Statistics Canada, *Perspectives on Labour and Income* 16,
    no. 3 (2004): 5–13.

Alberta. Economic Development. *Alberta Wage and Salary
    Survey,* 2003.
Alberta. Financial Investment and Planning Advisory Commis-
    sion. *Report and Recommendations,* 2008.
Alberta. Health and Safety Conference, 21 October 2008.
Alberta. Municipal Affairs. "Alberta's Official Population from
    1960 to 2002." http://www.assembly.ab.ca/lao/library/
    egovdocs/alma/2002/136927.pdf.
Alberta. *White Paper: Proposals for an Industrial and Science
    Strategy for Albertans, 1985 to 1990.* Edmonton: Queen's
    Printer, 1981.
Canada. Census and Statistics Office. *Canada Year Book,*
    1916–17, 1922–23.
Canada. Citizenship and Immigration Canada. "Facts and
    Figures 2009 — Immigration Overview: Permanent and
    Temporary Residents." 2010. http://www.cic.gc.ca/english/
    resources/statistics/facts2009/index.asp.
Canada. Department of Labour. *Labour Gazette.*
Canada. Human Resources and Skills Development Canada.
    "Orders Suspending the Right to Strike or to Lock Out."
    Industrial Relations Legislation in Canada. Last modified
    12 March 2010. http://www.hrsdc.gc.ca/eng/labour/
    labour_law/ind_rel/index.shtml.
Canada. *Report of the Royal Commission on Aboriginal
    Peoples.* Vol. 1, *Looking Forward, Looking Back.* Ottawa:
    Indian and Northern Affairs, 1996.
Canada. Royal Commission on Industrial Relations. *Official
    Report of Proceedings.* National Industrial Conference of

Dominion and Provincial Governments with Representative Employers and Labour Men on the Subjects of Industrial Relations and Labour Laws. Ottawa: King's Printer, 1919.

Canada. Special Joint Committee of the Senate and the House of Commons on the Constitution of Canada, January 1981.

Census of Canada, 1901. Vol. 3, *Manufactures.* Ottawa: King's Printer, 1905.

Census of Canada, 1911. Vol. 1, *Areas and Population by Provinces, Districts and Subdistricts.* Ottawa: King's Printer, 1913.

Census of Population and Agriculture of the Northwest Provinces: Manitoba, Saskatchewan, Alberta, 1906. Ottawa: King's Printer, 1907.

Census of the Three Provisional Districts of the North-West Territories: 1884–5. Ottawa: Maclean, Roger and Co., 1886.

Edmonton Social Planning Council. *Annual Reports.* Edmonton: Edmonton Social Planning Council.

———. *Maternity Leave in Alberta.* Edmonton: Options for Women, 1975.

Ferrao, Vincent. "Paid Work." In *Women in Canada: A Gender-Based Statistical Report,* 6th ed., by Vincent Ferrao and Cara Williams. Ottawa: Statistics Canada, 2010. Catalogue No. 89-503-XIE. http://www.statcan.gc.ca/bsolc/olc-cel/olc-cel?catno=89-503-X&lang=eng.

Statistics Canada. "Ethnic Diversity and Immigration." Last modified 7 September 2007. http://www41.statcan.gc.ca/2007/30000/ceb30000_000-eng.htm.

Statistics Canada. *Labour Force Historical Review 2009.*

Statistics Canada. *Perspectives on Labour and Income,* various issues.

Statutes of the Province of Alberta.

Interviews

Alberta Labour History Institute

Allan, Helen, Edmonton, 25 May 2004

Arthurs, Jimmy, Calgary, 30 April 2009

Avramenko, Joyce, Edmonton, August 2003

Ballerman, Elisabeth, Edmonton, 23 March 2010

Basken, Reg, Edmonton, September 2003, 20 May 2005

Beauchamp, Vicky, Edmonton, 1998

Bezanson, Norman, Edmonton, May 2001

Botsford, Clare, Edmonton, 1 August 2001.

Bulloch, Brad, Calgary, 16 November 2005

Canmore nurses, n.d.

Charles, Barb, Medicine Hat, 31 November 2008

Cholak, Sam, Edmonton, 24 November 2007

Christie, Gordon, Calgary, 21 May 2008

Climie, Bill, Edmonton, 4 September 2007

Connelly, Kip, Edmonton, 14 July 1999

Duckworth, Archie, Brooks, 10 October 2007

Enright, Tom, Edmonton, 24 November 2007

Ethier, Marg, Edmonton, September 2003

Fagnan, Len, Calgary, 24 April 2009

Flookes, Bill, Calgary, 2005

Fontana, Al, Coleman, 10 November 2005

Fontana, Emma, Coleman, 10 November 2005

Fontana, Veronica, Coleman, 10 November 2005

Franklin, Betty, Hinton, 23 April 2005

Franklin, Gerald, Hinton, 23 April 2005

Gawne, G. Grant, Edmonton (Alberta Labour History Day Address to ALHI), August 2004

Gilbertson, Emma, Edmonton, 22 June 2004

Grandy, Ashley, Brooks, 1 November 2005

Grigel, Pauline, Coleman, 10 November 2005.

Grimm, Ted, Medicine Hat, 8 November 2005

Holbein, Peter, Edmonton, 11 November 1996

Hubler, Jack, Edmonton, n.d.

Jany, Peter, Brooks, 1 November 2005

Johnson, Albert, Red Deer, 24 October 2010

Jones, Cathy, Canmore, 18 November 2005

Keeler, Bernie, Edmonton, 6 May 2005

Keeley, Susan, Calgary, 11 September 2007

Kinnear, John, Coleman, 10 November 2005

Kitaguchi, Tets, Hinton, 28 October 2005

Kozlowska, Tamara, Edmonton, 13 July 2010

"L.D.," n.d.

Lacombe, Clarence, Red Deer, 2 May 2003

Land, Wally, Hinton, 2005

Lapierre, Noel, Hinton, 2005

Lee, Sam, Edmonton, 5 June 2004

Levine, Gil, Edmonton, n.d.

Mackenzie, Ken, 16 October 2010

Makowecki, Walter, Edmonton, n.d.

Marconi, John, Coleman, 10 November 2005

Marshall, Andy, Cochrane, 18 November 2005

McCallum Miller, Cindy, Edmonton, 11 November 2008

McGillivray, Bill, Medicine Hat, 3 June 2005

McGregor, Frank, Edmonton, n.d.

Mitchell, Eugene, Edmonton, 29 October 2002

O'Halloran, Doug, Calgary, November 2005

Olson, Karen, Edmonton, 22 March 2010

Ozipko, Anne, Edmonton, 4 April 2003

Panek, Alain, Coleman, 10 November 2005

Parcels, Susan, Edmonton, n.d.

Phillips, Jack, Vancouver, 2003

Plain, Dr. Richard, Edmonton, 27 March 2010

Potter, David William, Edmonton, n.d.

Poulton, Glen, Coleman, 10 November 2005

Proctor, Hazel, Calgary, 2001

Pyke, Fred, Edmonton, n.d.

Reimer, Neil, Edmonton, 25 October 2002, December 2004,
     November 2007

Root, Emily, Coleman, 10 November 2005

Root, Ray, Coleman, 10 November 2005

Royer, Lucien, Edmonton, 1 August 2009

Shaw, Wally, Edmonton, August 2003

Skura, Bill, Coleman, 10 November 2005

Smith, Guy, Edmonton, 4 March 2009

Stallknecht, Lorraine, Fort McMurray, 20 October 2005

Sustrik, Jane, Edmonton, 19 April 2007

Swankey, Ben, Burnaby, British Columbia, July 2003

Taje, Gary, Coleman, 10 November 2005

Tamton, Mike, Calgary, 16 October 2007

Taylor, Glen, Hinton, 2 May 2003

Tomlinson, Doug, Edmonton, n.d.

Tomlinson, Eva, Edmonton, n.d.

Van Schaik, Andre, Edmonton, n.d.

Ventura, John, Edmonton, 20 November 1998

Watt, Walter, Edmonton, n.d.

Werlin, Dave, n.p., n.d.

Wiley, Lorne, Medicine Hat, n.d.

Wiley, Agnes, Medicine Hat, n.d.

Wilgus, Mike, Edmonton, 16 November 2005

Wright, Myrna, Pincher Creek, 4 March 2009

Yeliga, John, Coleman, 10 November 2005

Alberta Union of Public Employees (*AUPE News*)
Broad, Bill, 3 October 2006

Charles Irby Collection
Toles, Willie, Amber Valley, 1970

Glenbow Archives
Ellis, Norma, n.d.

GWG Project (Catherine C. Cole)
Dotto, Assunta, Edmonton, 20 April 2004

Engley, Nellie, Edmonton, 21 April 2004

Hook, Norah, Edmonton, 12 May 2004

Kosma, Elizabeth, Edmonton, 12 May 2004

Romanuk, Mary, Edmonton, 2 April 2004

David Millar
Williams, Enoch, Library and Archives Canada, 1969.

Racialization, Immigration, Citizenship (RIC)
Female participant, Edmonton, 2009

Lafierre, Daniel, Edmonton, 2009

Members, Workers of Colour and Aboriginal Workers
     Committee, Edmonton, 2010

Oil worker from Trinidad, Edmonton, 2007

Professional worker, Edmonton, 2008

Newspapers and Magazines

Alberta Labour News
ATA News
British Medical Journal
Calgary Herald
Canadian Dimension
Crag and Canyon
Edmonton Bulletin
Edmonton Journal
Edmonton Sun
Lethbridge Daily Herald
Our Times
See Magazine
Victoria Colonist
Western Socialist

Secondary Sources

Abel, Kerry. *Drum Songs: Glimpses of Dene History*. Montreal and Kingston: McGill-Queen's University Press, 2005.

Adkin, Laurie. "Ecology and Labour: Towards a New Socialist Paradigm." In *Labour Worldwide in the Era of Globalization: Alternative Union Models in the New World Order*, edited by Ronaldo Munck and Peter Waterman, 199–217. New York: St. Martin's Press, 1999.

AFL (Alberta Federation of Labour). *The Horizon Project: Showdown over Labour Rights*. Edmonton: AFL, 2004.

———. *Running to Stand Still*. Edmonton: AFL, 2003.

AFL (Alberta Federation of Labour) Women's Committee. *Claiming Our Past . . . Shaping Our Future: A Collection of Essays in Celebration of the Alberta Federation of Labour's 75th Anniversary*. Edmonton: AFL Women's Committee, 1987.

Ahaja, Ravi. "State Formation and 'Famine Policy' in Early Colonial South India." *Indian Economic and Social History Review* 39, no. 4 (2002): 351–60.

Alberta Chambers of Commerce and Certified General Accountants Association of Alberta. *Vision 2020: Phase 1 Report: Demographic Impacts on Alberta's Provincial Budget — Fiscal Projections Through 2020*. September 2004. http://www.abchamber.ca/Portals/0/ACCResources/Vision2020/Phase1.pdf.

Avery, Donald. *"Dangerous Foreigners": European Immigrant Workers and Labour Radicalism in Canada, 1896–1932*. Toronto: McClelland and Stewart, 1979.

———. *Reluctant Host: Canada's Response to Immigrant Workers, 1896–1994*. Toronto: McClelland and Stewart, 1995.

Babcock, Robert H. *Gompers in Canada: A Study in American Continentalism Before the First World War*. Toronto: University of Toronto Press, 1974.

The Back Row: Labour's Cold War in Alberta. Videorecording. Produced and directed by Don Bouzek. Edmonton: D. Active Productions, 2005.

Baker, William M. "The Miners and the Mounties: The Royal North West Mounted Police and the 1906 Lethbridge Strike." *Labour/Le Travail* 27 (Spring 1991): 55–96.

Ball, Ann. "Organizing Working Women: The Women's Labor Leagues." *Canadian Dimension* 21, no. 8 (1988): 19–20.

Barnetson, Bob. *The Political Economy of Workplace Injury in Canada*. Edmonton: Athabasca University Press, 2010.

———. "Regulation of Child and Adolescent Employment in Alberta." *Just Labour* 13 (Spring 2009): 29–47.

———. "The Regulatory Exclusion of Agricultural Workers in Alberta." *Just Labour* 14 (Autumn 2009): 50–74.

Barrie, Doreen. *The Other Alberta: Decoding a Political Enigma*. Regina: Canadian Plains Research Centre, 2006.

Baskerville, Peter, and Eric W. Sager. *Unwilling Idlers: The Urban Unemployed and Their Families in Late Victorian Canada*. Toronto: University of Toronto Press, 1998.

Basran, G.S., and L. Zong. "Devaluation of Foreign Credentials as Perceived by Visible Minority Professional Immigrants." *Canadian Ethnic Studies* 30, no. 3 (1998): 6–18.

Bastien, Betty. *Blackfoot Ways of Knowing: The World of the Siksikaitsitapi*. Calgary: University of Calgary Press, 2004.

Beal, Bob, and Rod Macleod. *Prairie Fire: The 1885 Northwest Rebellion*. Edmonton: Hurtig, 1984.

Bedford, Judy. "Prostitution in Calgary, 1905–1914." *Alberta History* 29, no. 2 (1981): 1–11.

Bercuson, David Jay. *Confrontation at Winnipeg: Labour, Industrial Relations, and the General Strike*. Montreal and Kingston: McGill-Queen's University Press, 1974.

———. *Fools and Wise Men: The Rise and Fall of the One Big Union*. Toronto: McGraw Hill Ryerson, 1978.

———. "Labour Radicalism and the Western Industrial Frontier: 1897–1919." *Canadian Historical Review* 58, no. 2 (1977): 154–75.

Betke, Carl F. "The United Farmers of Alberta, 1921–1935." In *Society and Politics in Alberta: Research Papers*, edited by Carlo Caldarola, 14–31. Toronto: Methuen, 1979.

Boothe, Paul Michael, and Heather Edwards, eds. *Eric J. Hanson's Financial History of Alberta, 1905–1950*. Calgary: University of Calgary Press, 2003.

Bradbury, Bettina. "Gender at Work at Home: Family Decisions, The Labour Market, and Girls' Contributions to the Family Economy." In *Canadian Family History: Selected Readings*, edited by Bettina Bradbury, 177–98. Toronto: Irwin, 2000.

———. "Pigs, Cows and Boarders: Non-Wage Forms of Survival Among Montreal Families, 1861–91." *Labour/Le Travail* 14 (Fall 1984): 9–46.

———. *Working Families: Age, Gender and Daily Survival in Industrializing Montreal*. Toronto: University of Toronto Press, 1993.

Bradwin, Edmund W. *The Bunkhouse Man: A Study of the Work and Pay in the Camps of Canada, 1903–1914*. New York: Columbia University Press, 1928.

Braudel, Fernand. *The Mediterranean and the Mediterranean World in the Age of Philip II*, vol. 1. New York: Harper Torchbooks, 1975.

Breen, David. "1947: The Making of Modern Alberta." In *Alberta Formed, Alberta Transformed*, vol. 2, edited by Michael Payne, Donald Wetherell, and Catherine Cavanaugh, 539–64. Edmonton: University of Alberta Press; Calgary: University of Calgary Press, 2005.

Brennan, Brian. *Boondoggles, Bonanzas, and Other Alberta Stories*. Calgary: Fifth House, 2003.

Brennan, William, ed. *Building the Cooperative Commonwealth: Essays on the Democratic Socialist Tradition in Canada*. Regina: Canadian Plains Research Centre, 1985.

Bright, David. *The Limits of Labour: Class Formation and the Labour Movement in Calgary, 1883–1929*. Vancouver: University of British Columbia Press, 1998.

———. "The State, the Unemployed, and the Communist Party in Calgary, 1930–5." *Canadian Historical Review* 78, no. 4 (1997): 537–65.

———. "'We Are All Kin': Reconsidering Labour and Class in Calgary, 1919." *Labour/Le Travail* 29 (Spring 1992): 59–80.

Brink, Jack. *Imagining Head-Smashed-In: Aboriginal Buffalo Hunting on the Northern Plains*. Edmonton: Athabasca University Press, 2008.

Brown, Jennifer S.H. *Strangers in Blood: Fur Trade Company Families in Indian Country*. Vancouver: University of British Columbia Press, 1980.

Brown, Jennifer, and Robert Brightman, eds. *The Orders of the Dreamed*. Winnipeg: Manitoba Studies in Native History, 1988.

Buckley, Karen. *Danger, Death and Disaster in the Crowsnest Pass Mines, 1902–1928*. Calgary: University of Calgary Press, 2004.

Bullen, John. "Hidden Workers: Child Labour and the Family Economy in Late Nineteenth-Century Urban Ontario." *Labour/Le Travail* 18 (Fall 1986): 163–87.

Bumsted, J.M. *The Winnipeg General Strike of 1919: An Illustrated Guide*. Winnipeg: Watson and Dwyer, 1994.

Bunner, Paul. "Crash, Layoff, Exodus, Repeat: Welcome to the Lost Decade." In *Alberta in the Twentieth Century*, vol. 12, edited by Paul Bunner, 4–11. Edmonton: United Western Communications, 2003.

Burke, Helen. *The People and the Poor Law in Nineteenth Century Ireland*. Littlehampton, UK: Women's Education Bureau, 1987.

Burley, Edith. *Servants of the Honourable Company: Work, Discipline, and Conflict in the Hudson's Bay Company, 1770–1879*. Toronto: Oxford University Press, 1997.

Calliste, Agnes. "Sleeping Car Porters: An Ethnically Submerged Split Labour Market." *Canadian Ethnic Studies* 19, no. 1 (1987): 1–20.

Campbell, Peter. "Understanding the Dictatorship of the Proletariat: The Canadian Left and the Moment of Socialist Possibility in 1919." *Labour/Le Travail* 64 (Fall 2009): 51–73.

Canadian Pacific Railway. *Women's Work in Western Canada: A Sequel to "Words from the Women of Western Canada."* Winnipeg: Canadian Pacific Railway, 1906.

Caragata, Warren. *Alberta Labour: A Heritage Untold*. Toronto: James Lorimer, 1979.

Cardinal, Harold, and Walter Hildebrandt. *Treaty Elders of Saskatchewan: Our Dream Is That Our Peoples Will One Day Be Clearly Recognized as Nations*. Calgary: University of Calgary Press, 2000.

Carter, Sarah. "Britishness, 'Foreignness,' Women and Land in Western Canada, 1890s–1920s." *Humanities Research* 13, no. 1 (2006): 43–60.

———. *The Importance of Being Monogamous: Marriage and Nation Building in Western Canada to 1915*. Edmonton: University of Alberta Press and Athabasca University Press, 2008.

———. *Lost Harvests: Prairie Indian Reserve Farmers and Government Policy*. Montreal and Kingston: McGill-Queen's University Press, 1990.

Carter, Velma, and Wanda Leffler Akili. *The Windows of Our Memories,* vols. 1 and 2. St. Albert: B.C.R. Society of Alberta, 1988.

Chambers, Allan. *Fighting Back: The 1995 Calgary Laundry Workers Strike*. Edmonton: Project 2012, 2011.

———. *On the Line: The Struggles of Alberta's Packing Plant Workers*. Edmonton: Project 2012, 2010.

———. *Spirit of the Crowsnest: The Story of Unions in the Coal Towns of the Crowsnest Pass*. Edmonton: Project 2012, 2009.

Cho, Lily. *Eating Chinese: Culture on the Menu in Small Town Canada*. Toronto: University of Toronto Press, 2010.

Chodos, Robert. *The CPR: A Century of Corporate Welfare.* Toronto: James Lorimer, 1973.

Clark, G.L., and A.H.B. Monk. "The Legitimacy and Governance of Norway's Sovereign Wealth Fund: The Ethics of Global Investment." *Environment and Planning A* 42, no. 7 (2010): 1723–38.

Cole, Catherine C. "The Levi's Era." *Piece by Piece: The GWG Story*. virtualmuseum.ca. 2010. http://www.royalalberta museum.ca/virtualExhibit/GWG/en/history/thelevisera. html.

———. "Union Activities at GWG." *Piece by Piece: The GWG Story*. virtualmuseum.ca. 2010. http://www.royalalberta museum.ca/virtualExhibit/GWG/en/labourforce/local120. html.

Conley, James R. "Frontier Labourers, Crafts in Crisis and the Western Labour Revolt: The Case of Vancouver, 1900–1919." *Labour/Le Travail* 23 (Spring 1989): 9–37.

Cook, Tim. *At the Sharp End: Canadians Fighting the Great War, 1914–1916*. Toronto: Viking Canada, 2007.

Cooper, David, and Dean Neu. "The Politics of Debt and Deficit in Alberta." In *The Trojan Horse: Alberta and the Future of Canada*, edited by Gordon Laxer and Trevor Harrison, 163–81. Montreal: Black Rose Books, 1995.

Copp, Terry, and Bill McAndrew. *Battle Exhaustion: Soldiers and Psychiatrists in the Canadian Army, 1939–1945*. Montreal and Kingston: McGill-Queen's University Press, 1990.

Coulter, Rebecca Priegert. "Alberta Nurses and the 'Illegal Strike of 1988.'" In *Canadian Working-Class History: Selected Readings*, 3rd ed., edited by Laurel Sefton MacDowell and Ian Radforth, 407–17. Toronto: Canadian Scholars' Press, 2006.

———. "The Working Youth of Edmonton, 1921–1931." In *Childhood and Family in Canadian History*, edited by Joy Parr, 143–59. Toronto: McClelland and Stewart, 1982.

Cox, Kenneth. "The Bust." In *Running on Empty: Alberta After the Boom,* edited by Andrew Nikiforuk, Sheila Pratt, and Don Wanagas, 35–44. Edmonton: NeWest Press, 1987.

Craven, Paul. *An Impartial Umpire: Industrial Relations and the Canadian State, 1900–1921.* Toronto: University of Toronto Press, 1980.

Crosby, Alfred W. *Ecological Imperialism: The Biological Expansion of Europe, 900–1900.* Cambridge: Cambridge University Press, 1991.

Crowe, Keith J. *A History of the Original Peoples of Northern Canada.* Montreal and Kingston: McGill-Queen's University Press, 1991.

Crowson, Belinda. "Ethnic Diversity in Lethbridge's Red Light District, 1880s to 1944." *Alberta History* 57, no. 4 (2009): 2–9.

Cui, Dan, and Jennifer R. Kelly. "A Historical Exploration of Internationally Educated Teachers: Jamaica Teachers in 1960s Alberta." *Canadian Journal of Educational Administration and Policy* 100 (February 2010).

———. "'Our Negro Citizens': An Example of Everyday Citizenship Practices." In *The West and Beyond: New Perspectives on an Imagined Region,* edited by Alvin Finkel, Sarah Carter, and Peter Fortna, 253–77. Edmonton: Athabasca University Press, 2010.

D'Altroy, Terence N. *The Incas (People of America).* Oxford: Wiley-Blackwell, 2002.

Danysk, Cecilia. *Hired Hands: Labour and the Development of Prairie Agriculture, 1880–1930.* Toronto: McClelland and Stewart, 1995.

Dawson, J. Brian. *Moon Cakes in Gold Mountain: From China to the Canadian Plains.* Calgary: Detselig, 1991.

Dawson, J. Brian, and Nicholas Ting. *The Chinese Experience in Canada: Life Stories from the Late 1800s to Today.* http://www.abheritage.ca/pasttopresent/en/settlement/chinese_laundry_worker.html

Delâge, Denys, and Helen Hornbeck Tanner. "The Ojibwa-Jesuit Debate at Walpole Island, 1844." *Ethnohistory* 41, no. 2 (1994): 295–321.

Dembicki, Harry. *Unemployment — Reaping the Costs.* Edmonton: Edmonton Social Planning Council, 1986.

Dempsey, Hugh A. "Confessions of a Calgary Stenographer." *Alberta History* 6, no. 2 (1988): 1–15.

Den Otter, A.A. *Civilizing the West: The Galts and the Development of Western Canada.* Edmonton: University of Alberta Press, 1982.

Dick, Lyle. "The Seven Oaks Incident and the Construction of a Historical Tradition, 1816 to 1970." *Journal of the Canadian Historical Association,* n.s., 2 (1991): 91–113.

Dickason, Olive Patricia, with David T. McNab. *Canada's First Nations: A History of Founding Peoples from Earliest Times.* 4th ed. Toronto: Oxford University Press, 2009.

Dickinson, Harley, and Terry Wotherspoon. "From Assimilation to Self-Government: Towards a Political Economy of Canada's Aboriginal Policies." In *Deconstructing a Nation: Immigration, Multiculturalism and Racism in '90s Canada,* edited by Vic Satzevich, 405–21. Halifax: Fernwood, 1992.

Drugge, Sten. "The Alberta Tax Advantage: Myth and Reality." In *The Trojan Horse: Alberta and the Future of Canada,* edited by Gordon Laxer and Trevor Harrison, 182–94. Montreal: Black Rose Books, 1995.

Engelmann, Fred. "Seniors: The End of a Dream." In *The Trojan Horse: Alberta and the Future of Canada,* edited by Gordon Laxer and Trevor Harrison, 286–300. Montreal: Black Rose Books, 1995.

Equal Pay Coalition, "Other Provinces." http://www.equalpaycoalition.org/other-provinces/.

———. "Pay Equity and Unions." http://epc.grassriots.org/pay-equity-and-unions/.

Erickson, Lesley. "Constructed and Contested Truths: Aboriginal Suicide, Law, and Colonialism in the Canadian West, 1823–1927." *Canadian Historical Review* 86, no. 4 (2005): 595–618.

Evans, Patricia. "Eroding Canadian Social Welfare: The Mulroney Legacy, 1984–1993." *Social Policy and Administration* 28, no. 2 (1994): 107–19.

Ferguson, Will. *Why I Hate Canadians.* Vancouver: Douglas and McIntyre, 1997.

Field, Debbie. "The Dilemma Facing Women's Committees." In *Union Sisters: Women in the Labour Movement,* edited by Linda Briskin and Lynda Yanz, 293–303. Toronto: Women's Educational Press, 1983.

Finch, David, and Gordon Jaremko. *Fields of Fire: An Illustrated History of Canadian Petroleum*. Calgary: Detselig, 1994.

Finkel, Alvin. "The Cold War, Alberta Labour, and the Social Credit Regime," *Labour/Le Travail* 21 (Spring 1988): 123–52.

———. "Obscure Origins: The Confused Early History of the CCF." In *Building the Cooperative Commonwealth: Essays on the Democratic Socialist Tradition in Canada*, edited by J. William Brennan, 99–122. Regina: Canadian Plains Research Centre, 1985.

———. *Our Lives: Canada After 1945*. Toronto: James Lorimer, 1997.

———. "The Rise and Fall of the Labour Party in Alberta, 1917–42." *Labour/Le Travail* 16 (Fall 1985): 61–96.

———. *The Social Credit Phenomenon in Alberta*. Toronto: University of Toronto Press, 1989.

———. *Social Policy and Practice in Canada: A History*. Waterloo: Wilfred Laurier University Press, 2006.

———. "Trade Unions and the Welfare State in Canada, 1945–1990." in *Labour Gains, Labour Pains: Fifty Years of PC 1003*, edited by Cy Gonick, Paul Phillips, and Jessie Vorst, 59–77. Halifax: Fernwood, 1995.

Flanagan, Greg. "Not Just About Money: Provincial Budgets and Political Ideology." In *The Return of the Trojan Horse: Alberta and the New World (Dis)Order*, edited by Trevor Harrison, 116–35. Montreal: Black Rose Books, 2005.

———. *Sobering Result: The Alberta Liquor Retailing Industry Ten Years After Privatization*. Edmonton: Parkland Institute, 2003.

Flower, David. "Public Education as the Trojan Horse: The Alberta Case." *Our Schools, Our Selves* 13, no. 2 (2004): 89–94.

Foner, Philip S. *The History of the Labor Movement in the United States*. Vol. 4, *The Industrial Workers of the World, 1905–1917*. 2nd ed. New York: International Publishers, 1973.

Foster, Jason. "Conflict and Solidarity: How the Lakeside Workers Won Their Union." *Our Times* 24, no. 6 (December 2005–January 2006): 28–35.

———. "Making Temporary Permanent: The Silent Transformation of the Temporary Foreign Worker Program." Paper presented at the annual conference of the Canadian Industrial Relations Association, Fredericton, NB, June 2011.

———. "State of the Unions: Trends in Unionization in Alberta." Presentation to Organizing Institute Planning Committee, Edmonton, 27 June 2001.

———. "Talking Ourselves to Death." *Labor Studies Journal* 36, no. 2 (2010): 288–306.

Foster, John. "The Country Born in the Red River Settlement." PhD diss., University of Manitoba, 1973.

Fowke, Vernon. *The National Policy and the Wheat Economy*. Toronto: University of Toronto Press, 1957.

Frager, Ruth A., and Carmela Patrias. *Discounted Labour: Women Workers in Canada, 1870–1939*. Toronto: University of Toronto Press, 2005.

Friesen, Gerald. *The Canadian Prairies: A History*. Toronto: University of Toronto Press, 1987.

Fudge, Judy. "Labour Is Not a Commodity: The Supreme Court of Canada and the Freedom of Association." *Saskatchewan Law Review* 67, no. 2 (2004): 25–52.

Fudge, Judy, and Eric Tucker, *Labour Before the Law: The Regulation of Workers' Collective Action in Canada, 1900–1948*. Toronto: University of Toronto Press, 2004.

Gale, Brian. "Challenging Times for Early Hospital Staff." *Esplanade Archives Times,* Spring 2007, 11–13. http://esplanade.ca/media/public_files/documents/2011/Sep/22/ArchivesTimes2007.pdf.

Galeano, Eduardo. *Open Veins of Latin America: Five Centuries of the Pillage of a Continent*. Translated by Cedric Belfrage. New York: Monthly Review Press, 1997.

Geddes, Elaine. "Alberta Labour Legislation Under the Social Credit Government: 1935–1947." LL.M. thesis, University of Alberta, 1990.

Gereluk, Winston. *We Are the Friends of Medicare*. Edmonton: Friends of Medicare, 2010.

Goutor, David. *Guarding the Gates: The Canadian Labour Movement and Immigration, 1872–1934*. Vancouver: University of British Columbia Press, 2007.

———. "'Standing By Our Principles': The Trades and Labor Congress of Canada and Immigration, 1933–1939." *Just Labour* 11 (Autumn 2007): 55–65.

Gower, Dave. "A Note on Canadian Unemployment Since 1921." *Perspectives on Labour and Income* 4, no. 3 (1992).

Goyette, Linda, and Carolina Jakeway Roemmich. *Edmonton: In Our Own Words*. Edmonton: University of Alberta Press, 2004.

Graves, Donald E. *South Albertans: A Canadian Regiment at War*. Toronto: Robin Bass Studio, 1998.

Gray, James H. *Red Lights on the Prairies*. Toronto: Macmillan, 1971.

Gudwara, Jaswinder. *Splintered Dreams: Sikhs in Southern Alberta*. Calgary: Arusha International Development Resource Centre, 1985.

Guo, Shibao, and Per Andersson. *Non/Recognition of Foreign Credentials for Immigrant Professionals in Canada and Sweden: A Comparative Analysis*. Edmonton: Prairie Centre of Excellence for Research in Immigration and Integration, 2005–2006. Working Paper Series No. WP04-05, http://pcerii.metropolis.net/WorkingPapers/WP04-05.pdf.

Hall, C.T. *Redcliff's Fifty Golden Years: The Early History of Redcliff*. Redcliff, 1962.

Hall, Greg. *Harvest Wobblies: The Industrial Workers of the World and Agricultural Laborers in the American West, 1905–1930*. Corvallis: Oregon State University Press, 2001.

Harrison, Trevor. "The Reform-Ation of Alberta Politics." In *The Trojan Horse: Alberta and the Future of Canada*, edited by Gordon Laxer and Trevor Harrison, 47–60. Montreal: Black Rose Books, 1995.

———, ed. *The Return of the Trojan Horse: Alberta and the New World (Dis)Order*. Montreal: Black Rose Books, 2005.

Haycock, Ronald. *Sam Hughes: The Public Career of a Controversial Canadian, 1885–1916*. Waterloo: Wilfrid Laurier University Press, 1986.

Hildebrandt, Walter. *Views from Fort Battleford: Constructed Visions of an Anglo-Canadian West*. Edmonton: Athabasca University Press; Regina: Canadian Plains Research Centre, 2008.

Hiller, Harry H. *Second Promised Land: Migration to Alberta and the Transformation of Canadian Society*. Montreal and Kingston: McGill-Queen's University Press, 2009.

Hobbs, Margaret, and Joan Sangster, eds. *The Woman Worker, 1926–1929*. St. John's, NL: Canadian Committee on Labour History, 1999.

Hooks, Gwen. *The Keystone Legacy: Reflections of a Black Pioneer*. Edmonton: Brightest Pebble, 1998.

Hughes, Karen, Graham Lowe, and Allison McKinnon. "Public Attitudes Toward Budget Cuts in Alberta: Biting the Bullet or Feeling the Pain?" *Canadian Public Policy* 22, no. 3 (1996): 268–84.

Humphries, Jane. "Enclosures, Common Rights, and Women: The Proletarianization of Families in the Late Eighteenth and Early Nineteenth Centuries." *Journal of Economic History* 50, no. 1 (1990): 17–42.

Hungry-Wolf, Adolf. *The Blackfoot Papers*. Skookumchuk, BC: Good Medicine Cultural Foundation, 2006.

Hunter, Robin. "Social Democracy in Alberta: From the CCF to the NDP." In *Socialism and Democracy in Alberta: Essays in Honour of Grant Notley*, edited by Larry Pratt, 57–87. Edmonton: NeWest Press, 1986.

Indian Brotherhood of the Northwest Territories and Métis Association of the Northwest Territories. "Past and Present Land-Use by Slavey Indians of the Mackenzie District." Summary of Evidence of Michael Asch, Department of Anthropology, University of Alberta, before the Mackenzie Valley Pipeline Inquiry, Yellowknife, NWT, April 1976.

Jackson, Andrew. "Gender Inequality and Precarious Work: Exploring the Impact of Unions Through the Gender and Work Database." Paper presented at the Gender and Work: Knowledge Production in Practice conference, York University, 1–2 October 2004. http://www.genderwork.ca/conference/Jackson_edited_final.pdf.

Jakobowski, Lisa M. *Immigration and the Legalization of Racism.* Halifax: Fernwood, 1997.

Jamieson, Stuart Marshall. *Times of Trouble: Labour Unrest and Industrial Conflict in Canada, 1900–66.* Ottawa: Information Canada, 1968.

Johnstone, B. "Interview: Alberta Labour at the Crossroads." *Athabasca University Magazine* Special Labour Supplement 10, no. 5 (May 1987): 19–20.

Judd, Carol M. "Native Labour and Social Stratification in the Hudson's Bay Company's Northern Department, 1770–1870." *Canadian Review of Sociology and Anthropology* 17 (November 1980): 305–14.

Jung, John. *Chinese Laundries: Tickets to Survival on Gold Mountain.* Cypress, CA: Yin and Yang Press, 2007.

Kaye, Frances W. *Goodlands: A Meditation and History on the Great Plains.* Edmonton: Athabasca University Press, 2011.

Kealey, Gregory S. "State Repression of Labour and the Left in Canada, 1914–1920: The Impact of the First World War." *Canadian Historical Review* 73, no. 3 (1992): 281–314.

Kealey, Gregory S., and Douglas Cruikshank. "Strikes in Canada, 1891–1950." In Gregory S. Kealey, *Workers and Canadian History,* 345–418. Montreal and Kingston: McGill-Queen's University Press, 1995.

Kealey, Linda. *Enlisting Women for the Cause: Women, Labour and the Left in Canada, 1890–1920.* Toronto: University of Toronto Press, 1998.

Kinsman, Gary, and Patrizia Gentile. *The Canadian War on Queers.* Toronto: University of Toronto Press, 2010.

Kiss, Simon. "Selling Government: The Evolution of Government Public Relations in Alberta." PhD diss., Queen's University, Kingston, 2008.

Kramer, Reinhold, and Tom Mitchell. *When the State Trembled: How A.J. Andrews and the Citizens' Committee Broke the Winnipeg General Strike.* Toronto: University of Toronto Press, 2010.

Krasowski, Sheldon. "Mediating Treaties: Eyewitness Accounts of Treaties Between the Crown and Indigenous Peoples, 1871–1876." PhD diss., University of Regina, 2011.

Laliberte, Ron, and Vic Satzewich. "Native Migrant Labour in the Southern Alberta Sugar-Beet Industry: Coercion and Paternalism in the Recruitment of Labour." *Canadian Review of Sociology/Revue canadienne de sociologie* 36, no. 1 (1999): 65–86.

Lambertson, Ross. "'The Dresden Story': Racism, Human Rights, and the Jewish Labour Committee of Canada." *Labour/LeTravail* 47 (Spring 2001): 43–82.

Lambrecht, Kirk N. *The Administration of Dominion Lands, 1870–1930.* Regina: Canadian Plains Research Centre, 1991.

Langford, Tom. *Alberta's Day Care Controversy From 1908 to 2009 — and Beyond.* Edmonton: Athabasca University Press, 2011.

———. "An Alternate Vision of Community: Crowsnest Miners and Their Local Unions During the 1940s and 1950s." In *A World Apart: The Crowsnest Communities of Alberta and British Columbia,* edited by Wayne Norton and Tom Langford, 147–57. Kamloops: Plateau Press, 2002.

———. "'So Dauntless in War': The Impact of Garth Turcott on Political Change in Alberta, 1966–71." *Prairie Forum* 34, no. 2 (2009): 405–34.

Langford, Tom, and Chris Frazer. "The Cold War and Working-Class Politics in the Coal Mining Communities of the Crowsnest Pass, 1945–1958." *Labour/Le Travail* 49 (Spring 2002): 43–81.

Langille, David. "The Business Council on National Issues and the Canadian State." *Studies in Political Economy* 24 (Autumn 1987): 41–85.

Laxer, Gordon, and Trevor Harrison, eds. *Trojan Horse: Alberta and the Future of Canada.* Montreal: Black Rose Books, 1995.

Leier, Mark. *Red Flags and Red Tape.* Toronto: University of Toronto Press, 1995.

———. *Where the Fraser River Flows: The Industrial Workers of the World in British Columbia.* Vancouver: New Star Books, 1990.

Lenihan, Patrick. *Patrick Lenihan: From Irish Rebel to Founder of Canadian Public Sector Unionism*, edited by Gilbert Levine and with an introduction by Lorne Brown. St. John's: Canadian Committee on Labour History, 1998.

Levine, Gil. "The Waffle and the Labour Movement." *Studies in Political Economy* 33 (Autumn 1990): 185–92.

Lisac, Mark. *The Klein Revolution*. Edmonton: NeWest Press, 1995.

Logan, H.A. "Rise and Decline of the One Big Union in Canada." *Journal of Political Economy* 36, no. 2 (1928): 240–79.

Lukasiewicz, Krystyna. "Polish Community in the Crowsnest Pass." *Alberta History* 36, no. 4 (1988): 1–10.

Lux, Maureen K. *Medicine That Walks: Disease, Medicine, and Canadian Plains Native People, 1880–1940*. Toronto: University of Toronto Press, 2001.

Maclachlan, Ian. *Kill and Chill: Restructuring Canada's Beef Commodity Chain*. Toronto: University of Toronto Press, 2001.

Macleod, R.C. *The North-West Mounted Police and Law Enforcement, 1873–1905*. Toronto: University of Toronto Press, 1976.

Mandelbaum, David G. *The Plains Cree: An Ethnographic, Historical and Comparative Study*. Regina: Canadian Plains Research Centre, 1979.

Mardiros, Anthony. *The Life of a Prairie Radical: William Irvine*. Toronto: James Lorimer, 1979.

Martin, Don. *King Ralph: The Political Life and Success of Ralph Klein*. Toronto: Key Porter Books, 2002.

Masson, Jack F., and Peter Blaikie. "Labour Politics in Alberta." In *Society and Politics in Alberta*, edited by Carlo Caldarola, 271–86. Agincourt, ON: Methuen, 1979.

Mathieu, Sarah-Jane. "North of the Colour Line: Sleeping Car Porters and the Battle Against Jim Crow on Canadian Rails, 1880–1920." *Labour/Le Travail* 47 (Spring 2001): 9–41.

May, David. *The Battle of 66 Street: Pocklington vs. UFCW Local 280P*. Edmonton: Duval House, 1996.

McCallum, Margaret E. "Keeping Women in Their Place: The Minimum Wage in Canada, 1910–25." *Labour/Le Travail* 17 (Spring 1986): 29–56.

McConnell, Terry, and J'lyn Nye, with Peter Pocklington. *I'd Trade Him Again: On Gretzky, Politics and the Pursuit of the Perfect Ideal*. Toronto: Fenn, 2009.

McCormack, A. Ross. *Reformers, Rebels and Revolutionaries: The Western Canadian Radical Movement, 1899–1919*. Toronto: University of Toronto Press, 1977.

McCrorie, Aaron. "PC 1003: Labour, Capital, and the State." *Socialist Studies* 10 (1995): 15–32.

McKay, Ian. *Reasoning Otherwise: Leftists and the People's Enlightenment in Canada, 1880–1920*. Toronto: Between the Lines, 2008.

McKenzie-Brown, Peter, Gordon Jaremko, and David Finch. *The Great Oil Age: The Petroleum Industry in Canada*. Calgary: Detselig, 1993.

McMillan, Melville, and Allan A. Warrack. "One Track (Thinking) Toward Deficit Reduction." In *The Trojan Horse: Alberta and the Future of Canada*, edited by Gordon Laxer and Trevor Harrison, 134–62. Montreal: Black Rose Books, 1995.

McPherson, Kathryn. *Bedside Matters: The Transformation of Canadian Nursing, 1900–1990*. Toronto: Oxford University Press, 1996.

Melnyk, George. *Beyond Alienation: Political Essays on the West*. Calgary: Detselig, 1993.

Melnyk, Olenka. "Dreaming a New Jerusalem in the Land of Social Credit: The Struggles of the CCF in Alberta." In *Socialism and Democracy in Alberta: Essays in Honour of Grant Notley*, edited by Larry Pratt, 40–56. Edmonton: NeWest Press, 1986.

Mildon, Marsha. *A Wealth of Voices: A History of the Edmonton Social Planning Council, 1940–90*. Edmonton: Edmonton Social Planning Council, 1990.

Miller, J.R. *Shingwauk's Vision: A History of Native Residential Schools*. Toronto: University of Toronto Press, 1996.

Milloy, John. *A National Crime: The Canadian Government and the Residential School System — 1879 to 1986*. Winnipeg: University of Manitoba Press, 1999.

Mitchell, Tom, and James Naylor. "The Prairies: In the Eye of the Storm." In *The Workers' Revolt in Canada, 1917–1925*, edited by Craig Heron, 176–230. Toronto: University of Toronto Press, 1998.

Monod, David. "The End of Agrarianism: The Fight for Farm Parity in Alberta and Saskatchewan, 1935–48." *Labour/Le Travail* 16 (Fall 1985): 117–43.

Montgomery, David. *The Fall of the House of Labor: The Workplace, the State, and American Labor Activism, 1865–1925.* New York: Cambridge University Press, 1987.

Moore, William. "The Determinants and Effects of Right to Work Laws: A Review of Recent Literature." *Journal of Labor Research* 19, no. 3 (1998): 445–69.

Morton, Desmond. *When Your Number's Up: The Canadian Soldier in the First World War.* Toronto: Random House of Canada, 1993.

Morton, W.L. *The Progressive Party in Canada.* Toronto: University of Toronto Press, 1950.

Mowat, Farley. *And No Birds Sang.* Toronto: Key Porter Books, 2003. First published 1979.

Murphy, Emily. *The Black Candle.* Toronto: Thomas Allen, 1922.

Murphy, Jonathan. "Workfare Will Make You Free: Ideology and Social Policy in Klein's Alberta." In *The Trojan Horse: Alberta and the Future of Canada*, edited by Gordon Laxer and Trevor Harrison, 315–31. Montreal: Black Rose Books, 1995.

Naylor, R.T. "The Canadian State, the Accumulation of Capital, and the Great War." *Journal of Canadian Studies* 16, nos. 3–4 (1981): 26–55.

———, ed. *Dominion of Debt: Centre, Periphery and the International Economic Order.* Montreal: Black Rose Books, 1985.

Nichols, Roger L. *Indians in the United States and Canada: A Comparative History.* Lincoln: University of Nebraska Press, 1998.

Nikiforuk, Andrew. "The New Quarterback." In *Running on Empty: Alberta After the Boom*, edited by Andrew Nikiforuk, Sheila Pratt, and Don Wanagas, 114–27. Edmonton: NeWest Press, 1987.

———. *Tar Sands: Dirty Oil and the Future of a Continent.* Vancouver: Greystone Books, 2008.

Ogmundson, R., and M. Doyle. "The Rise and Decline of Canadian Labour, 1960 to 2000: Elites, Power, Ethnicity and Gender." *Canadian Journal of Sociology* 27, no. 3 (2002): 413–54.

Owram, Doug. "1951: Oil's Magic Wand." In *Alberta Formed, Alberta Transformed*, vol. 2, edited by Michael Payne, Donald Wetherell, and Catherine Cavanaugh, 567–86. Edmonton: University of Alberta Press; Calgary: University of Calgary Press, 2005.

Paavo, Adriane. "Union Workload: A Barrier to Women Surviving Labour-Movement Leadership." *Just Labour* 8 (2006): 2–9.

Palamarek, Michael. *A History of Women and Politics in Alberta, 1900–1988: A Report for Senator Martha P. Bielish.* Canada, 1989.

Palmer, Bryan. *Working-Class Experience: Rethinking the History of Canadian Labour, 1800–1991.* Toronto: McClelland and Stewart, 1992.

Palmer, Howard, and Tamara Jeppson Palmer. *Alberta: A New History.* Edmonton: Hurtig, 1990.

Pannekoek, Frits. *A Snug Little Flock: The Social Origins of the Riel Resistance of 1869–70.* Winnipeg: Watson and Dwyer, 1991.

Peck, Trevor R. *Light from Ancient Campfires: Archaeological Evidence for Native Lifeways on the Northern Plains.* Edmonton: Athabasca University Press, 2011.

People's Food Commission. *The Land of Milk and Money: The National Report of the People's Food Commission.* Kitchener, ON: Between the Lines, 1980.

Phillips, Paul, and Erin Phillips. *Women and Work: Inequality in the Canadian Labour Market.* Toronto: James Lorimer, 2000.

Pierson, Ruth. "Women's Emancipation and the Recruitment of Women into the Canadian Labour Force in World War II." Canadian Historical Association, *Historical Papers* 11, no. 1 (1976): 141–73.

Piva, Michael J. *The Condition of the Working Class in Toronto, 1900–1921*. Ottawa: University of Ottawa Press, 1979.

Podruchny, Carolyn. *Making the Voyageur World: Travelers and Traders in the North American Fur Trade*. Lincoln: University of Nebraska Press, 2006.

Pok, Joe. "Oil Sands Development in Alberta and the Implications on Sulphur Supply." Presentation to the International Fertilizer Industry Association Annual Conference, Quebec City, 16 October 2002.

Pollock, Allyson M., Jean Shaoul, and Neil Vickers. "Private Finance and 'Value for Money' in NHS Hospitals: A Policy in Search of a Rationale?" *British Medical Journal* 324 (May 2002): 1205–9.

Potrebenko, Helen. *No Streets of Gold*: *A Social History of Ukrainians in Alberta*. Vancouver: New Star Books, 1977.

Pratt, Larry. "Energy, Regionalism and Canadian Nationalism, 1982–86." *Newfoundland Studies* 1, no. 2 (1985): 175–99.

———. "Energy: The Roots of National Policy." *Studies in Political Economy* 7 (Spring 1982): 26–59.

———. "Grant Notley: Politics as a Calling." In *Socialism and Democracy in Alberta: Essays in Honour of Grant Notley*, edited by Larry Pratt, 1–37. Edmonton: NeWest Press, 1986.

Pratt, Larry, and Garth Stevenson. *Western Separatism: The Myths, Realities and Dangers*. Edmonton: Hurtig, 1981.

Pratt, Sheila. "The Grip Slips." In *Running on Empty: Alberta After the Boom,* edited by Andrew Nikiforuk, Sheila Pratt, and Don Wanagas, 102–13. Edmonton: NeWest Press, 1987.

Prescott, Lisa. *Un-accountable: The Case of Highway Maintenance Privatization in Alberta*. Edmonton: Parkland Institute, 2003.

Ramsey, Bruce. *The Noble Cause: The Story of the United Mine Workers of America in Western Canada*. Calgary: UMWA District 18, 1990.

Ray, Arthur J. *I Have Lived Here Since the World Began: An Illustrated History of Canada's Native People*. Toronto: Key Porter, 2010.

———. *Indians in the Fur Trade: Their Role as Trappers, Hunters and Middlemen in the Lands Southwest of Hudson Bay, 1660–1870*. Toronto: University of Toronto Press, 1974.

Ray, Arthur J., and Donald Freeman. *Give Us Good Measure: An Economic Analysis of Relations Between the Indians and the Hudson's Bay Company Before 1763*. Toronto: University of Toronto Press, 1978.

Rennie, Bradford. *The United Farmers and Farm Women of Alberta, 1909–1921*. Toronto: University of Toronto Press, 2000.

Reshef, Yonaton, and Sandra Rastin. *"Unions in the Time of Revolution": Government Restructuring in Alberta and Ontario*. Toronto: University of Toronto Press, 2003.

Richards, John, and Larry Pratt. *Prairie Capitalism: Power and Influence in the New West*. Toronto: McClelland and Stewart, 1979.

Richardson, Sharon. "Frontier Health Care: Alberta's District and Municipal Nursing Services, 1919 to 1976." *Alberta History* 46, no. 1 (1998): 2–9.

Richmond, A.H. *Comparative Studies in the Economic Adaptation of Immigrants in Canada*. Toronto: York University, Institute for Behavioural Research, 1981.

Roberts, Wayne. *Cracking the Canadian Formula: The Making of the Energy and Chemical Workers Union*. Toronto: Between the Lines, 1990.

Robin, Martin. *Radical Politics and Canadian Labour, 1880–1930*. Kingston: Industrial Relations Centre, Queen's University, 1968.

Ronda, James P. "'We Are Well as We Are:' An Indian Critique of Seventeenth-Century Christian Missions." *William and Mary Quarterly*, 3rd ser., 34 (1977): 66–82.

Roome, Patricia. "Amelia Turner and Calgary Labour Women, 1919–1935." In *The Prairie West: Historical Readings*, edited by R. Douglas Francis and Howard Palmer, 424–49. Edmonton: Pica Pica Press, 1992.

Royal Alberta Museum. "Piece by Piece: The GWG Story." virtualmuseum.ca. 2010. http://www.royalalbertamuseum.ca/virtualExhibit/GWG/en/index.html.

"The Royal Charter for Incorporating the Hudson's Bay Company, A.D. 1670." *The Solon Law Archive.* Last modified 30 June 1997. http://www.solon.org/Constitutions/Canada/English/PreConfederation/hbc_charter_1670.html.

Sampert, Shannon. "King Ralph, the Ministry of Truth, and the Media in Alberta." In *The Return of the Trojan Horse: Alberta and the New World (Dis)Order*, edited by Trevor Harrison, 37–52. Montreal: Black Rose Books, 2005.

Sangster, Joan. *Transforming Labour: Women and Work in Postwar Canada.* Toronto: University of Toronto Press, 2010.

Saskatchewan Union of Nurses and United Nurses of Alberta. *100 Years of Nursing on the Prairies.* www.100yearsofnursing.ca/english/frames.html.

Sautter, Udo. "The Origins of the Employment Service of Canada, 1900–1920." *Labour/Le Travail* 6 (Autumn 1980): 89–112.

Sayers, Anthony M., and David K. Stewart. "Is This the End of the Tory Dynasty? The Wildrose Alliance in Alberta Politics." *University of Calgary School of Public Policy Research Papers* 4, no. 6 (2011): 1–28.

Scammell, G.V. *The World Encompassed: The First European Maritime Empires, c. 800–1650.* London: Methuen, 1981.

Schneider, Elise. "Addressing the Issues: Two Women's Groups in Edmonton." *Alberta History* 36, no. 3 (1988): 15–22.

Schultze, David. "The Industrial Workers of the World and the Unemployed in Edmonton and Calgary in the Depression of 1913–1915." *Labour/Le Travail* 25 (Spring 1990): 45–75.

Seager, Allen. "Socialists and Workers: Western Canadian Coal Miners, 1900–21." *Labour/Le Travail* 16 (Fall 1985): 23–59.

Seager, Allen, and David Roth. "British Columbia and the Mining West: A Ghost of a Chance." In *The Workers' Revolt in Canada, 1917–1925*, edited by Craig Heron, 231–67. Toronto: University of Toronto Press, 1998.

Seager, Charles Allen. "A Proletariat in Wild Rose Country: The Alberta Coal Miners, 1905–1945." PhD diss., York University, 1981.

Selby, Jim. "Women Win 'Illegal' Restaurant Strike in Edmonton in 1935: Action Overcomes Employer Abuse and Government's Blind Eye in the Great Depression." *Union Magazine Online* (Spring/Summer 2008). http://www.afl.org/index.php/component/option,com_unionmag/Itemid,8/mag_id,13/view,unionmag/.

Sellers, Nigel Anthony. *Oil, Wheat, and Wobblies: The Industrial Workers of the Work in Oklahoma, 1905–1930.* Norman: University of Oklahoma Press, 1998.

Shaffer, Ed. "Oil, Class and Development in Alberta." In *Socialism and Democracy in Alberta: Essays in Honour of Grant Notley*, edited by Larry Pratt, 112–30. Edmonton: Hurtig, 1986.

Shewell, Hugh. *"Enough to Keep Them Alive": Indian Welfare in Canada, 1873–1965.* Toronto: University of Toronto Press, 2004.

Sprague, D.N. *Canada and the Métis, 1869–1885.* Waterloo: Wilfrid Laurier University Press, 1988.

Stacey, C.P. *Arms, Men and Governments: The War Policies of Canada, 1939–1945.* Ottawa: Department of National Defence, 1970.

Stainsby, Cliff, and John Malcolmson. "The Fraser Institute and the Government: Corporate Free Lunch." Vancouver: Solidarity Coalition, 1983.

Stanway, Paul. *The Albertans: From Settlement to Super Province, 1905–2005.* Edmonton: CanMedia, 2005.

———. "When Alberta Got Too Rich, Ottawa Unleashed the NEP." In *Lougheed and the War with Ottawa, 1971–1984*, edited by Paul Bunner, 00–00. Edmonton: CanMedia 2006.

Stewart, Walter. *The Life and Political Times of Tommy Douglas.* Toronto: McArthur, 2003.

Strikwerda, Eric. *The Wages of Relief: The City and the Depression on the Canadian Prairies, 1929–1939.* Edmonton: Athabasca University Press, 2012.

Strong-Boag, Veronica. "The Girl of the New Day: Canadian Working Women in the 1920s." *Labour/Le Travailleur* 4 (1979): 131–64.

Swankey, Ben. "Reflections of a Communist: The Hungry Thirties." *Alberta History* 27, no. 4 (1979): 1–12.

Swyripa, Frances. "The Ukrainian Image: Loyal Citizen or Disloyal Alien." In *Loyalties in Conflict: Ukrainians in Canada During the Great War*, edited by Frances Swyripa and John Herd Thompson, 47–68. Edmonton: Canadian Institute of Ukrainian Studies, 1983.

Taft, Kevin. *Shredding the Public Interest: Ralph Klein and Twenty-five Years of One-Party Government*. Edmonton: University of Alberta Press and Parkland Institute, 1997.

Taylor, Jeffery. "Capitalist Development, Forms of Labour, and Class Formation in Prairie Canada." In *The West and Beyond: New Perspectives on an Imagined Region*, edited by Alvin Finkel, Sarah Carter, and Peter Fortna, 159–80. Edmonton: Athabasca University Press, 2010.

———. "Compulsory Arbitration and the Right to Strike: The Experience of Alberta's University Faculty." *Socialist Studies* 2, no. 1 (2006): 99–127.

———. "Labour in the Klein Revolution." In *The Trojan Horse: Alberta and the Future of Canada*, edited by Gordon Laxer and Trevor Harrison, 301–13. Montreal: Black Rose Books, 1995.

Thomas, Alister, ed. *The Super Roughneck: Fifty Years of Canadian Oilpatch History as Reported in* The Roughneck. Calgary: Northern Star Communications, 1992.

Thompson, David. *Explorations in Western America, 1784–1812*. Edited by J.B. Tyrell. Toronto: Champlain Society, 1916.

Thompson, John Herd. "Bringing in the Sheaves: The Harvest Excursionists, 1890–1929." *Canadian Historical Review* 24, no. 4 (1978): 467–89.

Titley, Brian. *The Frontier World of Edgar Dewdney*. Vancouver: University of British Columbia Press, 1999.

———. *A Narrow Vision: Duncan Campbell Scott and the Administration of Indian Affairs in Canada*. Vancouver: University of British Columbia Press, 1986.

———. "Red Deer Indian Industrial School: A Case Study in the History of Native Education." In *Exploring our Educational Past*, edited by Nick Kach and Kas Mazurek, 55–72. Calgary: Detselig, 1992.

Tobias, John L. "Canada's Subjugation of the Plains Cree, 1879–1885." *Canadian Historical Review* 64, no. 4 (1983): 519–48.

———. "Protection, Civilization, Assimilation: An Outline History of Canada's Indian Policy." *Western Canadian Journal of Anthropology* 6, no. 2 (1976): 13–30.

Treaty 7 Elders and Tribal Council, with Walter Hildebrandt, Sarah Carter, and Dorothy First Rider. *The True Spirit and Original Intent of Treaty 7*. Montreal and Kingston: McGill-Queen's University Press, 1996.

Tucker, Eric. "The Constitutional Right to Bargain Collectively: The Ironies of Labour History in the Supreme Court of Canada." *Labour/Le Travail* 61 (Spring 2008): 151–80.

———. "Diverging Trends in Worker Health and Safety Protection and Participation in Canada, 1985–2000." *Relations Industrielles/Industrial Relations* 58, no. 3 (2003): 395–426.

UFCW (United Food and Commercial Workers). *Collective Bargaining in Canada: A Human Right or Canadian Illusion*. Ottawa: United Food and Commercial Workers, 2004.

UNA (United Nurses of Alberta). *United Nurses of Alberta: Twenty-five Years of History*. Edmonton: United Nurses of Alberta, 2002.

———. *The First Twenty-Five Years*. Edmonton: United Nurses of Alberta, 2003.

United Nations World Commission on Environment and Development. *Our Common Future*. Oxford: Oxford University Press, 1987.

Van Herk, Aritha. *Mavericks: An Incorrigible History of Alberta*. Toronto: Penguin Canada 2001.

Van Kirk, Sylvia. *Many Tender Ties: Women in Fur-Trade Society in Western Canada, 1670–1870*. Norman: University of Oklahoma Press, 1980.

Venne, Sharon. "Understanding Treaty 6, An Indigenous Perspective." In *Aboriginal and Treaty Rights in Canada: Essays on Law, Equality and Respect,* edited by Michael Asch, 173–207. Vancouver: University of British Columbia Press, 1997.

Vivone, Rich. *Ralph Could Have Been a Superstar: Tales of the Klein Era.* Kingston: Patricia Publishing, 2009.

Wahl, Asbjørn. "Building Progressive Alliances." *Global Labour Column.* Global Labour University, 5 July 2011.

Waiser, Bill. *All Hell Can't Stop Us: The On-to-Ottawa Trek and Regina Riot.* Calgary: Fifth House, 2003.

———. *Park Prisoners: The Untold History of Western Canada's National Parks, 1915–1946.* Saskatoon: Fifth House, 1995.

———. *Saskatchewan: A New History.* Calgary: Fifth House, 2005.

Wardhaugh, Robert A. *Mackenzie King and the Prairie West.* Toronto: University of Toronto Press, 2000.

Weaver, John C. "Edmonton's Perilous Course, 1904–1929." *Urban History Review* 2 (October 1977): 20–32.

Whitaker, Reg, and Gary Marcuse. *Cold War Canada: The Making of a National Insecurity State, 1945 to 1957.* Toronto: University of Toronto Press, 1996.

White, Julie. *Mail and Female: Women and the Canadian Union of Postal Workers.* Toronto: Thompson Educational Publishing, 1990.

———. *Sisters and Solidarity: Women and Unions in Canada.* Toronto: Thompson Educational Publishing, 1993.

Wilkinson, Richard, and Kate Pickett. *The Spirit Level: Why More Equal Societies Almost Always Do Better.* London: Allen Lane, 2009.

Williams, Glyndwr. "Highlights of the First 200 Years of the Hudson's Bay Company." *The Beaver,* special issue (Autumn 1970): 4–63.

Worswick, Christopher. "C.D. Howe Institute Backgrounder No. 81: Immigrants' Declining Earnings: Reasons and Remedies." Toronto, ON: C.D. Howe Institute, April 2004.

Woywitka, Ann. "Strike at Waterways." *Alberta Historical Review* 20, no. 4 (1972): 1–5.

Wright, Ronald. *Stolen Continents: Conquest and Resistance in the Americas.* Toronto: Penguin, 1992.

CONTRIBUTORS

DAN CUI is a doctoral student in the Department of Educational Policy Studies, University of Alberta. Her earlier research work on the Chinese head tax and discourse analysis focuses on the early history of Chinese immigrants in Canada. Her research interests include Chinese immigrants, youth, ethnic relations, social justice, and social theory. She is the co-author, with Jennifer Kelly, of "'Our Negro Citizens': An Example of Everyday Citizenship Practices," in *The West and Beyond: New Perspectives on an Imagined Region* (Edmonton: Athabasca University Press, 2011).

ALVIN FINKEL is professor of history at Athabasca University. Author, co-author, editor, or co-editor of twelve books, he is president of the Canadian Committee on Labour History and former book review editor for *Labour/Le Travail*. His books include the best-selling, multi-edition, two-volume *History of the Canadian Peoples* (with Margaret Conrad), *The Social Credit Phenomenon in Alberta, Business and Social Reform in the Thirties, History of Canadian Social Policy*, and *The Chamberlain-Hitler Collusion* (with Clement Leibovitz). He joined the Alberta Labour History Institute in 1999 and has been an executive member since 2000.

JASON FOSTER is academic coordinator for Industrial Relations at Athabasca University. Before joining the faculty at AU, Jason worked for many years as the director of policy analysis with the Alberta Federation of Labour, dealing extensively with industrial relations practices, government employment and labour policy, and the operation of trade unions. He also brings experience in non-profit sector employment relations. He has published work on union activism in Canada and on tripartism in Canada and Europe. He is currently co-investigator on a research project examining the training and education experiences of temporary foreign workers in nursing and the building trades.

WINSTON GERELUK has spent most of his career within the labour movement, after a brief career as a schoolteacher. He was research and education director of the Alberta Federation of Labour in the late 1970s and subsequently held a number of positions in the Alberta Union of Provincial Employees and the AFL, and was thus intimately connected with the events that he discusses in this book. In recent years, he has represented the Canadian labour movement in a variety of international forums, including the International Labour Organization, and was also academic coordinator of Industrial Relations and Human Resources at Athabasca University. A member of the Alberta Labour History Institute since 1999, he has served on its executive for many years. He is the chair of the steering committee for Project 2012.

JENNIFER KELLY is associate professor and department chair of the Department of Educational Policy Studies at the University of Alberta. Among her many publications are two books, *Borrowed Identities* (New York: Peter Lang, 2004) and *Under the Gaze: Learning to Be Black in White Society* (Halifax: Fernwood, 1998). Her current SSHRC-funded three-year research project, "Racialization, Immigration and Citizenship: Alberta 1900–1960s," explores how processes of immigration and racialization affected the social formation of African-Canadian communities in Alberta.

She is also conducting an ongoing oral history research project with Jamaican teachers who immigrated to Alberta during the 1960s. In addition, she is continuing to publish research on youth, media, and production of black subjectivities. Jennifer is a long-time activist with the Alberta Labour History Institute and has held executive positions at the ALHI.

JAMES MUIR is assistant professor of history at the University of Alberta. His work focuses on the intersection of law, colonialism, and the economy, with an emphasis on the early history of Nova Scotia. He has also studied liability and tort law in nineteenth-century Nova Scotia, laws related to the natural environment in New Zealand between 1840 and 1920, and labour regulation in Hudson's Bay Company posts in the eighteenth century. He is an active member of the Alberta Labour History Institute board.

JOAN SCHIEBELBEIN is the director of CAPS, the University of Alberta Career Centre. She began working with CAPS in September 1988, eventually taking on responsibility for developing and managing the unit's career education programming and Career Peer Educator (CPE) program. In addition to her work with CAPS, Joan currently serves on the University of Alberta's Community Service-Learning Advisory Board and the Work and Learning Network for Research and Policy Advisory Board, which is based in the Department of Educational Policy Studies. She has been an activist with and executive member of the Alberta Labour History Institute for many years and is a key figure in Project 2012.

JIM SELBY is a lifelong labour activist and author of left-wing publications. He was research and communications director at the Alberta Federation of Labour for ten years and then research director for another fifteen years. He researched and wrote policy papers and briefs to all level of government on a wide range of social and economic issues.

ERIC STRIKWERDA teaches history at the University of Alberta and at Athabasca University, including working-class history and western Canadian history. He also teaches courses at Athabasca University in labour studies. His book, *The Wages of Relief: The City and the Depression on the Canadian Prairies, 1929–1939*, will be published by Athabasca University Press in 2012. He has also published articles on relief policies in western Canadian cities during the Great Depression.

INDEX

bold page numbers indicate photos

A

A-Channel, 231, **232**
Aberhart, William, 102, 103
Aboriginals. *See* First Nations; Natives
accidents: and city employees, 150; in coal mining, 57–58, 165; in construction, 141; in meat-packing, 164; and Workers Compensation Board, 158, 180; workplace fatalities, 287–88. *See also* health and safety on the job
Action Canada Network, 183, 197
adolescent workers, 235
advocacy groups, 215–16
African-Canadians: immigration of, 270, 271, 280–281; labour options for, 272–73, 274, 280–81, 282; and Lakeside Packers, 235–37, 283–84; as railway porters, **266**, 277–78
agricultural economy, 33, 71–73, 115, 117, 302n85. *See also* farming/farmers
Ahtahkakoop, Chief, 33
Aircraft Repair, 251
airline industry, 190
Alberta, Government of: anti-union attitudes of, 109, 125, 179–80, 195, 221–22, 223–24, 250; and Bill 44, 182–84; and civil servants, 86–87, 144–45; cuts to public spending, 176–77, 240; during Depression, 103, 105; and diversification,

7, 143–44, 151, 174, 238; fight against public sector workers, 144–45, 225; finances of, 187–88, 199, 293, 294; and human rights legislation, 170, 279; labour legislation of, 86, 115, 129, 130–31, 158, 162, 194–95, 278; Labour members of, 93; and maternity leave, 259, 260; and nurses, 146–47, 178, 245; and prosecuting employers, 235, 287–88; and rat-killing crusade, **108**, 109; and social programs, 127–28; support for employers, 117, 181; and temporary foreign workers, 234–35, 285. *See also* Klein government; Lougheed government; Manning government
Alberta Advantage, the, 215
Alberta Alliance, 311n91
Alberta and Great Waterways Railway, 83
Alberta Association for the Advancement of Coloured People, 278
Alberta Association of Registered Nurses (AARN), 146, 147
Alberta Board of Industrial Relations, 123, 130, 133, 152, 157–58
Alberta District Nursing Service, 245
Alberta Energy Company, 151
Alberta Environmental Network (AEN), 197–98
Alberta Factory Act, 86, 253
Alberta Farmers' Union (AFU), 117
Alberta Federation of Labour (AFL): and Alberta

Labour Act, 130, 158; and Alberta Labour History Institute, 4; and building trades, 186; fights anti-union legislation, 182–84, 194–95, 222, 224; fights for fair union legislation, 115, 278; fights Klein cuts, 215, 217, 220; financial problems of, 225; founded, 69; future of, 295; and industrial unionism, 89; merges with IFLA, 133–34; and public sector workers, 144, 148; and safety legislation, 162, 288; social activism of, 143, 170, 197–98, 202, 230, 233; and Social Credit, 128, 134–35, 139, 152–53, 168, 291; strike support from, 199, 218, **228**; support for farm workers, 234; and tar sands, 238; ties to NDP, 166, 200, 225, 239, 240; 2008 election strategy, 239–40; and unemployment centres, 185; views on non-European immigration, 276–77; and wage controls, 168–70, 179; women involved with, 254, 264; and workers of colour caucuses, 284
Alberta Federation of Labour Women's Committee, 258, 264
Alberta Government Telephones (AGT), 151
Alberta Health Care Association, 261
Alberta Heritage Savings Trust Fund, 294
Alberta Hotel Association (AHA), 132–33
Alberta Human Rights Association (AHRA), 280
Alberta Human Rights Branch, 279
Alberta Labour Act, 130–31, 152–53, 158

and mine workers, 92; role in labour struggles, 4; and women workers, 255

company unions: government support for, 153; legislation on, 30, 32, 152; supported by industry, 44, 149, 156

Comrie, Dan, 192

Congress of Industrial Organizations (CIO), 107

Connelly, Kip, 192

conscription, 85–86

construction industry: accidents in, 141; and Dandelion movement, 183; and destruction of unions in, 181–82; and spin-off companies, 158; and unions, 61, 159, 162, 186

consumer boycotts, 231

consumerism, 126–27, 142

Continuous Passages Act, 276

contracting out, 212, 214, 227

Corbin, AB, 106

Cormack, Audrey, 260

corrections workers, 145–46

Corse, Mary, 255

Council of Canadians, 196

Council of Christians and Jews, 279

courts, 224, 261

CPR. See Canadian Pacific Railway (CPR)

craft unions: compared to industrial, 61–64, 88–89, 105; description of, 61–63, 75; and Social Credit, 103; strikes involving, 63–64, 105; and women's auxiliaries, 255

Crawford, Neil, 259

Cree: education of, **36**; and horses, 22; in North-West Resistance, 32; social organization of, 14, 15–16; traditional religion of, 10; and treaty negotiations, 34

Crowsnest Pass, 50–51

cruise missile campaign, 186, 198

Curtis, Edward S., 8

Czaja, Ed, 176

D

Dandelion movement, 183

Daniel, Bill, 176

Danysk, Cecilia, 72

Davison, Andy, 114

daycare, 141–42, 258, 263

Dean, Carol Anne, 211

Decore, Laurence, 208

Delaney, Adam, 9

Dene, 14, 16

Dent, Ivor, 167

Depression, the Great: and Chinese labour, 274; conditions of, 95–96, **101**; and Hunger March, 97–100; and Social Credit, 103; strikes in, 96, 105–7

Depression of 1913–1914, 70–72, 77, 81

Dewdney, Edgar, 34

Diamond Bus Lines, 157

Dickason, Olive, 196

Dickinson, Harley, 269

Dinning, Jim, 209

disease, 20–21, 24, 45

District 18 of United Mine Workers of America, 51, 53–56, 68–69, 75

domestic work, 246–47, 250, 280

Dominion Labour Party (DLP), 92–94

Dotto, Assunta, 111–12, 247

Douglas, C.H., 102

Drumheller, AB, 80, 83, 92, 119

Duckworth, Archie, 236, 237

E

economic booms, 70

economic crisis of 2008, 240

Edmonton: and Depression of 1913–14, 70, 81; early growth of, 61; general strike in, 90; GWG plant, 111–12; and Hunger March, **76**, 97–100; immigration to, 282; life in, 64, 66;

meat-packing industry in, 107; and recession of 1980s, 175; and teachers' strike, 148; unionization in, 86; and WWI, 80, 81, 85

Edmonton, City of, 259

Edmonton District Labour Council, 201

Edmonton Food Bank, 185

Edmonton Trades and Labour Council, 68

Edmonton Voters Association (EVA), 201

education, 35–37, 190, 209–10, 269, 280

Ellis, Norma, 281

employee associations, 129, 132. *See also* company unions

employment: during 1913 Depression, 70–71, 81; in early 1920s, 91; legislation, 278; on railways, 39, 40, 81, **268**; and recession of 1980s, 175, 184, 185, 188; and recession of 1990s, 206; during settler years, 39–40; in 2000s, 284; of women, 66–67, 91, 250–52; during World War I, 77–78

Energy and Chemical Workers Union (ECWU), 153, 173, 187, 192–93, 195, 198

Engley, Nellie, 114

environmental movement, 197–98, 238

Ethier, Marg, 147, 178

ethnic groups, 55–56, 84–85. *See also* African–Canadians; Chinese–Canadians

Europeans, 10, 17, 19–21

Evans, Jack, 131

Evans, Slim, 92

Ewasiw, John, 191

F

Factory Act (1917), 86, 253

Fagnon, Len, 218

family allowance, 128

famine, 34, 35

Farm Workers Union of Alberta, 234

Farmers' and Workers' Unity Leagues, 97, 105

United Nurses of Alberta (UNA): and Bill 27, 224; collective action in late 1990s, 226; growth of, 146–47; and maternity leave, 261; merges with Health Sciences, 225; and privatization of medicare, 220; strikes of, 177–78, 190, 199–200

United Packinghouse Workers of America (UPWA), 124–25

United States, 28–29

University of Alberta, 149, 196

V

Van Schaik, Andre, 150

Ventura, John, 181, 191, 192

Vietnamese-Canadians, 282

visible minorities, 283, 292, 315n53

voyageurs, 23, 24

Vriend, Delwin, 233

W

Waffle group, 168

wage controls, 146, 168–70, 179

wage labour: on farms, 71–74; during 1920s, 90–91; for women, 246–47, 256–57; during WWI, 77–78, 82–83; during WWII, 111–12

Walker, J. Bruce, 267

Ware, John, **272**

warfarin, 109

Warren, Marilyn, 265

Watson, J.H., 63

Watt, Walter, 146

welfare, 210

Werlin, Dave: background, 186; and Bill 44, 182, 183; and Free Trade agreement, 202; and Gainers' strike, 191; as head of AFL, 200; hired

by City of Calgary, 139; on labour legislation of 1987, 194; and Zeidler strike, 193

West, Steve, 209, 212

Western Canada Coal Operators Association (WCCOA), 53–54

Western Federation of Miners (WFM), 50–51, 55, 254

Western Labour Conference, 77

White, Alan, 279

White, Fred, 93

White, Julie, 260, 263

Wigger, Ole Nelson, 131

Wildrose Alliance Party, 240–41, 311n91

Wiley, Agnes, 127

Wiley, Lorne, 127

Wilgus, Mike, 184

Williams, Enoch, 295

Winnipeg General Strike, 89–90

Winspear, Francis, 279

Wolseley, Garnet, 31

women: and daycare, 141–42, 263; and domestic work, 246–47; effect of government cuts on, 292; employment record of, 66–67, 91, 250–52; at GWG, **66**, 125, 246–47, 251; as hotel workers, 154; in labour movement, 250, 253–58, 263–65, 291; and maternity leave, 258–61; and nursing, 120–22; and prostitution, 249–50; as settlers, 243–44, **245**; and sexism, 263–64; and social activism, 197, 261–63; as teachers, 247–49, 251; and Unemployment Insurance, 127–28; in union leadership roles, 225, 264; in war time, 87, 111–12, 114, **242**, 251

women's auxiliaries, 254

Women's Labour Leagues, 254–56

Wood, Henry Wise, 92

Woodsworth, J.S., 101

Woodsworth-Irvine Socialist Fellowship, 166

work-life culture, 46–47, 83, 126–27

worker-employer councils, 87

worker safety. *See* health and safety on the job

Workers Compensation Board, 158, 180, 194, 214, 219, 288

Workers of Colour and Aboriginal Workers Committee (WCAWC), 284

Workers Party of Canada (WPC), 94

workfare, 208

Workmen's Compensation Board, 153. *See also* Workers Compensation Board

Workplace Hazardous Materials Information System (WHMIS), 195, 308n103

World War I: and conscription, 85–86; and corruption, 84; declaration of, 80–81; effect on returning soldiers, 77, 87; and internment camps, **84**, 85; reason for fighting, 75; soldiers' experiences of, 82

World War II, 109–11, 112–14, **242**, 251, 275–76

Wotherspoon, Terry, 269

Wright, Myrna, 226

Y

Yellow Cab, 190

Yorath, Christopher J., 274

Young, Art, **93**

Z

Zeidler, Fred, 193

Zeidler plywood plants, 193, 199

Zukarko, Bill, 117

Zukarko, John, 117

¶ This book was typeset in FF Celeste Serif and Sans designed by Chris Burke. It was printed on 80 lb Sappi Flo Dull Text.